Macmillan Building and Surveying Series
Series Editor: **Ivor H. Seeley**
Emeritus Professor, The Nottingham Trent University

List continued overleaf

List continued from previous page

Macmillan Building and Surveying Series
Series Standing Order
ISBN 0–333–71692–2 hardcover
ISBN 0–333–69333–7 paperback
(*outside North America only*)

You can receive future titles in this series as they are published by placing a standing order. Please contact your bookseller or, in the case of difficulty, write to us at the address below with your name and address, the title of the series and the ISBN quoted above.

Customer Services Department, Macmillan Distribution Ltd
Houndmills, Basingstoke, Hampshire RG21 6XS, England

URBAN LAND ECONOMICS AND PUBLIC POLICY

Fifth Edition

PAUL N. BALCHIN
Ph.D., B.Sc.(Econ.)
Reader in Urban Economics
University of Greenwich

GREGORY H. BULL
B.A., M.A., Doctorate
Senior Lecturer in Economics
University of Greenwich

JEFFREY L. KIEVE
M.Phil., B.Sc.(Econ.), A.I.A.S.
Property Investment Consultant

First edition 1977
Reprinted 1979
Second edition 1982
Reprinted 1983
Third edition 1985
Reprinted 1986
Fourth edition 1988
Reprinted 1990, 1993
Fifth edition 1995

Published by
MACMILLAN PRESS LTD
Houndmills, Basingstoke, Hampshire RG21 2XS
and London
Companies and representatives
throughout the world

ISBN 0–333–62903–5

A catalogue record for this book is available
from the British Library.

10   9   8   7   6   5
04   03   02   01   00

Printed in Great Britain by
Antony Rowe Ltd,
Chippenham, Wiltshire

Contents

List of Figures

List of Tables

Preface to the Fifth Edition

While this book, like the first four editions, is a basic text for students registered on degree courses in Estate Management/Land Economics, Building Surveying and Quantity Surveying, it serves as an essential reader where there are degree or diploma courses (or specialisms) in urban economics, urban geography or town planning. In addition, the book should remain an important reader for students preparing for the examinations of many professional bodies concerned with land – for example, the Royal Institution of Chartered Surveyors and the Royal Town Planning Institute.

Between us we have lectured on courses in land economics and town planning for over two decades and have been involved in the preparation of both honours degree and postgraduate syllabuses. We have found that while there is an ever-increasing flow of new literature on urban land economics, often the product of intensive research, the student's problem of a restrictive range of suitable books still remains partly unresolved. By combining theory with the applied aspects of the subject, this book is intended to eliminate this deficiency.

In recent years there has been a dramatic change in the economic strategy of government in the United Kingdom – most notably with the rise and decline of monetarism, financial deregulation and the implementation of programmes of privatisation, not least within the field of property. This edition therefore considers public policy at greater length than in earlier editions – a facet reflected inevitably in the coursework and examination questions of the relevant academic and professional institutions. By placing welfare considerations near the middle of the book, it is hoped that a bridge will be formed between the initial chapters, which concentrate mainly on the private market, and subsequent chapters, which deal more with public intervention.

A new feature in this edition is an entire chapter devoted to examining the problems of urban decline and renewal. The economic and social problems of these areas are dealt with in the framework of current issues in urban policy, local government and planning. In addition, much material has been updated, revised or rewritten and, although extended in coverage, the general layout and emphasis of the book remains largely unchanged.

The subject matter of the book progresses from the general to the specific. Chapter 1 is an attempt to provide a background account of population change; the process of urbanisation; and the basic features of land as a factor of production; it also considers the role of urban land economics. Chapters 2 and 3 seek to explain the locational determinants of economic activities. Chapters 4 and 5 deal with property investment; investment appraisal in the private sector and the economics of development, and redevelopment and rehabilitation. Chapter

6 considers the relationship between welfare economics and land, and examines the question of pollution. Chapter 7 sets out to explore urban congestion in the context of both private and public transport. Chapter 8 examines the process of urban decline and urban regeneration, and the development of public policy in this area. Chapter 9 analyses the problems of housing, particularly within the context of recent house price fluctuations. Chapter 10 looks at the performance and organisation of the construction industry.

In compiling all editions of this book, every effort has been made to ensure that legislative and statistical detail is accurate or at least undisputed at the time of writing.

We must acknowledge the debt we owe our colleagues past and present who have advised us, particularly with regard to amendments to later editions. As before, we would particularly like to thank Professor Ivor Seeley, who read and edited the initial manuscript painstakingly and without whose help the publication of this text would not have been possible. We would also like to extend thanks to all those who helped in the production of the new-edition and in particular to Sue Brimacombe, who helped to type and collate material for this edition, and to Sue Lee and Peter Stevens, who produced many of the drawings. Finally we would like to thank our respective families for the patience they showed throughout the preparation of this book.

Paul Balchin
Gregory H. Bull
Jeffrey L. Kieve

Acknowledgements

The authors and publishers wish to thank the following who have kindly given permission for the use of copyright material:

Academic Press (London) Ltd for table 3.8, from J. Michie (ed.), *The Economic Legacy 1979–93* (1992), table 7.2.

Carfax Publishing Company for the adapted table 2.3, from J. Potter, 'External manufacturing investment in a peripheral rural region: the case of Devon and Cornwall', *Regional Studies*, 27 (1993), table 6, p. 201.

Hillier Parker May and Bowden for table 10.5, from 'International Property Bulletin', (1990), table 4.3 from 'Hillier Parker Rent Index Digest 1993', and table 3.2 from 'British Shopping Centre Development Master List' (1993).

Hodder & Stoughton Publishers for the adapted table 8.4, from A. G. Champion and A. R. Townsend, *Contemporary Britain* (Edward Arnold, 1990), table 7.8.

Pion Ltd and the authors for figure 10.6, from R. Barras and D. Ferguson, 'A spectral analysis of building cycles in Britain', *Environment & Planning A*, 1985, 17 (1985), Figures 3(a) and (c), pp. 1369ff.

Urban Studies for table 2.4, from R. L. Moonmaw, 'Agglomeration economies: localisation or urbanisation', *Urban Studies*, 25 (1988).

Central Statistical Office, Newport, for figures 6.16 and 10.5.

Office of Population Censuses and Surveys, London, for tables 8.1, 8.2 and figure 8.1.

Financial Times for figure 4.3: 'Share price movements 1973–87' (*Financial Times*, 24 October 1987).

HMSO, *Housing and Construction Statistics*, for table 10.1 and figures 10.2 and 10.4.

Michael Laurie for table 4.2: 'Investment media: comparison of real rates of return, 1979–92' (*MLG-CIG Property Index*, 1993).

Every effort has been made to trace all the copyright-holders, but if any have been inadvertently overlooked the publishers will be pleased to make the necessary arrangement at the earliest opportunity.

1

Introduction

Urbanisation

An increasing proportion of the rapidly growing world population is attempting to satisfy its economic and social needs and desires in an urban context. The enormous migration of people into cities and towns has produced a very distinct possibility of an uncontrollable urban explosion – an unprecedented increase in population, greater demands on the urban infrastructure, higher rates of pollution and a decrease in the non-material (and in some cases material) standard of life.

There are five major forces determining the pace of urbanisation throughout the world: economic growth and development; technological change; a rapid growth in the world population; a large scale movement of people from rural areas to cities; and, in some countries, a net outward-migration of population from cities to towns and villages. Despite recessions in most Western industrial countries in recent years, the world production of goods and services continues to increase. As a result of improvements in transportation and the supply of power, production becomes *more* concentrated rather than less in those locations offering the greatest comparative advantages. These tend to be increasingly large metropolitan-centred market areas. This trend is compounded by the simultaneous growth of large, often multinational, companies which, with their increasing market dominance and internal and external economies of scale, form an interdependent relationship with areas of large population and high purchasing power.

The increased pace of industrial growth commencing in western Europe in the eighteenth and nineteenth centuries has had a direct effect upon mortality. An improved food supply and better living conditions and medicine have all led to a decline in death-rates – in Britain, for example, the death-rate has fallen from 30 per 1000 of the population in 1750 to 11.3 per 1000 in 1991. While birth-rates in industrial countries have also been declining – in Britain from 35 to 13.8 per 1000 between 1750 and 1986 – the rate of fertility has remained very high in many developing countries, often being in excess of 40 per 1000. Recently the population of the world has been growing by about 1.9 per cent per annum, a rate of increase unparalleled in history. Although it took from Palaeolithic times to 1850 for the world population to reach 1000 million, by 1925 this number had doubled and by 1962 it had trebled. In 1993, the world population exceeded 5000 million.

Table 1.1 *Percentage of active population employed in agriculture in selected advanced capitalist countries, 1955, 1973 and 1990*

	1955	1973	1990
Italy	40.8	18.3	9.0
Japan	37.9	13.4	8.5
France	26.7	11.4	6.1
Canada	18.0	6.6	4.2
United States	9.7	4.2	4.1
West Germany	17.8	7.5	3.4
United Kingdom	5.4	2.9	2.1

Source: OECD, *Labour Force Statistics* (various).

Small urban settlements are incapable, however, of evolving into major cities solely through the process of natural population increase – the migration of people from the countryside is an equally or more important determinant of growth. Apart from the economic 'pull' of towns there is also the 'push' effect of agricultural change such as the establishment of enclosures, land reform or an acceleration in the application of capital-intensive farming. The proportion of the working population employed in agriculture in economically developed countries began to decline in the late nineteenth century, and the share of civil employment in agriculture has continued to diminish in recent decades (table 1.1).

In global terms there has been a decrease in the ratio of the overall rural population to the total population, and a reciprocal increase in the proportion of the urban population. Today about 40 per cent of the world population is urban but whereas in rural areas population increase is at a rate of 1 per cent per annum, in towns and cities the growth is on average 3.5 per cent per annum, with an even greater increase in developing countries. In the ten years 1950–60 the number of cities with populations in excess of 500 000 grew from 158 to 234, and agglomerations with populations greater in number than 2 million grew from 20 to 26 (of which 12 were within the developing countries). In Britain, not only did the population increase from 10.5 million to 56 million between 1801 and 1991, but the proportion of the population which was urban grew from 21 to 80 per cent – an increase in both relative and absolute terms. In 1750 there were only two cities in Great Britain (London and Edinburgh) with populations greater than 50 000, by 1851 the number had increased to 29 and by 1991 there were over 150 cities with populations in excess of this size.

As part of this process of urbanisation, industry (and particularly manufacturing) replaced agriculture as the dominant economic activity in terms of employment. But in all advanced capitalist countries since the 1950s, increasingly services have superseded industry as the largest sector (tables 1.2 and 1.3).

Notwithstanding the dramatic increase in the pace of urbanisation in a global context, there has been a recent tendency in advanced countries for sectoral employment shifts to be accompanied by urban decentralisation.[1] Within the

Table 1.2 *Percentage of active population employed in industry in selected advanced capitalist countries, 1955, 1973 and 1990 (percentage in manufacturing in brackets)*

	1955		1973		1990	
West Germany	45.5	(33.8)	47.5	(36.6)	39.8	(31.5)
United States	37.6	(28.5)	33.2	(24.8)	35.7	(22.2)
Italy	29.2	(20.0)	39.2	(28.5)	32.4	(22.5)
France	36.2	(26.9)	39.7	(28.3)	29.9	(21.3)
United Kingdom	47.9	(36.1)	42.6	(32.3)	29.0	(21.0)
Japan	24.8	(18.4)	37.2	(27.4)	27.4	(23.5)
Canada	34.0	(24.1)	30.6	(22.0)	24.5	(15.9)

Source: OECD, *Labour Force Statistics* (various).

Table 1.3 *Percentage of active population employed in services in selected advanced capitalist countries, 1955, 1973 and 1990*

	1955	1973	1990
Canada	48.0	62.8	71.3
United Kingdom	46.7	54.5	68.9
Japan	37.3	49.4	64.1
France	37.1	48.9	64.0
United States	52.7	62.6	60.2
Italy	30.0	42.5	58.6
West Germany	36.7	45.0	56.8

Source: OECD, *Labour Force Statistics* (various).

European Community (EC), for example, between 1960 and 1970 the population of non-urban areas grew at a faster rate than the population of urban areas, but in the period 1970–5 in Italy, France, Denmark and probably West Germany, urban population growth not only remained relatively slow but it also decelerated. The urban populations of Belgium, the Netherlands and Britain, moreover, declined in absolute terms during this period (table 1.4) – a trend particularly indicative of the economic and social malaise affecting the urban areas of north-west Europe.[2] A similar process of urban decentralisation also occurred in the United States.

Except for averting a catastrophic war or famine, there are few challenges and problems that appear as daunting and intractable as the problems of urban areas. To many, the city has seemed synonymous with civilisation, with the height of man's achievement in the arts and sciences, in technology and in administration. To others, especially since the Industrial Revolution, the city has offered poverty, misery and disease. Yet while economic processes may have brought about distress to millions, economics as a discipline has helped

Table 1.4 *Population growth in urban and non-urban areas, 1960–70 and 1970–5*

| | Average annual growth (%) | | | |
| | 1960–70 | | 1970–5 | |
	Urban	Non-urban	Urban	Non-urban
Belgium	0.78	4.52	−0.58	3.74
Netherlands	2.97	10.55	−0.35	9.04
Great Britain	1.16	5.06	−0.03	3.45
West Germany	3.41	5.09	n.a.	n.a.
Denmark	3.79	3.81	0.43	3.51
France	3.36	7.55	1.58	7.18
Italy	4.35	2.30	2.51	2.93

Source: L. Van den Berg *et al.*, *Urban Europe: A Study of Growth and Decline* (Pergamon, 1982).

to solve many of the problems of the human condition. As yet, however, it has not been applied on any scale to these problems within a specifically urban context. In the United Kingdom, this is illustrated by reference to the long boom of the 1950s–70s and its aftermath. In the twenty or more years prior to the oil price shock of 1974, the long boom facilitated the extension of the housing stock and the improvement in the urban infrastructure.[3] But with the adoption of monetarist policy in the late 1970s, a further oil price hike in 1979 and the application of free-market ideology (marked by continuous programmes of privatisation) in the 1980s–90s, it became evident that any further improvement in the urban environment would at best be patchy. Except for small areas of commercial development, the inner cities were debilitated increasingly by deprivation and a resurgent housing crisis, and it was evident that there was a glaring and widening mismatch between, on the one hand, 'need' and, on the other, unused land, labour and construction capacity. The plight of our cities was, of course, intensified by the recession of the national economy in the early 1980s. Unemployment soared from 5.2 per cent in 1979 to 13.9 per cent in 1985 and was very largely associated with deindustrialisation. The pace of deindustrialisation (and a less than compensatory growth of service employment) was not only more rapid than in most other advanced capitalist countries, it also produced new divisions of labour and disparities of growth between cities and suburbs, and metropolitan areas and provincial towns (in addition to a widening 'north–south divide').[4] The recession of 1989–early 1990s was particularly marked by a rise in unemployment which reached 10.6 per cent in 1993, but since service industries were now the principal victims of deficient demand, the south-east rather than the industrial regions of the north and west suffered disproportionately – delaying the processes of urban regeneration in London and narrowing the north–south divide.

The Resource of Land

Urban land shares most of its basic features with land in general. To the classical economist, land is defined as being all the free gifts of nature which yield an income. Agricultural land would obviously be included, but so would minerals, water resources and forests with all their natural flora and fauna. Although structures on land have been regarded as part of the factor of production capital, the distinction is of little concern to the urban or land economist. He often finds land and capital so interdependent that separate identification may either be impossible or inconvenient. A lawyer's definition of land is thus more appropriate to his/her needs – land is 'the surface of the earth together with all the subjacent and super-jacent things of a physical nature such as buildings, trees, minerals'.[5] Land has a number of features which in aggregate are not entirely possessed by other factors, especially if the classical definition of land is accepted. Land is characterised by the following.

The relative fixity of supply

Traditionally, economists have argued that the total supply of land is fixed. If one type of use is increased in area (for example, farmland) it will be at the expense of another (for example, forests). But the land economist is not directly concerned with this global definition of land and its implication. He knows that productive land *can* be both increased *or* decreased through man's actions – Dutch polderland and the dustbowls of the United States often being cited as respective examples. He also knows that land can be increased by more intensive use; for example, by constructing a multistorey office block on a formerly low density residential site (or decreased by a reversion to less intensive use). Yet it must still be accepted that, when compared with capital (as an independent resource), labour or entrepreneurship, land is the least flexible factor of production, its supply being comparatively fixed.

No cost of creation

Man has, of course, the power to increase his/her own numbers, and s/he can also produce capital and evolve entrepreneurial skill. But s/he cannot *make* land in its broadest meaning; it was there before him/her and it cost him/her nothing to create. But when land is developed, costs are incurred. It then becomes like the other factors of production, no longer a free resource.

Heterogeneity

To the user of land each site and building is different, but even so, land can be classified into a number of economic categories – sub-marginal land having no remunerative use, break-even marginal land, and profit- or surplus-yielding intramarginal land.

Table 1.5 *Diminishing returns to land*

Units of land	Number of men employed (each with equal amount of farm capital)	Total output per year (tonnes of potatoes)	Average output	Marginal output
1	1	8	8	8
1	2	18	9	10
1	3	30	10	12
1	4	44	11	14
1	5	56	11.2	12
1	6	66	11	10
1	7	74	10.6	8
1	8	80	10	6
1	9	84	9.3	4
1	10	86	8.6	2
1	11	86	7.8	0
1	12	84	7	−2

Yet the boundaries or 'margins of transference' between these different categories of land frequently change. If, for example, the price of cereals increased or the cost of cultivation fell (or both), wheat cultivation might expand from its intra-marginal land into mainly oat areas (normally break-even land for wheat) and these in turn might extend into livestock rearing areas (usually break-even land for oats and sub-marginal land for wheat). Conversely, if cereal prices fell or costs increased (or both) the margins of transference would shift in the opposite direction. In urban areas similar shifts occur. If office rents and relatively lower residential rents increased or the cost of construction in real terms fell (or both), office use would expand into residential areas and these in turn would extend into agricultural areas, sub-marginal land becoming break-even land and break-even land becoming intra-marginal land. The converse could happen in theory but it rarely does in practice.

The Law of Diminishing Returns

Nineteenth-century economists, in particular David Ricardo and his followers, believed that land was unlike other factors in that it was subject to the Law of Diminishing Returns. The law states that 'after successive applications of labour and capital to a given area of land, first the marginal output, then the average output and eventually the total output diminishes'. Table 1.5 shows that marginal output increases to 14 tonnes when the number of men employed is raised to four, average output increases to 11.2 tonnes when five men are employed, and total output rises to 86 tonnes when the labour force increases to ten or eleven men. Above these levels of output it can be seen that diminishing returns set in.

In a free market economy the producer would employ additional men until marginal output reached its maximum (in table 1.5, four men would be employed, producing marginally 14 tonnes of potatoes). If the extra men available were re-employed elsewhere, according to the same criterion there would not only be a marked increase in overall output but each producer would maximise his/her profits (assuming factor costs per unit of output and product prices remained constant). But the quality of land and capital can be improved and farming skills might become more sophisticated, and in consequence diminishing returns could be delayed. Table 1.5 could equally show diminishing returns of a building development – the number of storeys could substitute for the number of men employed, total rent income could replace total output, and marginal rent and average rent income could substitute for marginal and average output. If construction costs were the same for each storey, a building of four storeys would provide the maximum profit. Yet improved technology and lower real costs of development would enable more storeys to be constructed prior to the onset of diminishing returns.

The absence of a market for 'land'

While in market economies other factors of production can be bought or sold in their own right, in most, if not all, countries land deals are transactions not in land itself but in interests or rights in, on, under and over land. Since at least feudal times land has been owned only by the Crown or State, and various forms of tenure have been bestowed on individuals, firms, or institutions enabling them to use land subject to various conditions. In English Law these rights in aggregate are known as 'real property'.

Economic or scarcity rent

The word 'rent' originally referred only to the factor of production land – classical economists realising that the comparative scarcity of land produces a return quite different in character from that normally earned by labour or capital.

(1) *Agricultural rents* Until the early nineteenth century it was generally believed that the price of food largely reflected the rent charged to tenant farmers. It was thought that landlords would charge rents directly in relation to the fertility of the land and that farmers would attempt to pass on these rents to the consumer in the price of farm produce. But in 1817, Ricardo suggested an alternative explanation of the relationship between food (especially corn) prices and rents. Although conceding that rent represented

> that portion of the produce of the earth which is paid to the landlord for the use of the original and indestructible powers of the soil[6]

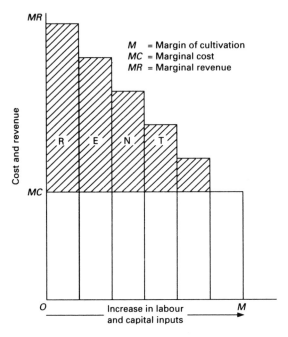

Figure 1.1 *Relationship between labour, capital inputs and rent*

he argued that food prices determine rents rather than vice versa. Aware of a decreasing supply of corn from the Continent as a consequence of the Napoleonic Wars and the effects of an increasing population, s/he postulated that 'corn is not high because rent is paid, but a rent is paid because corn is high'. Ricardo further argued that if either the supply of corn increased with the resumption of imports, or the demand decreased, prices would fall, the demand for land for corn would decrease and rents would consequently diminish. Clearly, therefore, the demand for land was a derived demand. Land was not required for itself but for the value of its product.

Ricardo thus believed that rents were determined by the interaction of supply and demand. Given a fairly fixed supply of farmland, land of high fertility would yield a high marginal output (in response to a constant marginal increase in labour and capital inputs) and would therefore command a high rent – a surplus equal to the marginal revenue of the product less the marginal cost of labour and capital (figure 1.1). Land of low fertility would attract the least demand and therefore command little or no rent.

To modern economists the Ricardian concept of rent is inadequate. Although in colloquial terms rent can refer to any regular payment for the hire of a product (for example, a motor car or a television set), in a more specific economic sense the term 'rent' relates to factors of production not perfectly elastic in supply, with land as the principal example. The payment for the use of land is known as *commercial rent*, but there are two constituents of commercial

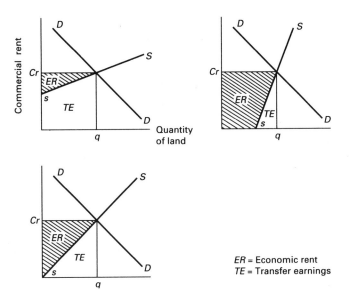

Figure 1.2 *Economic rent and transfer earnings*

rent – *transfer earnings* and *economic* (or *scarcity*) *rent*. Transfer earnings occur because most land is capable of being used for many different purposes and there is competition between various potential interests to secure the right to use it. They are the minimum sums which have to be paid to retain land for its current economic purpose, and if the land has no maintainable use the transfer earning is zero. Economic rent is a payment reflecting the scarcity value of land in excess of its transfer earnings.

Although most farmland contains elements of transfer earnings and economic rent, the proportions vary according to the elasticity of the supply of land. If land were plentiful, supply would be relatively elastic and a high proportion of rent would be in the form of transfer earnings and comparatively little of the payment would be economic rent. But in an intensively farmed area, land would be fairly inelastic in supply, and consequently economic rent would account for a high proportion of total rent. It is not impossible, of course, for some types of farmland to command equal proportions of transfer earnings and economic rent – a situation obtaining if supply were of unitary elasticity (figure 1.2).

If there was a completely free market, land would transfer to its most profitable or *highest and best use*. Each user would be paying more for his/her land than any of his/her competitors would be willing or able to pay. Every eventual user will pay for land either an outright purchase price or rent appropriate to the expected profit s/he can realise from his/her use of the land. Therefore the capital value of land is determined indirectly by the profitability of its use, and directly by the annual rental value. An example of this is the annual value of farmland being derived from the difference between the cost of production and the revenue from the sale of farm produce.

(2) *Urban rents*   Whereas in the country the demand for farming land is derived from the demand for farm produce, in towns 'the demand for land is a demand for space which can be varied by structural changes through the allied processes of property development, redevelopment and conversion'.[7] In contrast to the farmer, the developer may find him/herself constrained by the relative inflexibility of his/her capital and labour inputs. Location and siting, while being of only general significance to the farmer, may thus be of crucial importance to developers in urban areas.

Within urban areas land use is subject to fewer changes; location is therefore of greater importance, and advantages and disadvantages of location are longer-lasting. If there is scarcity of land within the central business district and a high level of demand for central sites, rents will be high. No instant increase in the supply of land in central areas is possible, although in the long term supply might be increased if there is a more intensive use of land and there is an increase in the spatial extent of the central area through an 'invasion' of the surrounding zone.

There is no exact similarity between the determinants of agriculture and urban rents. Relatively higher urban rents are not paid to dissuade landlords from converting their land to farmland, but are the consequence of competition between different urban users. Urban transfer earnings are thus paid to prevent land from transferring from one urban use to another. Yet as urban land is fairly inelastic in supply – increasing in inelasticity towards the central business district – economic rent is also large and its proportion of the total rent also increases towards the centre. On key sites within the central business district economic rent may be as high as 100 per cent of the total rent because of the impossibility of expanding supply. Any increase in demand will increase the economic (and total) rent. In contrast, in the outer suburban area an expansion of supply – in response to an increase in the demand for a particular use – will result in relatively little extra economic rent over and above transfer earnings.

Urban Land Economics

The subject is mainly concerned with the economic implications and consequences of the scarcity and choice of essentially urban property rights. Yet despite the recent interest shown in urban land economics, especially in the United States, the discipline is still in its infancy. This is because conventional economic analysis cannot easily be applied to an urban situation. The market is absent for many products, especially those associated with the urban infrastructure, there are many externalities, and investment decisions are usually undertaken without reference to the urban structure in general and to external scale economies and diseconomies in particular. It is thus difficult or impossible to allocate resources optimally, either within the public sector or between the public and private sectors.

Where there are markets (for example, in the case of owner-occupied houses) they tend to function imperfectly. The scarcity or glut of specific uses is common and often transactions do not occur when market prices are offered. The property market is quite unlike the Stock Exchange or a commodity market. It is not organised and there is no central buying or selling place. It consists of an aggregate of a vast number of deals, large and small, involving heterogeneous buildings and sites. The land professions attempt to bring together buyers and sellers, generally within a fairly local context.

The complexity of urban life proves an obstacle to the application of economic analysis. There is no satisfactory resource allocation model (with a manageable number of variables) which can determine the optimal combination of factors of production in an urban economy – an economy which changes both over time and in space. Yet economic analysis can and must be applied to the many problems relating to urban land use. Spatial structure and urban growth, the location of urban land uses, the property market and planning, the processes of development and techniques of investment analysis, welfare considerations, the economics of urban decay and renewal, housing, the condition of the construction industry – these and other areas provide the economist with the opportunity to apply his/her special powers of analysis and to investigate in specific contexts the productive and distributive processes of urbanised society.

REFERENCES

1. P. Hall and D. Hay, *Growth Centres in the European Urban System* (Heinemann, 1980).
2. L. Van den Berg *et al.*, *Urban Europe: A Study of Growth and Decline* (Pergamon, 1982).
3. M. Edwards, 'Planning and the Land Market: Problems, Prospects and Strategy' in M. Ball *et al.*, *Land Rent, Housing and Urban Planning: A European Perspective* (Croom Helm, 1984).
4. D. Massey, 'In What Sense a Regional Problem', *Regional Studies*, 13 (1979).
5. G. C. Cheshire, *Cheshire's Law of Real Property* (Butterworth, 1972).
6. D. Ricardo, *Principles of Political Economy and Taxation* (Penguin, 1971).
7. R. H. Wright, 'The Property Market 1', *The Architect and Surveyor* (January/ February, 1971).

2

Spatial Structure and Urban Growth

The ability of activities to compete for sites depends upon whether they have the means to benefit from accessibility and complementarity within the urban framework. But economic conditions, population, other land uses both public and private, and the size of the urban area continually change, subjecting the urban land market to forces of perpetual adjustment.

The underlying influences upon urban growth are both national and regional. At a national level the size and rate of growth of the gross national product (GNP) *per capita* determine the quantity and quality of urban land use activity. Yet the less industrialised the country, the greater the potential rate of urbanisation, while countries with high GNP *per capita* may witness a decline in their city centres and an increased rate of suburbanisation and decentralisation. Nationally, non-economic forces reinforce economic factors. Population growth and migration to urban areas tend ultimately to increase living standards and to lower death-rates. Technological development similarly raises real incomes and affects the urban land use pattern. For example, improved construction techniques allow the development of taller buildings and new production methods might necessitate larger buildings on the periphery of cities. Government intervention, even where it is minimal, imposes a national influence over urban growth. But if the government is concerned with such issues as the nationalisation of development land, the taxing of increased values and strategic planning rather than with merely controlling, say, public health or building standards, the degree of influence is substantial and the economic consequences immense.

Regional or local economic, social and political factors may result in some cities growing more rapidly than others. An area may be endowed with expanding industries and, because of greater job opportunities and other attractions, there may be a net inward migration of population. Conversely, other areas may be disadvantaged by declining industries, an outdated infrastructure and an outward migration of population. The structure of local government and the impact of its policies may or may not be favourable to the growth or improvement of the urban area.

Urban Rent – Land Values – Density

Urban growth alters not only the pattern of land use and land values, but also the intensity of site use. As the supply of land in an urban area is fixed in the short term, this will create scarcity. Commercial users will double-up and may operate less efficiently, households may have to live in shared dwellings. Only in the medium and long term will business and residential development extend the city outwards. In the meantime, rising rents will increase the degree of competition for sites within the existing built-up area.

The medium- and long-term supply of land is elastic provided that there is an absence of constraints such as green belt controls and use-restrictions, and assuming the availability of transport. With the extension of the radius of the urban area the supply of land increases in geometric proportions, and if the demand for sites is relatively inelastic any increase in demand should cause site values and rents to fall. But it would be wrong to assume that outward-decreasing site values and rents are due to higher transport costs, and that higher values and rents inward are due to a saving in transport costs. Urban rent is determined by productivity (or profitability), which is highest at the place of maximum accessibility, that is, the central business district. Even if general accessibility begins to diminish when congestion in the centre increases to severe levels, values and rents may continue to rise if sites benefit from some form of special accessibility. In the same location within the urban area, large sites may be more valuable than small ones, as economies of scale can be realised even if the site has many uses.

Land value gradients vary from city to city, and because of higher incomes and internal and external scale economics, peaks are generally higher in larger cities. But the rate of fall in value is not the same for every use. Competition among commercial users in the central business district produces a very steep slope, but further out the slope becomes gentler as competition diminishes. The residential gradient is very gentle as values may be adversely affected in the inner areas of cities because of small sites. The gradient may be flattened out by decentralisation and the diffusion of journey destinations. Smaller peaks may be found at suburban route foci and especially in outlying business districts.

Values continually change because of changes in general and special accessibility. Planning controls, especially those concerning residential and commercial densities, may modify the gradient, and green belts might create local areas of scarcity and so raise values. Rating differences between local authorities also affect gradients. Where there is an absence of industry (for example, in high-income residential areas) a high rate poundage could depress residential values, but this might be more than offset by the appreciating effect of amenity.

There is, of course, a general reduction in population density with the increase in the radical distance from the inner areas of cities (although the central business district may have an almost complete absence of a residential population). In the case of older cities, where employment and housing evolved centrally, the density gradient can be quite steep, whereas in cities of recent

origin there is a greater dispersal of commercial, industrial and residential use
and the gradient may flatten out and comprise numerous outer peaks. If the
public transport system is highly developed in the inner areas of cities and if
there are social customs such as workers returning home for lunch, gradients
will be very steep. Although gradients of the daytime population density or of
net residential densities may produce smoother slopes, it is probable that the
gradient of gross population density is a preferable measure of urban structure.

Accessibility and Demand

Profitability and utility are largely determined by accessibility. The greater the
accessibility of a location (and the lower the net economic cost of movement
in terms of distance, time and convenience), the greater the comparative advantage and the greater the demand for property at that location.

In the case of business use, general accessibility refers to nearness to transport facilities (rail termini, bus stations, motorways), labour, customers, and
service facilities such as banks and post offices. Special accessibility exists
when complementary uses are in close proximity to each other, for example in
London lawyers are close to the Law Courts, stockbrokers are near the Stock
Exchange, commercial and merchant banking is located adjacently, and the
wholesale and retail clothing industry is situated in the Oxford Street area.
(Special 'inaccessibility' is desirable when there are incompatible uses, for instance noxious heavy industry and new high-income housing, or take-away food
shops and retailers of luxury merchandise.) The importance of accessibility to
residential land is illustrated when the utility of particular sites depends upon
monetary factors such as schools, shops, public and private open space, and
travelling costs to work and upon non-monetary considerations such as peace and
quiet (or the reverse), compatible neighbours, fresh air and other less tangible amenities.

The greater the accessibility (general or special) and the greater the relevance of accessibility to the user of land, the higher the value of the land in
question. Therefore the pattern of accessibility creates a pattern of urban land
use which will be concomitant with the pattern of land values. In addition
there is a relationship between accessibility, land uses and values, and the intensity of utilisation. As demand is greatest for those sites with the highest
degree of accessibility, it is more feasible to develop those sites intensively.
Users able to put the site to its most productive use would be prepared to pay
the highest price or rent to acquire the developed property.

The relationship between accessibility, land uses and land values was first
set out in Heinrich von Thünen's theory of rural land use. In 1826, in the light
of empirical evidence, von Thünen[1] postulated that around a 'central town',
rural land of constant fertility assumed different forms, land use diminishing
intensively in inverse relationship to increased distance from the town. The
land use pattern from the centre outwards would comprise the following concentric
belts: horticulture and dairying, silviculture, intensive arable rotation, arable

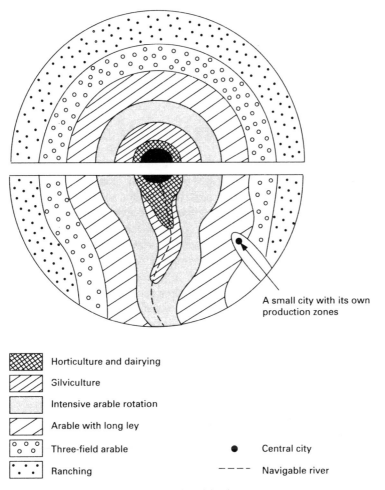

Horticulture and dairying

Silviculture

Intensive arable rotation

Arable with long ley

Three-field arable   ●   Central city

Ranching   – – – –   Navigable river

A small city with its own
production zones

Figure 2.1   *Von Thünen's model of agricultural land use*

with long ley, three-field arable and ranching (figure 2.1). Although in part
influenced by practicality (for example, milk could not be transported great
distances to the market prior to refrigeration, therefore dairying would be close
to the town), land in greatest demand would be that land as near as possible to
the market because of low transport costs. The highest rent would be gained
for this advantage and the highest value output per hectare would accrue. In
the outer belt there would be little demand for land because of high transport
costs, rents would be low and the value of extensive production would be cor-
respondingly low.

The overall land use pattern might be modified by the existence of a navigable river. In contrast to fairly high transport costs over land, costs of river
transport are low, especially for bulky commodities. The river wold have the
effect of extending the different land uses almost parallel along its course. A

further modification might occur if a small city with its own production zones was located within the land use pattern of the main settlement.

Although the von Thünen model has been criticised because it assumed unlikely conditions such as production taking place around an isolated market and soil being of constant fertility, it nevertheless established a distance–cost relationship which has recently become the basis of urban location theory.

THE URBAN LAND USE PATTERN

As with rural land, there are, of course, wide differences in the land use patterns of different urban areas. Varying topographical features have an effect on land use; so do climatic conditions, past and present social and religious customs, legislation and legal decisions, demand for goods and services (including varying consumer preferences), and the policy of local and central government in the supply of public utilities and social services. These variations provide different frameworks within which competition between the existing and potential land users decides the pattern of land use in any urban area. Within these frameworks and subject to the imperfections of the market, the forces of demand and supply provide the means by which land is developed up to its highest and best use. It is as a result of this process that a general pattern of land use has evolved in most urban areas, which in the industrialised world comprise the following areal components: the central business district, the zone of transition, the suburban area and the rural–urban fringe.

The Central Business District

Having the maximum overall accessibility to most parts of the urban area, the central business district is the focus of intra-city transport routes. Competition for sites among commercial users raises land values and the intensity of development to a peak. Population increase and economic growth increase densities within the central business district, development usually being vertical rather than horizontal. The central business district becomes a decreasing proportion of the expanding urban area. If a number of urban areas merge into a conurbation, the central business district with the greatest comparative advantage in terms of accessibility will become the most intensively developed centre at the expense of the other centres.

Within the larger central business districts the shopping area is usually separated from the main office area, although office users will produce a demand for more localised retail services. A separate entertainment area may emerge, but the dispersed siting of cinemas, theatres and concert halls may make it difficult to delineate its boundaries.

The central business district merges almost unnoticed into the surrounding transitional zone, but usually its boundaries are marked by public transport (especially rail) termini reflecting the general absence of the lateral growth of the central business district since the nineteenth century.

The Zone of Transition

In most industrial nations over the last hundred years an area of mixed use has developed around the central business district. This consisted of warehousing and light manufacturing (serving the commercial activities of the central business area) interspersed with transport facilities and residential land. Housing initially would have been for the middle and higher income groups, but generally it has become decayed and dilapidated due largely to its conversion into multiple occupancy low-income dwellings. There are also areas of local authority and charitable trust housing, much of which is old and in need of renewal. Almost alone, London has some transitional areas (such as Belgravia and South Kensington) which have retained their status as high-income enclaves.

The transitional zone is generally beset with many social and economic problems, for example mass deprivation (including homelessness, disease and delinquency). Land might be continually blighted because of the slow pace at which planning proposals are implemented, and many landlords (both private and public) may forgo rents, keeping their properties empty pending redevelopment. The maintenance or improvement of dwellings may be impeded by rent regulation and vagaries in public policy concerning housing rehabilitation. The zone of transition is often referred to as 'the twilight zone'.

Yet new development within the zone does take place. To some extent the market enables land to be developed to its highest and best use as commercial development takes place along the radial routes towards the suburbs or in areas specifically designated for publicly-assisted regeneration.

The Suburban Area

The predominant use in this area is moderate or low density residential land. Housing is segregated by socio-economic class or ethnically, and there is clustering close to railway stations and the main road foci – the area being dependent upon easy access to the employment opportunities and the general attractions of the central part of the city.

Although there is a scattering of schools, churches, public houses and medical facilities, shops tend to be more concentrated into parades and neighbourhood shopping centres. Where office development takes place on a sufficiently large scale, shopping and other commercial and social facilities may have been developed comprehensively to form an 'outlying business district'.

Since the expansion of motor transport and electricity supply, manufacturing industry has been attracted to suburban locations. Sites adjacent to major routes are particularly favoured, making it easy to distribute goods not only to the urban area but also to the regional or national market. Manufacturers also benefit from relatively low-cost sites convenient for further development.

Interspersed with other uses, there are generally extensive areas devoted to golf courses, race tracks, parks, cemeteries, allotments and public open space.

The Rural–Urban Fringe

As the density of the suburban area becomes less, and the built-up parts become largely residential, public open space is replaced by market gardens or farmland. There may also be extensive 'green belt' areas for the purpose of constraining urban expansion. The rural–urban fringe is mainly a commuter belt, its high-income adventitious population now usually outnumbering those engaged in horticulture and agriculture.

THEORIES OF URBAN STRUCTURE

Although the character of the physical structure and population of cities is heterogeneous, the city is a unit of social behaviour. It is also an aggregate of smaller homogeneous areas, all focusing on the central business district. The spatial structure of a city is a product of centripetal forces of attraction and congestion, centrifugal forces of dispersion and decongestion, and forces of areal differentiation. Many theories of spatial structure and urban growth are unsatisfactory because they fail to take into account sufficiently suburbanisation, decentralisation, the development of sub-centres, greater flexibility of location, improvements in technology and transportation, and the effects of central and local government policies. It tends to be the more complicated theories which have lost their credibility, and ironically it is the earliest and simplest ones which are still valid, however loosely.

Concentric Zone Theory

This emerged from a study of Chicago by Burgess[2] and was essentially an application to urban land use of von Thünen's earlier theory relating to rural land around a city (see p. 19). It was suggested that any city extends radially from its centre to form concentric zones and that as distance from the centre increased there would be a reduction in accessibility, rents and densities. Land use would assume the following forms from the centre outwards: the central business district, a zone of transition, an area of factories and low-income housing, an area of higher-income housing, and a commuter zone (figure 2.2). There would also be declining proportions of recent immigrants, delinquency rates, poverty and disease as distance increased from the centre.

The concentric zone theory allows for underlying conditions to change continually. Natural population increase, in-migration, economic growth and income expansion will all result in each zone within the urban area 'invading'

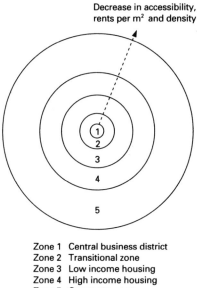

Decrease in accessibility,
rents per m² and density

Zone 1 Central business district
Zone 2 Transitional zone
Zone 3 Low income housing
Zone 4 High income housing
Zone 5 Commuter zone

Figure 2.2 *The concentric zone theory*

the next zone outwards. But there may not be a simple transformation in land use outwards. As the central business district expands, the locational advantages of central sites might diminish, the transitional zone (awaiting redevelopment) might become more and more a twilight area, and as suburban populations increase, new outlying business districts may evolve. There are further effects upon the spatial structure as traffic flows become more complex in response to decentralisation.

Many criticisms can be made of the theory. Land uses within many parts of the urban area are heterogeneous – shops, offices, factories and housing may all be located close to each other, although they may have potentially different site and locational requirements; and there may be many possible locations for different activities which do not all conform with the idealised model. Accessibility may be a relatively unimportant consideration for many uses, especially housing, and commercial users may find it disadvantageous to agglomerate if there is an opportunity to corner an undeveloped market. Decentralised shopping centres and offices may further distort the pattern, and the central business district might experience a decrease in rents and density following the reduction in its accessibility through congestion. The concentric zone model also ignores physical features, takes little account of industrial and railway use, and disregards the effect of radial routeways upon land values and uses. It is more likely that a star-shaped pattern of land use will emerge; travel time rather than transport costs often being more important as a determinant of use. An axial development model (figure 2.3) modifies the concentric zone pattern,

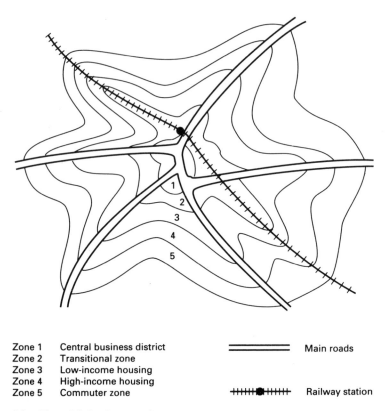

Zone 1	Central business district
Zone 2	Transitional zone
Zone 3	Low-income housing
Zone 4	High-income housing
Zone 5	Commuter zone

================ Main roads

++++++●++++++ Railway station

Figure 2.3 *The axial development theory*

taking into account the effect of transport route. The assumption of a single focal point remains, though maximum accessibility need no longer be found at a central location.

However, even in its modified form, the concentric zone theory is little more than descriptive, showing *how*, rather than *why*, urban growth takes place. It is deterministic and assumes that social groups have to accord with a specific urban structure. Its greatest weakness is that it assumes a free or perfect market, it ignores imperfections (such as locational inertia, sub-optimal use and long leases) and takes no account of planning controls. It disregards the purchasing of sites for future development, with current use being retained at a sub-optimal value. But the pattern of urban land use is not wholly irrational and is not subject to an incomprehensible welter of paradoxes and anomalies. The concentric zone theory is illuminating it shows that, in general, accessibility, rents and densities diminish with increased distance from the central business district, and that the process of invasion is responsible for changing land use.

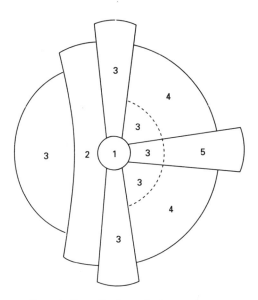

Sector 1   Central business district
Sector 2   Manufacturing and warehousing
Sector 3   Low-income housing
Sector 4   Middle-income housing
Sector 5   High-income housing

Note: The diagram assumes a prevailing wind from the east. The manufacturing sector is thus located to the west of the high incoem housing sector. In the United Kingdom the reverse conditions usually apply.

Figure 2.4   *The sector theory*

Sector Theory

This theory, as presented by Hoyt,[3] propounds that growth along a particular transport route takes the form of land use already prevailing and that each sector of relatively homogeneous use extends outwards from the centre (figure 2.4). Compatible land uses would lie adjacent to each other (for example, warehousing and light manufacturing, and low-income housing) and incompatible uses will be repelled (for instance, high-income housing, and warehousing and light industry). Residential uses will tend to be segregated in terms of income and social position, and will expand in different directions in different parts of the city. As with the concentric zone theory there is a process of invasion as economic and population growth takes place. When the inner areas are abandoned by high-income households they are infilled (usually at a higher density) by lower-income households.

The criticisms of the theory are broadly the same as those made of the concentric zone theory, and so are the merits. But while recognising the relationship between accessibility, land use and values, and densities, Hoyt believed

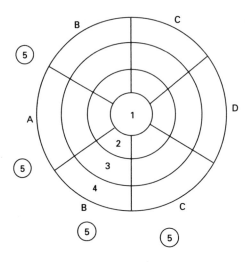

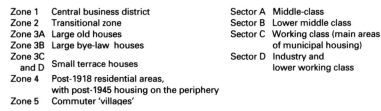

Zone 1	Central business district	Sector A	Middle-class
Zone 2	Transitional zone	Sector B	Lower middle class
Zone 3A	Large old houses	Sector C	Working class (main areas
Zone 3B	Large bye-law houses		of municipal housing)
Zone 3C and D	Small terrace houses	Sector D	Industry and lower working class
Zone 4	Post-1918 residential areas, with post-1945 housing on the periphery		
Zone 5	Commuter 'villages'		

Figure 2.5   *The structure of a hypothetical British city*

that the interdependence of these variables expresses itself differently in terms of the spatial structure of the city.

Concentric Zone–Sector Theory

Both the previous theories were developed in the United States following studies undertaken of a number of cities, the concentric zone theory being related to Chicago. But Mann[4] produced a hybrid model of the structure of a hypothetical British city – an urban area large enough to have distinct internal differentiation, but not too large to exhibit the complexities of a conurbation. The main additional feature is the existence of commuter villages separated from the built-up area of the city (figure 2.5).

In considering theories of urban growth it has been assumed so far that zones or sectors 'invade' each other, generally outwards, low-income housing moving into the high-income housing area, and the latter expanding into the commuter belt. But with increased costs of commuter travelling the inner areas of cities have again attracted higher-income households – invasion and 'gentrification' taking place inwards. If, simultaneously, the central business district expands outwards, the area of low income housing will be squeezed

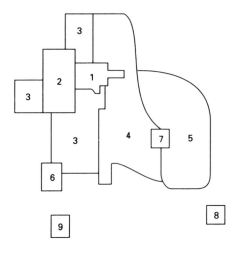

Nucleus 1 Central business district
Nucleus 2 Wholesale and light manufacturing
Nucleus 3 Low-income residential
Nucleus 4 Middle-income residential
Nucleus 5 High-income residential
Nucleus 6 Heavy manufacturing
Nucleus 7 Outlying business district
Nucleus 8 Residential suburb
Nucleus 9 Industrial suburb

Notes: (i) The diagram assumes a prevailing wind from the east.
(ii) It is assumed that land use boundaries coincide with the main traffic routes of a 'grid-iron' street pattern.
Neither of these conditions are applicable to cities in the United Kingdom.

Figure 2.6   *The multiple nuclei theory*

between two invading forces. Increased occupancy of the remaining low-income dwellings, migration to country towns or homelessness will consequently be compounded.

Multiple-nuclei Theory

Unlike the theories of urban growth considered so far, which have all assumed that cities grow from one central point, the multiple-nuclei theory produced by Harris and Ullman[5] in the United States is based on the assumption that urban growth takes place around several distinct nuclei. The nuclei could include the first urban settlement (probably a market town), a nearby village, a factory, a mine, a railway terminal or waterside facility. Ultimately they would be integrated into one urban area largely agglomerated by residential use and intra-city transportation. The original nuclei would help to determine current use, for example the market town might become the central business district, the village an outlying business district, the factory site might evolve into an area of wholesaling and light manufacture, and the mine or waterside facility could become an area of heavy industry (figure 2.6).

Within the urban area, compatible uses are attracted to each other – for example, low-income residential land would be close to wholesaling and light manufacturing and near-heavy industry, and the medium- and high-income residential areas would surround the outlying business district. Incompatible uses would remain far apart – for example, high-income housing and heavy manufacturing. The number of nuclei would generally be greater in large urban areas than in small cities and there would be a greater degree of specialisation within each nucleus.

The multiple-nuclei model related initially to cities within the United States where grid-iron road patterns separated land uses geometrically. But less regular route patterns and use boundaries in other countries do not invalidate the basic principles of the theory.

Theories of urban spatial structure are as much descriptive as analytical. They explain how cities change their form, and very rarely will a single theory be adequate for this task. The concentric zone theory, while recognising that the transitional zone experiences deterioration prior to eventual redevelopment, ignores the same trend occurring elsewhere – for example, on the rural–urban fringe. None of the theories explains satisfactorily the significance of sub-centres to urban growth, and none pays sufficient attention to agglomeration; most ignore the important changes that occur within the central business district and which affect the urban area as a whole; and, perhaps more importantly, all fail to consider the process of decentralisation.

The Development of Individual Urban Sites

Whichever of the theories of urban spatial structure is being considered, it is assumed that land uses invade each other and that there is a varying pace of renewal. Changing property values are both a cause and a consequence of these processes. Urban property has two basic values – the capital value of buildings and sites in their *existing use* and the capital value of cleared sites in their *best alternative use*. In a period of price stability, the capital value of the building and site in existing use falls as the building becomes obsolete or wears out, but the value of the cleared site in its best alternative use remains constant (figure 2.7a). During inflation, both values increase although the capital value of the cleared site for the best alternative use would probably rise more quickly than the capital value of the building and site in existing use – the latter value eventually declining (figure 2.7b).

When redevelopment occurs it will usually be for a more intensive use and, assuming planning consent, to higher buildings. But there are economic limits to height. On the supply side, the state of building technology could mean that sub-ground conditions are unsuitable. Increasing costs occur as additional storeys are added because of the necessity for increased hoisting and more costly foun-

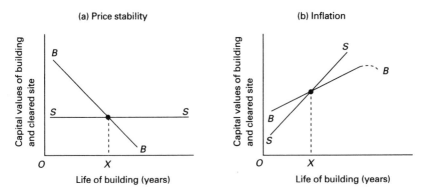

Note: *BB* = capital value of building and site in existing use
SS = capital value of cleared site in its best alternative use

Figure 2.7 *The maximum economic life of a building*

dations. There is an increasing percentage of unremunerative space which needs to be devoted to servicing and maintenance of buildings. On the demand side, there may be limits, although penthouses command high values. Basically, the developer may go on adding storeys until the marginal yield from the additional storey is equal to the marginal cost of providing it subject to statutory approvals and structural considerations. Beyond this point, further storeys would be unprofitable. For housing developers, terraces of narrow-fronted housing achieve higher density and lower site costs. Stone[6] contends that the real costs of providing and maintaining dwellings rise more rapidly than the requirement for land falls; hence the real costs per hectare of land saved increase with the number of storeys. Frequently, the use of high-density development is advocated as a means of housing more people nearer the centre of the city and nearer their work; however, additional space must be made available for local shopping and other facilities, this increases the amount of land required and hence reduces the numbers that can be housed near the centre.

In figure 2.7 redevelopment should take place after *X* years, *ceteris paribus*. But because of the durability of buildings (and often because of their architectural merit or historic interest) redevelopment might not take place until the buildings are structurally unsound. In other cases inaccurate valuation of the cleared site or building (or both) may create inertia. The multiplicity of interests, properties being retained by their existing owners for non-monetary reasons, and the length of leases and legal rights of tenants may also inhibit the redevelopment of a site. The continued use of the building after *X* years therefore implies that the land is being used inefficiently or sub-optimally, although it must be recognised that non-economic or indirect influences may be important.

On the rural–urban fringe, the direct value of agricultural or horticultural activities may be considerably less than the capital value of sites. Again, redevelopment may be restricted through planning controls – not least by green-belt restrictions. In both urban and rural areas when the capital values of

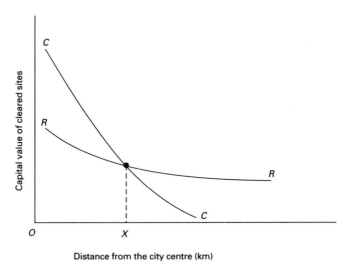

Distance from the city centre (km)

Note: *CC* = commercial site values
       RR = residential site values

Figure 2.8   *Site values of competing uses*

buildings fall below the capital values of cleared sites, the possibility of the
nationalisation of development land and the taxation of increased values might
deter development – sub-optimal use consequently resulting.

The micro-economic aspects of the change (or lack of change) in the use of
individual sites is consistent with macro-economic explanations of the urban
structure and the theories of urban growth. Firey[7] argued that although accessibility and the capital value of sites diminish outwards from the centre of the
city, the rate of fall in site value is not the same for each use. There is a
greater rate of decline of those uses most dependent on accessibility, namely
the commercial uses of the centre. Where the site value of one use becomes
less than that of another, change to the higher value will occur eventually. In
figure 2.8 commercial use will replace residential use when the distance from
the city centre becomes less than *X* km. Any remaining residential sites within
the central area will probably be redeveloped as commercial properties.

Firey's hypothesis of site value is closely related to Alonso's theory of
rent (see p. 51). Both approaches help to clarify the rationale of the numerous models of urban structure discussed earlier in this chapter, and the theories of urban growth offer explanations of why the underlying determinants
of the capital values of cleared sites and buildings fluctuate – the values
reflecting the levels of economic activity, technological application and
government policy.

THEORIES OF URBAN GROWTH

Urban economics is in its infancy and therefore as yet cannot be expected to produce satisfactory models to explain urban growth. The complexity and diversity of urban growth, social and cultural influences (in addition to economic forces) and inadequate data make the economist rely heavily on demographic variables and persuade him/her unavoidably to equate an increase in population with an increase in urban growth. It must not be assumed, however, that population growth can be related immediately to an increase in welfare – congestion, a higher cost of living and poorer housing could be direct results of an increase in the urban population, and even if the GNP *per capita* rises following increased urbanisation, this could be attributed to higher incomes being realised in rural areas.

It is important to draw a distinction between the dynamics of spatial structure (discussed earlier in this chapter) and the theories of urban growth. The former attempt to explain how cities grow, and the latter (now to be considered) help to identify the reasons why urban areas grow (or decline).

Central Place Theory

Christaller[8] hypothesised that the distribution of centralised services accounts for the spacing, size and functional pattern of urban centres. On the assumption that urban settlements locate on a uniform plain, centralised service centres would be distributed regularly within a systematic pattern. Market areas or spheres of influence would take the form of a hexagonal mesh. This would avoid either certain areas not being served, or other areas being served by overlapping hinterlands – consequences of a pattern of circular market areas. The main function of each town would be to supply goods and services to the countryside – town and country being interdependent.

A hierarchy of centres would evolve. Towns with the lowest level of specialisation would be evenly spaced and surrounded by their hexagonally-shaped market areas. For each group of six towns there would be a larger city with more specialised functions which would be located an equal distance from other cities with the same degree of specialisation. Such cities would have larger hexagonal hinterlands for their own specialised services. Even larger and more specialised settlements would have larger market areas and be situated at an equal distance from each other. Christaller believed that the lowest-ranked centres were likely to be located 7 km apart. Settlements of the next highest rank would serve three times the area and three times the population. Thus they would be situated 12 km apart ($\sqrt{3} \times 7$). Similarly, the market areas of centres of the next rank would again be three times larger (table 2.1, figure 2.9). Since the number of settlements of successively lower rank follows a geometric progression (1, 3, 9, 27, ...) the pattern is referred to as a $k = 3$ hierarchy. Towns within the hierarchy would grow as a result of an increase in the production

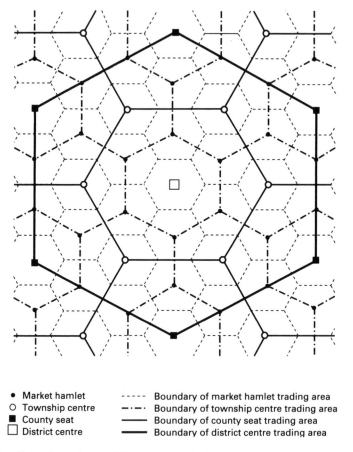

●	Market hamlet	- - - - -	Boundary of market hamlet trading area
○	Township centre	— · — ·	Boundary of township centre trading area
■	County seat	——	Boundary of county seat trading area
☐	District centre	▬▬	Boundary of district centre trading area

Figure 2.9   *Christaller's theory of the arrangement of central places*

of goods and services to satisfy an increased demand from a growing population within their zones of influence, but generally they would remain within their rank and the rule of three would persist.

Christaller recognised that the hierarchy would be modified by long-distance trade, by transport routes and by administrative functions. Towns influenced by these factors would have larger populations than their local market would imply, and would be part of a $k = 4$ or even $k = 7$ hierarchy. Settlement would tend generally to be clustered along main routes and be larger at route junctions. Large-scale manufacturing industry would also have an agglomerating influence, increasing population out of proportion to the size of the immediate service hinterland.

The central place theory is criticised as it is dependent upon the evolution of settlement on a uniform plane – Christaller largely ignored variable topography. The influence of manufacturing industry both past and present and below a large scale is also discounted, the production of goods and services for

Table 2.1 *The urban hierarchy in South Germany (after Christaller)*

Market centre	Distance apart (km)	Population	Tributary area size (km²)	Population
Market hamlet (*Marktort*)	7	800	45	2 700
Township centre (*Amstort*)	12	1 500	135	8 100
County seat (*Kresstadt*)	21	3 500	400	24 000
District centre (*Bezirksstodt*)	36	9 000	1 200	75 000
Small state capital (*Gausstadt*)	62	27 000	3 600	225 000
Provincial head capital (*Provinzhauptstadt*)	108	90 000	10 800	675 000
Regional capital city (*Landeshauptstadt*)	186	300 000	32 000	2 025 000

Source: E. L. Ullman, *American Journal of Sociology*, 46 (1941) 857.

distribution to other areas is not considered, local specialisation is ignored, and it is not appreciated that growth generates the internal needs of cities (for example, schools, hospitals, and general service and manufactured requirements). Neither the growth of industrial suburbs nor of outlying business districts fits in with the central place theory, and there is no consideration of the effect upon the size of towns of a large in-migration of labour.

But the central place theory is useful in that it stresses the relevance of the market area to the size of a town's population, and it introduces the idea of the urban hierarchy. It has led to the introduction of the 'rank–size rule' which states that the population of a given urban area tends to be equal to the population of the largest city divided by the rank of the population size into which the given urban area falls, the population of settlements thus being arranged according to the series $1, \frac{1}{2}, \frac{1}{3}, \frac{1}{4}, \ldots 1/n$. If plotted on a graph this produces the result exhibited in figure 2.10.

Whereas the central place theory was idealistic, not being derived from empirical information, the rank–size rule is based on the study of actual population data. Yet generally the rank–size rule is in accord with the central place theory. Both imply that there are very few large cities, and where Christaller's urban hierarchy would produce a stepped arrangement of population sizes and the rank–size rule shows a smooth progression of settlements through the ranks, this divergence is largely illusory. Christaller's theory is most relevant to small rural areas and to the lower ranks of the hierarchy, whereas the rank–size rule is particularly relevant to a large area – possibly a whole country. Because of

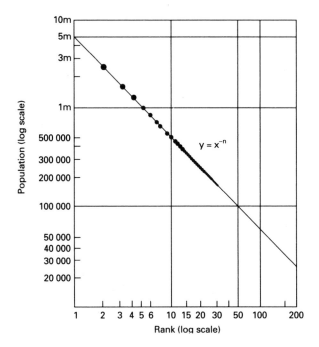

Figure 2.10   *The rank–size rule: the hypothetical population of cities in relation to their ranking*

regional variations in the degree of industrialisation, the development of transport services and administrative structures, a series of stepped hierarchies merge together to produce a relatively smooth population curve blurring the edges of individual hierarchical systems. The rule depends upon the assumption of a stable relationship between the populations of central places and the population of the market areas served by them. The principal weakness of the rank–size rule is that in most countries the largest city is larger than the rule would suggest.

Central place theory and rank–size rule provide an efficient basis for administering urban regions and for allocating resources. Investment decisions must take the urban hierarchy or rank–size into account if the desired private or social returns are to be realised.

Based on empirical studies made in 1938, Smailes[9] suggested that the urban hierarchy in England and Wales comprised seven ranks of settlement: that is, major cities, major towns, towns, sub-towns, villages, and hamlets. To qualify as a fourth-rank, 'fully-fledged' town, an urban settlement would need to possess at least three banks, a Woolworth's store, a secondary school, a hospital, a cinema and a weekly newspaper. Settlements which did not possess this complete range of services were categorised as sub-towns or villages. In contrast, a city would have all the services of a town and would also possess department stores, specialised hospital services and an evening newspaper. A major city would in addition have the regional offices of private firms and government departments; and when the research was being undertaken, a major city would also have its daily morning newspaper and a civic university. But Smailes was not prepared to identify market areas and recognised that the location and spacing of urban settlements showed no hexagonal pattern.

Smith,[10] using a much larger number of indicators of urban rank than Smailes had used in his 1938 classification, showed that the urban hierarchy in England and Wales had remained very stable. Of the 606 urban centres, only 138 rose in rank, and 78 declined over the period 1938–78. Change occurred mainly among the lower-order centres, especially in the north, but the south and east were particularly stable because of the dominance of London. In research funded by the Royal Institution of Chartered Surveyors and the Economic and Social Research Council,[11] it was also shown that the hierarchy of shopping centres in Britain had changed little over the period 1961–84.

In the United States, central place theory has been further developed. Berry and Garrison[12] suggested that the concepts of 'range' and 'threshold' control the distribution of central places. The range of a good or service is the distance over which people are prepared to travel to obtain that product, and the threshold is the minimum amount of purchasing power necessary to support the supply of a good or service from a central place. The range of a product is limited at the upper level by the degree of competition from other central places supplying the same product, and at the lower level by the threshold necessary to permit it to function. As more specialised products require a larger threshold they usually need a more extensive range, therefore it is logical for an urban hierarchy to evolve based on the degree of specialisation of central places.

The central place theory and considerations of urban rank have been generally concerned with towns as service centres. But Pred[13] argued that (at least in the United States) the rate of development of a city is related functionally to the diversification of its manufacturing sector, and that city size depends largely on the number of extent of its overlapping hinterlands.

Urban Base Theory

Unlike the central place theory, which was concerned with the distribution of products from an urban centre to its hinterland, the urban base theory involves a consideration of demand from anywhere outside the boundaries of the settlement.

The more a city specialises, the more it destroys its self-sufficiency. Urban growth will thus depend upon the urban area's ability to export goods and services to pay for its imported needs. The production of goods and services for export is known as a 'basic' activity and the output of products for distribution solely to the urban area itself is referred to as a 'non-basic' activity. According to the theory, the growth of an urban area depends upon the ratio of basic to non-basic activities – the higher the ratio, the greater the rate of growth. Non-basic industries will be dependent upon the basic sector, employees in the latter providing much of the demand for the products of the former.

The theory assumes that once the underlying economic, technological and

Table 2.2 *The basic–non basic equilibrium*

	Number	I Initial equilibrium ratio to basic employment	Number	II Disequilibrium ratio to basic employment	Number	III Eventual equilibrium ratio to basic employment
Basic employees	10 000	1.0	12 500	1.0	12 500	1.0
Non-basic employees	15 000	1.5	15 000	1.2	18 750	1.5
Total employees	25 000	2.5	27 500	2.2	31 250	2.5
Total population	50 000	5.0	55 000	4.4	62 500	5.0

social structure of a country has stabilised, the basic–non-basic ratio of an urban area and the ratios of these activities (separately or combined) to the total population remain constant. If there is an injection of basic employment into the town, eventually non-basic employment will have to increase to meet the higher local demand for goods and services, and the total dependent population will also increase. Thus any temporary instability resulting from an initial increase in basic employment will be eliminated through an upward adjustment in both non-basic employment and total population (table 2.2). The extent of the overall change will therefore be at a multiple of the initial injection of basic employment.

The urban base theory also suggests that if an urban area loses some basic employment, less non-basic employment will be required and the town's population will decline at a multiple of the initial withdrawal of basic employment.

Many criticisms have been expressed regarding the validity of the theory. There is unlikely to be a constant basic–non-basic ratio for an urban area even if the overall underlying conditions remain fairly stable. Total non-basic activity increases in relative importance as urban areas increase in size, and individual basic and non-basic activities may experience economies of scale (and possibly eventual diseconomies) thereby altering ratios. Undue importance is attached to basic employment; non-basic employment may sometimes be more important in determining economic activity in an urban area, and while the theory argues that non-basic employment is dependent upon basic employment, the reverse is often true. Well-developed non-basic activities will attract basic industry, which will be dependent upon the non-basic activities' ability to supply goods and services, capital, ancillary labour and developable land. The theory only suggest what might happen if there is a change in basic activity; it gives no indication of what future changes may be anticipated in an urban area. But a major weakness is that it ignores the importance of imports. If all the increase in export earnings of basic activities was spent on imported goods and services there would be no increase in demand for the products of non-basic industries. Any application of the urban base theory (or one where non-basic activities were assumed to be dominant) would involve the difficult problem of first defining and then identifying basic and non-basic activities and employ-

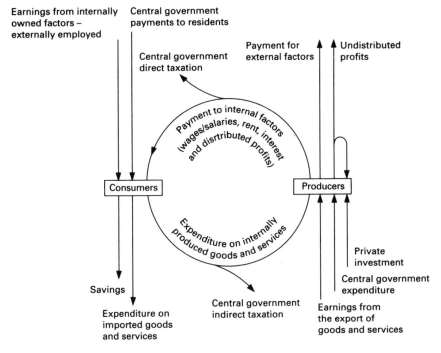

Figure 2.11 *Money flows circulating around, injected into and withdrawn from an urban area*

ment, since industries, institutions, firms and employees may not demarcate between production for the local market and production for export.

Nevertheless, although the numerical aspects of the theory are unrefined, in many urban areas (especially in medium-sized and small towns) changes in overall economic activity and in population depend largely upon changes in basic activity. The theory also shows that there is a multiplier effect following initial injections (or withdrawals) of activity. In general it should be assumed that there is interdependence between basic and non-basic activities, and that the multiplier of each activity is different and varies over time and over different population and income levels.

Keynesian Theory

Whereas the urban base theory concentrated upon urban employment, additions to the level of employment and multiplier effects upon the total population, the flow of money theory is essentially concerned with the economic growth of an urban area expressed in monetary terms. It involves the assessment of the effect upon total income of the circular flow of money between producers and consumers, export earnings and import expenditure, investment and savings and public spending and taxation (figure 2.11).

This approach developed with regard to the national economy by Keynes[14] in the 1930s identifies money inflows as export earnings, the earnings of externally-employed factors, and national government expenditure; money outflows are identified as import expenditure, payment for externally-owned factors (used by producers located in the urban area) and national government taxes. Investment and saving may or may not be retained for use within the town, but net investment is an injection into the money flow, while net savings would be a withdrawal.

The income of the urban area would grow if there was an increase in the circular flow of money between producers and consumers, money inflows exceeded money outflows, and investment exceeded savings. If the opposite trends occurred the income of the urban area would decline.

A multiplier would result in any initial increase (or decrease) in income having a more than proportionate effect on the eventual urban income. The greater the marginal propensity to consume (MPC) or the smaller the marginal propensity to save (MPS) the larger the eventual increase in income. The extent of the multiplier is measured accordingly:

$$K = \frac{1}{1 - \text{MPC}} \text{ or } K = \frac{1}{\text{MPS}}$$

where K is the multiplier. (Note: the marginal propensity to consume and the marginal propensity to save are the additions to consumption and savings resulting from an increment of income expressed as fractions of that income.)

Although the money flow theory of growth is as relevant to an urban area as it is to a national economy, its weakness is that data at a local level are largely unavailable and that even if information were to hand the theory would not predict when a change in variables would occur. But like the urban base theory it suggests that there is a causal relationship between the export activities of an urban area and its rate of growth, and that basic and non-basic activities are mutually dependent. While the urban base theory is primarily concerned with employment and assumes that incomes within the urban area will increase at some proportion to an increase in population, the money flow theory is mainly concerned with income. If increased, urban income might or might not be associated with a subsequent increase in population but it would probably have an effect, possibly substantial, on the built environment.

Input–Output Analysis

Developed by Isard,[15] Leontief and Strout,[16] input–output analysis requires the construction of a matrix to show the production and distribution of the industries of an urban area, the nature of the interrelationships between those industries, and the interrelationship between those industries and other economic sectors both within and outside the urban area. For each industry it is necessary to know its purchases of inputs (labour, capital, raw materials, transport services, property) from all other industries and sectors of the economy located inside or outside the town or city. A similar analysis should then be made of the distribution of the output of those industries.

Although input–output analysis does not indicate why initial changes in inputs and outputs occur, nor takes sufficiently into account the change input–output relationships resulting from technological improvement, its use is pertinent to the understanding of urban growth. By showing the dependence of one industry or activity on all other industries and activities it allows the chain of repercussions stemming from a change in that industry or activity to be traced until the adjustments necessary to restore stability have been made. This is of relevance to government policy since at a central and local level it can encourage, deter or prohibit industrial development.

LOCATION THEORY

Production of goods and services in the economy involves the combination of factors of production by the most efficient means possible. Producers who are able to minimise production and distribution costs may gain an advantage over competitors which will enable them to extend their markets. Both production and distribution costs will to some degree be influenced by location, which will affect the cost of purchasing and combining inputs and the cost of supplying markets. Indeed, even at the wider level of regions themselves, one can talk of the general locational advantages an area possesses that make it attractive to producers – the cost and availability of land, buildings, energy, labour and capital, access to specialised business services, and good access to the transport network and wide markets.

Inevitably, firms will have different preferences depending on their required combination of factors of production. Some industries, such as coal-mining, are clearly restricted by the location of natural resources. Industries with a high bulk-to-value ratio for materials or products may find transport costs are their main priority in deciding on a location. Such industries are *transport-oriented*, and will tend to locate either close to the source of raw materials (if they lose weight in the production process), or close to the market (if they gain weight in the production process). The latter case may at first appear rather odd, but in practice there are several industries which experience weight gain in this sense, either because of some generally available resource such as water (for example, in beer production) or because of the need for bulky packaging, as in glass production.

Other types of industry, such as textiles, may instead be attracted to areas with abundant and cheap labour. These industries – often termed *labour-oriented* – occur where labour costs represent a high share of total costs, and where other considerations (such as transport costs) are less important. However, it may often be wrong to generalise for any particular industry, since even within the same industry different lines of production may require very different

Table 2.3 *Pull factors influencing decisions to locate green-field units in Devon and Cornwall,* (n = 68)

	Number of plants	Percentage %
Central government regional assistance	37	54.4
Labour factors:		
Availability of semi-skilled labour	29	42.7
Low cost of labour	12	17.7
Site/premises factors:		
Suitable site available	22	32.4
Cost of premises	10	14.7
Owner/director had connections with the region	11	16.2
Attractive residential environment	9	13.2
Good road and rail connections	4	
Good air and water quality (food and drink/ chemicals plants)	4	
Access to regional market	4	
Availability of raw materials	4	

Note: Respondent may identify factors in more than one category.

Source: Adapted from J. Potter (see note 18).

combinations of factors – some products may require more labour-intensive techniques (for example, car assembly in contrast to car components), or perhaps a higher degree of skilled labour.

In addition, Alonso[17] suggests a further category of *amenity-oriented* industries which appear to be gaining in importance. Such industries (for example, electronics) are often research intensive and require highly skilled engineers and scientists, at least for some parts of the production process. Transport costs, due to a low bulk-to-value ratio, are often insignificant. It is in these instances that firms may be attracted by a wide variety of amenity factors relating to the general infrastructure and environment: proximity to research establishments and universities, good access to motorway networks and major airports, a good residential environment, good schools, a pleasant climate and cultural facilities. Some of these factors may in reality represent inputs into the production process, while others may be required more generally to ensure an attractive living and working environment for key workers and management.

A recent study which examined the locational factors behind the establishment of new green-field branch factories in Devon and Cornwall highlights the relative importance of these factors.[18] Table 2.3 summarises the survey results. It is important to bear in mind that the factors mentioned are clearly influenced by the locational characteristics of the area itself and the nature of the firms interviewed (that is, branch plants). In this context and in common with other peripheral locations, it is likely that incoming firms will place less emphasis on transport connections either because they are mainly supplying local or regional markets or because they are able to trade off higher transport costs against reduced labour costs, lower cost of premises or regional aid.

The conclusion of the study was that the availability of regional aid, the cost and availability of semi-skilled labour and the availability of a suitable site were the main factors influencing green-field branch plant establishment in Devon and Cornwall. Given that most firms in the survey would have set up before the abolition of automatic Regional Development Grants (1988), the implication is that inward investment in such peripheral areas in the 1990s may well end up lower than in previous decades.

This view is supported by an earlier study which examined how – at the national level – spatial variations in cost components would influence the profitability of a range of firms.[19] One of the main results was that unit input costs tended to be higher in the large conurbations than in their surrounding hinterlands (especially in London, Birmingham, Sheffield, Liverpool and Newcastle). For example it was suggested that the profitability of the majority of manufacturing industries could be increased (by more than 20 per cent) by a move of at least 100 miles away from Inner London. The study also suggested that many non-urban locations in areas not eligible for regional aid, but in relatively close proximity to London and Birmingham, might offer similar (and often better) profitability by comparison with peripheral locations benefiting from regional aid. If a substantial majority of firms dispersing from the conurbations can improve profitability by means of such relatively short-distance moves to nearby (non-assisted) rural areas, it is indeed difficult to see how many peripheral areas would continue to attract inward manufacturing investment in the absence of continuing regional assistance to firms. For example, firms leaving London might be more inclined to move to an area such as East Anglia (non-assisted) or parts of the Birmingham hinterland in preference to, say, Merseyside or Northumberland. Also, given the current problems facing urban areas themselves, it can be argued that more should be done to help improve the profitability of manufacturing firms in these areas. Indeed, as we shall see below, many manufacturing firms and processes still retain strong links with highly urbanised locations.

A final set of locational considerations involves the rather complex interrelationships between the location decisions of different firms once these are considered together rather than separately. In a simple case, for example, the location decisions of a number of small supplier firms may hinge critically on the decisions of one or two major purchasers. However, in most cases such interrelationships are more diffused and concern the broad advantages firms in *similar* or *different* industries obtain from locating in proximity. Benefits of this type may be subdivided usefully into economies of *localisation* and economies of *urbanisation*.

Localisation economies are found between firms in the same industry and involve benefits such as the availability of a specialised labour force and service facilities peculiar to the industry, the minimisation of transport and information costs with regard to supplier firms, and the advantages of being able to follow closely the marketing strategy and production technology of competing firms.

Urbanisation economies are more general and arise from the close proximity of a large number of different economic activities; these include a large and diverse labour market, good urban transport facilities, and a wide range of professional and commercial service facilities, the availability of which tends generally to increase with urban size. However, we should hasten to note that as urban areas grow in size, so urbanisation economies may eventually turn into diseconomies – congestion of transport facilities and eventual labour shortages may push up operating costs and, over time, any remaining benefits may become capitalised in inflated land values and passed on as higher industrial and commercial rents. For as long as they exist, however, external economies may have the effect of reducing long-run average costs as production becomes more efficient.

Internal economies (economies of scale) – which also reduce unit costs – are likely to be gained by firms that are able to supply large markets and can therefore benefit from longer production runs, greater specialisation and an organised distribution network. Internal economies are likely to be more significant in larger urban areas, because only with large labour markets and plants will some firms be able to achieve the economies of large-scale production. However, in most cases such economies will only exist between given levels of output, disappearing after a certain output is reached. Certainly, a firm which aims to supply an entire national (or even the single European) market will have to weight very carefully the advantages of lower transport costs resulting from a dispersed pattern of production against any loss of scale economies that a greater number of plants would entail.

Together, *external* and *internal* economies are referred to as (business) agglomeration economies.[20] They have the potential to produce enhanced competitiveness, higher productivity and, in turn, higher wages and incomes. Other forms of economies exist, such as social and consumer agglomeration economies,[21] reflecting the influence of urban size on the cost and availability of public- and private-sector services respectively. Discussion of these will be taken up in the following section.

There have been numerous studies undertaken which confirm the importance of external economies (localisation and urbanisation) in production. A study by Townroe and Roberts[22] also confirmed the existence of internal economies of scale for a wide range of industries (with the notable exception of electrical engineering). The distinction between localisation and urbanisation economies is of considerable significance for urban areas. If localisation economies dominate, then the manufacturing fortunes of cities will be tied to those of the industries in which they specialise. If, however, urbanisation economies are more important, then a large diversified set of industries would provide the main source of advantage. In an attempt to separate out these effects, Moomaw[23] produced the results given in Table 2.4 for the USA. By examining the degree to which these industries tended to be located within large cities, the author

Table 2.4 *Classification of industries by external effects*

	Group	Industry
a	Localisation economies and urbanisation diseconomies	Primary metals and Chemicals
b	Localisation economies only	Instruments, Fabricated metals, Rubber products, Paper products and Stone, Clay and Glass
c	Localisation economies and urbanisation economies	Printing and Electrical machinery
d	Urbanisation economies only	Apparel and Food products
e	No external economies	Non-electrical machinery, Petroleum refining, Transportation equipment, Leather products, Furniture, Textiles and Wood products

Source: R. Moomaw (see note 23).

was also able to assess the extent to which localisation and urbanisation economies provided the basis for the observed locational pattern of these industries. Significantly, agglomeration economies were found for eleven of the twelve most urbanised industries. For example, industries in group (a) tended to be highly urbanised, and here localisation benefits appeared to outweigh urbanisation diseconomies. In general, the conclusion reached was that external economies were predominantly localisation economies rather than wider urbanisation economies. Notable exceptions were 'apparel' and 'food products' in group (c), which appeared to benefit most from urbanisation economies – both being highly urbanised in practice. Finally, it should be noted that a wide range of industries – in group (e) – exhibited few signs of either localisation or urbanisation economies.

While it is difficult to generalise on the subject of external economies it would appear that many industries do in practice benefit from locating near other firms within the same industry. The role of urbanisation economies, although significant in a few industries, is less clear overall. Whilst Carlino, for example, found urbanisation economies to be significant in twelve out of a sample of nineteen industries studied, he also found diseconomies to be significant in ten industries.[24] On average for populations above 3.3 million, agglomeration diseconomies appeared to outweigh economies.

The question of agglomeration economies in general is of considerable significance for regional and urban planning and development. It is sometimes argued, for example, that at the national level the selection of only a few major centres – and their promotion by means of, say, enhanced infrastructure provision – would be more efficient than the alternative of following a decentralised pattern of regional and urban development. Although the latter course might involve a greater number of (smaller) urban settlements and thus lower agglomeration economies, it would help to promote a balanced spatial pattern of national growth and a more dispersed pattern of employment opportunities.[25]

At the level of the European Union, it is possible that large multi-national firms may find that agglomeration economies in locations at the heart of the new Single European Market outweigh the additional transport costs of supplying peripheral markets where these had formerly been served by a more geographically dispersed production pattern. Any move to consolidate production in fewer (central) locations would almost certainly result in a substantial increase in goods and materials movement throughout the Union. This would in turn add to congestion in such central and often highly urbanised locations.

SIZE, URBAN GROWTH AND OPTIMALITY

Optimal city-size theory defines the non-monetary as well as the monetary costs and benefits of urban size and examines these in a welfare economic framework. Such considerations are important and may have far-reaching implications for urban and regional planning. The theory may help determine, for example, whether the size of the largest cities should be controlled and, at the other end of the scale, whether there exists some minimum urban size. Unfortunately, many of the non-monetary costs and benefits relating to city size – such as congestion, pollution and crime – are difficult to measure precisely and even more difficult to evaluate monetarily, in common with other costs and benefits. Nevertheless, some attempt should be made if such factors are likely to have important effects on welfare.

The benefits of large city size for consumers lie in a greater choice and range of goods and services created by the demands of a large urban population. This follows directly from central place theory. For producers the benefits are essentially twofold. First, external economies are derived from firms in different or similar industries locating close together. Secondly, internal (scale) economies can be obtained by firms operating with larger factories and workforces, and more specialised equipment. Internal and external economies have the effect of reducing unit production costs and can therefore be expected to result in higher levels of output (and earnings) per worker.

The cost of increasing city size involves, first, the direct costs to the public sector in providing urban services and infrastructure. These are generally assumed to form a 'U' shape with average costs initially falling as urban size increases, remaining fairly flat for a while, but eventually rising for large cities. Although various studies suggest that average costs fall and rise at different rates for different activities, the overall view for a wide range of countries is that public expenditure per capita rises significantly in the largest cities, often caused by the rising costs of public works, transport, staff, public security and social services. For example, in one study of local authority expenditure (per capita) in eight European countries it was found that when compared to the (national) average for towns of around 15–50 000 inhabitants, expenditure in larger towns was between 5 per cent and 213 per cent higher, and for the largest cities expenditure was between 49 per cent and 484 per cent higher.[26] To some extent such estimates for large cities may be unduly high, since large centres provide high-level services for smaller centres nearby, as well as for their own populations. But overall, it is unlikely that differences in service structure between urban areas could explain away easily such sizeable disparities in per capita expenditure – especially notable in the largest urban conurbations.

One social cost related to urban size concerns the time and cost involved in the journey to work. In 1940 the Barlow Report on the distribution of industry in Britain condemned the economic and social consequences of excessive travel to work, in particular concerning the London conurbation. More recent figures from the Department of Transport confirm that average distance and travel time to the urban centre tend to be higher for London and the major conurbations, in contrast to smaller urban areas and rural areas.

Again, in terms of the indirect costs of city size, much evidence would appear to suggest a close relationship between size and atmospheric pollution. Although it is often difficult to separate out the influences of other variables such as climate, topography, physical layout and industrial structure, the relationship for a number of pollutants appears fairly regular when urban areas of similar sizes are grouped together. For example, Hoch[27] found that for the United States, sulphur dioxide, nitrogen dioxide and particulate concentrations showed a fairly clear increase with city size. Vanhove and Klassen,[28] using Belgian data, found a strong correlation between sulphur dioxide concentrations and city size.

A third social problem strongly associated with city size involves the incidence of crime. Figures for England and Wales show a steady rise in crime rates, especially major crime rates, as population size increases.[29]

One of the undoubted complexities in assessing how social costs vary with city size is that low-income, central-city residents may suffer disproportionately more from the social ills of pollution, crime and congestion than do other groups. High-income residents may find they are more easily able to escape these problems by relocating to the suburbs, and may continue to benefit disproportionately more from the cultural facilities of the big city. As a result, it can be argued that cities optimally sized for the middle class are often too big from the point of view of those on lower incomes.[30] The latter are seen as benefiting relatively little from central-city amenities and suffering relatively greatly from the social problems generated by big cities. One implication of this argument is that it becomes difficult – if not impossible – to distinguish optimality from distributional considerations in determining the 'optimal' city size. What is optimal for one social class may well be too large for another.

In practice, given the difficulties of placing monetary values on social costs and benefits, most studies on city size have restricted themselves to examining only a few of the indicators discussed so far. Cost data are generally based on local authority expenditure, while measures of urban benefits have tended to

Table 2.5 *Gross domestic product (GDP) per head by county at factor cost and household disposable income (GDP per head UK = 100)*

GDP per head (UK = 100)		County/Metropolitan area	Household disposable income per head 1987 (UK = 100)
1977	1987		
98	87	Tyne & Wear	92
111	92	Cleveland	92
110	96	West Midlands	89
100	95	Greater Manchester	88
94	80	Merseyside	92
107	103	South Glamorgan	97
141	147	Great London	110

Source: CSO Regional Accounts 2, *Economic Trends*, HMSO (various).

rely on earnings (as a proxy for output per worker). Concerning the latter, most studies show that average benefits tend to rise with increasing city size.[31] As Richardson[32] points out, this relationship still holds true when incomes are corrected for the higher cost of living associated with large cities. Such costs rise with city size because of higher land values and urban rents. These in turn push up housing costs and consumer costs in retailing and so on. According to Hoch,[33] cost of living differences explain between a half to two-thirds of the wages differential between city sizes (in United States' cities). However, the various unpriced costs mentioned above are not reflected in any cost-of-living index, and could well help to offset the benefits of large cities.

In a broad sense, therefore, higher incomes must reflect both the productivity gains as well as the inconveniences of big cities. In support of this view, Porrell[34] has shown that employees are found to trade off a range of disamenities against higher wages, and amenities against lower wages. After accounting for cost of living and amenity–disamenity effects Hoch[35] suggests that influences on migration will emerge if wage rates in an urban area are more or less than expected. Following this line of reasoning, if output or income per worker is observed to decline in cities relative to elsewhere – reflecting a relative decline of urban productivity – we would expect to observe a rise in net out-migration (or fall in net in-migration).[36] Table 2.5 shows UK national accounts estimates at county level, where these appear to match closely the major metropolitan areas. Gross domestic product (GDP) per head clearly declined relative to the rest of the UK in all major metropolitan areas shown, apart from Greater London, over the 1980s. Perhaps more significant, however, is the fact that most such areas now appear to have levels of output per head not only below the national average, but in some cases below that of surrounding areas. For example, in the West Midlands region in 1987, Warwickshire achieved a level of GDP per head similar to that given in Table 2.5 for the West Midlands

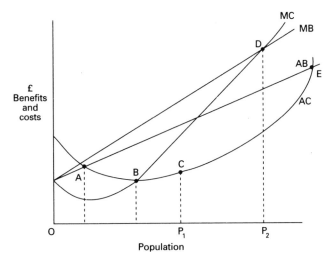

Figure 2.12   *The benefits and costs of city size*
MB = marginal benefits
MC = marginal costs
AB = average benefits
AC = average costs
Source: Adapted from W. Alonso, *The Economics of Urban Size, Regional Science Association Papers*, vol. 26 (1971).

metropolitan area. However in 1977, GDP per head in Warwickshire had been considerably lower in relative terms, only achieving an index of 75 against an index of 110 for the metropolitan area. Furthermore, in 1987 Warwickshire achieved a level of household disposable income of about the national average, whereas in the metropolitan area disposable income was more than 10 per cent lower.

Finally, one suggestion has been to use land values as an index of net urban benefits.[37] This approach assumes that all benefits and costs – even those of a non-monetary nature – are fully internalised in the land market and therefore capitalised in higher or lower urban land values. Unfortunately there is little agreement on the extent to which external effects such as pollution and congestion are fully internalised. Walker,[38] for example, argues that the land market accounts only very imperfectly for the costs of urban living, and he suggests that imperfect knowledge and ignorance of external effects tend to inflate land values, rendering them a false index of net urban benefits.

From the preceding discussion, it should be clear that the measurement of costs and benefits associated with city size presents considerable problems. Nevertheless, a useful generalisation is given in Figure 2.12. The average benefits (AB) curve is shown rising fairly steadily as population increases, although it is possible that urban diseconomies at larger city sizes could eventually cause average benefits to decline.

The results from a number of studies suggest that the average cost (AC) curve might be expected to reach a minimum point at a population size some-where 100 000 and 500 000 inhabitants.[39] After this point the average (or unit) cost would rise.

Several population sizes are of significance and deserve some discussion. The first occurs at point A where AC = AB; this is the *minimum efficient city size* below which the unit cost of providing urban infrastructure and services exceeds the average benefit (AC > AB). Point B corresponds to the least-cost city size (minimum AC), but this is clearly not an optimum since no account is taken of average benefits rising with population size. Point C – population size P_1 – is the optimal city size from the point of view of the city's residents. It corresponds to the point where the distance between the AB and AC curves is greatest (and the slopes of these curves are the same), that is, where net benefits per capita are highest (maximum AB–AC). Any further increase in population size beyond this point would clearly reduce the level of net benefit (AB–AC) for existing inhabitants.

Point D (P_2) represents the optimal city size from the view of maximum social welfare. This can be seen from the fact that below P_2 the marginal cost (MC) of adding another inhabitant is less than the marginal benefit (MB) to society (MC < MB); hence by expanding city size up to the point where MC = MB, the total (net) benefits are maximised. In practice, however, cities else-where in the urban system may be well below this optimum size, so that ex-panding these smaller cities would increase total welfare by more than if expansion were limited to only a few centres of population P_2. One recent study has suggested that the optimum city size may be below 0.5 million population,[40] if so, it seems likely – for many countries – that expansion of a larger number of smaller centres would generally be preferable to allowing over-concentration of national resources in capital cities.

A final possibility – and one that strengthens the case for planning – is to consider what might happen if no efforts were made to control expansion of the city and further in-migration beyond P_2. Then, the population would prob-ably increase up to point E (where AC = AB). Pressure for expansion would indeed be great since new entrants in reality tend to face average costs and benefits rather than marginal costs and benefits, as assumed in the previous case. On the cost side, this occurs because, in practice, charges and taxes for urban services are averaged over *all* service users and cannot distinguish be-tween new (high-cost) and existing (low-cost) residents (or firms). Also, new residents (or firms) do not face the rising marginal external costs (of conges-tion, pollution, noise and so on) inflicted on other city residents. In the ab-sence of control there may therefore be a tendency for cities to grow well beyond an optimum size (P_1 or P_2).

In practice, optimal city size theory has received some criticism. One objec-tion is that many urban costs and benefits may be specific to particular conur-bations and related to factors such as density, industrial structure or road layout rather than city size itself. Some research has shown, for example, that polycentric as opposed to monocentric cities are less prone to problems of congestion.[41]

Urban economic structure may also influence optimal city size; research has suggested that the optimum from the point of view of business services, for example, may well be larger than the optimum for manufacturing or construction.[42]

Furthermore, the theory tells us nothing about the desirable spatial distribution of the population in the context of the national urban hierarchy, and it sits uneasily with other theories (such as central-place theory) which do. From the point of view of planning, the loss of (net) benefits of urban size might be outweighed by the benefits of greater spatial accessibility if a more dispersed pattern of smaller urban settlements is considered. On the latter point, if, as previously suggested, the average cost curve is rather flat around the least-cost city size (point B), it is probably that there would exist a broad range of city sizes over which net benefits per capita (AB–AC) are fairly similar (compare net benefits at B with those at C and D in figure 2.12).

Given that average costs appear to rise substantially in the largest conurbations there would seem to be a strong case for encouraging a settlement structure of medium-sized towns and cities rather than one involving only a few large cities. While productivity may well be higher in large cities, as we have seen, the evidence is not so compelling as to suggest that any loss from encouraging smaller urban sizes would be at all substantial. Perhaps a few major capital cities with significant international functions (for example, London, Tokyo and New York) may have to remain very large in order to carry out effectively their world roles. For others, particularly the burgeoning megacities of the developing world, there must remain a question mark over their economic and social viability. Indeed, the recent experience of declining cities in many developed countries (see Chapter 8) may perhaps be taken as evidence to suggest that the agglomeration economies which existed in the past, are now much less significant.

REFERENCES

1. H. von Thünen, *Der Isolierte Staat*, 1826; English translation by C. M. Wartenberg, *Von Thünen's Isolated State* (Pergamon, 1968).
2. E. W. Burgess, 'The Growth of the City', in R. E. Park *et al.*, *The City* (University of Chicago Press, 1925).
3. H. Hoyt, *The Structure and Growth of Residential Neighbourhoods in American Cities* (Federal Housing Administration, 1939).
4. P. H. Mann, *An Approach to Urban Sociology* (Routledge & Kegan Paul, 1968).
5. C. D. Harris and E. L. Ullman, 'The Nature of Cities' in P. K. Hatt and A. J. Reiss (eds), *Cities and Society* (The Free Press, 1951).
6. P. A. Stone, *Urban Development in Britain: Standards, Costs and Resources, 1964–2004, Vol. 1, Population Trends and Housing* (National Institute for Economic and Social Research, Cambridge University Press, 1970).
7. W. Firey, 'Ecological Considerations in Planning for Urban Fringes', in P. K. Hatt and A. J. Reiss (eds), *Cities and Society* (The Free Press, 1951).
8. W. Christaller, *Die Zentralen Orte in Suddeutschland* (Fisher, 1933).
9. A. E. Smailes, 'The Urban Hierarchy in England and Wales', *Geography*, 29 (1944).

10. R. D. P. Smith, 'The Changing Urban Hierarchy', *Regional Studies*, 2 (1978).
11. R. Schiller, 'A Ranking of Centres Using Multiple Branch Numbers', *Estates Gazette* (23 March, 1985).
12. B. J. L. Berry and W. L. Garrison, 'Recent Development of Central Place Theory', *Papers and Proceedings of the Regional Science Association*, 4 (1958).
13. A. R. Pred, *The Spatial Dynamics of U.S. Urban–Industrial Growth 1800–1914* (M.I.T. Press, 1966).
14. J. M. Keynes, *The General Theory of Employment, Interest and Money* (Macmillan, 1936).
15. W. Isard, *Location and Space Economy* (MIT Press, 1956).
16. W. Leontief and A. A. Strout, 'Multiregional Input–Output Analysis' in T. Barna (ed.), *Structural Interdependence and Economic Development* (Macmillan, 1963).
17. W. Alonso *et al.*, *Regional Development and Planning: A Reader* (M.I.T. Press, Cambridge, Mass. 1975).
18. J. Potter, 'External Manufacturing Investment in a Peripheral, Rural Region: The Case of Devon and Cornwall, *Regional Studies*, 27 (1993).
19. P. Tyler and B. C. Moore, 'Geographical Variations in Industrial Costs', *Scottish Journal of Political Economy*, 35 (1988).
20. W. Isard, *Location and Space Economy*, (John Wiley, 1956).
21. H. W. Richardson, *Regional Growth Theory* (Macmillan, 1973).
22. P. N. Townroe and N. J. Roberts, *Local–External Economies for British Manufacturing Industry* (Gower, 1980).
23. R. L. Moomaw, 'Agglomeration Economies: Localisation or Urbanisation', *Urban Studies*, 25 (1988).
24. G. A. Carlino, 'Manufacturing Agglomeration Economies and Returns to Scale: A Production Function Approach, *Paper and Proceedings of the Regional Science Association*, 50 (1982).
25. See H. Louri, 'Urban Growth and Productivity: The Case of Greece', *Urban Studies*, 25 (1988), for an example of this line of argument. It can be noted that almost half of all economic activity in Greece is concentrated in the Athens region.
26. Commission of the European Communities, 'Le Cout des Concentrations Urbaines et la Dépopulation Rurale dans la CEE', Working Paper (European Commission, 1975).
27. I. Hoch, 'Urban Scale and Environmental Quality', in R. G. Ridker (ed.), *Population, Resources and the Environment*, US Commission on Population Growth and the American Future Research Report III (USGPO, Washington DC, 1972).
28. N. Vanhove and L. H. Klassen, *Regional Policy: A European Approach* (Saxon House, 1980).
29. F. McLintock and N. Avison, *Crime in England and Wales* (Heinemann, 1968).
30. K. R. Cox, *Location and Public Problems* (Basil Blackwell, 1979).
31. V. R. Fuchs, *Differentials in Hourly Earnings by Region and City Size* (National Bureau of Economic Research, Washington DC, 1959); W. Alonso, 'The Economics of Urban Size', *Regional Science Association Papers*, 26 (1971); I. Hoch, 'Income and City Size', *Urban Studies*, 9 (1972); I. Hoch, 'City Size and US Urban Policy', *Urban Studies*, 24 (1987).
32. H. W. Richardson, *Regional and Urban Economics* (Penguin, 1978).
33. I. Hoch, 'City Size Effects, Trends and Policies', *Science*, 193 (1976).
34. F. W. Porrell, 'Intermetropolitan Migration and Quality of Life, *Journal of Regional Science*, 22 (1982).
35. I. Hoch, 'City Size and US Urban Policy', *Urban Studies*, 24 (1987).
36. This outcome could also arise from a sudden large rise in rural/urban migration or international migration, if either produced significant downward pressure, on urban wage rates in particular. This is, however, thought to be less likely in the North European context and is not considered further.

37. H. W. Richardson, *Regional and Urban Economics.*
38. B. Walker, *Welfare Economics and Urban Problems* (Hutchinson, 1981).
39. N. Vanhove and L. Klassen, *Regional Policy.*
40. B. Begovic, 'The Economic Approach to Optimal City Size', *Progress in Planning*, 36, (1991). The study is, however, confined to business agglomeration economies.
41. P. Gordon, A. Kumar and H. W. Richardson, 'Congestion, Changing Metropolitan Structure and City Size', mimeo, School of Urban & Regional Planning, University of Southern California (1987).
42. B. Begovic, 'Economic Approach to Optimal City Size'.

3

The Market and the Location of Urban Land Uses

Regardless of the geographical location, origin or size of an urban area, a rational pattern of land use evolves. Normally after an assessment of various advantages and disadvantages, the location of any activity is determined either by the desire to maximise (or realise satisfactory) profits in respect of business users of land, or to maximise (or obtain acceptable) utility in the case of residential and other non-business users. The urban land use pattern is determined mainly by activities competing for sites through the forces of demand and supply – demand being the quantity of property required at given prices or rents, and supply being the amount of property available at those prices and rents.

The demand for land is a reflection of the profitability or utility derived from its use by current or potential users. The greater the benefit to be obtained from using a site for any particular purpose the higher the rent or price the would-be user is willing to pay. Since capital values are derived from annual rental values, so the higher the levels of rents the greater will be the capital values. As with any other form of investment, the prices of property interests rise in anticipation of future increases in rent incomes. Property investors may therefore be prepared to accept low yields or returns in relation to current property income in order to obtain the future benefit of an increased income and the possibility of additional capital gains.

The total supply of land in any country is fixed, except in cases of territorial gains and losses or reclamation and dereliction. But the supply of land for different uses can be either increased or decreased. Change in supply occurs when, for example, land transfers from one agricultural use to another, from farming to urban use, from residential to office or retailing use, and from private to public use.

The supply of land for specific uses is comparatively static in the short term. The underlying conditions of supply (the state of construction technology, sources of materials and other factors of production, number and type of public utilities, and the transport system) remain fairly constant. Because supply is slow to react to increases or decreases in demand, it is demand which is the major determinant of rental values, and consequently of capital values. In Britain from the 1950s until the late 1980s there was a substantial increase in property values because of the effect of increased demand for urban property upon a more slowly changing pattern of supply. The increased demand was the product of four

Table 3.1 *United Kingdom population 1951–91*

Year	Population (millions)	Birth-rate (per 1000)	Death-rate (per 1000)
1951	50.2	15.8	13.4
1956	51.2	16.0	12.5
1961	52.8	17.8	12.6
1966	54.4	17.9	11.8
1971	55.6	16.2	11.6
1981	56.3	13.0	11.8
1986	56.3	13.3	11.8
1991	57.2	13.8	11.3

distinct factors: inflation, credit availability, population growth and increased affluence.

(1) Until the late 1980s inflation not only increased property values in step with the rise in the general level of prices, but because property was regarded as a 'hedge' against inflation, and because of its scarcity in relation to demand, values increased ahead of general price levels. Property therefore became very attractive to developers and speculators.

(2) The availability of finance from institutional investors, not least from building societies, compounded the rate of increase in the level of effective demand. Interest rates on mortgages barely kept pace with the increased prices of property. After tax allowances on interest payments were taken into account the real financial cost of purchasing property was either very small or nil.

(3) The population increased over the period mainly as a result of changes in birth- and death-rates, by 1991 being over 12 per cent greater than in 1951 (table 3.1).

(4) An increase in population by itself would have had little effect upon the level of property values. But this increase occurred simultaneously with an increase in real incomes. These two factors led to an increase in the quantity of demand for property, and to qualitative changes, the result of changing social, economic and cultural characteristics. Changes included the earlier age of marriage and the dispersal of the family unit into separate dwellings, with young people leaving home at an earlier age, the demand for improved quality and higher standards of both new and older properties and the demand for second homes – the latter decentralising increased values throughout the country – especially where there was an increase in accessibility resulting from motorway development.

Influenced by changes in the underlying conditions of demand, land within the market transfers to the user who is prepared to pay the highest price or rent (demand and supply forever moving towards an equilibrium situation). This monetary value will reflect utility in the case of householders, and profit levels in respect of commercial and industrial users.

Although the property market can be described as an economic mechanism rationing land between competing and occasionally conflicting users, it is one of the most imperfect markets and one of the most susceptible to change in underlying conditions.

The Inefficiency of the Market

The property market is one of the least efficient markets of all. The imperfect knowledge of buyers and sellers, the 'uniqueness' of each site and building, the strong preference of establishments for existing sites, the unwillingness of some owners to sell despite the certainty of monetary gain, the absence of easily recoverable investment in costly and specific developments, the immobility of resources once they are committed, the possible loss on initial investment, the time-absorbing and costly process of seeking and acquiring new locations, the expense and legal complexity of transferring property, the length and legal rights of property interests, the influence of conservationists, the slowness of the construction industry to respond to changing demand, the monopoly power of planning authorities, property companies, mortgage institutions, sellers of property and the design professions – these are some of the factors which prevent land from transferring smoothly to its most profitable use. The pattern of land use changes only slowly over a long period and at no time is the market in a state of equilibrium with all resources being optimally used.

Even where market prices (as determined by comparable valuation) are offered, a transaction may not take place as the owner may weigh non-monetary factors more heavily than monetary considerations.

Despite these imperfections the market still attempts to assert itself, albeit inefficiently. While there is a perpetual state of disequilibrium between demand and supply resulting in either the scarcity or overabundance of different land uses, a change in the demand for a specific use will ultimately have an effect on prices and rents and subsequently will produce a change in supply.

URBAN LOCATION THEORY

Location theory not only explains the pattern of land use, but by indicating a solution to the problem of what is the most rational use of land, it suggests ways in which the current pattern can be improved. Very rarely is an activity's location determined by a single locational requirement; a mixture of interacting influences usually explain each locational decision. A location may be selected only after an appraisal has been made of the advantages and disadvantages of alternative locations for the particular activity.

As the price mechanism largely decides the profitability or utility of goods and services, it determines subsequently the location of activity and the spatial structure of the urban area supplying those goods and services. But although land is developed to its highest and best use, the process is lengthy and is frustrated by changes in underlying market conditions and by severe market imperfections.

Factor inputs may be equally important in determining location. High levels of accessibility within the central business district are reflected in low transport costs, thus attracting the greatest demand for sites, especially from commercial users. Conversely, low overall accessibility and high transport costs within the suburban areas and the rural–urban fringe will attract a much lower level of demand, especially from commercial users.

There may be some general reduction in the cost of factor inputs because of internal and external economies of scale being realised within a city. Up to a certain population size the economies will become greater. Richardson[1] argued that these will increase at a rate more than proportionate to an increase in population, but it is difficult both to quantify these agglomeration economies and to ascertain the optimum size of a city. He suggested that it would be useful to measure the per capita cost of retail and office services and of urban transport facilities, social services and entertainment at different levels of population, and to estimate at what level of population agglomeration diseconomies take over from the agglomeration economies, and when net social costs replace net social benefits.

It has been difficult to devise a location theory about urban land use in general, or commercial and industrial land use in particular. Inertia, stability in the occupation of land and the pre-empting of sites result in most urban land being used sub-optimally. Land use models are usually very simplistic as changes in population, technology and transportation continually exert an influence on the built environment. Further pressures come from central area redevelopment, and local and central government policy. Often similar types of use are seen to be feasible in different locations within the urban area. For these reasons it is difficult to suggest where optimal locations should be. It is probable that there may be several optima for the same use and that these locations are continually changing.

Notwithstanding these difficulties, neo-classical theory became concerned with rent as a determinant of optimum location. In the 1960s Alonso[2] evolved an approach to urban location theory based on the principle that rents diminish outward from the centre of a city to offset both lower revenue and higher operating costs, not least transport costs. A rent gradient would emerge consisting of a series of bid-rents which would exactly compensate for falling revenue and higher operating costs. Different land uses would have different rent gradients (figure 3.1), the use with the highest gradient prevailing. Thus competitive bidding between perfectly informed developers and users of land would determine the pattern of rents throughout the urban area, and would allocate specific sites between users so as to ensure that the 'highest and best' use obtained – that is, land would be used in the most appropriate way to ensure the maximisation of profit.

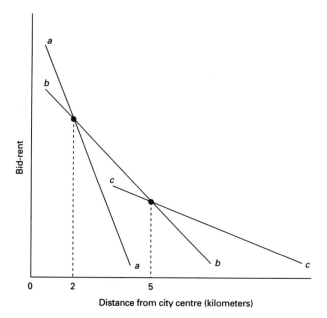

Figure 3.1   *Alonso's bid-rent–distance relationship*

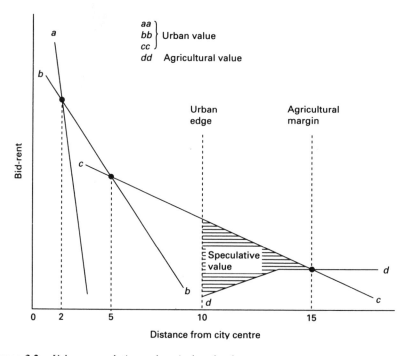

Figure 3.2   *Urban, speculative and agricultural values*

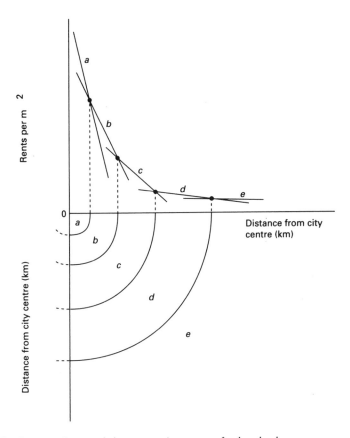

Figure 3.3 *Rent gradients and the concentric pattern of urban land use*

In figure 3.1 use *a* prevails up to a distance of two kilometres from the central business district, from two to five kilometres use *b* is dominant, and beyond five kilometres use *c* prevails. A change of use could be expected to take place through the price mechanism when one gradient falls below another. Although the Alonso model does not specify the type of land use associated with each bid-rent gradient, it must be assumed that on the edge of the urban area there is a separate agricultural rent gradient. It has been suggested[3] that outwards from the built-up area the proportion of the total value of land attributable to agriculture rises − until agricultural values exceed urban values and so dictate the predominant land use (figure 3.2). Inwards, speculative values increase as urban development becomes imminent and agricultural values become blighted.

Alonso's bid-rent concept adds a value dimension to Burgess's concentric zone theory (see Chapter 2). Figure 3.3 shows that where rent gradients intersect there would be a change of use to that activity which could afford to pay the higher rent. In Figure 3.3 rent gradient *a* could coincide with the central

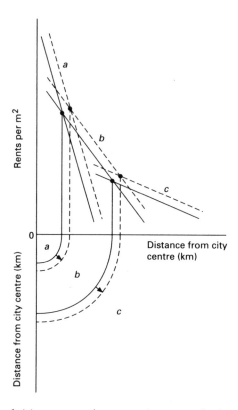

Figure 3.4   *The effect of rising rents on the concentric pattern of urban land use*

business district, category *b* with the transition zone, categories *c* and *d* with low- and high-income housing, and category *e* with the commuter zone. In the central business district the gradient would be steep because of intense competition for a very limited number of sites, but would be very slight in the outer zones with a comparative abundance of land.

With an increase in urban population and/or an increase in total urban income, the demand for land would increase – raising bid-rents throughout the urban area. This, in turn, would result in each land use zone invading the next outer zone (figure 3.4) – a process of urban expansion explained in non-monetary terms by Burgess.

The Alonso theory has been subject to much criticism. First, it can be argued that the information available to the developers and users of land is incomplete and this alone produces an imperfect market. The theory fails to take account of the very distinctive nature of buildings and their uses. For example, once offices, shops and factories have been built they cannot be moved or easily converted for other uses – there is considerable inertia resulting in sub-optimal use over time. Similarly, many large properties may not be suitable for sub-division or sub-letting at current use when demand for the complete property decreases.[4] It is also argued that since commercial, industrial and residential property is not homogeneous, varying in age, size, design, layout and location, each parcel of land is unique. This often provides the owner with a considerable degree of monopoly power which can be particularly exploited in urban areas. Alonso fails to take account of public sector land and ignores the external or spillover effects of specific land uses on other property. Alonso's theory is clearly a very idealised view of reality, but it has some merit in that it attempts to demonstrate the nature of the land market and emphasises the notion of efficiency in the use of urban land. If it can be assumed that public policy has a very variable effect upon the pattern of urban land use and values, then the bid-rent theory cannot be dismissed as an irrelevance – particularly if it is also assumed that even an efficient market in private urban property cannot be equated *per se* with a socially optimal pattern of land use.[5]

Because the Alonso model is general, it is necessary to consider separately the locational determinants of commercial and industrial use. To do so it is essential to identify the components of the cost and revenue gradients of business firms and to indicate the basis of their profitability.

Costs

The prices and rents of land fall with increased distance from the central business district though the gradient is rarely smooth. Wages are higher in the centre – local demand for labour being greater than local supply. Also, personal costs of commuting need to be offset by higher remuneration, but this might also apply to travelling to decentralised employment. Transport costs are more of a reflection of accessibility than distance. Locations close to junctions, nodes and termini are particularly favoured, maximising proximity to suppliers and markets. Although retailing is still generally attracted to the lowest overall transport cost location of the central business district, decentralised shopping centres are being developed following road improvements and increased car ownership. Modern manufacturing industry relies increasingly on heavy road vehicles for long-distance transportation and incurs lower transport costs on the fringes of cities than at more central locations. Capital costs (interest charges) are generally uniform and have little effect on location.

Revenue

Retailing revenue is determined by the size of the shopping catchment area or hinterland, not just in terms of population but also in terms of purchasing power. The distribution of the daytime population and points of maximum transit (where people cluster together) are also important. In the case of offices the spatial distribution, number and size of client establishments determine revenue.

In general, revenue is greatest within the central business district and so are aggregate costs. But as the distance from the centre increases, while revenue falls, aggregate costs (after falling initially) rise in suburban locations and beyond. This is mainly because of the upward pull of transport costs, which are no longer offset sufficiently by economies in the use of land and labour. Only within fairly short distances from the central business district are commercial users able to realise high profitability.

Costs, Revenue and Decentralisation

So far in this discussion it has been assumed that rents generally diminish outwards from the centre of an urban area, and in a Ricardian sense reflect a centrifugal reduction in population density and the level of economic activity. However, since the late nineteenth century, both the population density and employment gradients have been flattening out as a result of decentralisation[6] – in Western Europe population out-migration preceding employment change, and in the United States employment change pre-dating population out-migration. Rent gradients have also flattened out, but not always to the same extent, because of imperfections in the property market. The monopolistic ownership of central area land and restrictive planning policies have kept rents at a high level in the urban core long after the process of decentralisation was begun. An implication of decentralisation is therefore that costs do not necessarily fall continuously from the central business district and neither does revenue. Indeed, both costs and revenue may begin to rise when evolving outwards as increasing numbers of firms decentralise to exploit spatially expanding markets.

Profitability

To maximise profits firms need to locate where they can benefit from both the greatest revenue and from the lowest costs. But there is no single location where this can be achieved in absolute terms. Nevertheless, in an attempt to realise maximum revenue, specialised functions and activities serving the urban market as a whole might continue to locate centrally; firms requiring large sites and those attempting to reduce costs of overconcentration will be attracted to the suburbs. Firms locating close together to benefit from complementarity will incur lower costs because of external economies and enjoy higher revenue because of joint demand. Outlying business districts may be at least as attractive as the central business district in terms of profitability and more attractive than the relatively high-cost and low-revenue locations of the suburban belt in general.

But there is a high degree of inertia, most firms not operating at maximum profit locations. As with the level of output, firms find it difficult to adjust their locations to the optimum. A satisfactory rather than an ideal location is usually the best that can be achieved. The pattern of location, moreover, is stabilised by zoning and land use controls.

RETAIL LOCATION AND DEVELOPMENT

Retail efficiency is highly dependent upon location, and within a location highly dependent upon site. Within short distances one site may be very superior to another. Often the selection of the right site means the difference between business success and failure. The number and type of shops which can locate profitably in an urban area is very limited and is dependent upon the determinants of revenue (see above) and the degree of competition among retailers for a portion of that revenue. Retailers may wish to break down mass markets into segments (*market segmentation*), and respond differently to variations in the social class, age and lifestyle of consumers; and increasingly retailers are undertaking *niche-marketing*, attempting to satisfy the very specialised needs of relatively high-income, credit-worthy and closely-defined groups of consumers.[7] Low-income shoppers, on the other hand, are being catered for less and less in terms of new shopping development.

Shops (which in the UK had a total floorspace of 86 million m^2 in 1991) can be classified broadly into five categories.

Convenience shops

Customers purchase goods from these shops fairly regularly at short intervals spending only a very small proportion of their net weekly incomes. Although retail turnovers and rents per m^2 are low, convenience shops are viable with only a small catchment area, a low consumer purchasing power and a small floorspace – say less than 280 m^2. Newsagents, tobacconists and confectioners, grocers, bakers and greengrocers are examples of shops in this category.

Over the past two decades, convenience shops have been unable generally to withstand competition from larger retailers; for example, the number of independent grocer shops in the United Kingdom fell from over 56 000 in 1971 to less than 40 000 in 1991 and their share of grocery turnover nationally plummetted from 42 to under 20 per cent. There has, however, been a renewed interest in the development of local convenience retailing.[8] Small shops are proving viable if they remain open up to ten (or more) hours a day, seven days a week, are located close to the focal point of residential areas (particularly in the outer suburbs of Greater London and elsewhere in high-income areas of the South-East) and cater particularly for pedestrian and impulse shoppers. Development (and refurbishment) has recently been undertaken by specialist companies (for example, Cullens and Misselbrook & Weston), voluntary groups (such as Spar and Mace), the Co-operative Wholesale Society, and petrol stations (notably those operated by BP) – rather than by independent traders. It is anticipated that up to 6000 convenience stores of this type will be trading by the mid-1990s.

Shopping shops

Goods are purchased from these shops less regularly and at longer intervals, with shoppers spending a higher proportion of their net weekly incomes. Turnovers and rents per m² will be higher than in the case of convenience shops, but larger catchment areas and a greater purchasing power will be necessary. Examples of shops in this category include clothes shops, ironmongers, hairdressers and some soft furnishing stores.

Speciality shops

Customers buy goods at very irregular and lengthy intervals and may spend a multiple of their net weekly incomes. The turnover and rent per m² of this category of shop can be very high and profitability may be dependent upon a very large catchment area and a high purchasing power. Jewellers, furriers and furniture, antique and musical instrument shops fall into this category of retailing.

Department and multiple stores

In one building a department store will be concerned with convenience, shopping and speciality activity. Increasingly key traders (Marks & Spencer, Boots, W. H. Smith and Woolworth) are extending their range of merchandise and assuming many of the functions of deparment stores.

Service shops

These shops are often workshops and sometimes partly wholesale premises. Turnovers and rents per m² are usually small. Even though customers may spend a multiple of their net weekly incomes they do so at very irregular intervals thus making a service shop dependent upon a large catchment area with a high purchasing power. Examples of shops of this type include furniture renovators and re-tread tyre dealers.

This classification of shops can be incorporated into the hierarchy of shopping centres, the structure of the hierarchy being as follows:

The central shopping area

This coincides approximately with the central business district except where there is exclusively office use. Generally shops co-locate with offices. Office employees are often the principal customers, and retailers may specialise in supplying offices with stationery, machinery, fittings and furniture. Moreover, as shops very rarely utilise space above the ground floor (except in the case of department and multiple stores) office use at higher levels ensures that valuable sites can be developed to their maximum.

Some large cities may have more than one central shopping area. It may be linear or nuclear in form. Except for service shops, all the other categories of retailing are well represented. Department stores and key traders may locate solely in the central shopping area because of this area having the maximum accessibility to the largest catchment area and greatest purchasing power. Cus-

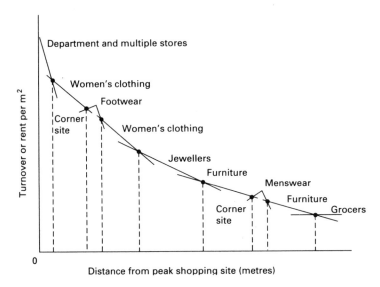

Figure 3.5 *Hypothetical turnover or rent gradient within a major shopping centre*

tomers may be attracted from all regions of the country and from abroad.

Within the central shopping area the relationship between retail turnovers and rents per m² is particularly pronounced. There is little inertia and, with the exception of the major retailers, shops are continually changing use as increasing demand raises rent levels. The 'turnover–rent gradient' may slope steeply or gradually away from the key or '100 per cent' sites, but in general as distance from the key sites increase shops change in the use from being department or multiple stores to women's clothing, jewellery, furniture and grocery shops. Corner sites are especially favoured where window display is important, for example in the case of footwear and menswear (figure 3.5). Throughout the central shopping area turnovers and rents are usually higher on the side of the street which receives the most sunshine, this being the northern (south-facing) side in the northern hemisphere.

With the redevelopment of bombed city centres after the Second World War, the central shopping area became increasingly important in the 1950s and 1960s, mainly because of the economies of scale associated with the growth of multiple stores, the wider range and larger stocks of goods that can be carried when turnovers are high, the rise in rents forcing out small independent retailers, and the effective end of resale price maintenance after the Resale Prices Act 1964. In the 1970s planning authorities continued to concentrate new retail investments in city centres rather than on the periphery. Either in the form of large regional shopping centres of more than 40 000 m², or smaller centres of 5000–40 000 m², these developments could blight not only other shops within the same city if central positions suddenly became off-centre locations but also other shopping centres in the regional or sub-regional hierarchy. By the 1980s,

Table 3.2 *The largest town centre and out-of-town shopping schemes, Great Britain, 1992*

Location	Town	Scheme	Floorspace m^2
Town centre	Manchester	Arndale Centre	128 000
	Milton Keynes	Central Milton Keynes	114 000
	Newcastle upon Tyne	Eldon Square	84 000
	Redditch	Kingfisher Centre	83 960
	Telford	Telford Shopping Centre	83 420
Out-of-town	Dudley	Merry Hill Centre	192 670
	Gateshead	Metrocentre	175 800
	Thurrock	Lakeside	123 800
	Sheffield	Meadowhall	118 400
	Hendon	Brent Cross	81 806

Source: Hillier Parker, *British Shopping Centre Development Master List*, 1993.

however, the average size of town centre schemes was decreasing and was significantly less than that of out-of-town development. In 1986, the *average* floorspace of town centre schemes under construction, with planning consent and proposed, ranged from only 11 600 m^2 to 13 200 m^2, whereas the average floorspace of out-of-town shopping centres at all stages of development ranged from 22 500 m^2 to 40 700 m^2.

Central shopping areas are currently posing considerable problems for investors and retailers. The purpose-built centre – first developed in the 1960s to consolidate urban shopping – is in danger of being forsaken by the major national retailers who increasingly favour decentralised locations. Institutional investors in town-centre shops, experiencing a decline in the value of their investments, are thus attempting to redesign, remodel and refurbish their properties to raise standards to those demanded by major retailers and their customers – an important objective being to secure the location of 'anchor tenants' such as the John Lewis Partnership and Marks & Spencer.

Anchor tenants and other national multiples undertake or commission increasingly sophisticated market research in determining retail location. *Local expenditure zone analyses* (defining consumer expenditure and preference within a system of non-overlapping retail zones), *geodemographic analyses* (classifying neighbourhoods by socio-economic indicators) and *isochronic maps* (showing access to shopping centres in terms of time rather than distance) are each used in this process.[9]

City centre investment is usually at the expense of small independent shops which cannot compete effectively with the multiples for trade or sites. The decline of shop numbers in the United Kingdom from 542 000 in 1960 to about 350 000 in 1991 indicates the vulnerability of the small shop. In view of the fact that most major shopping development schemes are undertaken by a partnership of a local authority and a property company, it is remarkable how little the proposals are subject to public scrutiny. The United Kingdom is, however, still over-provided with retail space, though much of it is in the wrong place. It is clear that the traditional High Street has become increasingly obsolescent and unappealing because of a confusion of architectural styles, the inappropriate floorspace and layout of shops, and the problems of traffic congestion, parking and shelter. It has been suggested that national multiples may soon no longer be satisfied with their town centre shops – redesigned and refurbished every two to three years – and instead employ, once and for all, the easier option – decentralisation.[10] It is important, however, not to exaggerate the scale of the problem. Of the 748 shopping centres in excess of 4645 m^2 (50 000 ft^2) developed between 1965 and 1992, 682 were located in town centres and only 66 centres (excluding retail warehouses) were located out of town, respectively accounting for a total of 10.2 million m^2 and 1.3 million m^2.[11] The larger town centre schemes, moreover, are broadly comparable in size to the out-of-town centres (table 3.2) indicating that, in terms of scale, they are similarly viable.

Ribbon shopping

This extends along the main radial roads towards or beyond the suburban shopping centres. There will be the greatest concentration of shops in the direction of the most densely populated or highest-income areas. Generally, department and multiple stores are absent and the only speciality retailers are motor traders – convenience and shopping shops predominate. From central areas outwards, accessibility, turnovers and rents diminish, although gradients are not smooth and small peaks occur near suburban centres.

Ribbon shopping development is faced with numerous problems. The distribution of shops may be over-extended for convenient shopping, motorists may face parking restrictions, there may be no recognisable shopping centre (though key traders may be located in 'hot spots'), traffic or even physical barriers divide shopping frontages, and there may be many redundant shops occupied by non-retail uses.

Suburban centres

These are usually of recent growth, although their origins may be old, in some cases dating from medieval times. The larger suburban centres may be part of an outlying business district with shops relating to offices in the same way as in the central business district. There are signs of substantial expansion where access to the central shopping area is poor, and where the suburban population and its purchasing power is high. In many cases car parking and servicing facilities are comparatively good. The same types of shop as are found in the central shopping area will be located in the suburban centre, although turnovers and rents per m^2 will not be as high.

Neighbourhood centres

These will either be in the form of small parades of shops or small shopping precincts dependent on a restricted catchment area and a fairly low purchasing power. Turnovers and rents per m² are relatively low. Convenience shops will be profitable, though shopping or speciality shops will be less viable. Yet even in neighbourhood centres compound trading is ousting the small independent retailer.

Local corner shops

Though tending to disappear, the corner shop will remain if it can truly retain its convenience function. The catchment area is small and the required purchasing power is very low. In consequence turnovers and rents per m² are also very low.

Decentralised shopping facilities

These consist of the activities of most types of shops – convenience, shopping, speciality – perhaps in a number of different buildings under different leases, and possibly with one retailer dominating; alternatively, the activities may be concentrated in one building operated by one firm. Out-of-town shopping centres were first developed in the United States – where there were 2000 centres in 1956 (increasing to 28 500 by 1985) – but in recent years decentralised shopping has expanded in Europe, especially in France and the former West Germany, but less so in the United Kingdom.

Increased congestion and reduced accessibility have rendered retailing less and less profitable in the central areas of many cities in the United States, motivating the development of shopping centres in out-of-town locations. In Europe it is improbable that central shopping areas have reached the same level of congestion and subsequent decline, yet the viability of decentralised centres and stores has been recognised in spite of the continuing (and often increasing) profitability of central area locations.

There are six types of decentralised shopping facility:

(1) Out-of-town shopping centres – complexes of shops dominated by department stores with catchment areas of at least 250 000 people. In the United Kingdom by 1980, despite a number of applications, only the Brent Cross development had been permitted – a centre of 71 257 m². (It is often argued, however, that Brent Cross is not an out-of-town development at all, but rather a strategic suburban shopping centre.) Similar restrictions were placed on developments of this scale in France and the former West Germany. By 1986 only the Metrocentre in Gateshead had been added to the list of major out-of-town developments, but by 1992 a number of large-scale developments had been completed, notably Meadowhall in Sheffield, Merry Hill in Dudley and

Lakeside in Thurrock (see table 3.2). Many other major out-of-town schemes proposed during the consumer boom of the late 1980s were shelved during the recession of the early 1990s or failed to obtain planning permission.

(2) Edge-of-town centres – complexes of shops dominated by supermarkets or variety stores with catchment areas up to 100 000 people. Planning permission has been more readily forthcoming than in the case of out-of-town centres.

(3) District shopping centres – smaller complexes of shops dominated by convenience trades, wtih catchment areas rarely in excess of 10 000 people.

(4) Hypermarkets – large free-standing stores of up to 23 000 m² combining food trades with the sale of a variety of cheaper household goods. They may contain banks, restaurants, hairdressers and other service trades. Although hypermarkets have proliferated in France (which had over 1000 in 1993) and in Germany, only a small number have been permitted in Britain (for example in Caerphilly, Eastleigh, Irlam, Telford and Merton).

(5) Superstores – also large, free-standing stores but with up to only 10 000 m² of floor area. Similar to giant supermarkets, they concentrate on food and household goods. In contrast by hypermarkets, a large number of superstores have been developed in the United Kingdom in recent years, often as nuclei of redeveloped town shopping centres or on inner city sites. Retailers such as the Argyll Group (Safeway), Asda, Sainsbury and Tesco have been notable in this field, and the number of superstores has increased (almost to the point of saturation in the major urban areas) from about 200 in 1980 to over 800 in 1993 – taking nearly 60 per cent of the retail food market. The growth in the number of superstores has been particularly rapid in London. Whereas in 1980 there were only 5 superstores in the capital, by 1993 the number had increased to 49, each in excess of 2500 m². Since every store provides about 350 new full-time and part-time jobs, local authorities have been reluctant to withhold planning permission, despite protests from small shopkeepers. Outside urban areas, however, applications for planning approval have often been rejected (largely on environmental grounds, not least within the green belt), although as many as 50 per cent of superstore appeals have been successful – compared with an average success rate of appeal of only 35 per cent.

(6) Retail warehouses – are normally large, single-storey buildings of up to 6500 m² (although there are plans for units of over 9000 m²). There have been three stages in their development since the early 1970s. *First generation* units were relatively small converted warehouse buildings (rarely in excess of 2300 m²), often located in industrial estates, and mainly concerned with DIY, carpets and furniture. *Second generation* units occupied prominent main road locations and provided adequate car parking. *Third generation* development consisted of retail parks – planned and purpose-built sites for clusters of warehouse 'shops' with scale economies such as shared car parking and advertising. Since the 1970s, Sainsbury, W. H. Smith and Woolworth have absorbed some of the earlier warehouse operators, and together with other national multiples (such as B&Q, Comet, Halfords and Texas) have operated from their own purpose-built warehouses – becoming more selective in their choice of sites. A *fourth*

generation of store appeared in 1993–4, the discount warehouse. Firms such as Cargo Club in Croydon and Costco at Thurrock offered customers the opportunity to buy at 'knock down prices' on bulk purchases, thereby posing a competitive threat to other decentralised shopping centres as well as to town-centre shops. It was likely that there was about 1.5 million m^2 of retail warehouse floorspace in the United Kingdom in 1993, but further growth was dependent upon a continuing increase in consumer spending, a further growth in car and home ownership, a retained interest in this sector by the major retailers, and, of course, planning consent.

Decentralised shopping development made considerable strides in the 1980s. It benefited from a consumer boom of unusual length and magnitude – starting in 1983 and continuing for at least six years (in 1987 alone, consumer spending in real terms rose by 5.8 per cent – the largest rise since 1972). There were significant reductions in direct taxation, there was large-scale credit expansion and wages rose significantly faster than inflation. Shop rents similarly increased ahead of inflation reflecting soaring retail profitability (particularly in 1986 and 1987). Apart from a favourable macroeconomic climate, however, decentralised shopping also requires the following conditions: a high car-owning population and ideally a high proportion of families owning at least two cars; a large proportion of married women employed, making it necessary for shopping to take place mainly once a week and at one point; a high proportion of households owning deep-freezers; a highly developed ring-road system making adjacent locations as accessible to as large a catchment area and as high a purchasing power as is enjoyed in the central shopping area; the availability of large and inexpensive sites for the development of shopping facilities and spacious car parks; and the availability of finance and development expertise.

Like central shopping areas, decentralised facilities generally benefit from high accessibility, but unlike central areas, rents per m^2 are initially low. Although turnovers per m^2 may also at first be low, the very large retail floor areas result in a high level of total profitability. Consumers also benefit because internal economies of scale are passed on in relatively low prices, and lower travel costs might be incurred on shopping journeys.

But there are a number of obstacles in the way of decentralised shopping development. In Britain land values in outer urban locations may not be very much cheaper than in the central shopping area or existing suburban centres, ring roads are far less developed in Britain than in, say, the United States or the former West Germany – central areas retaining the highest level of accessibility in the urban area; two-car families still account for a very small proportion of shoppers, urban land (even on the fringe of the built-up area) is scarce and out-of-town shopping may be considered wasteful of land, especially if there are already large-scale supermarkets in suburban areas, and government policy may be opposed to the further development of out-of-town centres. Under the Town and Country Planning (Shopping Development) Direction 1986, moreover, local authorities are obliged to consult with the Secretary of State for the Environment before granting planning permission for developments in excess of 23 325 m^2, although in 1993 the government revised its *Planning Policy Guidance Note 6* which stressed the need for a balance between in-town and out-of-town development. Despite opposition from retailers in established shopping centres, however, there was little evidence by 1987 that decentralised retailing development had had a harmful effect on the viability of traditional shopping locations. But with the rapid opening of new out-of-town centres and superstores in the late 1980s, decentralised shopping is increasingly accounting for a greatly increased share of the retail market to the detriment of retailing elsewhere. The Merry Hill centre, for example, has attracted about 70 per cent of local shopping away from Dudley, its nearest town. It would thus seem that the government needs to do more to vet schemes in excess of 23 325 m^2. It has been suggested that the Department of the Environment (DOE) must study the cumulative impact of these developments, and also should vet slightly smaller schemes since these could have a major impact on catchment areas. The DOE must recognise that local authorities may be unable to gain an overview of proposals (if some are within and some outside their boundaries), and that a few local authorities may wish to adopt a soft option by appearing to create employment by approving out-of-town schemes regardless of the cost to town centres.

Local authorities, however, usually pursue a cautious approach to out-of-town proposals. Developers are normally obliged to undertake *impact assessments* (IAs) in support of their planning applications, but invariably IAs show that the potential effect on town centres will be minimal. While the Secretary of State had not defined what was an acceptable impact, the 1986 Direction stated that in assessing the impact of a scheme, 'the vitality and viability of a nearby shopping centre as a whole' should be considered. The impact could, in reality, be enormous. According to the John Lewis Partnership (JLP), if 92 000 m^2 of out-of-town development is undertaken and turnovers amount to £1870 per m^2, then the total turnover of the new centre would be equivalent to that of a town centre the size of Exeter, Stockport or Watford. Out-of-town development could also have an unfavourable impact on the modernisation of many city centres. JLP reported that there was not enough demand (despite the consumer boom) in the late 1980s to support both out-of-town developments and the renewal of High Street shopping centres – a view shared with Tesco.

The abolition of the Greater London Council and the metropolitan county authorities in 1986 had a serious effect on the strategic planning of shopping centres in their areas. Faced with thirteen proposals for out-of-town shopping developments, the Association of Greater Manchester Authorities (aware that the defunct Greater Manchester Council's structure plan had aimed to strengthen existing town centres) commissioned Roger Tym and Partners to advise on these intended developments.[12] Their advice was that if the proposals went ahead they would jeopardise proposed town centre developments since there was insufficient projected consumer expenditure to support both forms of development. Similarly, the structure plan of the former West Midlands Council had emphasised the need to redevelop existing centres. But faced with edge-of-town shopping proposals, seven West Midlands boroughs commissioned Drivers Jonas to undertake an impact study on these proposals.[13] The study showed that only by ignoring the effects of two approved centres at Merry Hill and Sandwell could a further 60 000 m² be supported by 1991.

In justifying new out-of-town proposals, developers argue that there is enough – and growing – demand to support both town centre and out-of-town shopping provision. While research has shown that the majority of consumers have a preference for out-of-town rather than in-town shopping,[14] this does not contradict the view that there is still an important role for town centres. Developers therefore point out that whereas out-of-town centres facilitate bulk-buying by car-borne shoppers, town centres accommodate a wide range of specialist shops and are more accessible to pedestrians – and as such are complementary rather than competitive. In historic cities, out-of-town centres can usually divert traffic away from the centre, easing congestion and parking problems, and as such could be welcomed by city centre retailers.

Impact assessments, however, are not only very unreliable (different assessments could, for example, show a 10, 25 or 40 per cent impact on trade) but are very narrow. They do not take into account broader considerations such as the impact on the utilisation of energy. It might be pertinent, for example, to question whether at a time when future supplies of cheap oil are unpredictable it is rational to develop a new kind of shopping dependent very greatly on the extensive use of the private motor car, and to bear in mind that such developments are highly regressive, in so far as the low-income consumer will probably not own a car and will be disadvantaged by a diminishing number of accessible shops.

The rise of the shopping centre

The distinction between individual shops and shopping centres is diminishing. This is because of the growth of compound trading, the tendency towards one-stop shopping and the increased use of franchises within stores. These trends have been brought about by economies of scale, changing shopping habits due to more married women being in employment, improved storage of food (by refrigeration) and the increased use of private cars. In assessing the value of a shop location it is essential to consider the centre in which it is situated. The relevance of the centre to a specific shop depends on whether the trade is receptive (that is, it receives trade from incidental or impulse shoppers) or self-generative (it attracts intending shoppers). The former group may be situated anywhere in the centre where it can tap trade, but self-generative trades are often gregarious for competitive or complementary reasons.

Shopping centres are footloose. In London, for example, the centre of shopping moved westward from St Paul's Churchyard in the seventeenth century, to the Strand in the eighteenth century, to Piccadilly and Regent Street in the early nineteenth century, and to Oxford Street by 1900. In each period the

Table 3.3 *The consumer boom and slump*

	Growth in retail sales (per cent per annum)	Interest rates (%)[1]	Balance of payments (current account) as a percentage of GDP	£ exchange rate[2]	New construction orders (£m at 1985 prices)	Construction output (£m at 1985 prices)
1985	4.7	11.5	0.8	100	1022	738
1986	5.3	11.0	0.0	92	1066	938
1987	5.1	8.5	-1.0	90	1482	1207
1988	6.3	13.0	-3.3	96	1664	1255
1989	1.9	15.0	-4.0	93	1586	1418
1990	0.4	14.0	-3.1	91	1078	1313
1991	-0.7	10.5	-1.1	92	1086	1121
1992	0.7	7.0	-2.0	88	979	1047

Notes: 1. Retail bank base rate, end of year.
2. Trade weighted index, average for year.

Source: Central Statistical Office; Department of the Environment.

Table 3.4 *The impact of the recession of the early 1990s on the development of shopping centres in Great Britain*

	Town centre schemes			Out-of-town schemes		
	Annual openings		Change in floorspace (%)	Annual openings		Change in floorspace (%)
	Centres	Floorspace m²		Centres	Floorspace m²	
1989	30	494 800		5	183 427	
1990	31	520 005	+5.1	55	303 542	+65.5
1991	29	538 950	+3.6	3	71 580	−76.4
1992	18	488 790	−9.3	−	21 528*	−69.9

Note: * Addition to the floorspace of existing centres.

Source: Hillier Parker, *British Shopping Centre Development Master List*, 1993.

centre was the point of maximum accessibility, and as the means of transport changed there was a relocation of the transport node. As in the past, the future pattern of shopping will be determined largely by the pattern of transportation, and there is likely to be a continuation of current trends – the decline of small businesses and the falling number and increased size of shops. The pace at which this takes place will not only be dependent upon the rate of economic growth but also upon government policy concerning monopolies and consumer protection, and upon planning policy at a local and central level. Alternatively, with the increased decentralisation of population, electronic shopping from home could evolve or there might be a re-emergence of the small independent shop in the small country town or village. This would reflect a changing demand and a reaction against the ever-increasing scale of both central and out-of-town shopping centres.

*The recession of the early 1990s and its impact on shopping centre
development*

The consumer boom of the mid-1980s was characterised by falling interest rates, and a substantial increase in new construction orders and construction output in respect of retail property development. The subsequent slump was associated with a marked increase in interest rates (aimed at correcting a deteriorating balance of payments and the exchange value of the pound), and a decrease in new construction orders and construction output (table 3.3).

Although there was a squeeze of real profits and an increase in vacant shop units in the early 1990s, it soon became clear that town centres were more resilient to competition from out-of-town retailing than was previously estimated. Although edge-of-town and out-of-town shopping centres increased their share of retail spending from 4 per cent in 1980 to about 20 per cent in 1993, town-centre shops only experienced a very minor reduction in their share, from 56 to 53 per cent.[15] It was the relatively uncompetitive neighbourhood shop that suffered the greatest loss of trade – from 40 to 27 per cent of retail spending between 1980–93.

Because of the impact of diminishing retail profits and consequential reductions in rents on new lettings, there was a general reduction in retail development. But whereas the amount of newly completed out-of-town shopping floor space plummetted in 1991 and 1992 (the large retailers being more concerned with consolidating their position and cost-cutting than with expanding their activities out of town), the amount of newly completed town centre floor space, in contrast, decreased by a relatively small amount (table 3.4). The downturn in the development of out-of-town shopping centres was also much greater than the decrease in the rate of new floorspace added to retail warehouses – which (like the town centres) continued to attract developers and investors well into the recession. At the end of the recession, however, out-of-town centres might be the first to recover and signal a further boom in retail development, particularly in unsaturated areas on the edge of country towns such as Godalming in Surrey, Sevenoaks in Kent and Cirencester in Gloucester with their rural hinterlands.

OFFICE LOCATION AND DEVELOPMENT

Offices are of two kinds – those attached to factories and those which are independently sited. In the case of the former, location will be dependent upon the factors responsible for the location of factories (these will be considered later in this chapter), but in the latter, location is dependent upon general accessibility and in particular upon special accessibility to complementary firms and the offices of clients. Even so, location may be fairly flexible and the site might not be as important as in retailing. Office functions, moreover, do not have to be tied to the ground floor or lower floors of a building.

Independently located offices (with a total floorspace in the UK of over 50 million m^2 in 1993) can be classified into the following groups.

The Head Offices of Major Commercial and Industrial Firms

To benefit from accessibility and from a 'prestige' address, firms have demanded more and more office space within the central areas of cities and are attracted more to large rather than small cities – London being of foremost importance. In 1938 there were 8.8 million m^2 of office space in Central London, in 1966 the figure had increased to 16.7 million m^2, and by 1993 the area exceeded 22 million m^2. In the United Kingdom, office jobs as a percentage of the total workforce increased from 24 to 38 per cent, 1960–90, and the percentage growth in office employment was five times the increase in employment generally – an increase much greater than in most other countries, including those with higher gross national products (GNPs) per capita. Office rents increased simultaneously, rising from about £15 per m^2 in the 1950s to £165 per m^2 in the City of London in 1973. This contrasted with rents of up to £45 per m^2 in other cities. By 1987, during the property boom, rents reached nearly £470 per m^2 and £420 per m^2 in the City and West End respectively. Taking occupancy costs (rent, local property tax and service charges), only Tokyo had higher outgoings than the City of London in 1987 – £720 per m^2 compared to £650 per m^2. Costs in downtown New York were £440 per m^2; in Paris £430 per m^2; and £230 per m^2 in Frankfurt. Suburban London and the South East continued to increase in appeal with, for example, Windsor and Slough (adjacent to the M4) attracting rents of over £162 and £153 per m^2 respectively, and Redhill/Reigate and Crawley (close to the M25 and M23) commanding rents of over £125 and £102 per m^2. In other regions rents were much lower. For example, £79 per m^2 in Bristol and Birmingham, £69 in Manchester, £56 in Liverpool, £51 in Sheffield, and £44 in Newcastle upon Tyne and Plymouth. With such enormous regional disparities in rent, it was not surprising that 70 per cent of all new office investment in the United Kingdom in 1986 was in London.

By affording high rents and rates, office users usually push out alternative uses, except perhaps ground-floor retailing and in prestige retail districts such as parts of London's West End. High rents and rates are paid because of the intensive use of the floor area and because of substantial external economies of scale (such as access to labour, materials and service inputs, and where offices collectively provide a large market for advertising, accounting and legal services – each consequently supplied at low unit cost). Where earning capacity is dependent upon being sited in a specific area, users are simply willing to incur the expense. Firms place a premium on locations providing the maximum opportunity for face-to-face contact and maximum degree of access to information. As it is practicable to construct multistorey offices (in contrast to shops), those sites occupied by offices will be the most intensively developed and most valuable sites within the urban area.

But eventually the central business district becomes saturated. Further vertical development is too costly and, except for minor instances of infilling and redevelopment, horizontal expansion is impossible because of the lack of sites. Decentralisation thus offers the only possibility for an expansion in office space and the process has been adopted in most capitalist countries. In the United States, for example, 87 per cent of major firms were located in the central business district in 1956, but this proportion decreased to 71 per cent by 1974[16] and continued to decline into the 1980s. In the United Kingdom, following the Control of Offices and Industrial Development Act 1965 office development became strictly controlled. Office Development Permits (ODPs) were required for all office development in the South-East and Midlands when the proposed floorspace exceeded 3000 ft^2 (279 m^2), and in Central London there was a complete ban on office development. Although ODP limits were subsequently raised in 1967 to 10 000 ft^2 (929 m^2) outside the Metropolitan Area, to 10 000 ft^2 within the region (exclusive of Greater London) in 1969, and to 10 000 ft^2 in London in 1970, the effect in these years was to raise office rents substantially because of the inadequate supply of new development. Between 1965 and 1970 rents of new and old offices in central London increased by five- and four-fold, respectively (in contrast to increases of 39 and 23 per cent in the respective rents of new and old offices in Manchester and Liverpool). Were it not for economic uncertainty and financial stringency, the Greater London Council's policy of restricting office development in Central London in the mid-1970s would have produced a similar soaring of office rents.

Encouraged by the Location of Offices Bureau (established in 1963), and influenced by expiring leases, premises due for demolition and the need for more space (and to a lesser extent by rising rents and rates, higher wages, labour scarcity and travel inconvenience), many firms have moved all or most of their office requirements out of London. General administration, routine accounts, records and technical departments have been decentralised since it has been recognised that the need for face-to-face contact had been exaggerated, but small reception departments usually remained (and many firms doubled up on their use of office space) within the central area. Between 1963 and 1977 over 2000 office-using firms left Central and Inner London, accounting for about 145 000 jobs, yet suburban areas or towns within the South-East were usually preferred to other locations in Britain. Concentrated decentralisation in the South-East made possible the retention of contacts between firms without their needing to incur the high direct costs of locating in London.

The pattern of decentralisation has clearly been at the expense of provincial locations. Whereas, for example, the outer South-East increased its share of company headquarters from 7 to 15 per cent of the national total between 1968 and 1983 (a gain of 114 per cent), the North-West decreased its share from 8 to 5 per cent, Scotland from 5 to 4 per cent and the North from 4 to 2 per cent. The concentration of company headquarters in one region (the South-East) is in complete contrast with many other capitalist countries such as the United States and the former West Germany, where head-offices are widely distributed.

Within the Assisted Areas of the North and West, decentralised offices were induced not only by the absence of the need to obtain an ODP, but after 1973 by government grants paid to employees who moved with their work, and rent grants for periods of three to five years. Loans were also available at concessionary rates for normal capital needs, interest relief grants could be claimed, removal grants up to 80 per cent of cost were provided, and the government offset up to 80 per cent of the redundancy pay commitment of relocating firms. Under the White Paper, *Regional Industrial Development* (1983) some service sectors previously excluded from regional development grants (RDGs) (for example, advertising agencies, credit-card companies, cable television and football pools) now qualified for assistance. Regional aid was to be allocated largely in the form of RDGs (which were limited to a cost of £10 000 per job) or as job grants (of £3000 per job).

Table 3.5 *The office development boom and slump*

	Growth in financial & business service (per cent per annum)	Interest rates (%)[1]	Balance of payments (current account) as a percentage of GDP	£ exchange rate[2]	New construction orders (£m at 1985 prices)	construction output £m at 1985 prices)
1985	6.4	11.5	0.8	100	1775	1635
1986	11.0	11.0	0.0	92	2183	1839
1987	10.1	8.5	−1.0	90	2852	2112
1988	7.6	13.0	−3.3	96	3725	2513
1989	4.8	15.0	−4.0	93	4008	3472
1990	2.7	14.0	−3.1	91	3379	4112
1991	−2.5	10.5	−1.1	92	1969	3347
1992	−2.7	7.0	−2.0	88	1597	2072

Notes: 1. Retail bank base rate, end of year.
2. Trade weighted index, average for year.

Source: Central Statistical Office; Department of the Environment.

By 1977 the economic plight of the inner cities (not least Inner London) had been recognised. The Department of the Environment therefore altered the terms of reference of the Location of Offices Bureau to attract office development to the inner cities rather than exclusively to decentralised locations. The Inner Urban Areas Act 1978 further emphasised the importance of offices to the inner cities. But decentralisation was finally rejected in July 1979 when the incoming Conservative Government (favouring a *laissez-faire* approach) abolished ODPs and closed down the Location of Offices Bureau. An office boom in Central London was anticipated. Despite some major developments in the early 1980s, by the middle of the decade big increases in demand pushed up rents in Central London ahead of the rate of inflation – a trend dramatically boosted by the deregulation of the City's financial markets in 1986 (the 'Big Bang'). Deregulation created an intensified demand for office space from conglomerates, solo firms, companies with futures determined by the Financial Services Act of 1986, and from spin-off accountancy and legal services. Most important was the strong demand for offices (such as those developed in Broadgate and redeveloped in London Wall) built to sophisticated specifications to house the electronics of the Big Bang. By mid-1987, rents in the City were already exceeding £465 per m^2 and had increased by over £90 per m^2 since December 1986. Even small office suites were now commanding £370 per m^2.

There were substantial fears of shortages of office space in Central London. Normally, the vacancy rate in the United Kingdom is never much higher than 8 per cent (in the United States it often exceeds 30 per cent), but by the mid-1980s this was drastically reduced. Whereas in January 1983 there were 4.1 years of new office supply in Central London, by January 1986 this had plummetted to only two years, and in 1987 it was estimated that while supply amounted to 240 000 m^2, demand had soared to 353 000 m^2. This shortage was exacerbated by older offices being taken out of use for redevelopment or refurbishment. The immediate effects of this inadequacy of space were: the increased degree of pre-letting, particularly to the banking and financial sector (by 1987 over 70 per cent of total floorspace under construction in the City was pre-let); the increased extent to which firms acquired the freehold of their offices (this was particularly the case among foreign operators, not least Japanese companies); and an inflationary impact on the West End office market where rents rose to £418 per m^2 in Mayfair in 1987.

The recession of the early 1990s and its impact on office development

The growth in the output of financial and business services in the mid-1980s was associated with falling interest rates and a substantial increase in new construction orders and construction output in respect of office development. Subsequently, high interest rates and the associated slump had a detrimental affect on new construction orders and construction output (table 3.5).

In 1993, during the property slump, average rents on new lettings in the West End of London plummeted to £430 per m^2 (from £756 per m^2 in 1988) and in the City of London fell to £323 per m², but were fairly stable at £226 per m² in Manchester and £182 per m² in Glasgow – regional divergence in the 1980s giving way to convergence in the early 1990s. Taking occupancy costs, however, only Tokyo's central business district had higher average outgoings than the West End of London (£1612 per m² compared to £732 per m²), while costs in the City of London were £649 per m², and £545 per m² in Hong Kong, £431 per m² in Paris, £409 per m² in Berlin, £397 per m² in Frankfurt and £362 per m² in mid-town New York.

The property slump in London can be attributed largely to an excess supply of new development in the City as a result of a substantial amount of speculative office development in the late 1980s (for example, 1.1 million m² of new office space was completed in the City in 1989, nearly four times as much as in 1986), and a deficiency of demand in the West End.

A number of very large developments were completed in the City, notably the later phases of Broadgate and all of London Wall, and up to 930 000 m² of office space at Canary Wharf in the London docklands became available. By 1992, there were 3.7 million m² of unoccupied office space in London, about 20 per cent of the capital's stock and equivalent to two and a half years' supply of new office space.

Other Offices

Offices of professional institutions

While central locations are desired, maximum or special accessibility is less important than in the case of business firms; nevertheless, prestigious sites are sought after. Accountancy, architectural, medical and surveying institutions may pay fairly high rents or own valuable properties adjacent to parks or in squares or crescents of historic interest.

Offices of small professional firms and branch offices of commercial organisations

Accessibility to a residential population is important, thus location in the high street of a suburb or small town is appropriate – sites close to a railway or tube station being particularly attractive. Whereas building societies, banks and estate agents prefer ground-floor situations, solicitors and accountants often utilise office space above shops. Turnovers and rents per m² are generally moderate to low.

Local government and civil service offices

In the nineteenth century and earlier, town halls and civil service deparments occupied central locations to signify the importance of the function of government. But except where comprehensive redevelopment has occurred in recent years, and where costs of development are shared with commercial interests, local and central government offices have tended to be located on less costly sites within the urban area, although there are many examples of civil service departments having taken the lead in decentralising offices to the Assisted Areas or to the overspill towns. Over 55 000 civil service jobs were dispersed to offices outside London between 1963 and 1975, and following the recommendations of the Hardman Report[17] it was announced in 1974 that a further 31 000 civil service posts would be moved from London, mainly to the Assisted Areas. But with cuts in public expenditure the dispersal programme was postponed in 1979.

Accessibility may be an exaggerated reason for offices in general being attracted to central areas. Tradition may have played a substantial part in firms choosing city centres as a base for their activities, and while leases continue, inertia militates against decentralisation. The use of the telephone, the telex and the increasing employment of computers provide the same degree of accessibility between firms almost regardless of location. Nevertheless, the centre of a city has for generations been both a market place and a social meeting place and it is unlikely that the central area of a town will cease to be attractive as a major location for offices.

Business parks

In recent years a large number of business parks have been developed, on comparatively low-cost land in edge-of-town or out-of-town locations, to satisfy a demand among office firms for relatively low rents and labour costs, more suitable premises, a more attractive (and possibly landscaped) environment and often good road accessibility. In 1991, for example, there was a total of 138 development schemes of 9290 m^2 more under way, with the largest providing 139 354 m^2 of office space.[18] Notwithstanding the many advantages of business parks, many office firms will continue to show a preference for the inherent attributes of the central business district, notably general accessibility as facilitated by public transport.

INDUSTRIAL LOCATION

During the Industrial Revolution of the eighteenth and nineteenth centuries, most of the larger British cities were essentially raw material locations for industry (often based on coal and iron supplies), market locations, ports and areas benefiting from agglomeration economies. But the development of road transport, the use of electricity and the availability of large and relatively low-cost and spacious sites in peripheral areas encouraged manufacturing industry (which in total occupied about 230 million m^2 of floorspace in 1990) to move from central locations to the edge of cities or beyond. Table 3.6 shows that,

Table 3.6 *Location of industrial floorspace in England and Wales*

	Manufacturing floorspace (million m^2)		Change (%)
	1967	1985	
Rural areas	16.5	25.1	+52.1
Small towns	44.3	57.0	+28.7
Large towns	29.7	32.8	+10.4
Free-standing cities	37.2	38.8	+ 4.3
Conurbations	65.8	58.0	−11.9
London	26.7	20.5	−23.2
England and Wales	220.1	232.2	+ 5.5

Source: Department of the Environment, *Commercial and Industrial Floorspace Statistics: Statistics for Town and Country Planning.*

for example between 1967 and 1985, the amount of manufacturing floorspace in rural areas and small towns increased dramatically, whereas there was a considerable decrease in the amount of manufacturing floorspace in London and the conurbations.

But the out-migration of industrial investment and employment must be seen within the context of de-industrialisation. Whereas the proportion of the working population of the United Kingdom employed in manufacturing decreased from 36 per cent in 1955 to 21 per cent in 1990, the proportion employed in this sector in the larger urban areas (and particularly in the inner cities) decreased at a significantly faster rate.

It has been suggested[19] that the urban–rural shift in manufacturing employment could be explained by any one of the following theories: *First*, the constrained location theory postulates that since site dimensions affect both *in situ* changes (expansions and contractions) and unit turnovers (openings and closures), cramped sites inevitably account for a high rate of loss from both contractions and closures, especially in Inner London and the inner cities of the North.[20] Manufacturers, moreover, are unable or unwilling to match the rents paid by competing land users (such as office firms, retailers and warehouse operators) to secure the space necessary for survival in the inner city. It is notable that in periods of relatively fast economic growth (for example, 1967–75, and 1986–9) the decentralisation of manufacturing was most marked, while in times of recession the pace of decentralisation was much slower (such as in the periods 1976–83 and 1990–3) – the degree of competition for urban sites and the attraction of alternative locations being greater at a time of growth than at a time of recession.

Second, the production cost explanation suggests that higher operation costs in urban areas (directly – the higher cost of land and labour, and indirectly – the cost of congestion and inconvenience) have adverse effects on profitability, investment, competition and employment, particularly *vis-à-vis* small firms.[21] Such firms would need to decentralise or risk closure.

Third, the capital restructuring theory maintains that in order to apply new techniques and to counter competition, large multiplant and often multinational corporations shift their operations from cities to rural areas to exploit less skilled, less unionised and less costly labour.[22]

Of these three explanations, the first might be considered to be the most credible, while the second approach is still subject to research. The third explanation is sometimes criticised on the grounds that spatial differences in union strength and labour costs are too small to be significant attractions *per se*.

Two further reasons could be offered to explain the decentralisation of manufacturing industry. First, the out-migration of population (especially the professional, managerial and skilled manual classes) has been an important factor in attracting decentralised employment; and, second, planning policies played a major part in the decentralisation of employment, particularly from London. Through the medium of new towns, expanded towns, industrial development certificates and office development permits, 'the coordinated decentralisation of population and employment from London [became] . . . a central element in strategic planning for the South East in the first thirty years or so after the war'.[23] However, most decentralisation has been independent of public policy and almost certainly would have occurred in the complete absence of regional planning.

Industrial inertia nevertheless exists. Some firms may have a traditional preference for central sites, or economies of agglomeration may compensate for the internal diseconomies of cramped sites and often obsolete and multistorey factory premises. Once a firm is located in a particular place it may eventually find difficulty in disposing of its old factory building, it might be reluctant to establish additional space elsewhere because of technical difficulties of splitting production, and it may be unwilling to incur the disruption of a move.

Industrial Location in a Regional Context

In spatial terms, contemporary de-industrialisation became apparent first in the 1960s in London and the other conurbations – old urban bases of nineteenth-century industry. In the 1970s and 1980s, the Development Areas again stagnated, having been centres of depression in the 1930s, but the West Midlands and the South-East were beginning to show signs of even greater manufacturing decline. In the early 1990s, the West Midlands suffered the greatest manufacturing job losses in proportionate terms, while the South-East not only experienced the greatest decrease in manufacturing employment in absolute terms but its manufacturing workforce decreased at a more than proportionate rate (table 3.7).

In addition to the decreasing supply of manufacturing labour, there are serious problems relating to the supply of industrial property. In the early 1990s there

Table 3.7 *Manufacturing job loss, United Kingdom, 1990–92*

| | Manufacturing employment change 1990–92 | |
	(000s)	(%)
West Midlands	−104	−18.2
South-West	−51	−15.8
South-East	−154	−13.8
North-West	−74	−12.9
East Anglia	−16	−9.7
Wales	−21	−9.5
East Midlands	−39	−8.8
Yorkshire & Humberside	−40	−8.7
Scotland	−31	−8.4
Northern Ireland	−7	−7.1

Source: Department of Employment, *Employment Gazette* (various).

was a low rate of new investment in factory floorspace, a substantial mismatch between the property requirements of firms and the sites they occupied, little likelihood of industrial regeneration in London and the conurbations, and in general an uncoordinated and unregulated supply of industrial property.

According to Fothergill *et al.*, if it were assumed that manufacturing output were to increase by 3.5 per year (by means of a 3 per cent increase in productivity and a 0.5 per cent increase in employment), then 3.5 per cent more floor space would be required each year.[24] Also taking into account demolitions and factories no longer suitable for use, the total additional floorspace required would amount to 190 million m² (or 12.5 million m² per year). This would necessitate an annual investment of £4.6 billion (at 1990 prices), £1.8 billion more each year than in the 1980s. Half of the 190 million m² would be needed in new units (as opposed to extensions/refurbishments), but this would require 31 600 ha. Although the amount of land available for industrial development is probably in excess of this, not all of it (suggest Fothergill *et al.*) is 'in the right place, available at the right time, of the right size and the right price'. This is particularly the case in London and the conurbations. Elsewhere (such as in the green belts) restrictive planning policies limit the supply of land.

Since it would be a tragedy if the possibilities of sustained economic growth were thwarted by a shortage of industrial buildings and land, public policy (argue Fothergill *et al.*) must ensure that investment funds are available for industrial property development, and that the mismatch between the demand and supply of both buildings and land is eliminated.[25] In this context, it is necessary for the policies of the Department of Enterprise and Department of the Environment to be co-ordinated, but there must also be the maximum degree of partnership between the public and private sectors.

Public-sector developers could play an important part in supplying the required industrial floorspace. English Estates, the Scottish Development Agency, the Welsh Development Agency, the New Towns Development Corporations and the local authorities have all been instrumental in regenerating the depressed areas and in aiding decentralisation. It is unlikely that the private sector – if left to itself – would have promoted growth so effectively. Currently, urban development corporations and local authorities are involved in regenerating the inner city (Chapter 8). There is an urgent need for these bodies to facilitate national economic growth by tackling (in their areas) the problem of industrial buildings, and land. Fothergill *et al.* argue that the problem of land supply must be solved if the inner cities are to attract a larger share of manufacturing growth.[26] They argue that local authorities should redesignate land currently reserved for other uses and that the cost of clearance, demolition and reclamation should be more heavily subsidised. The government should also subsidise rents on publicly owned land or they should be willing to sell such land to industrial developers at subsidised prices.

Small firms – occupying buildings of less than, say, 500 m² – numerically dominate the stock of factory space (more than 65 000 units of this size account for over half the total number of industrial premises in Britain). While most small premises were supplied by speculative developers, many local authorities, in partnership with the private sector, have played a significant part in the formation and growth of small firms in recent years – an involvement which clearly needs to be continued.

It might be assumed that de-industrialisation is synonymous with an increase in vacant floorspace, with an increase in supply in relation to demand and with falling rents. However, a high proportion of factories (vacant or occupied) are outmoded (40 per cent were built before 1945), are multistoreyed and have little external space for storage or expansion, or vacant land adjacent to the site.[27] Although in 1985 there were nearly 12 million m² of vacant factory floorspace on the market for sale or rent (about 3 per cent of the total stock), this may be inadequate to meet demand despite de-industrialisation. Fothergill *et al.* have shown that although manufacturing employment decreased dramatically in the period 1967–85, the demand for factory floorspace has increased since employment densities decreased from 37 to 21 workers per 1000 m² (1967–85) (table 3.8) and are likely to continue to decrease.[28]

Fothergill *et al.* warn that as the economy (eventually) recovers, spare capacity will be utilised and vacant premises will become occupied.[29] Far more floorspace will be required, they argue, but they foresee bottlenecks in the development process, particularly in London and the conurbations. Whereas, for the most part, Wales, Scotland and the North have the greatest supply of available land for industrial development, London and most of the conurbations are disadvantaged with regard to the quantity, quality and price of industrial sites. With the economic upturn, therefore, the industrial prospects of London and the conurbations will remain bleak (unless these areas are able to attract small and medium-sized firms with modest site requirements), and, as before, the burden of industrial

Table 3.8 *Changes in manufacturing employment and floorspace in England and Wales, 1967–85*

	Manufacturing employment (000s)		Change (%)	Floorspace (million m²)		Change (%)	Floorspace per employee (m²)	
	1967	1985		1967	1985		1967	1985
North-West	1216	693	−43	48.0	42.9	−11	39.5	61.9
Yorkshire and Humberside	813	502	−38	31.4	28.4	−10	38.6	56.6
West Midlands	1162	682	−41	34.0	36.9	+9	29.3	54.2
North	450	288	−36	10.9	14.3	+31	24.2	49.7
Wales	311	202	−35	6.8	10.0	+47	21.9	49.5
East Midlands	621	479	−23	19.1	23.4	+23	30.8	48.9
East Anglia	174	176	+1	5.8	8.3	+43	33.3	47.2
South-West	423	347	−18	11.1	15.3	+38	26.2	44.1
South-East	2316	1519	−34	53.2	52.7	−1	23.0	34.7
England & Wales	7485	4888	−35	220.1	232.2	+6	26.9	47.5

Source: Department of the Environment, *Commercial and Industrial Floorspace Statistics: Statistics for Town and Country Planning.*

adjustment would be borne by the inner cities. Interregionally, too, there are major disparities in the demand and supply of vacant factories and industrial sites. With regard to both rents and land prices there remains North–South divide, particularly as the demand for high-tech buildings has substantially pulled up the price of sites in the South-East close to the motorways (especially the M3, M4 and M11).

Location Policy

Regional policies have had a substantial effect on the pattern of industrial location in the United Kingdom and need to be examined. From the introduction of the Distribution of Industry Act 1945 until the 1980s, industrial development in London, the South-East and the Midlands has been restricted by the government's unwillingness to grant industrial development certificates (IDCs) to firms wishing to expand. Initially, IDCs were required when proposed factory development involved floor space in excess of 5000 ft² (465 m²). In contrast, IDCs were freely granted for expansion within the development areas of the north and west of Britain. Under the Industry Act 1972, however IDCs were not required in the development and special development areas, but in the intermediate areas IDCs were necessary for expansion in excess of 15 000 ft² (1395 m²). In South-East England they were needed for development over 5000 ft² (465 m²) and elsewhere over 10 000 ft² (929 m²) – the thresholds rising in 1976 to 12 500 ft² (1162 m²) and 15 000 ft² (1395 m²) respectively.

As part of a general policy of attempting to eliminate regional imbalance (especially in terms of unemployment levels) the government since the Special Areas legislation of the 1930s has made loans, grants the tax allowances available to industrialists developing in the depressed regions. Throughout most of the 1970s manufacturers in the Assisted Areas were able to claim regional development grants (RDGs) of 20–22 per cent for new industrial buildings, plant and machinery, and could write off for tax purposes 100 per cent of their capital expenditure on new plant and machinery and 44 per cent of the construction costs of new industrial buildings. Firms were also encouraged to increase, or at least maintain, their employment of labour by means of Regional Employment Premiums which were up to £3.00 per employee per week in the mid-1970s. The result of these policies is that the quantity of industrial development around cities in the South-East and Midlands has probably been far less than would have been the case if market forces had been permitted to operate freely. Conversely, there is now more new industry around cities in the Assisted Areas than would have occurred otherwise. Regional policies have also had a qualitative effect on industry in the South-East and Midlands, manufacturing developed in many small and duplicate factories and workshops within IDC exemption limits. This otherwise might have been concentrated in larger buildings – manufacturers then not having to forgo internal and external economies of scale.

As part of their dual commitment to monetarism and free market industrial policy, Thatcher administrations halved regional aid, in real terms, to an average of £989 million per annum over the period 1979/80 to 1984/85 (table 3.9) – cutting RDGs in development areas from 20 to 15 per cent and withdrawing them completely in intermediate areas; rolling back the boundaries of the Assisted Areas so that they would contain only 27.5 per cent of Britain's working population (as opposed to 44 per cent previously); and relaxing IDC controls – the threshold rising generally to 50 000 ft^2 (4645 m^2) with IDCs no longer being required in any of the Assisted Areas. In 1982 IDCs were abandoned altogether. This was at a time when unemployment was escalating in the traditionally depressed regions of Britain. Whereas unemployment nationally increased from 5.3 to 13.1 per cent (1979–84), in the North it increased from 8.3 to 18.1 per cent, in Wales from 7.3 to 16.2 cent and in the North-West from 6.5 to 16 per cent. Although £20 billion had been spent on regional aid during 1964–83, creating 500 000 jobs (at a cost latterly of £35 000 per job), stark regional disparities remained.

The White Paper, *Regional Industrial Development* (1983) recommended that policy should be more selective and cost-effective (in accountancy rather than in social terms). In 1984, therefore, the boundaries of the Assisted Areas were partly redrawn to ensure greater selectivity (taking in 35 per cent of the working population of Britain) and RDGs were limited to a cost per job of £10 000, or alternatively companies could claim employment grants of £3000 per job. In 1988, the above grant limits were replaced by even more selective regional enterprise grants – steering aid particularly to small firms which otherwise

Table 3.9 *Government expenditure on regional aid, 1976/7 to 1993/4*

Incentive	Average annual expenditure (£)			Planned
	1976/77 to 1978/79	1979/80 to 1984/85	1985/86 to 1990/91	1991/92 to 1993/94
Regional Development Grants	518	473	74	18
Regional Selective Assistance	39	57	84	115
Government Advanced Factory Building and land reclamation and provision	51	118	53	65
Regional Employment Premiums and other labour subsidies	106	5	–	–
Business development incentives:				
Regional Enterprise Grants	–	–	1	12
Business Consultancy Initiative	–	–	10	55
Totals: At current prices (£)	714	653	222	265
At 1989–90 prices (£)	1835	989	242	221

Source: J. Michie (ed.), *The Economic Legacy 1979–1993*, Academic Press, 1992.

might not function profitably. In addition, regional aid was further reduced to an average of £242 million per annum (at 1989–90 prices) over the period 1985/86 to 1990/91. It was one thing, however, to promote greater efficiency, but quite another matter to cut total expenditure on aid at a time of soaring unemployment – with potentially disastrous effects on the depressed regions.

Whereas the growth in manufacturing output in the mid- and late 1980s (as in previous booms) was associated with comparatively low interest rates, a substantial increase in new construction orders and construction output with respect to the development of industrial premises, and a North–South divergence of unemployment, the subsequent slump was attributable to a marked increase in interest rates (aimed at correcting a deteriorating balance of payments and depreciating pound) and was characterised by a large decrease in new construction orders and construction output and a North–South convergence of unemployment (table 3.10 and figure 3.6).

In the early 1990s, unemployment (in percentage terms) in parts of the South-East and South-West had risen to at least the level of that in the Assisted Areas, soaring, in these regions as a whole, from 3.9 and 4.5 per cent respectively in 1989 to 10.4 and 10.2 per cent in 1993. From 1990 to 1993, rates of unemployment in the regions, at a time of recession, had converged (as they had during the recession of the early 1980s) – in contrast to a divergence during the boom years (1987–9) (Figure 3.6). Therefore many small areas of high unemployment, mainly in the South-East and South-West, were added to the list of those eligible for assistance, and a number of areas (mainly in the traditionally depressed northern regions) were descheduled. Consequently, from 1 August 1993, the Assisted Areas covered only 34 per cent of the working

Table 3.10 *The industrial development boom and slump*

	Growth in manufacturing per cent per annum)	Interest rates (%)[1]	Balance of payments (current account) as a percentage of GDP	£ exchange rate[2]	New construction orders (£m at 1985 prices)	Construction output (£m at 1985 prices)
1985	2.7	11.5	0.8	100	1818	2566
1986	1.3	11.0	0.0	92	1975	2364
1987	5.2	8.5	-1.0	90	1979	2594
1988	7.0	13.0	-3.3	96	2446	2822
1989	4.3	15.0	-4.0	93	2327	3054
1990	-0.5	14.0	-3.1	91	2085	2789
1991	-5.2	10.5	-1.1	92	1635	2384
1992	-0.7	7.0	-2.0	88	1374	2101

Notes: 1. Retail bank base rate, end of year.
2. Trade weighted index, average for year.

Source: Central Statistical Office; Department of the Environment.

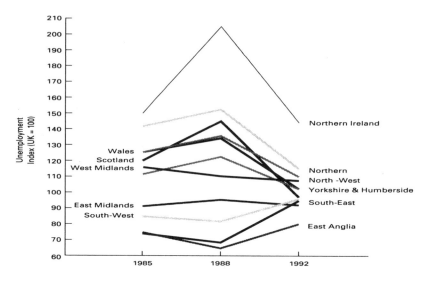

Figure 3.6 *Regional divergence and convergence in unemployment*

population of Britain, slightly less than in 1984, while regional assistance, planned to average £221 million per annum (1992/3–1993/4), was destined to fall further. Undoubtedly, there had been a major shift of emphasis from a policy of promoting the revival of the depressed regions to a policy of regenerating the inner cities (see Chapter 8), but this was of little consolation to entrepreneurs having to make decisions within a regional context.

RESIDENTIAL LOCATION

Housing constitutes the largest urban land use (in some towns over 50 per cent of the total area) and may account for over 25 per cent of personal expenditure. There is a great variety of types of housing but most residential land is fixed in area and location. Forced out of areas of good business accessibility, housing land is less frequently redeveloped compared with other uses, but marginal changes may have important economic and social ramifications. Although there is a relationship between personal income, place of employment and place of residence, this relationship is subject to different and conflicting interpretations. There are basically three explanations of the rationale of private-sector housing location.

Travel cost minimisation theory

It has been argued that if travel costs to work are nil or very low, householders will be prepared to pay the highest rents or prices for accommodation. Through the working of the price mechanism this would imply that the rich live very close to the central business district and the poor live in less expensive outer areas. But the converse is generally true. Low-income earners live close to their work (usually within the inner areas of cities) to minimise their travelling costs rents are mainly regulated, and housing densities are high. As incomes rise, there has been a tendency for people to live further away from their work in areas of lower density and more expensive housing. Moreover, the outward spread of cities would only be compatible with travel cost minimisation if employment was simultaneously decentralised and this usually does not take place.

But the theory is valid to some extent. Although house prices may be very high in the commuter belt, residential values per m^2 tend to diminish outwards from the central area as competition from business uses becomes less. Both in the cases of the unregulated furnished tenancies in the 'twilight' areas in inner London (up to 1974) and the exclusive leasehold properties in Belgravia and Mayfair, values could only be as high as they are because of the very large demand from persons unable or unwilling to incur high travel costs to gain access to employment and the other facilities of inner and central London.

Travel cost and housing cost trade off theory

A perfect trade off assumes that households of the same income group are prepared to pay, over a period, the same real aggregate cost of travel and housing – regardless of distance from a city centre (figure 3.7 (a)). But often there is not a perfect trade off and therefore it is assumed that households will attempt to minimise aggregate costs. Thus in the context of commuting into the city centre, there will be a migration of households inwards if travel costs rise, but a migration outwards if travel costs fall (figure 3.76 (b)). If, on the other hand, housing costs rise, there will be an out-migration, but if housing costs fall there will be an in-migration (figure 3.76 (c)).

Although there is an inverse correlation between site values and travel costs around many cities (for example, London), the same is not true of house prices and travel costs. High-income commuters do not have to trade off travel costs and housing costs – they can afford both; the rich may prefer to live in the commuter belt where they can benefit from a better environment and open space and where they can segregate themselves from lower socio-economic groups; and it may only be within the outer areas of cities that sites are available for the construction of new and expensive houses. Motorways, moreover, may make outer locations more accessible than many inner suburban locations from the central business district.

Even if there were an inverse correlation between house prices and travel costs, however, it is unlikely that householders would trade off. Housing expenditure (including rates as well as mortgage interest payments) and travel costs change frequently but households may only alter their location at intervals of five or more years. There is usually a long time-lag before householders react to changing costs, and there is a high degree of immobility as

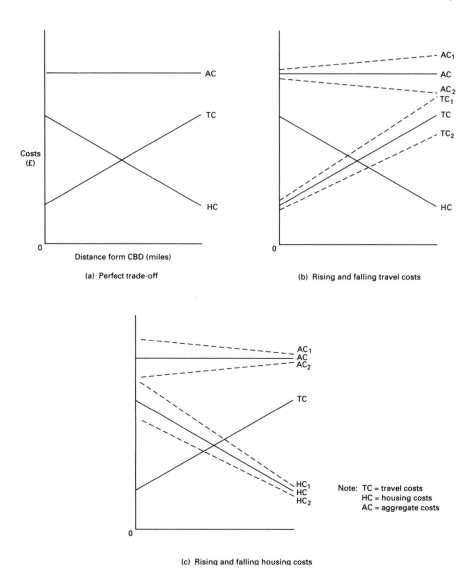

Figure 3.7   *The trade-off theory of residential location*

non-economic reasons may outweigh economic considerations in determining locational choice. The main reasons why householders change residence may be due more to a change of job, marriage or a change in the size of family than to a changing relationship between travel costs and house prices. It is completely unrealistic to assume that a householder is free to locate anywhere from the central business district to the outer commuter belt. His choice is fairly restricted and the point on the housing cost curve will be determined largely by mortgage availability.

A trade-off model of the above sort is least satisfactory in explaining residential location within a conurbation where there may be several central business districts and a complex pattern of commuting. Patterns and relationships will also be distorted by the decentralisation of employment. Nevertheless the trade-off hypothesis has been extended by Evans[30] who suggested that if a household's income increased, and the demand for household space increased, the household might move further out from the centre; but if the household's income increased and the demand for space remained constant, the household might move nearer the centre (the increase in the rate of pay and the resulting increase in the valuation of travel time could mean that the total saving in travel costs would offset higher house prices). Therefore, when incomes increase there are two opposing forces influencing locational choice. The direction of change, if any, will depend upon the relative strength of these two opposing forces. Evans further suggested that following a general increase in pay, higher income households out-bid lower income groups both on the periphery of urban areas and in the inner cites, in the latter case often by means of 'gentrification' (chapter 9). The resulting pattern of household distribution (a more than proportionate number of high-income households in both inner and peripheral areas and a more than proportionate number of lower- and middle-income groups in between) is well marked in British conurbations, particularly in Greater London and the Home Counties, as the data above demonstrate.

Maximum housing expenditure theory

This states that income and the availability and conditions of mortgage finance (including the effects of tax allowances) determine residential location. The theory is based on the assumption that house-buyers will attempt to acquire a house as expensive as they can afford with the maximum mortgage which they can raise in the area of their choice. But although house-buyers may seek a property over a wide area, transport costs may be a relatively minor consideration and may be variable in relation to the distribution of houses within a specific price range. Environmental and social factors (and the prospects of capital appreciation) are likely to be a much greater influence over choice. This hypothesis, evolved by Ellis[31] and Stegman,[32] implies that there is no overall relationship between income, travel cost/time and place of work, and that there is no effective trade-off.

In formulating policies, central and local government need to know why people live in a certain area, what types of houses should be constructed and in which locations, how significant are journey-to-work considerations, how far is it desirable to decentralise employment, how should investment in either improved transport (to the central and inner areas) or in residential environmental improvement be decided, and – if regional growth points are likely to provide a preferable environment and facilitate a more efficient transport system – how should investment decisions be made. Richardson[33] suggests that if it is thought that there is a trade-off between housing expenditure and travelling

costs then policy should concentrate on reducing travelling costs to work and/
or developing high density housing in the inner areas of cities. Alternatively, a
policy of decentralising employment would benefit particularly low-income
householders in the outer suburbs. But if it is found that environmental conditions influence householders more than travelling costs, policies would need to
concentrate on providing satisfactory residential environments rather than on
reducing the cost of the journey to work.

REFERENCES

1. H. W. Richardson, *Urban Economics* (Penguin, 1971).
2. W. Alonso, 'A Theory of the Urban Land Market', *Papers and Proceedings of the Regional Science Association*, 6 (1960); *Location and Land Use* (Harvard University Press, 1964); 'A Reformulation of Classical Location Theory and its Relation to Rent Theory', *Papers and Proceedings of the Regional Science Association*, 19 (1967).
3. R. Sinclair, 'Von Thünen and Urban Sprawl', *Annals of the Association of American Geographers*, 57 (1967); R. Goodchild and R. Munton, *Development and the Landowner. An Analysis of the British Experience* (George Allen & Unwin, 1985).
4. S. Fothergill, M. Kitson and S. Monk, *Property and Industrial Development* (Hutchinson, 1987).
5. G. Keogh, 'The Economics of Planning Gain', in S. Barrett and P. Healey (eds), *Land Policy: Problems and Alternatives* (Gower, 1985).
6. P. Hall, 'A Problem with its Roots in the Distant Past', *Town and Country Planning* (February 1985).
7. J. Carr, 'Malls Laugh as the High Streets Die', *Observer* (28 June 1987).
8. P. Jones, 'Small Shops, Big Implications', *Town and Country Planning* (June 1986).
9. Hillier Parker, *British Shopping Centre Development Master List* (1993).
10. J. Carr, 'Malls laugh'.
11. P. Cheeseright, 'An Awful Lot of Shopping in Manchester', *Financial Times* (6 March 1987).
12. P. Cheeseright, 'A Shop-around for the West Midlands Planners', *Financial Times* (20 March 1987).
13. P. J. McGoldrick and M. G. Thompson, *Regional Shopping Centres: Out-of-town Versus In-town* (Avebury, 1992).
14. Ibid.
15. B. Laurance, 'High Street Shopping Not Dead Yet', *Guardian* (3 October 1992).
16. I. Alexander, *Office Location and Public Policy* (Longman, 1979).
17. *The Dispersal of Government Work from London*, Cmnd 5363 (HMSO, 1973).
18. S. Shrouder, 'Down to Business', *Chartered Surveyor Weekly* (24 January 1991).
19. D. Keeble, 'Industrial Change in the United Kingdom', in W. F. Lever (ed.), *Industrial Change in the United Kingdom* (Longman, 1987).
20. R. D. Dennis, *Changes in Manufacturing Employment in the South East Region between 1976 and 1980* (Department of Trade and Industry, 1981); S. Fothergill and G. Gudgin, *Unequal Growth: Urban and Regional Employment Change in the United Kingdom* (Heinemann, 1982).
21. W. F. Lever, 'Urban Scale as a Determinant of Employment Growth or Decline', in L. Collins (ed.), *Industrial Decline and Regeneration* (Department of Geography, University of Edinburgh, 1982); B. Moore, J. Rhodes and P. Tyler, 'Geographical Variations in Industrial Costs', *Discussion Paper 12* (Department of Land

Economy, University of Cambridge, 1984); P. A. Wood, 'The South East', in P. J. Damesick and P. A. Wood (eds), *Regional Problems, Problem Regions and Public Policy in the United Kingdom* (Clarendon Press, 1987).

22. D. Massey and R. A. Meegan, 'Industrial Restructuring Versus the Cities', *Urban Studies*, 15 (1978).
23. N. Buck, I. Gordon and K. Young with J. Ermisch and L. Mills, *The London Employment Problem* (Oxford University Press, 1986).
24. S. Fothergill, M. Kitson and S. Monk, *Property and Industrial Development*.
25. Ibid.
26. Ibid.
27. Ibid.
28. Ibid.
29. Ibid.
30. A. W. Evans, *The Economics of Residential Location* (Macmillan, 1971).
31. R. H. Ellis, 'Modelling of Household Location – 'A Statistical Approach', *Highway Research Record*, 207 (1967).
32. M. A. Stegman, 'Accessibility Models and Residential Location', *Journal of the American Institute of Planners*, 35 (1969).
33. H. W. Richardson, *Urban Economics* (Penguin, 1971).

4

The Property and Investment Markets and Town Planning

PROPERTY INTERESTS

Fundamentally, the subjects of real property transactions are not the land and buildings themselves but interests in rights over land, which in aggregate are known to English law as property.[1] Land is merely the medium in which property rights subsist. The greatest bundle of rights in property is the 'fee simple absolute', an unencumbered freehold estate free from any sub-interest. Freehold rights are, however, not unlimited; they will be subject to the provisions of planning and other legislation. The freehold interest may be purchased subject to obligations entered into by the previous owner. For example, a property may be purchased with an existing tenant who has a leasehold interest. The freeholder has purchased the right to receive rent from the tenant, the right to regain possession at the end of the lease, and then to use the property within the constraints of planning or local authority regulations. The durability of real property enables more than one interest to exist; in particular, ownership and right of use may be separated.

A leaseholder may use the building subject to conditions laid down, in return for which s/he agrees to pay a specified rent. Many alternative forms of leasehold interest may be created by the freeholder. S/He may grant a building lease on condition that a building is erected on the site; at the end of the lease both land and buildings revert to the landlord. The rent agreed, the ground rent, may be nominal or a 'peppercorn rent' not necessarily representing the full value of the land; thus in addition to the rent a capital sum may be paid. The sum paid as rent or as capital will depend on various factors, especially tax. Where rents are chargeable against taxable income, and capital payments are not, the tenant may prefer a higher rent to any capital payment. An alternative arrangement is where the ground rent is reviewed periodically and related to site value, an arrangement beneficial to the freeholder.

The range of possible interests in property is exceedingly diverse: the head-lessee may be entitled to sub-let, grant his/her own leases and state the obligations and rights of the sub-lessee. Freeholders may borrow through a mortgage with the freehold as collateral; the mortgagee will have rights and interests in the freehold until the mortgagor clears the debt. In default of repayment, the mortgagee may exercise his/her right to foreclose and force the sale of the interest in order to repay the debt.

THE PROPERTY MARKET AND PRICE DETERMINATION

The property market deals in rights and interests in land and buildings; transactions involving heterogeneous units of high value in many sub-markets – shops, offices, houses – reflect variations in buyers, sellers, local knowledge and unique locational factors. The market has no formal organisation, central agency or institution such as the London Stock Exchange or Lloyds.

The property market is very imperfect; nevertheless there is an underlying rationale arising from the effectiveness of market price in allocating resources between different users. Transactions occur between sellers and buyers of property, and in the long run rights and interests will be controlled by those users who bid the highest price for these interests.

A property may be purchased either for owner-occupation or for investment. If the former the purchaser's return is in occupational benefits; if the purchase is for investment, the return may be as an annual rent or as a capital gain following a successful planning application either changing the use or the density of existing use.

Assuming rational behaviour, the investor will be seeking to maximise returns in profitability or satisfaction from either owner-occupation or investment. The decision to rent or purchase will depend upon the current level of rents, interest rates, the availability of credit, expectations about future trends, and personal financial factors. If anticipated rents are less than interest charges the owner might be induced to sell rather than rent, unless there is a prospect of capital gain. Similarly, a potential purchaser will compare interest payable on borrowings and their availability with rents payable. The opportunity cost of capital must be considered, whether renting or buying.

When a potential user decides to rent rather than purchase, s/he must offer a rent high enough to induce the owner to let; the greater the potential profitability and utility to him/her of the use of a building, the higher the rent s/he will offer. Similarly, the potential purchaser will bid a price determined by expectations regarding likely profits from ownership of that building. Bids will reflect the different expectations. Owners will similarly differ on how much they think they should receive for giving up interests in their property.

Real properties are heterogeneous and this adds to the complexity of supply and demand analysis. The market price of real property reflects economic assessments on the part of various buyers and sellers regarding anticipated net income and profitability.

Whether renting or purchasing, the investment aspect is present; the essence of investment is the giving up of a capital sum in return for income over time. The purchaser or potential occupier needs to discount the stream of anticipated income and benefits from the property to a present value at the appropriate rate of interest, probably the marginal cost of financing the project and according to present income and capital, the degree of risk and the probable return on capital in alternative investments with similar risks. Potential occupiers or purchasers will consider differing advantages from occupations so that each will arrive at a different place influenced by the price and availability of substitute properties. For any property interest there will be a maximum price which buyers will be prepared to pay. Similarly, potential sellers will value their interests and establish minimum prices influenced by the selling price of comparable properties, expectations regarding future price changes, economic policy and prospects, and the cost of equivalent reinstatement elsewhere. Thus, deals will occur provided potential buyers have maximum prices above the minimum prices of potential sellers. Where the buyer's maximum price is above the seller's minimum price, the price fixed will be determined by the competition among buyers and their expectations as against the number of properties on offer and the expectations of sellers.

If there is only one potential buyer of a particular property with a maximum price higher than the seller's minimum price, the market price will be fixed somewhere between the two points of bargaining. The two prices fix a limit on the possible movement of market price at any time; the situation may change as expectations or conditions within the property market vary. The stronger the seller's bargaining position the closer the market price will be to the maximum price; the weaker the seller's position, the closer the price will be to the buyer's maximum (or seller's minimum).

Thus prices within the various sub-markets will be determined by the various maxima and minima determined by prospective buyers and sellers bidding against each other. Equilibrium prices may be reached at which the amount of real property offered for sale is taken up by buyers; however, a characteristic of the property market as a whole, and of sub-markets such as private housing, is that it lacks the flexibility to clear itself. At times, property remains unsold because the minimum price asked by owners is higher than the maximum price of bidders. That the property remains unsold may bring about an adjustment in the owner's minimum price or buyer's maximum in a subsequent market period. Alternatively, the owner may keep to his/her price hoping that buyers will raise their maximum price as economic conditions change. In the depressed housing markets of 1974–6, 1981 and 1989–94 many new houses remained unsold because developers' minimum prices exceeded the limit of many prospective buyers. Within the commercial property market, prevailing uncertainty adversely affected many sales. The Centre Point office block in London, completed in 1966, remained largely unlet until 1980 because the minimum rental demanded by the owners exceeded the maximum rental bid by potential occupiers.

Any potential buyer of real property (rights to use land) is likely to view several properties before making a purchase, and a potential seller will await a number of bids before making a sale. However, few people are able to investigate all alternatives; where a potential buyer lacks information or buys too quickly s/he is more likely to pay a price which may be higher than the market level generally. Similarly, the potential seller lacking information or making a hurried sale will receive a lower-than-the-market price. Where a potential seller purchased a property in boom conditions and is under no pressure to vacate, s/he may hold out for a price that will cover his/her expenditure even though conditions may have changed fundamentally. Conversely, where the original owner dies, his/her heirs may consider the property as a windfall and sell quickly for a lower price than they might otherwise have obtained. Negative equity, where the capital value of a property is less than the mortgage outstanding was a significant factor in the United Kingdom housing market of the early 1990s, depressing the number of transactions.

The imperfection of the property market is especially significant in submarkets, such as for land. Similar plots in the same area may be bought or sold at different prices according to the expertise or lack of experience of the buyer. Herein lies the chance of making speculative profit because one person is more astute than the market in anticipating future trends. If perfect knowledge were available as to future events regarding land, there would be no opportunity for speculative gains because all future potential and therefore value would be fully and accurately discounted to the present. Speculative gains can only be made in an imperfect market. Similarly, when there are few sales involving a particular type of property and where buyers and sellers are not fully informed, relative skill in bargaining is significant in determining price. Market imperfections may mean a heavy reliance on professional middlemen, leading to monopoly power.

The typical method of conducting transactions in the property market is by private treaty between buyer and seller. The price will be determined by the offer and counter-bid process described. The transaction is likely to be carried out discreetly through the medium of professional middlemen. Because of market imperfections the seller will not know exactly what price s/he will obtain; the final selling price of a real property is rarely revealed. A more open method of buying and selling real property is through auctions, which are used where there is great uncertainty as to property values because of unique factors or where the market conditions are so fluid as to produce rapidly changing values. Auctions were particularly popular in the United Kingdom between 1971 and 1973 and again between 1985 and 1989, when prices increased sharply and seller wished to ensure that they received a current, higher price. Conversely, in a buyer's market, auctions are normally a less attractive method of selling, although the transaction is completed in a much shorter period than under private treaty.

Auctions are also used for sales by special bodies such as public trustees. If the necessary minimum price required (the reserve) is not reached, the property may be withdrawn and possibly put up for sale at a later date. Another method used where market conditions are exceptionally unstable or where the property is unusual is the tender; potential buyers are invited to submit a sealed bid by a set date. The seals are not opened until this date and, provided the tender is acceptable (the reserve is reached), the highest bidder secures the property. The tender may secure the highest possible price for the seller, as potential buyers will tend to put in a maximum bid without having the advantage of knowing competitors' bids, which they would at an auction; also buyers will not have the opportunity normally of resubmitting a tender. There are also many other transactions between divisions of a large company or members of a family, completely sheltered from the market processes and where prices will be determined by unique features.

Typically only a very small proportion of real property of any type is on the market at any one time. Because of the durability of buildings, the inelasticity of supply for relatively long periods, institutional and legal factors, change is slow and at any moment in time the market is in a state of disequilibrium.

INSTITUTIONS AND THE PROPERTY MARKET

A feature of the post-1945 property market in the United Kingdom has been the extent of institutional investment. Insurance companies and pension funds predominantly but also other major institutions such as property bonds, property unit trusts and the Church Commissioners have acquired interests, mainly in prime shops and offices and modern industrial property. Institutional investment in property has reflected expectations relating to the security of income and the extent to which it is believed that rents, and therefore capital values, will increase faster than the rate of inflation. Property has been seen as a secure, long-term investment that maintains earning power in real terms. Expectations were fully justified between 1962 and 1980 when property capital values (offices, shops and industrial) increased from base 100 to 880. The *Financial Times* Actuaries all-share index increased from 100 to 227; the retail price index increased from 100 to 462. Thus commercial property values in real terms increased from 100 to 194, despite a very sharp fall in rentals in real terms between 1974 and 1977.[2]

However, the period 1980–5 saw economic recession with little recovery and with virtually no rental growth in real terms. Between 1982 and 1983 capital values fell, the only exception being shops, which continued to outpace both offices and industrials. Average annual real rates of returns from property, 4.8 per cent between 1977 and 1987 were inferior to equities, 13.0 per cent, although better than gilts, 3.5 per cent.[3] Consequently institutional investment in United Kingdom property declined from 1982 (see table 4.1) as the performance gap between property and equities continued to widen when share markets entered a long bull market which lasted to 1987 (see table 4.2). With lower inflation, institutional investors could disregard the security offered by property and concentrate their efforts on short-term gain with privatisation issues and the expansion of the unlisted securities market ensuring a ready supply of investments. With a booming owner-occupier market in 1986–7, insurance companies extended their interests into the residential market by incorporating

Table 4.1 *Institutional investment into property, 1979–92 (£ millions) (not deflated)*

	1979	1982	1985	1987	1989	1990	1991	1992
Insurance companies	628	1059	815	755	1510	1080	1483	595
Pension funds	498	797	590	240	92	−491	564	342
Total	1106	1856	1305	995	1602	589	2047	937

Source: *Money into Property* (Debenham Tewson & Chinnocks, 1983).

networks of established estate agencies able to offer a range of financial services. The potential for profit in the cross-fertilisation between the financial sector and the buying and selling of houses appeared clear.

Before 1939 insurance companies had been virtually the sole institutional investors in property. From the 1950s they steadily acquired property assets as values accelerated and commercial rents increased. By the late 1970s, land and property were 19 per cent of total investments compared with 11 per cent in 1964. There was heavy emphasis towards prime areas of central London and other large United Kingdom cities. Over 50 per cent of total property holdings were invested in offices, with the balance in 100 per cent shop sites and modern industrial units. Residential investments were avoided as being too likely to be subject to statutory interference.

Despite a reduction in real terms, insurance company property assets in the United Kingdom increased throughout the 1980s, peaking in 1989 when total property assets exceeded £42 billion – a leap from the previous peak of £22 billion reached in 1986.[4] In 1990–1 the first significant reduction in money terms in the size of the portfolio occurred, to around £35 billion, reducing property investment to about 7 per cent of total investment. This was reversed in 1992. Indicative of a downturn in property investment in the 1980s was the rise in property disposals measured by the turnover rate. This increased from 1.5 per cent in 1980 to 4.7 per cent by 1986, and 9 per cent in 1987.

The insurance companies suffered from the collapsed residential housing market, as did building societies. Their costly investment in estate agency chains was decimated by a disastrous housing market, resulting in their decision to dispose of the chains, with substantial losses. Payment of mortgage indemnity claims added to losses as capital values fell and repossessions soared.

Pension funds have invested in property since 1955, although only in the early 1970s was there significant large investment. By 1980, over 13 per cent of total investment was in property. Public-sector funds were investing close to a third of their cash flow in property on behalf of approximately 12 million people in occupational schemes. Some funds carried out their own developments and also invested in property in the EEC and the USA. Throughout the 1980s the total investment in property assets rose, and peaked in 1989 at £28 billion – approximately 10 per cent of assets. The 1990–3 period saw a steady

Table 4.2 *Investment media: Comparison of real rates of return, 1979–92 (percentages)*

	1979	1980	1981	1982	1983	1984	1985	1986	1987	1988	1989	1990	1991	1992	Annualised rate Dec 1977 to Dec 1992
ML–CIG Property Index	3.8	4.2	2.8	2.2	4.2	5.0	3.0	6.5	20.4	19.3	8.7	−14.5	−10.2	−4.4	3.7
Office	–	–	–	–	–	–	–	–	–	–	–	–	–	–	3.2
Retail	–	–	–	–	–	–	–	–	–	–	–	–	–	–	5.0
Industrial	–	–	–	–	–	–	–	–	–	–	–	–	–	–	4.8
Pooled Property Funds	4.9	2.3	1.7	3.5	2.8	4.1	2.6	4.2	11.6	21.4	7.3	−13.7	−2.3	0.3	3.7
FT Actuaries Property Share Index	3.8	25.5	−6.4	−10.1	28.4	18.1	2.4	20.4	19.1	19.7	−1.9	−25.1	−17.3	−15.1	3.0
FT Actuaries All Share Index	−5.7	17.6	1.4	22.8	22.4	26.2	14.2	22.9	4.1	4.4	6.4	−17.4	15.5	17.3	10.7
FT Actuaries All Stocks Index	−10.4	3.8	−6.7	34.3	7.9	4.1	6.0	7.5	11.1	nil	0.5	0.3	11.1	15.6	4.6
FT Actuaries Index-Linked All Stocks Index	–	–	–	10.7	−4.6	0.9	−4.2	3.0	2.8	4.9	6.3	−3.2	0.9	13.5	0.6*

Note: * Annualised rate for the period 1982–92.

Source: *The ML–CIG Property Index 1978–1992* (Mangan Grenfell Laurie, 1993).

decline in property investment with fund net disinvestment in 1990 coinciding with the property market collapse. Nevertheless, it seemed likely that institutional investment might re-emerge in 1994/5, provided that rental values showed good evidence of firming up.

Typically, the cash flow of the pension funds has been squeezed since the mid-1980s. Inroads made by personal pensions, fund surpluses, employer contribution holidays and large redundancies in many of the old nationalised industries eroded the flow of funds into superannuation schemes. As cash flow stabilised, the bidding for investment funds became tighter, with any increased cash allocation to a particular asset class being obtained primarily at the expense of other investment media. This will be particularly critical in the 1994–6 period if the government's public sector borrowing requirement demands record gilt-edged sales. In this event, institutions will become heavy buyers of gilts, in contrast to the position in the late 1980s when they were net sellers. Inevitably, it appears that fewer funds will be available for non-gilt assets such as property.

In the late 1960s, the property bond and the property unit trust developed. The property bond enabled a person with limited capital and income to purchase a stake in commercial buildings through regular premiums which were used by life assurance companies to buy a portfolio of properties. The portfolio is divided into units which are then allocated to the policy-holder proportionate to the premium. The first property bond was launched in 1966[5] and by the early 1980s funds exceeded £1000 million. Bonds continued to thrive throughout the 1980s, peaking around 1989.

The property unit trust (PUT), first launched in 1966, was more limited in its appeal, being restricted originally to pension funds too small to be able to invest directly in a well-balanced property portfolio, but later spreading to local authorities and charities. The trusts have provided a tax-efficient channel through which smaller institutions are able to invest in property without having to pay capital gains or corporation tax, to which the trusts are not liable. The stagnation of the property market during the period 1982 to 1986 and the collapse in 1990–3 saw PUTs generally in decline with a significant net outflow of funds, resulting in a net surplus of disposals.

Among other institutions, significant in the property market are the Church Commissioners, long-term land-owners, and, since 1945, major investors in commercial property. The value of properties owned was over £1000 million by 1986, comprising 44 per cent offices, 15 per cent residential investments (the Commissioners are one of the largest private landlords in London), 22 per cent agricultural holdings, and the balance in shops and industrial investment. They were also actively involved in redevelopment schemes. The Commissioners suffered severely in the property decline of the early 1990s.

Until 1957 there was no separate property section listed on the London Stock Exchange because it was not considered to be sufficiently important. The ending of building licensing and the 100 per cent Development Levy in 1954, together with the vast areas of land available in city centres for redevelopment,

How far property is a protection against inflation is determined by the rental provisions in the lease. Increasingly, property investors have secured concessions on rent review periods; the accepted normal period has been revised downwards from thirty-five years to seven and even five years in a twenty-one-year lease. Alternatively, escalated rents are agreed before the lease is signed, or a turnover rent, especially popular in the United States, based on annual turnover. Rents may be indexed to the cost of living as in much of Europe. Increasingly, tenants will be offered short, renewable leases. Inflation in the post-1945 period has brought the reverse yield gap. Traditionally, fixed interest yields have been lower than the yield on ordinary shares because of the security of income, while equity dividends are dependent upon the profitability of firms and may therefore fall to zero. With accelerating inflation the average yield on equities has fallen below that on fixed interest stocks. By 1981 the reverse yield gap was over 8.5 per cent, emphasising investors' preference for future income and capital growth over high fixed current income. The property yield gap, the relationship between property returns and gilt-edged prices, also peaked at 10.3 per cent. By the early 1990s the reverse yield gap had fallen to 4.6 per cent, reflecting low inflation, high real interest rates and slow economic growth. The yield on property exceeded that on gilt-edged stock, indicating the extent of disenchantment with property investment.

(7) Tax rates vary according to status as individual, corporation, pension fund or charity. The latter two institutions are not liable for corporation or capital gains tax and can therefore aim for either high income or capital growth. Individuals paying high rates of tax on income may prefer to invest in low-yielding assets with the prospects of capital gains where the rate of tax is lower. Companies too may prefer to invest in low-yielding assets with potential for capital appreciation against which they will be able to borrow.

The rational investor will consider all factors. The net attractiveness of the investment will be reflected in its yield. The higher the risk, the less protection against inflation; the less the prospect of capital gain, the greater will be the current income required to compensate. This pattern is general throughout the investment market, whether property or stocks and shares.

Property yields do not exist in a vacuum; there is an interrelationship between yields from different property investments. Similarly, there is a relationship between yields in different sectors of the stock market. Clearly there is also a relationship between property and non-property yields, each reflecting assessments of present and future risk characteristics of the different investments.

The general level as compared with the pattern of yields in a sector is influenced fundamentally by the state of the economy and by government economic policy. The minimum lending rate (MLR) at which the Bank of England was prepared to lend money to the money market was broadly the key to the level of yields until 1981. It was then replaced by base rate. When MLR (bank rate to 1972) was increased, so too were most other rates, borrowing became more expensive throughout the economy and yield consequently increased.

Between June 1972 and December 1973, MLR was increased from 5 to 13 per cent, establishing a new high plateau for interest rates which lasted to the mid-1980s. Yields on all fixed interest investments rose. In 1975, the yields on long-dated gilts rose to 17 per cent while capital values fell. Yields on all property investments increased – though less dramatically. Prime offices selling on a 3.7 per cent yield in November 1972, a post-war low, were on offer at approximately 7 per cent by December 1974; consequently, property capital values fell sharply. Conversely, the resilience of prime property as an investment was shown between 1978 and 1980. Average bank base rates increased from 8.5 to 16.5 per cent. Prime office yields remained relatively stable at around 5 per cent, while yields on both fixed interest stocks and equities increased as capital values fell.

Assuming rational behaviour, the potential investor will consider each property on offer in comparison with other property and non-property investments. Fundamentally, property and non-property interests are competing for investment yields. A price movement in one sector will affect demand for investment in the other.

DIFFERENCES BETWEEN PROPERTY AND NON-PROPERTY INVESTMENT

The essential differences between property and non-property investment derive from the unique characteristics of the property market. The absence of a central institution, imperfection of knowledge and the uniqueness of individual properties lead to problems of valuation and marketability not faced by stock market investors. In addition there are other significant factors:

(1) Investment in property necessitates the employment of professionals such as surveyors and solicitors. This increases the expenses of property transactions and also delays completion; the title to each individual property interest will need to be proved before any sale can take place. With stocks and shares it is not essential for an investor to employ professional advice, though many may choose to do so, especially if large sums are involved.

(2) Unlike stocks and shares, property cannot be purchased direct in small units and it is therefore out of the question for the small investor; most direct investment in property is by institutions. The small investor may obtain an indirect stake in property through investing in shares of property companies or being a policy-holder with an insurance company. Direct investment in property, with a portfolio spread and management expertise, has been the great attraction of property bonds.

(3) The property market may often be vulnerable to legislation. Residential rent controls, taxation of development gains and betterment, and the freezing of commercial rents under the Prices and Incomes Policy 1972–4 are examples of public intervention which affect both incomes from real property and investment

values. The refusal or grant of planning consent can destroy, create or redistribute wealth.

(4) Generally the income on real property can only be adjusted periodically, typically in the United Kingdom at the end of a lease or when a rent reversion is due. Therefore incomes from property investments tend to adjust more slowly to changing conditions than does income from comparable investments, and higher yields may be necessary to compensate. Generally, the nearer in time to a reversion and the larger its extent in relation to current income, the more it will influence the yield in a downward direction. The advantage of property investment is that the date when income variation may take place is known with relative certainty. This does not apply to investment in equities where future income is uncertain; hence the commercial property rent freeze brought great uncertainty into the property sector.

CYCLES: POST-WAR PROPERTY MARKET BOOMS AND BUSTS, 1972–93

In a boom, credit is easily available, effective demand rises, asset values and share prices rise, and yields fall. Confidence is high, and investors anticipate growth in dividends, profits and continued capital gains. Within the property market, rents increase, yields fall and capital values increase. In a recession, effective demand will fall as confidence ebbs with tighter monetary and fiscal measures, and banks become unwilling to lend. Incomes, employment and share prices fall and yields rise. Property investors, attracted by higher yields, may consider switching out of property, as will institutions with new money to invest. Property sales slow down, prices fall and yields rise. The process will continue until a new equilibrium is reached in which investment funds have been recycled to yield maximum utility to investors.

The boom of the early 1970s was fuelled by a combination of inflation and an imbalance between the supply and demand for space. It gathered impetus as governments imposed restrictions on new developments. The demand for agricultural land continued to boom and property bonds continued to be popular with small investors. Office rents in London surged by 50 per cent in 1972–3. The apparently inevitable increase in property values created a situation in which property companies indulged increasingly in deficit financing, whereby the income from the property purchased fell far short of the interest on the borrowings used to fund the purchase. Clearing, merchant and secondary banks provided as much as 100 per cent of the finance for a scheme. A combination of uncertainty over the duration of the rent freeze, penal interest rates, and the prospect of fiscal measures to curb development profits hit the property market at a time of international and political crisis. Values fell and with them secondary banks, whose fortunes were intimately connected with the property sector. Major property groups collapsed. It was necessary for the Bank of England and major clearing banks to launch a lifeboat operation to save widespread collapse as it became apparent that many secondary banks would have a deficit of net tangible assets, if valued on a break-up basis, because of the fall in property values. There was grave concern that property bonds, many of which downvalued their units, might suffer from heavy withdrawals. Such turmoil in the financial system would ultimately have an indirect effect on industry and foreign confidence in the City of London would be undermined. Thus in 1974 the first great post-war property boom collapsed.

In Central London and the provinces, rents fell by at least 20 per cent from the peaks reached in 1973. The implications for property values were grim. The attractions of a reversionary situation (with the possibility of increased income when the present lease ends) had in any case been undermined by the establishment of a rent control precedent; now they were virtually extinguished by the possibility that future leases might be made at rents lower than at the present time. For many property development companies there was also the question of how existing loans were to be serviced if expected increases in rent failed to materialise. Many British developers, in the face of an uncertain market, the Community Land Act (which threatened to eliminate many of the attractions of private development), and spiralling costs, abandoned schemes. The situation was worsened by approximately £2700 million of property overhanging the market as a result of the collapse of major property groups.

However, the collapse of the property market was relatively small compared with the catastropic fall in share values as measured by the *Financial Times* All-Share Index which fell to 60 in December 1974 following an unprecedented steep fall in values from a high of 230 in 1972. This crash was worse than that which preceded the Great Depression of the 1930s.

A result of the 1974–5 collapse was that many property companies were forced to sell off many of their portfolios of investment properties to financial institutions in order to improve cash flows. Consequently, the role of the property company as an investor declined, leaving development as its principal function so far as prime sites were concerned. The Bank of England 'lifeboat' scheme organised the orderly sale of vast amounts of property to the institutions in order to pay off debt. Even so, several property companies went into liquidation and most had to reduce their portfolios substantially. Between 1973 and 1977 the institutions acquired some £4000 million of property, of which £2000 million can be attributed to acquisitions under the 'lifeboat' scheme, much of this being in offices. These massive institutional acquisitions reached a peak of about 21 per cent of total investment in 1974. The institutions were operating in a buyers' market at this period, although subsequently a reduction in the supply of good-quality property forced yields downwards. The lesson of the mid-1970s crash was that even in a depressed market institutional funds flow and need to be invested, and that in a crisis the attraction of property is in its tangible asset backing, and also that a business defaults on rent only as a last resort.

Leading property indices indicated that between 1977 and 1984, adjusted for inflation, there was little real growth in commercial rents.[6] Shop rents had

Table 4.3 *Commercial rental index adjusted for inflation 1965–93 (May 1977 = 100)*

	1965	1973	1977	1980	1985	1987	1990	1993
All property	87	156	100	107	120	128	189	124
Shops	89	142	100	117	98	148	217	180
Offices	86	188	100	100	88	123	178	93
Industrial	88	114	100	108	106	92	145	109

Source: Hillier Parker, *Rent Index Digest* (1993).

risen in real terms by about 10 per cent but both office and industrial rents had fallen in real terms. Over this period, property investments had not yielded the returns achieved by other investors in equities or fixed interest stocks. The possible oversupply of offices and the continued economic recession contributed to the concern. Briefly, there was discussion that property had lost favour as an inflation hedge compared with government-issued index-linked stock. It was suggested that the prospect of a lower rate of inflation might remove part of the rationale for property investment. Essentially, rental growth was unlikely to accelerate until there was a sustained increase in economic activity with improved levels of profitability.

The property boom of 1986–9 saw rents in real terms increase by nearly 90 per cent and house prices double. The boom was based on rising real incomes, tax cuts, an inflation rate which fell to 4 per cent, and an acceleration of economic growth. Fundamentally, the boom was dependent on an ever-growing consumer and investor confidence in the inevitable rise of property values. This was backed by increasingly aggressive bank lending against a background of financial deregulation. Together with a shortage of prime sites, rental values for shops were higher in real terms than at any time since 1973. Office rents too achieved a rental growth not seen since the 1970s. The large rental increases in the City of London had a ripple effect on other locations, notably out-of-town 'campus sites' and prominent locations near motorway corridors. Previously stagnant industrial rents also achieved growth ahead of the inflation rate (see table 4.3).

Many of the sharp rises in London property values and office rents came from organic growth in the financial and service sectors. In London, and the City in particular, the deregulation of financial markets with the Big Bang meant additional demand from an influx of foreign banks and security houses. The expansion of domestic credit and the rising stock market added to demand. The type of space required by financial and professional firms changed; existing buildings could not provide the sizes of unit or infrastructure needed by large international and national organisations. Hence this additional pressure on the limited suitable space resulted in London rentals increasing by 35 per cent in the City core and by 70 per cent in some fringe areas. Even so, rents were only 65 per cent of 1973 levels in real terms. The long lead times on development cause short-term imbalances which lead to periods of fast rental growth that slacken when the new supply comes to the market (see the discussion on development cycles in Chapter 5). It was anticipated that at least 20 million ft^2 (2.5 million m^2) of office space would be built in the City and Docklands by 1989. The massive development at Canary Wharf on the Isle of Dogs would add 9 million ft^2 (900 000 m^2).

In October 1987, the long bull market in equities, which had lasted since 1975, ended. Share prices in London fell by 30 per cent in a week. The collapse of share prices was worldwide – in Hong Kong prices fell by 33 per cent in a day. The dramatic collapse of the stock market emphasised the volatile nature of equities after the Big Bang. It was to adversely affect the occupational demand for expensive new office space in the City of London and Docklands from international financial companies and ancillary services. The stock market was to recover so that by July 1989 the record levels of 1987 had been equalled. Although a subsequent fall in prices occurred in 1990, it was to continue upwards to reach new records in 1993.

Surprisingly, the stock market collapse of October 1987 had little immediate impact on property values. If anything, it underpinned the belief that property could not suffer such a severe setback. Values continued to rise throughout 1989 to reach a peak in the first quarter of 1990. Banks continued to increase their lending so that the percentage of loans to property companies doubled during 1986–9. Increasingly, debt-financed speculative development added to the supply of property without adequate consideration of the demand aspects. Developers who had pre-let or pre-sold were relatively secure; speculative developments were vulnerable, as were over-geared property companies with optimistically valued assets. The scale of the property building explosion and its rental implications became evident by mid-1990. It was then estimated that the volume of office space under construction was 110 per cent greater than the levels reached during the 1970s boom. In a growing number of centres actual or potential supply outstripped demand. The disequilibrium was most acute in central London where, at 17 per cent of stock, the availability of office accommodation reached a record level in the last quarter of 1992. The situation had been made worse because the City of London had relaxed planning restrictions to counter the perceived threat from the Docklands and Canary Wharf to the City as the core financial centre. The effect on rental values was dramatic. In many areas rents fell for the first time since 1976.

Fundamentally, the high service employment growth that had underpinned tenant demand since the Big Bang had ended, with redundancies and liquidations being commonplace. The slowdown, overlapped with a historic peak in new supply and high interest rates during 1989–92, when the United Kingdom left the Exchange Rate Mechanism (ERM). Inevitably, there was a spate of property and construction company failures. The most dramatic was that of Olympia and York, developers of Canary Wharf in London's Docklands which went into administration in May 1992 with estimated debts of $30 (U.S.) billion. Over 40 per cent of Canary Wharf's giant tower – the highest building in

Europe remained unlet, in line with the 41 per cent vacancy ratio in the Docklands. Other major property companies were technically in default with their bankers, many of them massively debt-laden. The property slump in Britain was mirrored in North America, Japan and Australia.

Many major banks were dangerously exposed and by 1992 commercial bank lending to property companies had risen to about £41 billion. It represented around 11 per cent of the banking sector's commercial loan portfolio, one of the highest exposures recorded to property. It had increased sevenfold between 1985 and 1991. Provisions against bad debts and doubtful commercial loans by major United Kingdom banks to property companies had reached £8 billion. Inevitably, banks were unwilling to provide further loans for development. However, falls in property values and rises in yields were likely to attract financial institutions back into direct property investment, thus providing support for property values. The relative attraction and security of property would once again be revealed and the recovery would commence with the upward swing of the cycle with investment and development of retail units leading the way.

THE PROPERTY MARKET AND TOWN PLANNING

In advanced capitalist countries, the property market is clearly an economic mechanism rationing land between competing and occasionally conflicting uses. But it is often subject to criticism for at least one of the following reasons:

(1) As a means of allocating land between different uses the market may seem to be inefficient, suffering from inherent imperfections – demand and supply overall being rarely in equilibrium (Chapter 3).

(2) The pattern of land use and values as determined by the price mechanism disregards the needs of the less profitable, and often unprofitable yet socially desirable, users of land for such purposes as schools, hospitals and public open space.

(3) The financial nature of the property market, with its stress upon private profit, maintains and frequently highlights national inequalities of income and wealth, and usually does so in a way that is a reflection of the 'monopolistic' nature of land ownership rather than an indication of entrepreneurial ability.

Although it might sometimes be argued that the State should intervene to replace the market, in the United Kingdom (as in other liberal democracies) governments merely modify the price mechanism within the contexts of planning objectives, social need and the distribution of income and wealth.[8]

Town Planning and Property Values

Since private and public land uses are mutually dependent, and as the value of privately owned land may be increased by changes in the public land use infrastructure, town planning can be seen as a means of increasing the values of private and profitable uses of land.

Yet fragmented and multiple private interests in land restrict private owners from altering radically or enhancing the overall pattern of use, and multiple ownership simultaneously retards the transfer of land to more profitable users and inhibits large-scale redevelopment. Therefore, in this context, town planning can be seen both as a means of establishing complementarity of land uses while keeping conflicting uses apart through such devices as zoning, and as a means of speeding up the transfer of land between uses. By creating a climate of greater certainty; the zoning and density control aspects of town planning eliminate some of the imperfections of the property market, and enable land to move more readily to its highest and best use.

Although the report of the Uthwatt Committee[9] stated that town planning cannot affect aggregate values but merely shifts or redistributes values from one place to another, since the Town and Country Planning Act 1947 this view has largely lost its credibility. The ability of town planning to increase aggregate values is fully recognised, for example, the granting of planning permission in 1973 for office development in London raised values by over £800 million – a sum which could hardly have shifted from other land uses. But it is equally recognised that although increased property values are publicly created through the planning process, they are private realised. Yet from 1953 to 1967, and again from 1970 to 1974, and from 1985 to the present they have not been subject to any specific form of betterment taxation.

In recent years, planning has been undergoing substantial change. Since the late 1960s *process planning* has become increasingly practised, reducing the significance of *blueprint planning,* which had previously developed particularly after the Town and Country Planning Act 1947. Blueprint planning evolved from the technical skills of the architect, engineer or surveyor. Urban problems were viewed largely in their physical context and proposed solutions were similarly physical – involving land-use maps, zoning, density controls, building regulations and planning standards. Although blueprint planning involved a high degree of public intervention, it removed some of the imperfections inherent in the property market. It could have been argued that by imposing a fairly rigid development framework, blueprint planning reduced uncertainty and lessened risk – the 'rules of the game' being clearly defined. In contrast, process planning is more of a continuous and flexible exercise better suited to a largely market economy. Since the Town and Country Planning Act 1968 it has been increasingly recognised that the complex problems of urban structure and organisation cannot be examined, and solutions cannot be found, purely in physical terms. Continual reference to economic and social considerations is necessary. Plans have to be reviewed constantly and adjustments made, with the aim of avoiding delay and ensuring that policy is relevant to changing circumstances. Whereas blueprint planning provided the framework in which the property market operated, the market very largely provides the framework in which process planning is undertaken.

Under the Town and Country Planning Act 1990, process planning is undertaken through the medium of structure plans – first introduced by the 1968 Act and prepared and implemented by county councils in England and Wales, and by regional and island authorities in Scotland. Blueprint planning, however, is still practised by district councils and National Park authorities through the preparation and implementation of local plans (also dating from the 1968 Act), while within the areas of the former Greater London Council and metropolitan counties London boroughs and the metropolitan districts have a duty to prepare and implement unitary development plans which combine the functions of both structure and local plans.

The planning system had become increasingly market-oriented during the Thatcher administrations of the 1980s, ostensibly to encourage the development or change of use of land up to its highest value. Under the Local Government, Planning and Land Act 1980, enterprise zones were set up which exempted developers and landowners from normal development controls in an attempt to encourage free-market activity in areas in need of regeneration (see Chapter 8). Similarly, the Housing and Planning Act 1986 introduced simplified planning zones (SPZs) whereby any development – conforming to 'blanket' planning permission for specified types of development – did not require separate planning permission for ten years from the time of the SPZ's declaration. While SPZs offered developers and landowners a saving in effort, time and money, local planning authorities also benefited, since a resulting inflow of private-sector funds helped to boost economic activity and to facilitate regeneration. Planning controls were further relaxed by the Use Classes Order 1987. The order introduced a new class, *B1.Business*, which grouped together offices (other than those providing financial and professional services), research and development (R&D) establishments, and 'environmentally-friendly' industrial uses. Landlords or developers could now, and without planning permission, convert small factories or workshops into offices in an attempt to raise capital values – a practice particularly likely in the higher rent areas of the inner city or central business district.

Market-Determined Values and Social Needs

It is recognised that in the long term, through the interaction of supply and demand, land will transfer to its highest and best use. This will occur because those users or would-be users who are capable of realising the greatest benefit from their use of land will be willing to pay the highest rents or prices, and owners will generally lease their land or sell their interest to the highest bidders. It is often thought that the most profitable use of land is also the most efficient use. As efficiency is synonymous with desirability, proponents of a *laissez-faire* free market economy equate the most profitable use of land with the most desirable use of it. This assumed relationship overlooks the importance of social considerations. An uncontrolled market ignores social needs – it only exists to maximise private profit and pecuniary satisfaction. Yet an unfettered market may be no more 'natural' than a society free from man-made laws. All markets are reflections of demand and supply conditions, and intervention to adjust demand and supply can create new conditions of decision-making which can modify land values and land-use patterns. Injected into the market will be social factors and other considerations – often political in nature – which will alter the relationship between demand and supply and consequently alter rent levels, prices, and the quantities of land used for different purposes. It is very important, however, that the intervening agencies fully appreciate the working of the market mechanism and are able to predict most of the direct and indirect consequences of their intervention.

The best example of the problem of social values is offered by the question of property development and redevelopment. The private developer is only concerned with the feasibility of a particular scheme. He compares those costs he will have to incur (private costs) with those gains he expects to receive (private benefits). Unless he is unusually altruistic, or there is public pressure, he will not be interested in either the costs he might inflict upon the community (social costs) or the benefits which might be gained by the community as a result of the development (social benefits). In central London in the 1980s there was a substantial amount of office development. It is unlikely that the developers undertaking such schemes gave much thought to the creation of the additional social costs of traffic congestion and the shortage of resources for other forms of development such as housing; or to the social benefits such as increased local retail trade and rateable values.

When the market mechanism fails to provide socially desirable developments, public authorities may become involved in the development process, but they sometimes find it impossible to evaluate and appraise their schemes by means of the conventional valuation techniques used by private developers. Monetary profit-and-loss criteria are irrelevant to the problem of how to evaluate projects where the price mechanism is not used as an instrument for rationing the end-product between consumers (for example, road construction) or where the end is not essentially profit (for example, a public swimming-pool or a museum).

The economic approach being used increasingly as a means of overcoming these problems is cost-benefit analysis. This attempts to provide a method of evaluation and appraisal intended to indicate not only the private or direct costs and benefits of development, but also the social or indirect costs and benefits. But as an analytical device it is imperfect and is still in the process of refinement; much more research needs to be done. Cost-benefit analysis is used mainly for assessing alternative proposals for development, and has been applied mainly to transport schemes and urban development projects. The best results are usually obtained when cost-benefit analysis is used for deciding between a carefully chosen range of alternatives and is undertaken in the context of a definite set of initial assumptions (Chapter 6).

Social considerations are further taken into account when local authorities attempt to secure planning gain from developers. Although the term 'planning gain' has no statutory significance, as is made clear by Circular 16/91 of the Department of the Environment, it can be applied *either* loosely to the practice of a local planning authority attempting to extract from a developer some 'payment in kind' not directly related to the development proposed, *or* (more specifically) to a situation where a local planning authority might seek to secure – in the public interest – modifications or improvements to a development proposal submitted for its approval, for example, when a low-cost housing development, a leisure facility or a public car park is incorporated into a retail or office development scheme. Inevitably, there has been much debate about the propriety of planning for gain. Under both the Town and Country Planning Act of 1971 (Section 52) and the Town and Country Planning Act 1990 (Section 106), some local authorities have included specific statements in their local plans about the need for voluntary agreements with potential developers, while others have not, and there is inconsistency in the type and amount of gain that has been secured. It could be argued, moreover, that taxation might be a preferable way of diverting some of the private benefits of development towards society in general.

With regard to housing, the planning system has made specific provision to satisfy social needs. Circular 7/91 of the Department of the Environment states that where there is a clear shortage of affordable housing, and in the case of new housing development on a substantial scale, planning authorities are expected to negotiate with the developers for the inclusion of an element of affordable housing in their schemes, and may set out policies in local plans indicating their intention to do so.

The Price Mechanism and the Inequalities of Wealth

A major criticism of the property market is that it perpetuates the unequal distribution of incomes and wealth stemming from private 'unearned' windfall gains and losses.

The ownership of interest in land usually results in a greatly fragmented pattern of land tenure, and because of the specific locational character of individual sites has brought with it many instances of monopoly. This gives the individual vendor the opportunity to force a hard bargain with a potential buyer. For instance, a developer, having purchased and integrated several parcels of land under one ownership, may find him/herself having to pay for the marginal site a price considerably above its comparable use value. As the developer is using borrowed money, on which substantial interest charges accumulate rapidly, s/he will consider the value of the site to him/her in terms of his/her cost of finance. If the vendor is fully aware of this, s/he will take advantage of the situation and his/her own monopolistic position.

The question of land tenure is also seen in the problem of the 'unearned increment'. Land values are not just reflections of their current uses but also of possible future uses. For example, farm output, production costs and prices

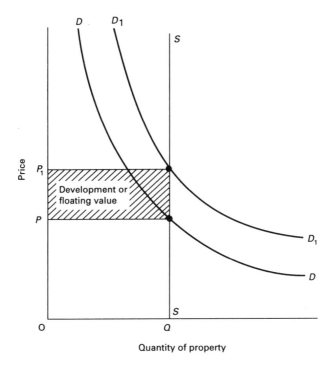

Note: P = existing use value
P_1 = market value

Figure 4.1 *The effects upon value of an increase in demand*

determine agricultural land values. If, however, it is thought that farmland could be used more profitably for some other purpose, such as housing or industry, then the land will increase in value. The rise in value occurs before the land is transferred to a new and higher use.

The difference between the now higher market value and the current use value is known as the 'development value' (or 'floating value' if there are only expectations of a change in use.) In figure 4.1 the demand for farmland is shown by the curve DD and the demand for housing land is shown by the curve D_1D_1. Where these curves intersect the supply line SS, the current use and market uses are determined and the difference between them is the development or floating value.

Not all landowners, believing their land to be saleable for development purposes, will be correct in their assumptions about the demand for their land. It is obviously not the landowner who causes the value of his land to rise, but rather the increased demand and the changing nature of demand which causes the value to increase to the level where it is profitable to transfer land from one use to another. Nevertheless it is the landowner who benefits from the enhanced value by making a substantial profit on the sale of his/her land. This profit is called the 'unearned increment', an income not for work done but for possessing a scarce resource.

Yet land can fall in value. Demand may decrease because of changes in its underlying condition. Not only might development values be completely eroded but current use values might also fall – in both instances not directly attributable to the action of the property owner.

'Betterment' and 'worsenment' are terms used to describe respective increases and decreases in the value of property, but because values change for many different reasons the terms need to be defined more specifically. In the narrow sense, betterment is the increase in property values resulting from an increase in real national income per capita, the effect of the increase in value of adjacent developments, or from inflation – the increased demand for a relatively fixed supply of property often causing values to rise at a greater rate than the increase in the general level of prices. Conversely, worsenment in the narrow sense implies falling values due to economic recession – a recession which might only be marked by a slowing down in the rate of inflation rather than a decrease in the general price level. In a broader sense, betterment is any increase in the value of property caused by central and local government policy. This may be manifested directly by the improvement of the infrastructure (for example, by means of better transport facilities) or indirectly through the exercise of planning powers. Development value depends on the granting of planning permission; however, the imposition of use restrictions and density standards also have a favourable effect on property values, if not on the property subjected to these constraints, at least on other properties in the locality. But public works schemes and planning policies are just as likely to cause worsenment. Values can also diminish in advance of a planning scheme through the process of blighting. Historically, betterment and worsenment have been subjects of much debate. Philosophically and pragmatically, there have been arguments both for and against imposing taxes on betterment values (and granting compensation for worsenment). There has also been much disagreement over the value at which compulsory purchase should take place – should it be the full market value, which might include a large element of betterment, or should it be a price omitting the betterment content? The problems involved in establishing equitable, efficient and acceptable legislation to deal with betterment, worsenment and compulsory purchase have been immense, and few (if any) satisfactory solutions have emerged.

THE POLEMICS AND EFFECTS OF GOVERNMENT INTERVENTION IN THE PROPERTY MARKET

Since the year 1066, land has been entirely owned *de jure* by the Crown. Individuals and private institutions have merely owned rights to use land – rights which in aggregate are known in English law as 'real property'. Consequently, 'land' deals are transactions not in land itself, but in rights in and over land.

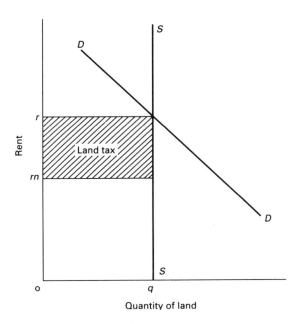

Figure 4.2 *Taxation and the supply of land*

This basically 'feudal' view of land has been manifested throughout the twentieth century. In 1936, mining rights were nationalised (and these rights were extended in recent years over half of the North Sea in connection with the exploitation of natural gas and oil), and since the Housing and Town Planning Act 1909 (with breaks in 1953–67, and 1970–3), development values have been wholly or partly siphoned-off by the Crown. Freehold rights were continually being withdrawn through the exercise of compulsory acquisition powers – local authorities (and other public bodies), by applying the rule of law reverting freehold to the Crown. But it has been more than 'feudal law' which has influenced land policy in the twentieth century – liberal and socialist thought during past century and a half has provided the underlying rationale of much of the recent legislation concerning land, and contemporary economic and social trends have been used to justify the measures.

In 1817, Ricardo[10] argued that land was different from other factors of production – it was fixed in supply and was a 'free' gift of Nature not capable of being created by humankind. Demand, rather than any action of its owner, determined the value of land – economic rent being entirely an 'unearned' increment, which Ricardo considered to be taxable. With the rapid growth of towns and the large migration of people into growth regions, economists became even more concerned with the problems of betterment. Writing an explanation of the programme of the Land Tenure Reform Association in 1870, Mill[11] argued that the government should be encouraged to claim for the benefit of the State the interception by taxation of the future unearned increase of the value of land. In California in the 1870s, George[12] (seeing that a substantial in-migration of population was pushing up rents and widening gaps between landowners and the landless) proposed a 100 per cent tax on economic rent. This, he claimed, would restrict the power of land monopoly, remove the incentive to speculate and keep land off the market, and eliminate inequalities arising from the ownership of property. In figure 4.2, with a given quantity of land (q) and a rent of r, the landlord's net income would be only $rn \times q$ since tax revenue ($r - rn \times q$) would be recouped for the benefit of the community. It is of note that the incidence of the tax falls entirely on the landowner, since the tax cannot push up the market rent above its equilibrium level at r.

Influenced by Ricardo, Mill and George, Tawney[13] in 1922 advocated a high level of taxation on large incomes flowing from land ownership. Yet, while believing that land should serve the community, he suggested that this should be achieved by public control since, compared with public ownership – as propounded by Green[14] – it was a preferable way of ensuring that property would fulfil a social purpose.

In twentieth-century Britain, the introduction of town planning legislation has complicated the arguments for governmental intervention in the market pricing of property. The main arguments for intervention in the price mechanism revolve around the inequalities of the planning system:

(1) Since at least the Town and Country Planning Act 1947, land use and land values have been decided largely by planning decisions concerning the granting (or refusal) of permission to develop. Land use and values are thus mainly determined by administrative decisions under the more-or-less effective control of a democratic political system.

There has emerged a very different pattern of use and values than would have occurred under *laissez-faire* free market conditions. Planning authorities have in fact created incomes and wealth – changes in land values depending greatly upon public policy rather than upon unimpeded market forces. According to Edwards,[15] the planning system has benefited elements of capital by limiting the supply of buildings which would have competed with those already within an area – for example, restrictions on development in conservation areas and in green belts, and on out-of-town shopping, benefit existing individual and corporate interests in both the protected areas and in urban centres. Planning control, moreover, might enable a residential development to be undertaken in locations which otherwise would accommodate commercial uses, while it could facilitate industrial development and agriculture in areas where these uses normally could not compete with housing (figure 4.3).

Overall, suggests Keogh,[16] local planning authorities should attempt to maximise social returns. If, for example, according to market forces, industrial use can out-bid agriculture over (say) 10 000 ha in the rural–urban fringe, then the local planning authority (taking into account external costs such as lost amenity, environmental affliction etc.) might deem the social value of agricultural land to be higher than the market value of the land, and reduce the amount

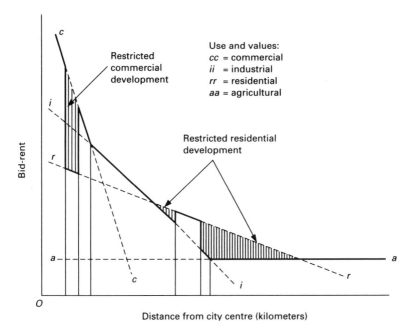

Figure 4.3 *The impact of planning control upon land use and values*

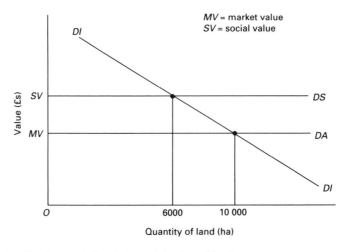

Figure 4.4 *Planning control and the social value of land*

available to industry to (say) 6000 ha. This is illustrated in figure 4.4 where *DI* represents the demand for land for industrial use, *DA* shows the demand for agricultural purposes, and *DS* indicates the social value of the land.

(2) The working of the price mechanism within the constraints of planning

legislation means that local authorities are often forced to pay high market prices for their use of land. Public facilities such as schools, open space or roads are thus expensive to develop or may have had to be diverted to cheaper but less socially desirable locations.

(3) With market pricing prevailing, local authorities are encouraged to compulsorily purchase economically (though not necessarily socially) 'obsolete' property. They are then compelled to undertake financially viable redevelopment (possibly in partnership with private developers) and largely have to ignore socially desirable renewal.

(4) Comprehensive development and redevelopment involve the ultimate creation of interests at new and higher market values. But local authorities (to the detriment of rate- and tax-payers) are not generally able to realise these enhanced values and the profits which they helped to create.

(5) However justified the government may be in imposing a tax on publicly created values, a high levy would almost certainly result in owners withholding land from the market. But land is practically indestructible and in total it is fixed in supply. The scarcity of land on the market, however, could be relieved by public ownership. There is no prima-facie reason why private land ownership is necessary to secure the best use of land.

(6) When the interdependent structure and local area plans have been finalised, there is still the need to allocate land use, or at least to produce a strategy for the future use of land. This is difficult when there is multiple private ownership and when market values prevail. Planning can only become a more effective means of economic and social policy through more substantial control of land.

In recent years the arguments against public intervention have been voiced increasingly by supporters of the free market. In essence, the arguments against intervention are as follows:

(1) Development profits are the result and not the cause of land scarcity and high values. Planning authorities have created the scarcity of building land through use restrictions, zoning and density regulations – measures which may not seem appropriate in a country where only about 12 per cent of the land is urban and where population increase has considerably slowed down. It was tight planning control which led (at times of inflation) to dramatic increases in the real value of commercial and residential property in the early 1970s and late 1980s. It was ironic that governments, when faced with soaring values in the past, instead of dismantling the restrictive aspects of planning, intervened still further by introducing betterment levies and plans to take land into public ownership. As Hayek[17] argued in the 1940s, a government's answer to the problems of intervention is yet more intervention.

(2) Most planning is prohibitive and negative. It restricts development which would be financially rewarding, and even public-sector development might squeeze out market-determined use of a sort consumers prefer. The opportunity cost to the community of these distortions could be immense. The cost is compounded by the expense incurred in applying for planning permission and in appealing

against refusal – particularly if appeals are rejected (70 per cent of appeals in the period 1986–7 to 1990–1 were turned down). No one has (or could) undertake a cost-benefit analysis of the overall effects of town planning, but it has often been suggested that it stultifies land use, restricts investment and curbs economic development.

(3) Land is heterogeneous and therefore needs a mechanism to allocate sites to the most efficient and most desirable uses. It is the price mechanism (it is argued) which, within legal limits and despite many market distortions, works as this rationing device. Critics argue that, at the level of the local plan, there is a cumbersome, unwieldly, expensive and bureaucratic system with every plot of land subject to an individual administrative and often political decision to decide its use. Land is, in fact, a commodity like anything else and should not be subject to planning by central or local government. Like other commodities, land can be rendered unusable and it is capable of being 'manufactured', improved or moved – by more intensive development on a site or reclamation constituting a change in its attributes.

But despite the free market nostrums of successive governments, it is improbable in the forseeable future that public intervention in the use and development of land will cease. A planning system has evolved since 1909 and its principal institution has gained the 'Royal' prefix (the Royal Town Planning Institute (RTPI)). It is therefore imperative that one should concentrate on examining some of the weaknesses of planning rather than contemplate its unlikely replacement by an unfettered property market.

Planning and the Loss and Recovery of Private Property Rights

Following the introduction of public health and housing legislation in the mid- and late nineteenth century during attempts to improve living standards in the United Kingdom's rapidly growing towns and cities, the early twentieth century witnessed the arrival of statutory planning.

The Housing and Town Planning Act 1909 introduced a 50 per cent levy on increases in value caused by the 'making of any town planning scheme'; conversely compensation could be awarded for any injurious effect of a scheme. Although the Act mainly affected suburban development – leaving virtually untouched values within the inner areas of cities – it was a legislative milestone. It introduced the principle that those who benefit from town planning (rather than from their own efforts) should be taxed and those who lose from such planning (rather than from their own mistakes) should be compensated.

Under the Housing and Town Planning Act 1919, county boroughs, urban district councils (with populations over 20 000) and municipal boroughs were compelled to produce planning schemes for suburban development. But only within declared 'interim development control areas' would the 50 per cent levy on betterment (previously introduced) apply – regardless of whether owners had or had not realised the appreciated value. The Town and Country Planning

Act 1932 increased the betterment charge to 75 per cent but the levy was only imposed when the market value was realised.

Unfortunately, local planning authorities lacked both professional staff and financial resources. Because of the difficulties in assessing and collecting betterment tax (shifting and floating values causing intractable problems), authorities were hesitant in producing plans which would also have involved incurring considerable compensation expense. This, together with costly delays in acquiring property under multiple ownership, impeded the production and implementation of plans for the redevelopment of town centres. Town planning depended very much upon local initiative. There were wide variations in the extent to which local authorities drew up plans and attempted to deal with problems of betterment and worsenment.

These problems were recognised by the Uthwatt Committee on Compensation and Betterment (1942). Believing that land values are largely created by community activity, it proposed that, in the case of the development of previously undeveloped land, rights should be nationalised, and if the land was required for redevelopment it should be purchased by the local authority at existing use value and then leased to a developer at a future use value. Land already developed should be compulsorily acquired when needed for redevelopment at the value appertaining on 31 March 1939; land with building plans prepared for it (but not implemented) should be treated as though it were undeveloped land – its development value being nationalised. In addition, the Uthwatt Committee suggested that there should be a 75 per cent annual tax on annual increases in site values (with valuations every five years) and that central government grants should be available to assist local authorities in undertaking compulsory purchase. It was thought that good town planning would only be possible if local authorities could acquire development land at a price they could afford, and it was considered reasonable that betterment should be largely returned to society, whose actions had created it.

The post-war Labour government based its Town and Country Planning Act 1947 largely on the principles of the Uthwatt Report, although the Act did not differentiate between provisions for developed and undeveloped land. All local planning authorities (then the county councils and county boroughs) were to produce plans for the whole of their areas and these were to be submitted to the Ministry of Town and Country Planning (set up in 1943) for approval. All development (specifically defined) requiring planning permission, and development rights were to be entirely nationalised. A development charge of 100 per cent was thus imposed on the developer, who would consequently ensure that all transactions were at existing use value. A Central Land Board was established to collect the levy (the problems of assessing shifting values being eased) and to handle compensation claims for the loss of development value on the enacting day – 1 July 1948. A £300 million fund was available for this purpose. Compensation would also be paid (by local authorities) if planning restrictions reduced existing use values. The Act should have enabled local authorities to have obtained land at a relatively low price, should have permitted them to undertake the 'right' amount of planning and should not have involved them in much compensation expenditure.

But the results of the 1947 Act were detrimental generally to the working of the property market. Different criteria for assessing development values led to much haggling between developers and district valuers, the cash flow of developers was seriously endangered by the levy being payable before development commenced, and there was anecdotal evidence that the complexity, uncertainty and stringency of the system prevented or deferred development, either by owners withholding land or developers being unwilling to acquire it. Yet the construction industry, with limited available resources, was working to full capacity, not least on local authority housing and new town development. There was also an increase in activity where there were exemptions from the levy; for example, conversions of houses into flats, small extensions to existing buildings, agricultural improvements, and construction involving no change in use. The most severely curtailed development was, of course, that which involved change of use, the end-product of which might have been shops or offices.

In 1951 the Conservatives came to office, and in 1953 and 1954 two Town and Country Planning Acts dismantled many of the provisions of the 1947 Act. The development levy was abolished, the Central Land Board was wound up and the compensation fund for the previous loss of development values was extinguished.

Compulsory purchase, however, continued to be at existing use values. Although confidence was restored to the market, much development was still held back as local authorities (probably because of political expedience) did not always wish to exercise their compulsory purchase powers – compensation at existing use value in relative terms falling further and further below rising market values.

Under the Town and Country Planning Act 1959 the dual market for land came to an end. By re-establishing market prices for compulsory purchase, all land transactions would be determined by the laws of supply and demand. For the first time in fifty years the government 'freed' the property market from fiscal distortions.

Except in green-belt areas (where owners may have felt that their development values were still nationalised), private development became increasingly speculative. From 1953 until the mid-1960s there were very many cases of site values increasing by as much as ten times – the development processes and the soaring increase in values being described very explicitly by Marriott.[18]

On returning to power in 1964, the Labour government began formalising its policy on land and favoured introducing a variant on what Lichfield[19] referred to as 'transient nationalisation' (the purchase of land at current use value and the creation of new leaseholds). The resulting Land Commission Act 1967 was intended to ensure that: the burden of the cost of land for essential purposes was reduced; suitable land was available at the right time for the implementation of national, regional and local plans; and part of the increased value of land arising from the possibility of changing its use or putting buildings on it returned to the community whose activities helped to create it – while at the same time the market would be left relatively free.

To achieve these aims a Land Commission was established which first had powers to purchase land and either to develop it itself or to make it available to public authorities and private developers. The Commission was equipped with the usual powers of compulsory purchase and could use the normal machinery for appeals and public inquiry. Land would normally be purchased at the market value and sold at the best possible price. A Crownhold would be granted subject to restrictions and with the future development value reserved for the commission. In the case of land for essential housing development, Concessionary Crownhold was created – sites being sold at sub-market prices.

Secondly, the Commission had powers to assess and collect a 40 per cent levy on net development value, the government believing that there was still enough of the development value left to provide an adequate incentive for owners to sell their land. The levy was payable when the whole, or a part, of the development value was realised. It was with these measures that the government hoped to release sites for development and to redistribute among the community part of the profits accruing to land.

But within the three years in which the Act was in force the Land Commission failed to achieve its objectives. At the time of the Act's repeal, the Commission had purchased only 2800 acres (1120 ha) (although a further 9000 acres (3600 ha) were in the pipeline) and only about 400 acres (160 ha) had been sold. In 1967 it was hoped that the Commission would assess 150 000 deals a year and collect £85 million per annum in levies, but by 1970 a total of only about 50 000 assessments had been made, yielding only £46 million. Even in mid-1971 (several months after the death of the Commission), over £30 million of betterment levy was still uncollected. The resources of the Commission (in terms of its 1000 staff and the £4 million per year allocated to it by the government) were clearly insufficient to handle the complexities of the legislation.

A major criticism of the Act was that, far from bringing down the price of land, it may have contributed to the further soaring of values. But although the observation was probably correct, the generally offered explanation was inaccurate. It had been argued that the 40 per cent levy was merely added on to prevailing prices, but this would have meant that either for some very improbable reason prices before 1967 were at sub-market levels, or that the levy could be passed on through higher prices because of a large surge of demand in the period from 1967 to 1970 – but there was no such increase in the level of demand. A more plausible analysis is that prices increased because owners reduced the supply of development land by withholding it from the market as they may not have wished to incur the levy, or they may have anticipated that the Act would prove to be unworkable and thence repealed, or that there would be a change of government and policy.

By 1970 the Land Commission was only just getting into its stride; given a few more years of life, it might have achieved its aims and objectives. In the short term it had created uncertainty, slowed down development and induced prices to rise. But during an election year land issues became polarised. Either the Land Commission had to be strengthened, betterment taxation simplified and the levy raised, or the Act had to be repealed as 'having no place in a free society'. After the defeat of the Labour government by the Conservatives in June 1970, the Act was indeed repealed and development land reverted to the free market. No central organisation was reconstituted for the purpose of acquiring land and no new tax specifically on betterment was devised.

The free market in the period 1970–3 produced severe planning problems associated with speculation and land scarcity. The repeal of the 1967 Act, the lifting of the 'Brown Ban' on office development in London, and the raising of the office development permit threshold from 3000 to 10 000 ft², all in 1970, heralded a great surge in land speculation. At best, compulsory purchase for 'essential' needs at market value did nothing to recoup for the community a share of the increased values which it helped to create; at worst, public planning policy decisions virtually eliminated public authorities from the market because of inadequate development funds.

In part, the corollary of speculation was land shortage, especially for housing and manufacturing industry. Low- and middle-income families were squeezed out as office and hotel development inflated site values in central and inner areas, and 'gentrification' led to reduced occupancy in rehabilitated housing. Manufacturers also moved out, often because there was insufficient space to modernise or expand, and they left behind higher unemployment rates and a narrower range of lower-paid and long-hour jobs in the service industries.

Faced with these problems, planners felt increasingly frustrated. Although they had to produce structure and local plans for 10–20 years ahead, they lacked initiative and control over development – having to confine their attention to the approval or rejection of planning applications and to major private development. They did not even manage indirectly any day-to-day public services. In the way plans were being prepared there was a danger that they would 'become a series of vague generalities – a mere reflection of the planner's own separation from reality. Land, the planners' resource was . . . peculiarly and manifestly not the planners' resource.'[20]

Based loosely on *Labour's Programme for Britain 1973* and the White Paper *Land*[21] 1974, the Community Land Act 1975 introduced a hybrid method of nationalising land which involved the ownership of land and the unification of development rights. The Act required that initially, and by means of a five-year rolling programme, local authorities would have the *power* to acquire all land needed for development over the following ten years. Land would be purchased at market value less development land tax (DLT) – DLT being introduced under the Development Land Tax Act 1976 at 66.66 and 80 per cent. Owner-occupied properties of up to 1 acre (0.45 ha), single house plots producing 10 000 ft² (929 m²), churches and charities, industrial schemes up to 15 000 ft² (1393 m²), agricultural, horticultural, forestry and mining land, and land owned or with planning permission attached on 12 September 1974 were all to some extent exempt from the scheme. Land acquired by local authorities (either by agreement or compulsorily) was to be leased at market values to developers with 99-year leases being established (including 60-year-old rebuilding clauses), except in the case of housing development, when the freehold would be sold. The Act was intended to ensure that a substantial part of the development value of land was recouped by the community as a whole. The Exchequer initially received 40 per cent of the surplus on land transactions, the local authority 30 per cent, and the remaining 30 per cent was shared among other councils. In 1978, the local authority's share was increased to 40 per cent at the expense of the Exchequer.

Eventually, local authorities would be given the *duty* to acquire all development land at current use value (except in the case of permitted exemptions). Effectively, the development value of this land would be nationalised and therefore DLT would no longer be imposed. This long-term provision of the community land scheme was, however, never implemented. The community land scheme (incorporate in the 1975 and 1976 Acts) was thus different from that originally proposed. Under the original scheme, all land was to be frozen at its value on the date of the publication of the White Paper (that is, 12 September 1974), and for the following ten years local authorities could acquire land at that value for development purposes. According to Silkin,[22] this would have stopped land speculation, eliminated land shortages and curbed the escalation of land costs for housing and public services.

The community land scheme was, however, welcomed by the Royal Town Planning Institute, the Town and Country Planning Association and many urban authorities (particularly before the swing from Labour to Conservative in the local government elections of 1976–7). It was thought that plan implementation would be greatly assisted, but it was also believed that the scheme could become a 'builders' charter'. Free from the need to accumulate land banks and identify profitable projects, developers and contractors would be able to enter into a viable partnership with the community. But the community land scheme affected builders adversely if they were accumulating land banks. The retention of a substantial proportion of development value was necessary to recompense builders for development risk, but most of this became liable to DLT.

The operation of the community land scheme was tragically similar to that of the Land Commission Act. At no time did it have more than a marginal effect on the purchase and sale of land. Over the three-and-a-half years to May 1979, the English local authorities acquired about 3600 acres (1458 ha) of development land, and of this sold only 700 acres (284 ha), producing a deficit of over £52 million (this was in contrast to the anticipated net surplus of over £300 million per year for the country as a whole). Although public expenditure was severely curbed in the late 1970s (as deflation followed the Land Commission Act in the late 1960s), local authorities failed to take up the money allocated to them for the scheme, therefore allocations under the White Paper,[23] *The Government's Expenditure Plans, 1978/79 to 1981/82* (1978) were reduced from £83 million to £54 million (1979–80), and for each of the subsequent two years cut from £102 to £64 million. At a local level there was a lack of political will to implement the scheme. The Conservatives were in control of most county and district councils, and the party vowed to repeal the 1975 Act as soon as it was returned to power nationally. Other councils were reluctant to move into a new entrepreneurial field. The scheme required an extra 12 750 to 14 000 staff (with a third or more being members of the land professions). Without this full complement of staff, local authorities were unable to operate the scheme as intended and could not fully utilise even the financial resources which were available. But some authorities (especially in areas attractive to developers) were generally opposed to further development. For these reasons, authorities were not induced to establish public development corporations for the purpose of acquiring and disposing of land and preparing it for development. In Wales, in contrast, the 1975 Act gave responsibility for operating the community land scheme not to local authorities but to a newly established Land Authority for Wales (LAW). As a public development corporation it was comparatively more successful in selecting, acquiring and reselling land for development than were the English local authorities, and it negotiated effectively with local planning authorities.

By 1979, the weaknesses of the community land scheme were being recognised; the scheme was particularly ineffective in the inner urban areas, where site values reached their peak. Local authorities were thus often inhibited from acquiring land for public development.

Soon after winning the general election in 1979, the Conservatives began to dismantle the community land scheme. The Budget of June 1979 cut DLT from 80 and 66.66 per cent to a single rate of 60 per cent, and raised the threshold from £10 000 to £50 000 (rising to £75 000 in 1984), and the Local Government, Planning and Land Act 1980 repealed the 1975 Act (although the LAW and its role were retained). The demise of the community land scheme marked the end of the third attempt since 1947 to deal with the problem of 'unearned' development profits, and once again the market prevailed – DLT finally being abolished by the Budget of March 1985, although there was little evidence that the tax had reduced the volume of development. Local authorities, however, had by then lost any initiative they might have had in the development process, being forced to pay market prices for land, and under the 1980 Act they became instrumental in the selling-off of public-sector land – although at prevailing rates of disposal it will take until the end of the century to clear the stock of publicly-owned land in inner cities. It became increasingly clear that by concentrating on the disposal of public-sector wasteland the government was putting in jeopardy its inner-city policies. It was thus proposed, in a publication by the Institute of Economic Affairs[24] (a body normally sympathetic to Conservative policies), that private land which had been vacant for a number of years should be taxed, as an incentive for owners to bring it into use – in other words, site value taxation (or site value rating) should be introduced selectively (see Chapter 8).

In conclusion, it might be useful to reflect on land policies in two other advanced capitalist countries. In France, land is frequently taken into community ownership by compulsory purchase when it is required for the provision of public services. Within zones of deferred development (ZDDs) (that is, where new town or urban renewal schemes are contemplated), public authorities have pre-emption rights in the purchase of land. Within these zones, the cost of acquisition is minimised, since compensation is based on values prevailing one year before the ZDD's declaration. In these cases, and in general, private-sector short-term profits are taxed as income, and long-term gains are subject to capital taxation (at up to 60 per cent on realisation). In addition, *a priori* ('equipment') taxes are imposed to facilitate the development of infrastructure when an owner either applies for a building permit or sells his property, and a tax of up to 100 per cent is levied on the value of any development in excess of permitted building coefficients (plot-ratios). French land policy thus differed substantially from that employed in Britain throughout the 1980s.

In Sweden, there is also a considerable degree of public intervention in the land market. Local authorities ('communes') have a statutory duty to build up land banks sufficient for 7–10 years' development. Financed on favourable terms from central government, the communes can either acquire land by agreement at approximately current use value, or by compulsory purchase at prices appertaining ten years prior to acquisition (with allowances for inflation) – a provision phased in from 1971. Land might then be used for public-sector use or released for private development at low market values (there being an absence of supply constraint), but private developers will be unable to realise any significant speculative gain since, in general, land profits are taxed as incomes and/or wealth, and in the case of housing development prices are regulated (Chapter 8). Unlike in Britain, where a very large proportion of development gain derives from land, financial returns from the development process in Sweden stem almost entirely from production.[25]

During the recession of the early 1990s, land shortages, land prices and land taxation were largely absent from political agendas. But when economic recovery gets fully under way, there will be increased demands on the planning system, and windfall gains will once more be a cause for concern. If a future government in Britain wished to adopt a land policy which would both facilitate positive planning and ensure that betterment was equitably distributed, it could well base its measures on successful policies employed abroad. In the meantime, a relatively free market for land will continue to allocate land uses inefficiently, largely disregard social needs and perpetuate inequalities of income and wealth.

REFERENCES

1. D. R. Denman, *Land in the Market*, Hobart Paper (Institute of Economic Affairs, 1964).
2. *An Analysis of Commercial Property Values* 1962–1992 (Michael Laurie & Partners, 1993).

3. *The MGL–CIG Property Index 1978–1992* (Morgan Grenfell Laurie, 1993).
4. *Money into Property* (Debenham Tewson & Chinnocks, 1993).
5. P. R. A. Kirkman and D. C. Stafford, 'The Property Bond Movement 1966–74', *National Westminster Bank Quarterly Review* (February 1975).
6. *ICHP Rent Index* (Hillier Parker, Investor's Chronicle).
7. Hillier Parker, *Rent Index Digest* (August 1993).
8. R. H. Wright, 'The Property Market 2', *The Architect and Surveyor* (March/April 1971).
9. *Report of the Expert Committee on Compensation and Betterment* (Uthwatt Report) Cmnd 6386 (HMSO, 1942).
10. D. Ricardo, *Principles of Political Economy and Taxation* (Penguin, 1971).
11. J. S. Mill, *Programme* (Land Reform Association, 1871).
12. H. George, *Progress and Poverty* (Hogarth, 1979).
13. R. H. Tawney, *The Acquisitive Society* (Bell, 1922).
14. T. H. Green, *Lectures on the Principals of Political Obligations* (Longman, 1913).
15. M. Edwards, 'Planning and the Land Market: Problems, Prospects and Strategy', in M. Ball *et al.*, *Land Rent, Housing and Urban Planning: A European Perspective*' (Croom Helm, 1984).
16. G. Keogh, 'The Economics of Planning Gain', in S. Barrett and P. Healey (eds), *Land Policy: Problems and Alternatives* (Gower, 1985).
17. F. A. Hayek, *The Road to Serfdom* (George Routledge, 1944).
18. O. Marriott, *The Property Boom* (Hamish Hamilton, 1967).
19. N. Lichfield, 'Land Nationalisation', in P. Hall (ed.), *Land Values* (Sweet & Maxwell, 1965).
20. R. Barras *et al.*, 'Planning and the Public Ownership of Land', *New Society* (21 July 1973).
21. Department of the Environment, *Land*, Cmnd 5730 (HMSO, 1975).
22. J. Silkin, 'A land value scheme that got away', *Town and Country Planning* (January 1987).
23. Treasury, *The Government's Expenditure Plans 1978/79 to 1981/82*, Cmnd 7049 (HMSO, 1978).
24. M. Chisholm and P. Kivell, *Inner City Wasteland: An Assessment of Market Failure in Land Development* (Institute of Economic Affairs, 1987).
25. S. Duncan, 'Land Policy in Sweden: Separating Ownership from Development', in S. Barrett and P. Healey (eds), *Land Policy: Problems and Alternatives* (Gower, 1985).

5

Investment Appraisal and the Economics of Development

THE NATURE AND TYPES OF DEVELOPMENT

Development is the process of carrying out works involving a change in the physical use or in the intensity of an existing use of land or buildings. Development may be a lengthy process from the original conception to change the existing use, to survey, design, estimates, preliminary discussion with various public bodies, land acquisitions, to the formal application for planning consent. Constant appraisal of the cost implications of the scheme and financial arrangements are necessary until successful completion.

There are two main categories of developers: public (including local authorities), and private (including property development companies and other institutions). There are significant differences in objectives and also in legal status. Only public developers have received special privileges, including extensive powers of compulsory purchase under legislation such as the Community Land Act 1975 (abolished 1980) – ultimately the public statutory duty. Much public development is non-profit-making or only semi-commercial, such as the building of libraries. Public developers take a longer, wider view than do private developers. The most economic development, given constraints, will be that showing the greatest return in terms of aesthetics or function to the community for the minimum capital invested. A local education authority must consider trends in the growth of the child population over the next decade; a highway authority may consider road proposals which cannot be achieved for twenty years. The indirect costs and benefits of the scheme in relation to other activities will be carefully appraised.

Private development is essentially profit motivated. The unity of the environment and its quality, externalities and the interplay of social, political and economic factors will not be considered. A function of planning authorities is to make private developers bear some of the indirect costs created by imposing planning conditions. It is clear that there can be divergence between the aims of planning authorities and private development.

Many developments are complex and costly. The risks are great, especially for speculative developments, as fundamental changes may occur in the market before the scheme is completed successfully. Many schemes fail because of unforeseen factors which have an adverse effect upon the initial calculations of the developer. Adverse legislation and changes in economic policy which may bring higher taxes and interest rates make marginal projects unprofitable; costs of labour and material may soar. Losses may occur because of unexpected capital expenditure, problems with underground services, or additional work needed to satisfy town planning requirements. Inadequate research into income and prices of existing houses may mean provision of dwellings for which the demand is limited, resulting in unsold buildings. Schemes fail because too high a price has been paid for land in anticipation of increases in prices continuing. There are four basic ingredients to a successful development: a well-located site, purchase at the right price, correct financing, and sufficient expertise to carry out the development.

SITE SELECTION

The acquisition of the site is usually the developer's first major commitment to the development project; from the limited land available, an ideal site satisfying all requirements can rarely be found. It may take a private developer many years to assemble a city-centre site. In selecting sites, therefore, the developer must usually make a compromise in his requirements. A multiple store can rarely sacrifice location, but a hypermarket may sacrifice location in order to obtain more space; an office requires a central location, while a single-storey factory needs space. Price may be the crucial factor, but each site has its own characteristics which will influence its suitability for development for a particular purpose.

Space

Requirements will vary greatly with the type, number of units and size of development proposed, the density of building allowed and whether any extensions to the scheme are likely.

Physical Characteristics

Industrial development requires a reasonably level site. Housing may be developed on sloping sites but this involves extensive earthworks and more expensive foundations. A cleared site will be preferred as site clearance involves additional expense. The sub-soil should have reasonable load-bearing capacity and the site should be free of soil pollution and from the possibility of flooding.

Public Utility Services

Developers require some or all services to be available, or to be made available. Private installations are expensive, both to provide and to operate. Industrial developments are especially demanding in their requirements for essential services. Inability to provide essential services at an economic cost effectively may prevent development from taking place.

Accessibility

A location and environment suitable for a housing development, with proximity to shops and schools, may not suit an industrial development requiring access to labour, raw materials and markets. Offices may require a central city location for external economies, the prestige of a central city address, and the possibility of better communication with other parts of the country. Out-of-town locations with access to motorways or ring-roads will also be demanded.

Legal Aspects

The leasehold or freehold interest needs to be acquired. There may be easements, restrictive covenants or public rights of way. It may be possible to overcome them: by payments, by offering alternatives ways, or by setting aside outmoded restrictive covenants. Public authorities may more easily overcome such impediments and have the power of compulsory acquisition. In addition, permission must be obtained from various public authorities, who may impose restrictions on the use and development of the site.

(1) *Planning authorities*   Structure and local plans will indicate the uses to which the site may be put and the permitted densities. They will indicate how adjoining areas are to be developed and the location and extent of major public works, such as new roads; planning authorities may impose requirements as to design or materials, or make preservation orders on trees which might possibly restrict the form and extent of development. There are often delays in obtaining the planning permission required for most forms of development unless it constitutes *permitted development*.

(2) *Highway authorities*   A developer is normally required to submit plans of any new streets for approval. Authorities may prescribe improvement lines, restricting development between the improvement line and the street. Building lines may also be prescribed beyond which no building will generally be permitted. In both cases the developer loses part of his/her site for profitable development.

(3) *Department of Trade and Industry (DTI)*   Permission was required until 1982 from the DTI for Industrial Development Certificates. Where certificates were refused by the DTI, no right of appeal existed and the local planning authority was unable to grant planning permission for the project.

(4) *Department of Environment (DOE)* Office development permits were required until 1979, and where these were refused, planning permission would not be granted. The DOE lists buildings of special architectural or historic interest which cannot be demolished or altered so as to seriously affect their character without obtaining local planning consent. A listed building can create a major difficulty in a development scheme.

(5) *Building requirements* Local authorities are responsible for ensuring that all building work is carried out to certain minimum standards of construction. For most of England and Wales the requirements are laid down in the Building Regulations. Even comparatively minor alterations and improvements require consent.

FINANCIAL CALCULATIONS FOR PRIVATE DEVELOPMENT AND THE PRICE OF LAND

Thus, prior to the purchase of a site a developer must know what development will be permitted and to what density. S/he also needs a financial appraisal including a projection covering building costs, finance charges and the probable rent or selling price of the completed development. It will indicate the feasibility of the scheme and is likely to include the following.

The Gross Development Value (GDV)

The anticipated value of the development on completion may be calculated for commercial property on an investment basis on the estimated total annual rent accruing from the development less the cost of outgoings. The net annual income is capitalised by multiplying by an appropriate year's purchase to obtain the GDV. The choice of multiple may create problems; the valuer advises on the basis of his/her knowledge of the market and current practice. However, there is no definitive method of valuation and much of it is intuitive. There is a fundamental difference between the valuer and the quantity surveyor, the latter being more cost conscious and working with tangible cost data.

The problem of valuation assumed a particularly acute form between 1971 and 1974, with sharper than normal movements in investment yields. For example, in early 1971 the yield on prime properties was around 6 per cent, by December 1972 yields had touched a post-war low of 3.75 per cent, indicating a sharp rise in the value of developments and completed buildings. The reverse occurred during 1974–6 when, plagued with uncertainty and financial collapse, the market in investment property came to a virtual standstill. Properties may be valued reflecting their future trading or redevelopment potential. A housing developer will estimate GDV on anticipated selling prices in the area based on local knowledge. Values will vary location, environment, character of the development and changes in the economic conditions.

Building Costs

Building unit rates are often computed per square metre of floor area to assess the total building costs of the development. A quantity surveyor's knowledge of cost analysis and data will be essential. Sharp increases occurred in building costs between 1973 and 1975 (weak demand conditions resulted in developers' inability to pass on these cost increases to purchasers). Sharply increased costs in the late 1970s saw housebuilders increasing their prices as demand allowed.

Professional Charges

The cost of specialist skill must be considered. The architects' and surveyors' fees cover the preparation of all drawings and contract documents, survey and supervision and financial arrangements for the contract. A large development organisation is likely to have its own 'in-house' design staff to carry out basic work, employing consultants to obtain variety and to cope with peak periods. It can also provide cost guidance and feedback from experience. It deals with abortive and *ad hoc* investigations and speculative work. It can advise on the appropriate fee for outside consultancy work. Legal costs are incurred on the purchase of the site, to buy out easements, to close rights of way and to prepare leases. Agents carry out research in an area and fees will be incurred on advertising and disposing of the property. This will be influenced by the number of units in the development; special fees may be negotiated where there is clear repetition of work. Approximately 2 per cent of the GDV may be allowed for agency and legal fees, and 10 per cent or more of the value of building work for architects' and surveyors' fees.

Cost of Finance

To purchase a site a developer will either borrow or will use his/her own capital. The interest paid or the revenue forgone should be charged to the development from the date of purchase of the site to when the completed building is let or sold. Building cost finance is usually calculated at market rate on half of the building costs for the full contract period, or the full costs for half of the contract period. The contractor will make full use of the funds available for only a limited period. Interest rate changes are a major development risk unless long-term finance with an institution has been arranged. A sharp rise can change a profitable scheme into a loss-making one.

The developer's profit is the return for the entrepreneurial risk-taking function, risk involving rising costs, falling rents, changing legislation and the inability to dispose of property on completion. The amount will depend upon the size and type of development, the degree of risk and gearing, and the time before completion.

Thus the price a developer can afford to pay for a site is restricted. On the one hand the rent or sale price of the finished development is determined by the market in relation to the size and quality of the building, and on the other, the price offered for the site is determined by the market in relation to its location and current demand. The developer must assess all costs of construction and finance against the likely selling price; since the stock of buildings is large compared with the annual amount of building, the market price for new building is determined more by demand than by the costs of construction. The price-bid for the site should enable the developer to cover all costs, including profits; it must also be sufficient to make it worthwhile for the owner to sell. Thus the maximum available for site expenditure will be a residual cost after all other expenditures have been taken into account. There is a relationship between the size and quality of a building and the price it will fetch. It may be worth spending more on a building if as a result it will sell for a higher price. The expected price of a building therefore implies a given size and standard; the development will only be worthwhile if it can be built within the price constraints, including land acquisition costs.

Table 5.1 illustrates a developer's budget for five terraced two-bedroom houses assuming a selling price of £60 000 each and interest charges of 15 per cent on maximum borrowings of £200 000 for six months with a total development period of one year, yielding a useful profit of £45 000. However, a 20 per cent increase in building costs to, say, £192 000, together with a lengthening construction period caused by problems on site increasing interest charges to £25 000 might change this profitable scheme into a loss-maker. Difficulty in disposing of all the houses at the price anticipated might also jeopardise the scheme.

SOURCES OF FINANCE FOR DEVELOPMENT

The type of finance required will depend on the development period and whether it is intended to retain the interest as an investment or to sell it. If the latter, the developer will need medium- or short-term finance, probably from the banks, for site acquisition and to cover construction costs. Long-term investment, generally the aim of property development companies in the United Kingdom, involves borrowing against the security of the development, or creating an interest which may be sold to an institution. Because a development company frequently retains its investment, its financial structure is somewhat unusual. Revenue is mainly rents and premiums paid for rent concessions. For a company to expand, it needs to raise equity capital or to borrow. Since most development companies do not trade but merely retain property, accumulated unrealised assets may change in value without affecting the profit and loss account, although

Table 5.1 *Developer's budget*

	£	£
Gross development value (GDV)		300 000
Building costs		
Costs of labour, plant and site overheads	160 000	
Costs of materials, sub-contractors' fees	24 000	
Interest charges at 15 per cent	15 000	
Total development expenditure	199 000	
Developers' profit, say 15 per cent of GDV	45 000	
Maximum available for site acquisition	56 000	
	300 000	300 000

they are reflected in the balance sheet. This distinction is significant, as property companies have been accused of making exorbitant profits from changes in the market values of their unrealised permanent investments. Programming expenditure is crucial to planning the development so that capital remains unproductive for as short a period as possible. There are significant differences between private and public developers' source of finance; the latter will be discussed later.

Short- and Medium-term Finance

This is generally available for periods of up to five years. It may be relatively expensive as there is limited security in the land and buildings during the construction period. The rate of interest which the developer will have to pay depends upon his financial status and the quality of the project. An established company may borrow at a lower rate. Because of uncertainties, the developer will prefer to keep short-term borrowings to a minimum, although this will depend upon the length of the scheme, current rate of interest and expectations regarding future trends in rates. Short-term rates are likely to vary directly with changes in base rate.

Clearing banks

These are the traditional sources of short-term credit in the United Kingdom. Provided projects are sound and the borrower is able to produce satisfactory collateral, funds may be available at 2–5 per cent above base rate. Banks generally loan up to 70 per cent of the value of the scheme and normally do not require equity participation. Sometimes an arrangement fee is charged, usually 1 per cent of the facility arranged. With stable rates of interest this is a satisfactory and relatively cheap way of raising funds.

Removal of controls over bank lending in 1971 saw the banks as major lenders to property companies. Between 1971 and 1975, bank advances to property companies increased more than sixfold. This rapid and very large increase was a factor in the general destabilisation and collapse of the property market in the mid-1970s. Following the collapse, the clearing banks reduced their commitments drastically, even to well-established companies, and from 1975 to 1979 were net dis-investors to property developers. With the property boom of 1986–7, bank lending on new development accelerated, so that by mid-1987 total loans to property companies and developers exceeded £5 billion or 4.5 per cent of total advances. This was some 40 per cent lower in real terms than the peak lending to the sector in the mid-1970s. Residential mortgages substantially exceeded loans to property companies.

Merchant and secondary banks

These were an important alternative source of short-term finance for property development until the financial crisis of December 1973. Groups with large equity backing, such as listed property companies or larger private development companies, were favoured.

Secondary banks were responsible for much of the new money between 1972 and 1974, and the concentration of debt on banks with a low capital base was a major factor in the subsequent collapse. Some banks lent incautiously and the collateral available from the property company was often inadequate. Gearing among property companies was very high and the proportion of short-term debt on variable interest rates was too high to withstand the abrupt change in economic conditions.

Interest rates were higher than those charged by the clearers but were sometimes fixed for up to two years. Funds were generally available for development but often on an equity participation basis. This frequently suited the developer since risks were shared and he paid out only realised profits. An established developer was able to borrow as much as 100 per cent of his development expenses, often on the basis of a revolving credit of a maximum amount being available for up to two years. The bank had the right to approve specific projects, on which it agreed to provide all development costs. The developer was obliged to offer all proposals to the bank which could call for properties to be revalued, and if the value was below the total costs incurred the bank might call for additional security or for the loan to be redeemed. As a result of the failure of several 'fringe' banks in 1974, the merchant banks became much more cautious in their lending to property companies – between 1975 and 1978 over £600 million in loans was called in.

In the mid-1980s the merchant banks were again active, although their role was confined largely to investment banking and underwriting. Lending to property companies as a percentage of merchant banks' total advances fell to 8.4 per cent during 1986.

Foreign banks

Since the 1960s, foreign banks in the United Kingdom have shown remarkable growth rates in the volume of business and also in numbers. By the early 1980s there were around 200. With the 'Big Bang' in 1986 this increased to over 400 banks in London alone. By 1987, foreign banks accounted for over £3.7 billion of loans, about 30 per cent of total loans to property companies.[1] North American, West European, Australian and Japanese banks predominated. Unlike the clearing banks, foreign banks were prepared for longer-term involvement, often in particularly large or complex development schemes. Most of these banks were subsidiaries of large parents based overseas and for whom they conducted foreign business; they thus had huge resources. Their rates were often cheaper than those of merchant and clearing banks and they have been prepared to loan up to 80 per cent on a suitable project. Large loans were syndicated among other banks, with only a small proportion of the total value held by the initiating bank.

Syndication

Syndicated loans became popular in the mid-1980s. Syndication allows a single bank to arrange an advance that exceeds its normal size limit and then to reduce the bank's exposure by inviting others to participate. Risk reduction allied to higher returns on very large projects have encouraged such arrangements. The increased activity in sharing debt among the banks has created new opportunities for borrowers and lenders alike. Syndication also allows smaller banks to participate in high-quality development that would normally be beyond their loan limits.

Limited recourse loans

Limited and non-recourse lending was an innovation of the late 1980s. Property companies were able to arrange special-purpose loans confined to an individual project. The exposure of the parent company is limited by this should any difficulties subsequently arise. A subsidiary or joint venture company is usually created for the specific development and the capital structure organised so that the sponsor company has less than 50 per cent equity. The evolution of this practice indicates the borrowing strength and degree of security offered by major development companies.

Trade credit

This is significant for most developers. It is the time interval between receiving plant and materials and paying for them. Trade credit, often 30 days, is therefore a useful source of working capital free of interest. Delays in payment may effectively reduce the capital required to fund a contract, although too long a delay in payment may undermine the commercial confidence in the company. As interest rates have risen, so builders' merchants have restricted both the credit amount and period allowed for payment, which might adversely affect cash flow for some developers.

Long-term Finance

The mortgage

Traditionally, funds were borrowed over 20–30 years at a fixed rate of interest and repaid at the end of the term. Mortgages are now repaid by annual instalments over the period of the mortgage. The lender thus recovers his capital over the term of the loan and may reinvest it at current rates; however, he still has no protection against inflation. The disadvantage to the borrower of repayment by annual instalments is that although interest may be charged against taxable income, capital payments cannot. In addition, income from the property may be insufficient to provide for both interest and capital, and there may be a negative cash flow. Generally, no more than 70 per cent of the value of the security may be borrowed by mortgage.

An alternative to the straight mortgage is the mortgage debenture. Funds are advanced against the security of a particular property, but in addition the lender has a charge over all the assets of the company. Should it be necessary to enforce repayment of the loan by selling the security and an insufficient sum is realised, the lender can claim on the other assets to liquidate the balance of the debt. Repayment of the mortgage debenture is at the end of the loan period. The lender has a fixed interest investment with a substantial security but no hedge against inflation. With real interest rates in the 1980s at exceptionally high levels, debentures and mortgages lost favour with developers as a means of financing projects.

A variation is the convertible loan stock. The lender has an option to purchase ordinary shares in the company at some future date at a fixed price in proportion to the amount of loan stock held. If the lender does not take up his option, he continues to receive interest at an agreed rate until the redemption date. The lender thus links the advantages of a fixed interest stock with protection against inflation. A further variation is where debenture holders receive both a fixed rate of interest and also part of the profits after the developer has received a fixed return on the total costs of development. These trends reflect the increasing sophistication of lenders in protecting their funds against the ravages of inflation.

The sale and leaseback

This method has been used increasingly since the 1960s as interest rates increased. The developer, having originally acquired the site and erected buildings, sells an interest to an institution, which then grants a lease to the developer. Thus the developer continues to have the use of the property while obtaining funds to finance another scheme. Initially, leases were as long as 99 years at a rent representing a percentage return to the institution for the acquisition of the interest. The rents are subject to reviews; the tendency has been for the reviews and leases to be at ever-shorter periods (reflecting inflationary pressures). Whereas in the 1950s a 50-year interval was not uncommon, by the 1980s reviews were often at 5- or 7-year intervals, while leases were for 25–35 years.

The advantage to the institution of the sale and leaseback is that the security of both income and capital is good. The transaction is not normally concluded until the property has been developed and let. The main types of development involved are prime commercial properties. Shops are especially favoured as their location is usually in central thoroughfares where site value is very high. The investor is relieved of management obligations since the development company takes the lease on full repairing and insuring terms. Under sale and leaseback, the developer may obtain 100 per cent of the value of the asset as compared with two-thirds with a mortgage – although the larger the sum raised the less the security of the purchaser, who will therefore require a higher yield. The disadvantage to the development company is that having disposed of a substantial part of its assets it only retains a relatively small profit rent; it has to meet a substantial head rent before it takes its profit. Should the developer wish to sell his profit rental to raise capital or to pledge it for security for temporary finance, it will be capitalised at a higher rate of interest (lower year's purchase) than the rate at which the total income might have been capitalised for raising a mortgage.

A variation on the sale and leaseback is the rent charge. The developer retains the freehold or leasehold of the building but grants the institution a charge on the property for as long as the developer's interest subsists. Rent charges can be made subject to periodic reviews in exactly the same way as rent under a lease. The stage at which the developer can obtain long-term finance, which is much cheaper than short-term, is critical. S/he must produce a scheme which can be presented to an institution for long-term funding with the risks and unknowns reduced to a minimum.

Various types of leaseback arrangement have evolved, the difference mainly centring on the split of the initial rental income, and subsequent rent increases, between the institutions and the development company. With 'geared leaseback' the institution typically takes the major share of the initial rent (say, 70 per cent) plus a small proportion of subsequent rent increases, so that over time its share of the total income declines, and that of the developer increases. With 'ungeared leaseback' their respective shares remain fixed over time; but with the institutional portion guaranteed, the return to the developer can be severely affected if some floor area remains unlet. With the 'reverse leaseback' the institution agrees to purchase a long lease and sub-lets back, enabling the developer to retain the freehold and therefore the certain and marketable bottom slice of income.

Where a developer is building for investment, it is sometimes possible to combine short- and long-term finance. Some institutions are prepared to finance development during the building period. On completion, rent is calculated at an agreed percentage on the total costs of developments. This method of finance is normally only available to well-established developers.

Joint companies

This is an arrangement by which the financing institution and the development company hold shares in agreed proportions. The institution acquires the site and grants a lease to the joint company at an agreed percentage of the total costs of the development. The hedge against inflation for the institution is provided by the equity stake in the joint company. In some cases the site owner becomes a participant, thus effectively creating a similar position to the local authority–private developer partnership where the local authority freeholder, in addition to the ground rent, requires a share in the equity, and the financing institution requires similar equity participation.

A problem of any large company is attracting entrepreneurial talent to its structured organisation. Several large property companies have backed new developers by providing them with finance, generally by forming joint companies in which the developer has the major shareholding while the public company retains financial if not voting control. The developer is free of financial problems while the public company vets the principles of each scheme. Projects too small for the public company are likely to be offered to the joint company.

Share issues

Companies quoted on the Stock Exchange are able to raise long-term capital by additional share issues. Existing shareholders may be given prior rights to subscribe for further shares. These rights enable shareholders to purchase new shares in proportion to their existing holding, and thus their voting power is not diluted. In addition, the rights issue is made at a privileged price lower than the current market price of existing shares. Many development companies have preferred to increase their gearing by increasing fixed interest borrowings, rather than by diluting the equity base of the company. However, with higher interest rates, many have resorted to rights issues with historically low levels of dividend yield and high stock market prices.

Smaller development firms are able to raise funds through 'Juning markets' – the unlisted securities market (USM) and the over-the-counter market (OTC). In both cases the expenses of quotation and the demands for a track record are less rigorous than on the main London Stock Exchange. The USM started in 1980. A USM quote gives advantages to existing shareholders in a private company, enabling them to release part of their investment without any change in control, and allows funds to be raised for company development. A quote gives the potential to use marketable securities for future acquisitions. The company must normally have been trading for at least three years and at least 25 per cent of the equity must be available, to ensure a spread of shares. OTC shares are quoted by licensed dealers who make the market in the shares.

Among medium-size development companies, internally generated funds may be critical to growth. It is only the large companies that are able to arrange a sophisticated financial strategy to meet changing needs; financial constraints still apply but the large company has a much wider range of options open.

Unitisation

By 1986 it was anticipated that a further source of funding would be created by unitisation. Shares or units in single property investment schemes would be traded on the London Stock Exchange. Three new property investment vehicles – property income certificates (PINCs), single asset property companies (SAPCOs) and single-property owned trusts (SPOTs) – were proposed.[2] Any of these schemes would be able to offer units directly to the public and to ensure 'tax transparency' – that is, investors should have any income and capital gains produced by their units taxed as if they had invested directly in property. Pension funds were expected to be major purchasers of the units. The Financial Services Act 1986 provided the framework for the legal establishment of these schemes.

It was anticipated that the new markets would add to the range of long-term funding available to developers. Large projects, in particular, would benefit by providing opportunities to a wider range of investors. Smaller funds would have a wider choice and opportunities to invest in schemes beyond their normal scope; market makers would ensure the liquidity hitherto lacking in property investment. Uncertainties related to the size and type of scheme to be offered, the problems of an after-market and at what price the new units would trade. Other criteria included adequate investor protection, a ban on insider dealings and access to data and information on buildings. It was likely that the creation of a liquid market in property units would have implications for the quality of building maintenance and the construction industry.

PROPERTY DEVELOPMENT AND INVESTMENT OVERSEAS

With freer capital and money markets, an increasing amount of development and investment overseas has been undertaken by British companies and institutions, particularly in the European Union (EU) but also in North America and Australia. The movement overseas developed in the 1960s, peaked in 1973 and then declined. Relatively high yields and good growth prospects initially attracted institutions. Typically, in 1972 Abbey Life Property Bond purchased Tour Madou, an office block in Brussels, which yielded 7 per cent as compared with the 4–5 per cent yields on comparable property in London.

British property companies did not venture overseas until the early 1960s. They concentrated on domestic expansion as boom conditions prevailed from

1954 onwards. For the British developer there were attractions in development overseas.

(1) Opportunities to participate in growth-oriented economies in which both income per capita and investment opportunities would be greater than those in the United Kingdom.

(2) Risk could be more widely spread.

(3) Unfulfilled demand for modern commercial and industrial developments.

(4) A strong local currency likely to give further capital appreciation compared to sterling.

(5) The necessary infrastructure in EU countries, the availability of adequate legal, accounting and tax advice on development and the problems of non-resident-controlled companies. Banks were prepared to lend for property investment and development, and competent professional advice and ancillary services were available. There was also the existence of a legal and tax structure not opposed to or penalising property companies.

(6) There were few native property development or investment companies with the expertise of the British companies.

Initially, the concentration was an office development in, for example, Paris and Brussels, but this has broadened into residential and also speculative industrial and warehouse development. Traditionally, in most EU countries, industrialists own their own premises but, as with the office market, a letting market emerged, especially around Paris and Brussels. The gradual acceptance of letting in areas where it has previously been unfamiliar is one major result of growing international influence in EU property markets. A factor was the increasing tightness of finance during the late 1960s; many industrialists began to see the wisdom of selling their existing premises and renting a building modified to their special requirements. Shopping development came later, because local companies were well established. British groups acquired shop investments in major cities such as Amsterdam, and out-of-town shopping centres were developed near Paris. Until 1973 there was a growing scale and widening of the geographical spread of investments, often away from the established centres and into new countries such as Germany, Spain and Italy.

The overseas property boom came to an abrupt halt in 1974. Many companies had as many projects as they could handle; also, because of the increased competition, there had been a drop in investment returns. More fundamental were the effects of the international financial blizzard which brought a rise in interest rates and credit restrictions in most of Europe and North America.

Thus the outlook for British developers overseas, especially in Europe, was uncertain. On the positive side, the sharp decline in building, following measures such as the control on the growth of offices in the Paris region, boosted lettings, and earlier fears of a temporary glut of office space and a subsequent fall in rents in centres such as Brussels diminished by the late 1970s. The companies with the major liquidity problems withdrew, and only the strongest survived. There was the need for new buildings of all types, and the EU countries with fast-increasing national incomes and potential growth situations could afford them. The strong inflow of international funds created a property market which did not exist before the British incursions. Several British property groups countered local measures against overseas companies by seeking European partners, and included their investments in continental-quoted companies. The efficient British company that really knows the market in which it operates, develops co-operative schemes with a local company or British agent and arranges its long-term finance soundly, will still emerge as a major force overseas, particularly in North America, where there has been an increase in the number of estate agents from Britain opening offices.

Major economic recession unprecedented in post-war history affected all EU countries from 1979. Many countries experienced negative real growth between 1980 and 1982, while unemployment in the EU increased to more than 30 million people. Real interest rates stimulated by high US rates rose to post-war peaks. United Kingdom developers and investors, freed by the abolition of exchange controls, looked further afield to the USA, Australia and Singapore.[3] This trend continued into the late 1980s.

THE DEVELOPMENT CYCLE

The production of commercial buildings, and particularly office floor area, has proved to be a very profitable activity since the Second World War because of the difference between the capital value of a completed building and its development costs. The capital value is determined by the rental income and the acceptable yield from investment in property. It is fluctuations in profitability compounded by the long lag between site acquisition and completion of a scheme which create successive cycles of development. The floor area produced in each cycle supplies two markets; the user market for occupiers of office space, and the investment market in which financial institutions acquire prime property as long-term assets. The interaction between supply and demand affects rent levels in the user market, and yields and capital values in the investment market. There has tended to be a declining rate of growth in office and industrial activity but an increasing growth in investment demand because of the returns from property investment and the growing weight of institutional funds.

It is the cyclical nature of development which provides the crucial link between profitability in the property sector, the user market and the investment market. The cycle of development proceeds as follows:

(1) The upward pressure of demand leads to increasing rents in the user market and declining yields in the investment market as existing space is taken up.

(2) Capital values rise, so increasing the potential profitability of development.

(3) Developers are encouraged to initiate schemes (although it may be some time before they are completed).

(4) If demand continues to grow, available space will continue to decline and new schemes will be initiated.

(5) The first wave of developments reach the market and there is potential over-supply from the volume of schemes started.

Although the boom appears to be at its height, the profitability of new schemes is much reduced, but only when the over-supply actually materialises does development activity slacken off. By this time the volume of newly developed space coming on to the market causes rents to stabilise or fall, yields to rise and capital values to fall. Development then continues at a low level until the supply of available space has declined sufficiently for the cycle to begin again.

There have been three major property booms in the United Kingdom since the Second World War. The boom of the late 1950s early 1960s and that of the early 1970s followed the pattern set out above. The boom of 1986–7 appeared likely to be followed by over-supply of space by 1989–90.

Analysis of the development cycle in the City of London by Richard Barras[4] shows significant differences between the first and second post-war booms, both in terms of conditions in the user and investment markets and the consequent extent of floor area redevelopment. In the immediate post-war years there was strong user demand for an increase in the stock of office space because of war damage, low levels of inter-war office building and high rates of growth in office-using activity. Much early development took place on war-damaged sites and the total supply of floor area grew rapidly, often on prime sites close to the City's banking core.

In the second boom, redevelopment of the existing secondary office stock was the dominant activity. Since the best sites in the core were already occupied by prestige offices, the larger redevelopment schemes were forced into the ring around the core.

Regarding cyclical fluctuations in profitability, it is clear that development conditions are most favourable in the early stages of a boom. Because of the time lag between the start and completion of a scheme, conditions decline to their least favourable for schemes started when the boom appears to be at its height. This explains why developers continue to initiate schemes when hindsight suggests that conditions are not so favourable. Also, typical valuation practice seems to encourage a short-sighted view of development profitability since the potential capital value and construction costs of a scheme are often derived from current rents and costs rather than being based on appropriate future estimates. This is particularly significant in that there is a long-term trend for construction costs to take up a decreasing share of development value, leaving an increasing share for site cost and development profit. This is principally because rents and capital values have, on average, been growing faster than construction tender costs. Between 1962 and 1977, capital values rose on average by 13 per cent per year, while construction costs rose by about 10 per cent per year.[5] The annualised rate of return on property averaged 13.7 per cent between 1977 and 1987.[6]

INVESTMENT APPRAISAL

Continuing government intervention, changing economic policies, higher inflation, mounting interest rates and building costs and the growing scale of development projects have made the investment decision increasingly complex. All
business decisions are made against a background of uncertainty about the future based upon assumptions regarding future needs and an evaluation of all
facts, administrative, legal and economic, relating to the viability, and social
and political acceptability of a scheme.

In reaching a decision the developer may need to choose between alternatives and will need to be equipped with techniques that assist him/her in his/her
choice. Each alternative will possess a range of respective costs and benefits, some
of which can be quantified in money terms, and other 'intangibles' which will
probably not be considered by a private developer but *will* be by a public body.

The increasing use of computers and operational research, together with an
increasing need for long-term planning, have contributed to the greater use of
rational methods of investment appraisal. Using the relevant techniques a firm
can identify the most profitable of a number of projects and, after considering
constraints, risk and uncertainty, make an objective choice.

Conventional Methods of Investment Appraisal

Many investment decisions are taken on the basis of entrepreneurial hunches
and experience, which do not take sufficient account of the timing of profits
derived from the investment; nor do they fully consider all costs and revenues
deriving from the project. Two methods of investment appraisal of this type
are (1) pay-back method and (2) average rate of return.

Pay-back method

This is a crude form of investment criteria used particularly for smaller projects.
The pay-back (PB) is defined as the period it takes for an investment to generate sufficient net profits, after tax, to recover its initial capital outlay in full.
Generally, the shorter the period in which the original capital outlay is expected to be recouped (the shorter the PB) the more favourable will be the
firm's attitude. PB recognises that earlier returns are preferable to those accruing later and it will have justification when later returns are particularly uncertain. The major weaknesses of the PB method are that it fails to measure long-term
profitability since it takes no account of the cash flows beyond the PB period.
It also takes no account of the timing of cash flows within the PB period.

Average rate of return method (ARR)

This is the ratio of net profit (after tax) to capital. However, net profit can be
either that made in the first year, or the average made over the lifetime of the

project. Similarly, capital can be taken to be either the initial sum invested or an average over time of all capital outlays over the life of the project. The process tends to be arbitrary and will give an inaccurate method of investment appraisal which might lead to the selection of projects yielding a sub-maximum return. The result depends on the number of years chosen and it takes no account of the timing of the cash flows.

DISCOUNTING AND THE TIME VALUE OF MONEY

Both ARR and PB fail to take into account that earnings vary over the life of the project and that a sum of money today tends to be worth more than the same amount at a later date. Money has a time value; a given sum now is usually worth more than an equal and certain sum at some time in the future. This is so even without inflation if the rate of interest is positive, because the sum of money now can be invested to earn a rate of interest and accumulate to more in a year. Alternatively, the sum can be used now to reduce borrowings and so avoid interest payments. Thus, if faced with the choice of £100 now or £100 in one year's time, the rational choice would be to take the £100 now. That sum could be invested, let us assume, at a risk-free market rate of interest (say, 10 per cent) and would have grown to £110 at the end of the period, $£100 \times (1 + 0.10)^1$, £121 in two years, $£100 \times (1 + 0.10)^2$, £133.1 in three years, $£100 \times (1 + 0.10)^3$. Thus if a sum of money (P) is invested at a rate of interest (r), the sum arising (S) after n years is given by the formula: $S = P(1 + r)^n$. Similarly, it can be seen that the offer of a certain £133.1 in three years' time is equivalent to the offer of £100 now. The present value or worth of any sum S due to be received in the future can be calculated by discounting the future sum at the appropriate rate of interest using the formula

$$P = \frac{S}{(1 + r)^n} \quad \text{for example } P = \frac{£133.1}{(1 + 0.10)^3} = £100$$

The present value of any future sum of money is dependent upon two factors: how far in the future is the sum and how high is the rate of interest. The further in the future the sum is or the higher the rate of interest or discount used, the less is the present value of that future sum. Using this discounting technique the potential investor can thus derive an exchange rate for cash flows over differing periods, enabling a rational comparison to be made. The two major techniques are the internal rate of return (IRR) and the net present value (NPV). These are based on the same theoretical approach and lead to identical decisions. Both methods involve the calculation year by year of the net cash flow (NCF) expected from the project, that is, the cash receipts and cash expenditures over its life. Once the cash flow has been estimated and discounted to present values by the appropriate rate it is possible to calculate both the present value and the yield on the development.

Net Present Value (NPV)

The NPV or earnings profile of a project is the sum of the present values of future cash flows for all years during the project's life. Basically, receipts and expenditures falling earlier are more significant than those occurring later; all foreseeable effects on other projects within the business must be incorporated in the calculations. Thus the effects on cash flow should be presented in the form of a timetable showing the estimated effects on outflows and inflows in each of a number of successive accounting periods.

To determine the NPV of a proposed development, the forecast net of tax cash flows are discounted to the time of the initial capital outlay. The rate of interest used to discount will tend to be the opportunity cost of the capital employed, the rate of return that could be earned by investing the money in the next best alternative, or the firm's marginal rate of financing. The NPV method calculates profitability by subtracting the present values of all expenditures when they occur from the present value of all revenues when they occur. Any project that has a positive present value (that is, greater than zero) is viable, and the one revealing the highest NPV is in purely financial terms the most profitable. It is possible that political, social or environmental factors make it less attractive. In addition, the most profitable solution could entail a capital expenditure beyond the borrowing powers of the developer concerned. However, all budgetary implications are exposed. Since all capital expenditure is included in the cash flow and an interest charge equal to the cost of finance to the company is implicit in the discounting process, no separate provision for depreciation or other capital charges is required. It will be apparent that the NPV of the project will vary with the rate used to discount the future cash flow. The lower the discount rate, the higher the NPV; and conversely, the higher the discount rate the lower the NPV. If the cash flows sum to zero, the return on the investment will be exactly equal to the discount rate, and it is a marginal investment. In this context clearly discount rate and interest are synonymous. If the present values of all expected net flows discounted to the base year at the appropriate rate of interest give a negative NPV, the project should not go ahead.

The operation of this technique is shown in table 5.2 with the example of an investment of £15 000 with anticipated annual income of £4000 over the next five years. The firm's cost of capital is 10 per cent. In this example the NPV is positive and at the rate of discount used the scheme will add to the wealth of the company; the return is greater than the 10 per cent cost of capital involved.

Internal Rate of Return (IRR)

The yield or rate of return of a project is the rate of interest which if used to discount the cash flow would make the NPV exactly zero. A project is worthwhile if its yield is greater than the firm's required rate of return. Thus the

Table 5.2 *The calculation of net present value*

Year	Net cash flow (NCF) (£)	Discount factor (DF) (10 per cent)	Present value (NCF × DF) (£)
0	− 15 000	1.0	− 15 000
1	+ 4 000	0.9091	+ 3 636
2	+ 4 000	0.8264	+ 3 306
3	+ 4 000	0.7513	+ 3 005
4	+ 4 000	0.6830	+ 2 732
5	+ 4 000	0.6209	+ 2 484
		NPV =	163

Table 5.3 *The internal rate of return*

Year	Net cash flow (NCF)	Discount factor of 10.4 per cent	Present value (NCF × 10.4 per cent)
0	− 15 000	1.0	− 15 000
1	+ 4 000	0.9058	+ 3 623
2	+ 4 000	0.8025	+ 3 282
3	+ 4 000	0.7432	+ 2 973
4	+ 4 000	0.6732	+ 2 693
5	+ 4 000	0.6098	+ 2 439
		NPV =	0

method employs the present value concept but seeks to provide an evaluation procedure that avoids the difficult choice of a rate of interest. Instead, it sets out to establish, by trial and error, a rate of interest that makes the present values of all expenditures incurred in a project equal to the present values of all revenues gained. That is, it determines the discount rate which reduces the NPV to zero. When calculated, this interest rate is known as the 'yield' of the investment. Having worked out the IRR, or yield, for each alternative, they should be compared with the cost of borrowing the capital. Any project or alternative having a higher return than the cost of borrowing is fundamentally 'profitable' and the highest return will be the most financially attractive. As with NPV, the IRR will generally be higher if the bulk of the cash flows are received earlier rather than later. Using table 5.2 for NPV, IRR will be equal to 10.4 per cent (table 5.3).

Internal Rate of Return and NPV

The relationship between the IRR and NPV methods can be seen in figure 5.1. An initial capital outlay of £15 000 generates revenues of £4000 in each of the

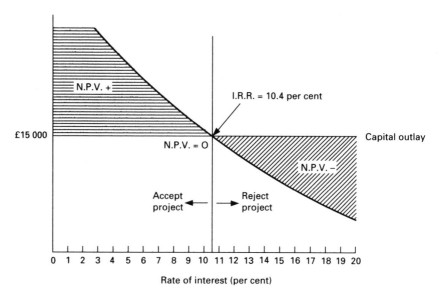

Figure 5.1   *Present value of income and expenditure*

Table 5.4 *Optimal investment criteria*

Project	Initial capital outlay	Project life (years)	Annual cash flow generated	NPV @ 9 per cent	IRR (per cent)
A	−500 000	5	140 000	44 544	12.5
B	−750 000	5	207 000	55 147	11.8
B-A	−250 000	5	67 000	10 603	10.8

ensuing five years. The present values of the positive cash flows arising from the project have been estimated for a range of interest rates. The difference between the present value curve and the initial capital outlay at any rate of interest represents the NPV of the project and thus the intersection of NPV and the capital outlay gives the IRR. Therefore, if a company's cost of capital is less than the IRR, the project would add to the firm's worth (NPV is positive) and should be accepted: if it is higher than the IRR, the project would not be profitable (NPV is negative) and should not be accepted.

No method of evaluation is ever precisely accurate, however. The purpose of investment appraisal is to examine all likely eventualities, given all the known and relevant data, in order to select the most probable solution. Where both NPV and IRR techniques are employed, the results will often be identical; there will also be situations in which different decisions will be indicated. This may be so when trying to decide which is the most profitable of two mutually exclusive projects (see table 5.4).

Using the NPV method, Project B appears to be more profitable than project A; but using the IRR method, A appears favourable to B. Different results are obtained because neither of the discounting methods makes allowance for the total capital involved in a project, nor for the time for which the capital is exposed to risk. However, by comparing the incremental cash flows that would result from carrying out Project B instead of Project A (that is B − A) with the extra capital cost required, a NPV and IRR for B − A can be obtained. Then if the return on the extra capital is deemed to more than compensate for the risks involved, Project B should be carried out rather than Project A.

This highlights one important advantage of the IRR method. The risks associated with the project are largely dependent on the quantity of capital involved and the length of the project. By showing a rate per unit of capital per unit of time of the project, the IRR shows the margin over the cost of capital that is being obtained in return for risk taken. It also avoids the controversial decision of selecting an interest rate.

Thus, once working hypotheses have been formed, techniques of investment appraisal can be used to predict the profitability of alternative courses of action. In some cases sophisticated appraisal techniques will be unnecessary. In relatively small developments decisions may be taken in the light of experience and market factors. In fact the principles of NPV and IRR underlie conventional valuation methods which frequently compute the profitability of the scheme by calculating the gross development value from the completion costs to the present. Variation can be allowed for by adjusting the capitalisation factor (years' purchase) or by setting aside sums for contingencies.

In effect, discounted cash flow analysis (DCF) differs only in being more sophisticated and risk-conscious in its consideration of time, and more flexible in investigating the possible range of variance in the factors underlying the investment decision. It is evident that costs, interest rates, schedules and rents can alter in the course of a development. DCF can be refined by the introduction of risks and uncertainty testing.

Uncertainty and Probability Theory

Uncertainty is defined as a situation in which neither the outcome of an event is known, nor the number of possible outcomes, their values or the probability of their occurrence. Risk is defined as a situation where the outcome lacks certainty, but the number of possible outcomes, their value and their probability of occurrence is known. Development appraisal is largely concerned with risk.

The evaluation of any plans, or developments, requires the measurement of the constituent factors forming the scheme, together with an estimation of their future performance. Such estimates depend largely upon an interpretation of what has happened in the past, and since the pattern of past events is never exactly repeated, future predictions can at best be imprecise approximations.

Sensitivity Analysis

It is necessary to list and examine the possible range of likely outcomes by using sensitivity analysis. This can take the form of estimating the worst and best possible outcomes of the project's cash flow. Decisions based on these extreme estimates tend to be misleading. A more precise approach is to define all the critical variables contained in the project and affecting its profitability – building costs, rents and the cost of borrowing – and to investigate their range together with the probability of their achieving any particular value in that range. The span of likely results occurring when these variables are combined, and their consequent estimates of probability for alternative schemes, can then be calculated. Consider a development proposal with three key variables which each have a 50 per cent probability of the 'best estimate' being correct, and which yields a return of 10 per cent. Assuming none of the factors are mutually determined, there is only a 12.5 per cent chance of the 10 per cent return being obtained $(0.50)^3$, and thus an 87.5 per cent chance of the return being either above or below 10 per cent. The greater the number of variables, and the less certain their performance, the lower the degree of reliability.

Assume a development project with three basic variables: construction costs of £200 000; the rental return estimated at £32 000; and a discount rate of 8 per cent. Calculations are made assessing the effect on the NPV of variations in the value of the variables. For example, it may be calculated that NPV becomes negative if construction costs increase by 5 per cent, if expected rents are 5 per cent short, or if the rate of discount is increased by 16 per cent. By testing of this nature it will be seen that the scheme is more sensitive to changes in construction costs and rents than to changes in the discount rate.

Ideally, the probability of the respective variables should be obtained from prior empirical investigation. In practice, it may be necessary to substitute subjective opinions which may be relatively inaccurate. Probabilities may be estimated from the statistical records and sensitivity variants obtained from experience or sampling. The larger the number of variables the more difficult becomes the appraisal. With the use of computers it is possible to process the simulation of multiple combinations of values and variables, and their relative returns and probabilities.

The list of returns and resulting probabilities can then be expressed graphically as a histogram, plotting returns against probabilities, and producing a risk/return profile. This approach is valuable where there are many variables with wide possible ranges, or where it is desirable to assess the characteristics of alternative investment proposals. One critical factor is the level of investment. In comparing alternative projects, it is possible that one project, while producing a favourable return, entails a considerably higher capital investment, and the risk involved at this level might militate against selection.

Thus in the financial evaluation of alternative plans the treatment of risk and uncertainty presents problems. The methods of appraisal discussed present no clear-cut answer, but both probability theory and sensitivity analysis provide a useful and significant improvement on conventional techniques. The presentation of data in the form of risk/return profiles is of considerably greater value than a single rigid estimate of the project's viability. Increasingly these techniques are being used in financial development appraisal in both private and public sectors. Conventional techniques are inadequate in their treatment of time and risk; they produce a too simplistic view of a problem.

OPTIMAL DEVELOPMENT

Since a positive relationship exists between the size and quality of a building and the price or rent it can command, we need to examine more closely the question of whether it is worth spending more on a building if, as a result, it will sell for a higher price.

With any given site there comes a point when the addition of further units of development capital produces successively smaller increases in the expected value of the development on completion. This situation is shown graphically in figure 5.2a. With the addition of successive units of development capital (each unit representing, say, £10 000) to a particular site, total returns (or GDV) will continue to increase, but at a diminishing rate. Finally, in the example shown, addition of the ninth unit of capital adds nothing to the expected GDV of the project, and adding a tenth unit of capital conceivably could start to reduce total returns. This could occur in the case of, for example, a housing development, where at higher density, properties would eventually be built too close together which would negatively affect the selling price of all units and the GDV of the development as a whole. In the case of industrial property, values would be affected adversely if site coverage became excessive; and in the case of retailing, multistorey development might add little if anything to the GDV, apart perhaps from special cases such as shopping malls.

In the example shown in figure 5.2a it would not generally be advisable for the developer to maximise the GDV or total returns. This can be seen by looking at the contribution to the GDV of the last few units of capital applied to the site; clearly no developer would add the ninth unit of capital which would add nothing to the GDV but the same would also apply to preceding units if these added less to the GDV than it would cost the developer to employ them.

Figure 5.2b illustrates this point by showing the additions to the GDV of each successive unit of capital (otherwise known as the marginal returns or marginal revenue product of capital). From this graph we can see, for example, that the marginal returns to the eighth unit of capital amount to only £5000. In other words, adding the eighth unit of capital adds only £5000 to the overall GDV – considerably less than it would cost to employ it in construction.

In order to answer the question of how many units of capital the developer should apply to the given site, we also need to know how much it would cost the developer to employ a unit of capital (defined as £10 000 of development costs including normal profit and professional fees). This will itself depend upon such factors as the rate of interest on borrowing and the length of time

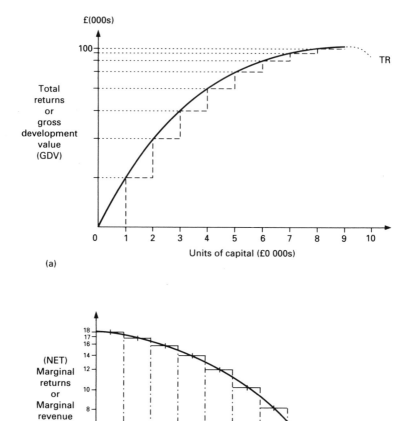

Figure 5.2 *Changes in gross development value (GDV) as successive units of capital applied to a given site*

that money is tied up in the development process. Let us assume for simplicity that this would add 10 per cent to the cost of a unit of capital, then the cost of additional units of capital (or the marginal cost of capital) would total £11 000. We can see from figure 5.2b that the first few units of capital employed on the project, up to and including the fifth unit, would produce marginal returns in excess of their marginal cost. However, the sixth and successive units of capital would each add more to the cost of development that they would increase the GDV. In other words, the marginal costs of employing these units of capital would exceed the marginal returns on so doing.

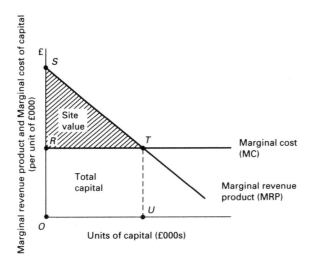

Figure 5.3 *Optimal site development and site-bid*

To maximise site-bid, development of a site should continue as long as the addition of an extra unit of capital increases the GDV by a greater amount than it adds to the total cost of development. This situation is analysed graphically in figure 5.3. The figure assumes a given use (such as offices) and standard of construction. The horizontal axis measures – in units of £1000 – the quantity of capital in the form of all construction and development expenditure applied to the site, including an allowance for normal profit. The cost of a unit of capital is measured on the vertical axis. We assume for simplicity that the cost of an additional unit remains constant, hence the marginal cost (MC) curve forms a horizontal straight line. The MC curve will be higher the greater the level of interest charges and the longer the capital is tied up in the development.

The marginal revenue product (MRP) curve shows the amount by which total returns (that is, GDV) are increased by the addition of one extra unit of capital. This estimate, as we saw earlier, could be based either on annual rental less outgoings or anticipated selling price on completion. MRP is shown to be declining as total capital applied to the site increases, illustrating the process of diminishing marginal returns to a fixed factor (that is, land). This may occur for several reasons: greater height may involve substantial additional expenditure on foundations; or car parking, lifts and fire escapes may be required; and construction costs may also rise. Rents on higher floors may also diminish, especially with retailing.

The optimum level of development is at point T where U units of capital are applied to the site and where the MRP of an additional unit of capital just equals the marginal cost of that unit. The total cost of capital is given by $ORTU$ (that is, £OR per unit x OU units), whereas total returns or the GDV is given by $OSTU$. The difference between the two is RST, representing the surplus or maximum amount remaining once costs are deducted. It is also the maximum sum the developer can bid for the site – at a higher or lower level of capital investment, maximum site-bid would fall below *RST*.

Factors Influencing Site-bid

Maximum site-bid will rise if either the MRP curve rises or the MC curve falls (and vice versa). A rise in the MRP curve could occur if: (1) the value of the finished product rose; (2) capital productivity rose, for example, through technological advance; or (3) there was a fall in the price of any inputs, such that a unit of expenditure on capital results in a higher level of output (and higher MRP, given a constant price for output). A fall in the marginal cost curve could arise if: (1) the interest rate falls; (2) there is a reduction in the construction time so that capital is tied up for a shorter period; or (3) with reduced risk, a loan on more favourable terms can be achieved. In practice, changes influencing any of the above factors are likely to affect different types of development in rather different ways, perhaps favouring some land uses relative to others.

Different land uses (such as offices, retailing or housing) will result in different site-bids because of differences in capital intensity (for example, offices may use more floors than retailing) and differences in the occupier's profitability from use of floor space – for example, High Street retailing as opposed to residential uses. If there were no controls over land use, then competition would ensure that a particular site would go to its highest and best use – that is, the use providing the highest possible site-bid. Although the developer would clearly like to pay less than this, competition between developers should ensure that each puts in a maximum bid in an effort to obtain the site. However, even among similar development schemes (for example, housing) different site-bids may result; while this may be due to differences in efficiency as between developers, it is important to recognise that it may also result from qualitative differences in layout, density levels or even construction standards.

In practice, the planning process may restrict the type of use to which land may be put, or limits may be placed on the maximum permissible height of buildings – thus restricting the amount of capital that may be applied to the site. Also, location will affect the profitability of any particular land use significantly.

Finally, MRP will decline at different rates in different land uses; for example, while office users may be largely indifferent to high-rise buildings, housing developers may find that as total capital and housing densities increase, so this may reduce the anticipated selling prices of *all* (and not just additional) units. Where units of capital are large and indivisible (for example, successive floors in office blocks) MRP declines in a stepwise fashion. This is shown in figures 5.4 and table 5.5, which also illustrate the point that rising costs result in higher capital outlays for successive floors.

Where several uses are considered together, the analysis becomes more complex. For example, increased site value may result from the addition of ground floor

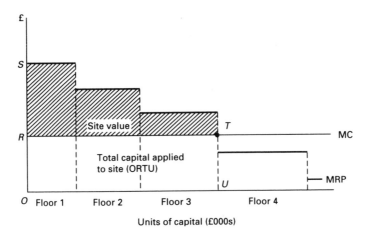

Figure 5.4 *Multistorey development*

Table 5.5 *The cost, revenue and site value of a hypothetical office development**

Floor	Capital outlay per floor (marginal cost) (£)	Capital value per floor (marginal revenue product) (£)	Residual (site) value per floor (£)
4	85 000	70 000	−15 000
3	75 000	80 000	5 000
2	60 000	90 000	30 000
1	50 000	100 000	50 000
Totals to third floor	Cost 185 000	GDV 270 000	Site value 85 000

* Present values.

shops to a residential block of flats (see figure 5.5). In the case shown, the optimal capital outlay remains unchanged at *ou* units.

On a larger scale, city-centre or out-of-town shopping and leisure developments will require very careful consideration in order to obtain the correct mix and location of activities and facilities (for example, adequate parking and access to public transport) to achieve a maximum value for the available site.

THE ECONOMICS OF REDEVELOPMENT AND REHABILITATION

Redevelopment and rehabilitation are often seen as alternative solutions to adapting buildings and sites to new demands and economic uses. Whereas rehabilitation

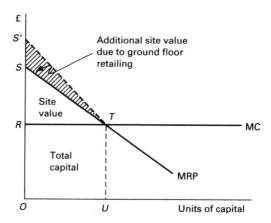

Figure 5.5 *Maximisation of site value for given capital investment*

involves maintenance, repair and adaptation in order to ensure a sound structure and some functional adjustment of the building, redevelopment implies
the total replacement of existing buildings. Redevelopment therefore offers wider
possible advantages in modifying land use, site coverage and density as well
as introducing new building techniques and standards of construction, specifi-
cation, design and layout. At the extreme, comprehensive redevelopment involving numerous buildings and activities may extend to large parts of an urban
area, examples being found in many city-centre schemes in Britain during the
1950s and 1960s. Bourne[7] suggested that for an individual building, the process of change and adaptation falls into a number of stages. We start from a
situation where the building is occupied by the use for which it was designed.
In the second stage the original use is replaced by another use representing a
higher order activity, or a more intensive use in the same activity (for example,
splitting up of large, formerly owner-occupied dwellings into smaller units for
private renting); at this stage there is little modification of the building. In the
third stage there is partial conversion or modification of the building to better
accommodate new uses and new occupants (for example, change of use of
city-centre residential properties to offices). To be worthwhile, this generally
requires a good location and accessibility. Finally, buildings are demolished
and replaced, either by a more intensive use (for example, retailing to offices)
or by a more intensive form of the existing use such as high-rise office space,
business parks, shopping malls or high-density residential flats. Bourne recognised that not all buildings fulfil this sequence, nor do similar buildings always
appear at the same stage at the same time (for example, because of locational
differences). Yet the sequence usefully describes the process of adaptation of
the built environment to accommodate changing demands. Moreover, Bourne
emphasises the fact that adaptation and replacement of buildings stems primarily from economic pressure rather than physical deterioration. This is particularly true in and around the Central Business District, where pressure for

change and adaptation is often greatest and where buildings may become obsolete over a relatively short period of time. Whereas the physical ageing of buildings depends on their initial construction and subsequent maintenance and repair, obsolescence depends on other factors:

(1) The rate of technical innovation and the adaptability of existing buildings (for example, to the increasing demands of office users for information technology); (2) problems caused by the changing pattern of urban growth and changes in the location of activities and population; and (3) negative external or neighbourhood effects on particular buildings or groups of buildings. Common examples include the effects of urban road schemes, planning blight brought about by expected change of use, and the impact of urban decay on surrounding areas as residents and firms come to fear risking capital outlays on improving or even on maintaining their own properties.

Whereas many modern buildings are usually designed for life spans of sixty years or slightly less,[8] the redevelopment of many types of building often occur over a much shorter time period. Equally, the life-span of other buildings may be extended through major refurbishment and/or rebuilding, particularly in the historic cores of many cities. Yet other buildings may suffer the fate of abandonment and dereliction due to a combination of obsolescence, rising repair or running costs, and the lack of new activities finding them a profitable source of investment. It is to the further examination of these activities and alternatives that we shall now turn.

Redevelopment

In order for redevelopment to be profitable, the value of the cleared site for the new development (effectively the developer's maximum side-bid) must exceed the value of the site and building in its existing use. We will consider the determination of cleared site value in more detail shortly, because this differs from site-bid theory, as discussed earlier, mainly due to the existence of sometimes substantial demolition and site preparation costs entailed by redevelopment. For the moment we need to start by examining changes over time in the capital value of the site and building in its existing use.

Over time, buildings tend to become increasingly unsuited for the demands placed upon them by the market, thus influencing achievable rents. As they age, more expensive repairs become necessary as materials weather or decay. In addition, periodic updating (which could involve anything from meeting new fire regulations to changing shop frontages or installing new heating or ventilation) often becomes more difficult and more costly.

This is illustrated in figure 5.6. In the upper diagram, expected operating costs (OC) are shown as rising over time because outgoings on repairs and maintenance increase in later years. By contrast, expected gross annual returns (GARs) – based on estimates of total annual rent – may eventually fall in real terms as competition with other developments increases or as the initial building

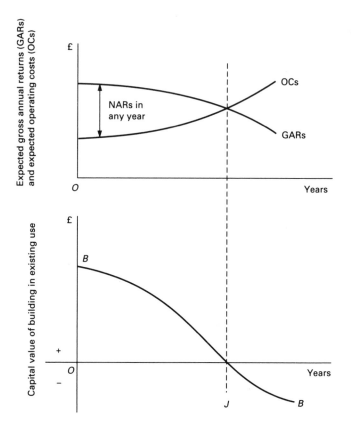

Figure 5.6 *Net annual returns (NARs) and capital value of a building in current use over time (price stability assumed)*

becomes increasingly obsolete relative to changing user demands. Net annual returns (NARs) for any year are given by the difference between GARs and OCs for that year. After *J* years, NARs fall to zero.

The lower diagram in figure 5.6 shows the capital value of the building – derived from future capitalised NARs – declining over time. This occurs because as we move closer to point *J*, there are fewer NARs remaining to be discounted to their present value. After *J*, capital value becomes negative, hence if redevelopment is not contemplated, the site and building would be abandoned and left derelict at this point; *J* years therefore represents the maximum technical life of the building.

However, when redevelopment is proposed, the capital value of the cleared site in its alternative use must exceed the capital value of the building and site in its existing use. To the developer, the capital value of the cleared site is determined by the present value of the site in its new use less the cost of clearing the site, any land preparation costs (for example, drainage) and the cost of rebuilding. This is illustrated in figure 5.7. It can also be seen that any

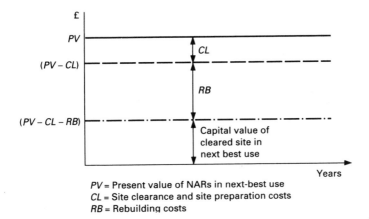

PV = Present value of NARs in next-best use
CL = Site clearance and site preparation costs
RB = Rebuilding costs

Figure 5.7 *Capital value of a cleared site in new use upon redevelopment*

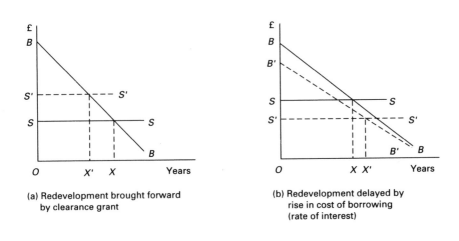

(a) Redevelopment brought forward
by clearance grant

(b) Redevelopment delayed by
rise in cost of borrowing
(rate of interest)

BB = Capital value of building (and site) in existing use
SS = Capital value of cleared site in best alternative use

Figure 5.8 *Factors influencing timing of redevelopment*

increase (decrease) in clearance and preparation costs (*CL*) or rebuilding costs (*RB*) will push down (up) the capital value of the cleared site – other things (such as rent) being equal. Although the capital value of the cleared site is shown as remaining constant at whatever point in time the redevelopment is contemplated, in practice shifts may occur over time because of changes in demand or supply factors; for example, technological change may lower the cost of rebuilding, or changes in demand (such as towards out-of-town retailing) could influence expected rents, or, again, public subsidy could reduce site clearance costs.

As shown in the following diagrams, redevelopment may occur (at point *X*) when the capital value of the cleared site in its next best use comes to exceed the capital value of the building in its current use. This point is known as the economic life of the existing building. Two examples of economic changes which may influence the timing of redevelopment are given in figure 5.8. In 5.8a a clearance grant is shown as raising the capital value of the cleared site and bringing forward redevelopment from X to X' years. In 5.8b, a rise in the rate of interest lowers both the capital value of the existing building (since future net earnings are capitalised at a higher rate) and the capital value of the cleared site – to $B'B'$ and $S'S'$ respectively. However, the current use is marginally favoured by this change, putting off redevelopment from X to X' years. This occurs for several reasons:

(1) the higher interest rate is applied to fewer net annual returns in the case of the existing building (this is why BB and $B'B'$ converge towards later years of project life); and (2) the next best alternative use will, in addition, incur higher development costs because of the higher cost of borrowing. Conversely, a fall in interest rates will tend to bring forward the pace of redevelopment.

Rehabilitation

Unlike redevelopment, rehabilitation involves improvement of the existing building, either in the same use or, not infrequently, in a more intensive use. On the one hand, rehabilitation may simply involve the reversal of neglect and decay, enabling the building to continue to provide an acceptable level of service. On the other it may involve major refurbishment or rebuilding in a general upgrading of the building. In all cases the objective is to raise future NAR's to an extent which will more than offset the outlay on rehabilitation. This is shown in figure 5.9. Rehabilitation taking place at point r in time produces higher attainable rents, thus raising GARs. In addition, some reduction in future operating costs is likely since, first, newer materials used in refurbishment will tend to age more slowly and require less maintenance than the ones they replace.

Secondly, it may be possible at the same time to undertake improvements that would reduce energy consumption; for example, by providing better standards of insulation. The combination of raised GARs and lower OCs improves net annual returns from point r onwards, as shown in figure 5.9b.

Whether expenditure on rehabilitation is worthwhile therefore depends upon whether the present value of the rise in NARs (shown as the shaded area in figure 5.9b) exceeds the present value of the cost of work undertaken. Alternatively, since the rise in NARs will produce a higher capital value for the rehabilitated building at point r, this increase in capital values can be compared directly with the cost of rehabilitation.

Shops frequently undergo refurbishment to keep up with new trends, and offices occasionally undergo major rebuilding for similar reasons. Large residential properties can often produce higher capital values by conversion into

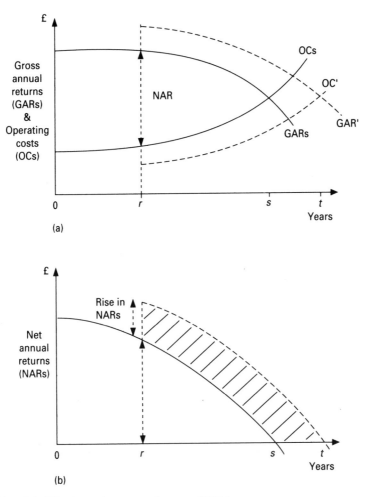

Figure 5.9 *Rehabilitation and net annual returns (NARs)*

smaller units, and even old industrial buildings or warehouses can sometimes be converted economically to better uses. Increasingly, however, with commercial properties, the decision whether to undertake major refurbishment has become complicated by the possibility of redevelopment in the not too distant future.[9] Prime examples are certain 1960s office blocks and shopping centres which, because the possibility of redevelopment is not far distant, may find that refurbishment would only extend their economic lives by perhaps another fifteen years. This problem can be illustrated as in figure 5.10 which also includes the cleared site value in the next best alternative use. Refurbishment of the existing building in year *r* would extend the economic life of the building from year *x* to *y*, but after this point is reached the value of the existing building becomes largely irrelevant if redevelopment is contemplated, since the cleared site value (CSV) is in excess of the value of the building and site

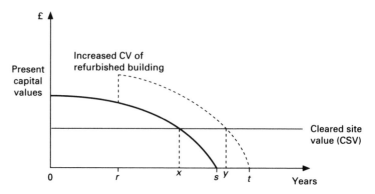

Figure 5.10 *Rehabilitation and the economic life of a building*

in its existing use. Clearly, as *y* moves left towards point *r* (that is, if CSV rises) so the advantages of rehabilitation become less clear and the more likely it becomes that property owners will 'sit it out' and await redevelopment, avoiding as much expenditure as possible on the existing building.

HISTORIC BUILDINGS

Economic analysis of the problems facing historic buildings can be undertaken largely within the framework of the preceding sections. In many cases such buildings require substantial rehabilitation, without which further decay and dereliction would eventually occur. Unfortunately, it is often the case that financial returns from continued use may not justify the outlays required on improvement works. In other cases historic buildings, while remaining economically viable, may nevertheless be under threat from redevelopment – particularly in expanding CBD's and where they do not represent an intensive use of their existing site (compared to high-rise offices, for example). As such, the CSV of the site they occupy may well be in excess of the value of the historic building itself. These alternative positions are analysed in figure 5.11a which shows the present capital values of the existing historic building as well as the cleared site value in the highest alternative use (for example, offices). The capital value of the historic building declines so that at year *x* redevelopment would be economically feasible, although if redevelopment was not contemplated, the building would be abandoned and left to decay after year *y*. Fig 5.11b shows how this may occur in practice. Although GARs may continue to rise as the historic building acquires a scarcity value over time, it is likely that OCs will tend to rise with structural wear and tear. If periodic major expenditure is required (for example, recasting of lead roofs) then OCs may increase in a stepwise fashion, falling off later. However, in many cases the situation may be even worse than that depicted. First, many historic buildings or monuments produce no direct revenue whatsoever, their public interest being entirely historical,

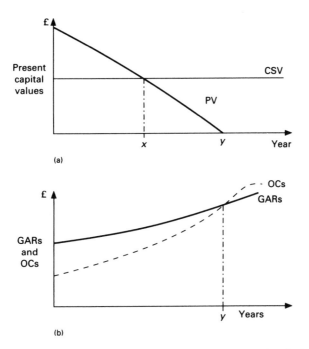

Figure 5.11 *Historic buildings – rising repair and maintenance costs offset higher gross annual returns*

social or architectural. Secondly, with many monuments, such as Hadrian's Wall, for example, it may not be practicable to try to enforce charges for visiting the facility. As a result, for many such buildings and monuments, GARs are frequently zero or at best negligible, and without public or charitable funding the costs of maintenance and repair could not be met.

But even where individuals or firms are prepared to place a value on living, working or simply visiting historic buildings, the market tends to ignore the wider valuation society as a whole places on them. This occurs for several main reasons:

(1) GARs measure only the private benefits accruing to those owning or renting such buildings. In addition to this are the external benefits derived by passers-by or other activities in the vicinity (for example, tourism, shops).

(2) Particularly if the consequences of decay are irreversible, individuals might be prepared to pay something just to keep open the option of visiting the building at a later date ('option' demand). For very important historic buildings or monuments people may feel there is some intrinsic value in maintaining these assets even though they may not personally be able to visit them ('existence' value). Although for any individual, 'option' and 'existence' values may be quite small, many

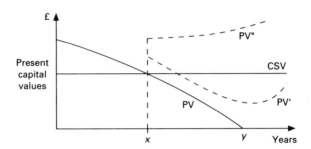

Figure 5.12 *Policy options for historic buildings*

people might be willing to contribute something: thus, overall, such values could become very substantial. Some idea of these values can be observed in the voluntary contributions made by a growing number of individuals to bodies such as the National Trust. Rising real incomes and growing leisure time may further increase the appreciation of architectural heritage and the desire to preserve it.

(3) Because of their often unique character, the scarcity value of such buildings is likely to rise over time, but it is unlikely that present-day markets will fully reflect such future benefits (which may in any case be largely external in character).

Even where market solutions are sought (for example, opening up stately homes to the public), the results may not always be successful, particularly since, for reasons mentioned above, the revenue raised is unlikely to reflect fully the value of the facility to society.

Figure 5.12 illustrates some of the policy options open to governments to help conserve historic buildings. First, designated buildings of architectural and/ or historical interest can be 'listed', which prevents demolition or alteration without the consent of the local planning authority. Under the 1967 Civic Amenities Act such considerations were extended to the wider urban setting of conservation areas (of which there are now 8000). While listing may prevent redevelopment from occurring at point *x* in figure 5.12 it will not necessarily prevent decay and dereliction by neglect (point *y*). Local authorities, even where this is permitted, only rarely take actions involving expense, such as restoration, since little finance is made available to them for these purposes. However, the powers of local authorities in this field have recently been increased, and under Section 54 of the Planning (Listed Buildings and Conservation Areas) Act 1990 they are able to execute urgent repairs for the preservation of unoccupied or partly unoccupied listed buildings (following the issuing of an urgent repairs notice). Local authority expenses can then be recovered from owners under Section 55 of the Act. Owners have a right of appeal but this is unlikely to be successful unless hardship can be proved. Following direction from the Secretary of State for National Heritage, urgent repairs powers can also be applied to unlisted buildings of importance in conservation areas. The full repairs procedure under Section 48 of the Act is more significant as it can be used on occupied buildings. The works specified in a full repairs notice should not, however, exceed those which are reasonably necessary for a building's 'preservation' – as opposed to its 'restoration'. Local authorities can now recover from owners through the County Courts the cost of works required by a relevant enforcement notice under the Planning and Compensation Act (1991). Failure to carry out the terms of a full repairs notice within two months can also lead to a compulsory purchase order (CPO) being made by the local authority. In practice it would appear that full repairs notice procedures only rarely end in local authorities having to undertake CPO action. This is presumably helped by the knowledge of owners that, first, (under the Historic Buildings and Ancient Monuments Act, 1953) local authorities may be able to defray the expenses they incurred, and secondly, if 'deliberate neglect' can be shown, then the local authority may request an order for 'minimum compensation' under the Planning (LBCA) Act 1990. Thirdly, it is also possible that a low value would be determined in any case as a result of a high cost of repairs – particularly since any development potential of the building would generally be ignored in calculating the basis for compensation.[10] Nevertheless, the comparatively low level of full repairs notices issued (in relation to the 36 700 listed buildings thought by English Heritage to be 'at risk')[11] would appear to reflect the financial worries of local authorities, as mentioned earlier.

The availability of grants (or, as has been suggested, tax incentives) towards repair and restoration costs at x could in theory raise NARs and capital values sufficiently (for example to PV^1 in figure 5.12) to prevent dereliction from occurring in year y. While GARs may then rise if the building gains subsequently in value (as shown by the upturn in PV^1), this would not, on its own, be sufficient to prevent redevelopment at point x. While a combination of listing and grants might prove successful, the amount of cash available from central government in the form of grants is, in practice, limited and tends to be restricted to around 6 per cent of the total of just over 441 000 listed buildings (that is, those classified as Grade I and Grade II* – although such classification does not in itself guarantee a grant).

Finally, the granting of permission for the building to be adapted to a more intensive use (for example, industrial or residential to offices) may sometimes provide a level of future NARs sufficient to cover not only the costs of repair and renovation, but also to prevent redevelopment from taking place (as shown by PV^2 in figure 5.12), thus safeguarding the building in the long term. Unfortunately, only a small proportion of historic buildings are likely to be conserved in this way and, even where alternative uses are found, their demands (especially offices) may require major alterations to many interior features (for example, floor-to-ceiling height).

In conclusion, the conservation of historic buildings will only occasionally be resolved by market forces[12] and, overall, greater financial support is required. Many historic buildings – provided they are not left to decay – have the potential not only to provide good service and tax revenues in the future,

but also to enhance the national and architectural heritage for future generations. Yet nearly a quarter of listed buildings are at risk from neglect or in
need of repair to prevent them becoming at risk. English Heritage alone has a
£56 million backlog of conservation work for over 400 national monuments
and historic buildings in its care.[13]

REFERENCES

1. *Money into Property* (Debenham Tewson & Chinnocks, 1987).
2. 'Unitization: Threat or Opportunity?', *Estates Gazette* (6 June 1987).
3. P. R. A. Kirkman and D. C. Stafford, 'The Property Bond Movement 1966–74',
   National Westminster Bank Quarterly Review (February 1975).
4. R. Barras, 'The Development Cycle in the City of London', *C.E.S. Research Series* 36.
5. R. Barras, 'The Returns from Office Development and Investment', *C.E.S. Research Series* 35.
6. *MGL–CIG Property Index 1978–86* (Morgan Grenfell Laurie).
7. L. S. Bourne, *Private Redevelopment of the Central City*, Research Paper No. 112
   (University of Chicago Press, 1967).
8. P. Larkham, 'Conservation and the Changing Urban Landscape', *Progress in Planning*, 37, Pt 2 (1992).
9. C. Pugh, 'The Refurbishment of Shopping Centres', *Property Management*, 10, 1
   (1992).
10. R. Picard, 'Listed Buildings: Strengthening of the Powers of Protection and Pre-
    vention', *Property Management*, 11, 2 (1992).
11. English Heritage, '*Buildings at Risk: a Sample Survey* (English Heritage, 1992)
12. J. Harvey, *Urban Land Economics*, 3rd edn (Macmillan, 1992).
13. English Heritage, *Annual Report and Accounts 1992–3*.

6

Welfare Economics, Land and the Environment

One only needs to cast a glance at urban activities to realise the degree to which actions are encouraged or constrained in some way in an attempt to bring about a more efficient allocation of resources: control of urban traffic flows, subsidies to public transport, planning controls and limits on permitted housing densities, to name but a few. In addition, public-sector infrastructure projects (such as roads, bridges and airports) will generally affect the well-being or welfare of a large number of individuals, and since many of these benefits (and costs) are of a non-monetary nature, economic theory must provide the means to assess such changes.

In the private sector, direct monetary costs and benefits (revenue) determine the profitability or otherwise of increased output and investment. In the public sector, all (not only monetary) costs and benefits for *all* individuals affected by an investment must in some way be evaluated. Welfare economics, then, is the study of how such economic changes can be assessed in terms of the welfare implications that affect individuals in society.

Welfare economics helps to address such problems as how to evaluate costs and benefits of a non-monetary nature, how to assess social benefit when no charge is made for a public facility (such as parks, open spaces and monuments) and how to adjust for market failure – for example, when decisions are made in the private sector or by private individuals which fail to reflect costs imposed on others (such as urban traffic).

First, it is necessary to consider how we can define and compare the welfare, utility or well-being of individuals in society. Secondly, the measurement and assessment of levels of welfare and changes therein must be addressed. Thirdly, the question of whether the free market can always be relied upon to maximise the well-being or welfare of society must be considered. Fourthly, the means by which the public sector evaluates the welfare implications of investment projects (cost-benefit analysis) must be looked at closely. Lastly, the case for public control over the urban environment must be examined, with reference to examples.

THE CONCEPT OF ECONOMIC WELFARE

Few people would argue with the observation that as an individual's consumption of goods and services increases, so his/her well-being, satisfaction or economic welfare might also be expected to increase. In practice, this could occur either because of a rise in the individual's income (with prices of goods and services unchanged) or because of a fall in the price of some goods and services consumed by that individual (assuming the individual's income remains unchanged). Of course, the individual's increased consumption of, say, cigarettes might conceivably do him/her some harm, but in general it must be assumed here that the individual knows best. In other words, his/her change in welfare must be measured as s/he him/herself values it – that is, in relation to what s/he is willing to pay to achieve a particular pattern of consumption. Problems arise, however, when we try to go further. For example, how is the welfare of different individuals to be compared? If it is realised that different individuals will generally have different capacities for deriving satisfaction from a unit of expenditure, the problem of making interpersonal comparisons of welfare becomes apparent.

To take a simple problem, how is a move from a situation where all the population have real incomes of £100 per week to one where half the population have £200 per week and the rest nothing, to be assessed? Both yield the same overall monetary value for society but with very different distributional consequences. While traditional measures of national output or consumption suffer from these (and other) problems of interpretation, we can for the moment fall back on another criterion for assessing economic changes which provides a more widely acceptable starting point.

In an attempt to remove the problem of interpersonal comparisons in assessing changes in social welfare, Vilfredo Pareto (1848–1923) suggested the following criterion: any economic change can be unambiguously said to improve social welfare only if at least one member's welfare increases while no other individual's welfare diminishes. Changes which satisfy this criterion are termed 'Pareto improvements' or 'gains'. This proposition is illustrated in figure 6.1.

The vertical and horizontal axes measure the level of satisfaction or utility of two individuals, *A* and *B*. At the initial position *r* the welfare levels of *A* and *B* can be seen by reading off the corresponding points on the two axes. Alternative situations *s* and *t* correspond to different bundles and distribution of goods between *A* and *B*. They yield situations where one individual is better off while the utility of the other individual is unchanged. However, at a position such as *u*, both individuals are better off. In contrast, at *v* both are worse off. Of all these changes, *s*, *t* and *u* all conform to the criterion for a Pareto improvement. In fact, any position between *s* and *t*, within the shaded area, also conforms to this criterion.

In practice, situations are likely to arise where although one or more individuals may suffer from a change, a great many others may, in fact, gain. Kaldor[1] and Hicks[2] suggested that as long as the gainers from such a change

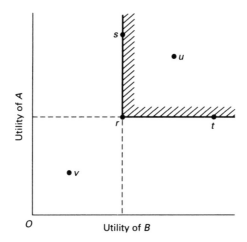

Figure 6.1 *Pareto gains and losses*

could fully compensate the losers while themselves remaining better off, the change could produce a net welfare gain for society in line with the Pareto criterion. Kaldor went on to suggest that the job of the economist was only to point out when such a gain was possible, the actual process of compensation being another matter – political, legal or interpersonal in nature. Such changes could then be termed *potential* Pareto improvements, and the concept is clearly more attractive and operational than one where no one should lose out from any project.

Again, the point can be illustrated using the same diagram as previously, but assuming this time that output is fixed and corresponds to a particular bundle of goods which may in principle be distributed in a variety of ways between individuals *A* and *B*. Line *11* illustrates this proposition (figure 6.2) and combinations of welfare between the two consumers may occur anywhere along this utility possibility curve depending on the distribution of goods. Similarly, *22* represents possible outcomes resulting from alternative distributions at a higher level of output.

The actual position of the individuals along any utility possibility curve or frontier such as *11* or *22* will be determined by the distribution of income between them. However, this will have been determined by the level of production itself, since the consumers are also the owners of factors of production within the economy. In sum, given the ownership of factors, any level of output automatically determines factor rewards and therefore the distribution of income. The latter in turn determines what goods the individuals may purchase and consequently their respective levels of welfare. If, for example, there is a move from *11* to *22*, it may be found that the two individuals move from a point such as *a* on *11* to one such as *b* on *22*. Individual *A* is clearly worse off at *b* since the income distribution and relative prices have moved against him. Nevertheless, a Pareto gain is possible: *B* could in principle take a cut in con-

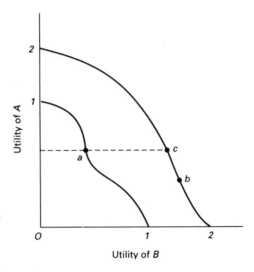

Figure 6.2 *Potential Pareto improvements*

sumption along *22*, donate goods to *A* and thus raise *A*'s welfare back to his/
her pre-change position at *c*. According to the Hicks–Kaldor criteria, the change
from *a* to *b* would be approved as a potential Pareto gain.

Of course, in the absence of lump sum taxes on beneficiaries such as *B*,
there is no way of actually compelling *B* to compensate *A* (unless *B* has in
some way infringed *A*'s property rights). Clearly, it is no good relying on *B*'s
altruism to solve this problem, but without payment of compensation a Pareto
gain remains only a possibility rather than an established event.

The problem of how to measure costs and benefits of an intangible nature
will be dealt with later. For the moment we need to look at how, in general,
non-priced benefits and costs relate to the present notion of social welfare and
changes within it.

WELFARE, EXTERNALITIES AND PUBLIC GOODS

In relating measures of welfare to output of goods and services in the economy,
such as gross national product (GNP), we are assuming implicitly that the welfare
of individuals and societies is dependent on the consumption of *marketed* as
opposed to *non-marketed* output. Hence, such measures of economic welfare
will largely avoid valuing the quality of, say, environmental services. In a broad
sense these include aspects of both the physical and the social environment;
for example, the quality of air and water, the countryside and access to it, and
the right to peace and quiet.

First of all, however, a general model needs to be developed which will
give a view of the components of the economic system as a whole. This model

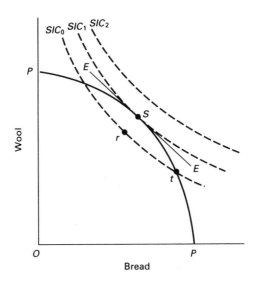

Figure 6.3 *Welfare maximisation: a simple model*

may then be adapted to include also non-marketed goods and services.

We shall start with a simple model which comprises two individuals, two marketed goods and two factors of production. Factor and good markets are assumed to be perfectly competitive. Combining the two factors (say, land and labour) in the production of different quantities of the two goods, the production frontier *PP* given in figure 6.3 can be derived. Moving along *PP* it can be seen how many units of one good can be exchanged in production for one unit of the other good. This is known as the marginal rate of transformation. The concave shape of *PP* illustrates that factors are not equally efficient in each sector, so that when resources are transferred from, say, wool to bread production, although the latter increases, it does so at a diminishing rate. Combinations of the two goods (here bread and wool) which are to the left of *PP*, such as *r*, are clearly *possible* but also *inefficient* and correspond to sub-optimal use of the two factors.

The two consumers' preferences for the two goods available are given by the series of social indifference curves, *SIC*. Higher curves denote higher levels of welfare for *both* consumers. Points along each curve denote bundles of the two goods between which the two individuals are indifferent (that is, yield identical levels of welfare).

For the two individuals to maximise welfare, production and consumption must occur at *s*, which corresponds to the highest attainable *SIC*. At this point, SIC_1 is at a tangent to the production frontier, and the slopes of both curves are therefore the same (*EE*). This indicates that the rate at which goods are exchanged in production along the production frontier (marginal rate of transformation) is equal to the rate at which the individuals wish to exchange the same goods in consumption (marginal rate of substitution). These rates are in turn equal to the market price ratio of the two goods *EE*, which can therefore be viewed as the price ratio under conditions of welfare maximisation. A point such as *t*, while being *technically efficient* in the sense of being on the production frontier, is *economically inefficient* in terms of welfare maximisation. This can be seen either because it corresponds to a lower level of social welfare, SIC_0, or because the marginal rates of substitution and transformation differ; specifically, at the margin, society would prefer to exchange bread for more wool in consumption even if the relative price of wool rises (as occurs when we move from *t* to *s*).

Unfortunately, imperfections in the functioning of the free market may in practice prevent a position such as *s* being reached. There are several potential sources of market imperfection which affect good or factor prices; they include monopolistic control of production, various distortions in factor markets and the non-pricing of certain resources. It is principally the latter which is of most concern for present purposes. The non-pricing of certain resources (for example, environmental services) is in practice quite common and results because production (or consumption) in one sector of the economy can have a negative influence on production (or consumption) in another sector, without any corresponding monetary (or other transfer) taking place. Such non-market effects are called 'externalities', and these will now be considered in more detail.

Externalities

Externalities can be defined as benefits or costs which accrue to an individual, group or firm as a direct result of *consumption* or *production* by another individual, group or firm for which no price is paid or no payment is received. In the following discussion we shall deal mainly with *negative* externalities that involve non-market costs between individuals/firms, individuals/individuals or firms/firms. *Positive* externalities involving non-market benefits also exist and their analysis is simply a mirror image of the former.

Let us assume that, still in the context of the previous model, we have a case of 'production on production' externality. Assume that two goods are produced (beer and leather), and that the factory producing leather dumps toxic waste products into the river, resulting in the beer factory downstream having to treat its water supply, which is required for brewing. The resultant increase in costs for the brewery may well be in excess of the cost if the waste had been treated initially at the tannery.

Let us assume this is the case and that for only a very small extra cost the leather firm could eliminate its waste – although quite clearly it will not do so unless there is some legal or financial constraint imposed. If the amount of labour available is fixed, we can illustrate the output possibilities in the two industries as in figure 6.4.

Lines *OL* and *OB* show the output possibilities for each industry considered *separately*. They show, for example, that if six units of labour are employed in

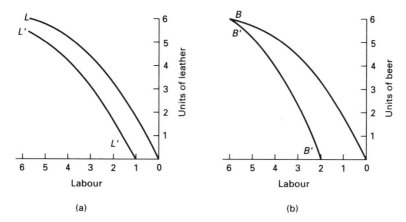

Figure 6.4 *'Production on production' externalities*

each industry, a total of six units each of leather and beer may be produced. However, since we have assumed that leather production imposes a negative externality on beer production, we need to establish the outcome when *both* industries are considered *together*. This situation is illustrated by *B′B′* and *OL*; leather production is unchanged (*OL*) but beer production is now lower for any number of labour units employed (assuming for simplicity that some units are employed in eliminating the source of the problem). As illustrated, *OB* and *B′B′* touch at a certain point. This is because we have assumed fixed resources (say six units of labour), so that the point of intersection of *B′B′* and *OB* corresponds to zero production of leather, where all units are employed in beer production.

The final line, *L′L′*, illustrates the position in the leather firm where costs of removing the toxic waste are taken into account. For simplicity it has been assumed that this involves a fixed cost of diverting one unit of labour towards some alternative method of waste removal.

The production frontier facing this society for any combination of employment between the two industries can now be derived. In figure 6.5, *SS* illustrates the production frontier when leather production is uncontrolled, and *S′S′* illustrates the case when the leather firm undertakes waste removal. The latter represents the 'true' production frontier reflecting the *social* (as opposed to the *private*) marginal rate of transformation, but will clearly only be reached if the leather producer has some incentive (or duty) to control waste disposal. Only if this occurs is society able to reach a higher social indifference curve SIC_1 which in this case also results in higher production levels of *both* goods (from *a* to *b*). In the presence of externalities (as discussed previously) such a move can be achieved by setting an appropriate tax on the firm or group which generates the externalities (more details will be given later). This process is referred to as '*internalisation*', that is, the setting of a market price on otherwise non-priced cost (or benefits). In this case, only if the external cost is

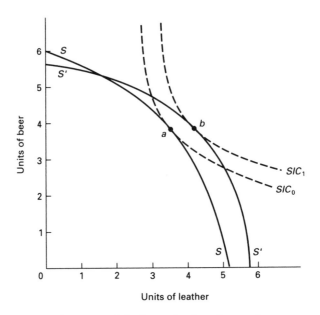

Figure 6.5 *Production frontiers and the internalisation of external costs*

made internal to the leather firm will optimal decisions regarding output and pricing be made in the economy.[3] As a result, social welfare can be maximised at point *b*.

One final comment on this example is that we have not included any estimation of the possible benefits accruing to other users of the river (for example, from fishing, bathing, etc.). If such benefits exist then the policy will clearly have resulted in both a greater production volume and an improved level of environmental quality. For other types of externality, such as those which impinge directly on the individuals' consumption of, say, environmental benefits, the analysis is complicated because such consumption does not generally rate in any standard monetary measure of national welfare. For example, while the construction of a new airport will bring measurable economic benefits, the disbenefits to nearby residents in terms of noise, congestion and pollution will not be included in measures of national welfare such as GNP. Nevertheless, it is clear that these external effects have a real impact on personal welfare.

The problem then is one of evaluating such non-monetary gains and losses and expressing them in monetary terms. This will be discussed, but before doing so there is another important category of goods, the provision of which involves externalities. Such goods are known as *public goods*.

Public goods

The reference to 'public' implies anything from a group of individuals to a locality or region, country or group of countries. A pure *public* good has characteristics which are opposite to those of a pure *private* good. The latter are *rival* in the sense that consumption of the good (for example, a shirt) by one person precludes its consumption by another person or persons. Following from this, it is clear that the greater the demand by consumers, the more units of the good must be produced and the more resources must be devoted to the production of these units.

Private goods also have the characteristic of *excludability* – a unit or units of the good can be consumed by one person to the exclusion of others, and consumption of the good affects the welfare of no other individual. The latter condition implies an absence of externalities.

In contrast, 'pure' public goods are both *non-rival* and *non-excludable*. They are non-rival in the sense that one unit can satisfy more than one consumer, implying that no additional resources are required as the number of consumers rises. Public goods are non-excludable in that once provided, it is impossible to exclude anyone from consuming them – in other words, the effects of providing a good are automatically extended to the whole community. As such, the good is associated with (positive) externalities (such as street lighting). Perhaps the most obvious example is national defence. The decision by governments to provide defence automatically extends the benefits to all, regardless of whether or not they have contributed to its expense (non-excludable). Also, the cost is essentially the same however many people are covered by defence (that is, non-rival). In practice, few goods are 'pure' public goods. Many goods, however, share certain public good characteristics.

One of the key points shared by public goods is that provision would either not occur or would be sub-optimal if left to the free market. This problem arises because, since provision automatically benefits everyone, it is in the interest of the individual to understate his/her preferences and avoid payment. In other words, individuals would attempt to 'free-ride' (that is, avoid payment) while still enjoying the benefits of the good. If this is true for each individual, then, taken as a whole, society may not provide the good even if it is in everyone's interest to do so. Of course, it is possible that one or more individuals who rate the good very highly in their scale of preferences might be prepared to foot the bill. One problem here is that the good may then reflect only the preferences of these individuals and be underprovided relative to the preferences of the rest of the community.

Clearly, also, no producer would wish to undertake marketed production of the good, since it would be impossible to prevent individuals consuming the good without paying (non-rival).

In contrast, the state will often be in a better position to estimate the demand for public goods, undertake their provision and organise payment via taxation. Nevertheless, problems may remain – in particular, some individuals may be taxed too highly relative to their valuation of the good, while others may be taxed too lightly. However, in the context of a large number of public goods, individuals may find that excess taxation for some public goods may be offset by undertaxation relative to their preferences for others.

While the case for supply via public institutions may appear clear-cut in the case of 'pure' public goods, it has been shown that many goods exhibit only *some* public good characteristics. Is there, then, a case for public supply of these goods? For example, while environmental resources such as air quality, water quality, peace and quiet, and open spaces are largely public goods in the sense that once provided they are widely available, they may nevertheless be rival and excludable in the sense that spatial opportunities for their consumption may differ. Facilities such as open spaces in urban areas may become congested so that additional users reduce the benefits to existing users. In particular, residential immobility may mean that different groups in society have unequal access to environmental resources. If income were evenly distributed and households perfectly mobile, spatial differences in access to environmental resources might not matter. Individuals with low environmental preferences could continue to live in, say, decaying inner cities, while those with high environmental preferences could choose to live in more peaceful locations with greater access to environmental resources. Other things being equal, substantial local differences in environmental services would eventually become capitalised in different property values. Since, however, assumptions relating to income distribution and housing mobility are probably not met, the likely result is that residents living in low environmental conditions are not so much those who place low values on such resources as those who cannot afford to move or who cannot find similar accommodation elsewhere.

Another important example of 'impure' public goods involves goods where, although it is possible to exclude consumers, it would be inefficient or suboptimal to do so. Examples of such goods are public roads, museums, bridges and parks, Here, as long as there is no congestion of the facility, there is no additional cost, either in provision or to other users, of adding one more consumer. In principle, a toll or other charge could be made, but such a charge (assuming no congestion) would lead to a lowering of welfare. This point can be illustrated by considering a major tunnel project.

Assume, first, that the welfare benefits of the project – that is, the sum total of the potential users' willingness to pay – can be measured accurately from the demand curve for the good in question.[4] It will also be assumed that the social (or opportunity) cost of the project is reflected accurately in the costs involved, measured in monetary terms, and that overall, the total benefits of the project outweigh the total costs.

In the present case, the demand curve for tunnel crossings could be estimated from analysis of existing traffic flows in the area plus some estimate of traffic likely to be generated by the new facility. A social cost-benefit analysis would also include indirect benefits (or costs) of the project such as reduction on congestion elsewhere, but for purposes of simplicity such effects will be ignored in the present case.

The estimated demand curve is given by *DD* in figure 6.6. It shows that at a zero price per crossing C_1 crossings would be undertaken, while at a charge of P_1 no crossings at all would be undertaken. If the tunnel is provided pub-

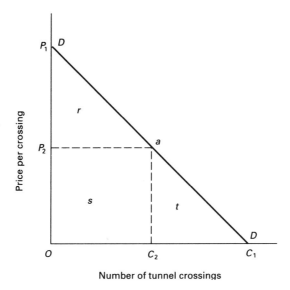

Figure 6.6 *Demand curve for tunnel crossings*

licly at zero user cost, then the total welfare gain (willingness to pay) is given by the area under the demand curve DD. If, however, the tunnel is provided and run by private individuals who charge a toll, the result will be different. Assuming revenue maximisation is desired, the private supplier will charge a toll such as P_2 per crossing. In this case only C_2 crossings will be undertaken, and $C_1 - C_2$ crossings will have been dissuaded by the toll. The benefit derived from C_2 crossings is given by the areas r and s, which represent the willingness to pay for these crossings. However, the actual revenue received is only area s (that is, $P_2 \times C_2$). The remaining area, known as the *consumer surplus* (area r) represents the difference between willingness to pay and the amount actually paid for the service.

It is immediately evident that the reduced number of crossings results in a lower level of consumer benefit – that is, area $r + s$ in contrast to area $r + s + t$, where no charge is made. Although revenue of area s is obtained by the tunnel operator, this is of no allocative importance; the tunnel would otherwise have been financed via taxation, and charging a toll merely constitutes another form of payment. Area t, however, is of allocative significance as it represents a lowering of welfare because fewer crossings are undertaken with a toll. A further feature is of note: if the total cost of the project had been estimated to be just above $r + s$ (which is still exceeded by total benefits of $r + s + t$, assuming zero user cost), then although the project would have produced a net welfare gain, no private supplier (charging a positive price) would have been able to provide the tunnel, assuming similar costs.

Are there ever circumstances under which even the public sector would be justified in charging a toll? In practice, such charges are observed on the Severn

Bridge and the Dartford Tunnel in London, and are widely observed on motorways, bridges and tunnels throughout Europe.

Several explanations may be put forward. First, the facility may be largely specific to a particular area or group of users, and in practice it may be impossible to distinguish such groups in order to cover construction and ongoing costs through taxation. In practice, however, with increasing long-distance private travel and haulage it may become more difficult to view any particular facility as region- or area-specific, thereby increasing the case for deriving revenue from road taxation or even personal or indirect taxation. This is especially true if there are important non-monetary costs involved in actually charging a tool, such as long delays.

Secondly, it is possible that excessive use of the facility will itself result in non-monetary costs – for example, too many visitors may result in damage to historic monuments or may affect the enjoyment of other visitors. If the facility becomes congested, causing damage, delay or other forms of externality, then a charge in proportion to the damage and inconvenience caused becomes justified, since it is now no longer the case that the good can be enjoyed by everyone, irrespective of the number of users.

A final and important category of public goods involves goods which, although mainly rival and excludable, nevertheless exhibit important external benefits. Such goods (known as merit goods) include health, education, housing, public libraries and fire services.

In principle these goods could all be provided by the private sector but, because of externalities, private provision would result in sub-optimal supply. Additionally, it may be felt that public provision at low or zero user cost is preferable to private provision, since even if the latter is subsidised, there may nevertheless be individuals who are too poor to afford even this. Moreover, the possible 'costs' of non-consumption by the individual may be high or so severe that public provision at zero user cost is considered indispensable (for example, the fire service).

There exist numerous types of activity which exhibit actual or potential externalities. While the case for direct public control does not extend equally to all such activities, indirect control in the form of taxes and subsidies can often achieve the desired result of optimal resource allocation.

HOUSING, EXTERNALITIES AND PUBLIC POLICY

Consider urban housing improvement where property-on-property type externalities exist. In such cases, properties are generally run-down and in need of renovation. This will involve substantial financial outlay for long-term improvements such as reroofing, rewiring, plumbing and glazing, as well as for shorter-term but more 'obvious' improvements such as redecorating. If all properties in the area were renovated then it is likely that property values would rise sufficiently to at least compensate owners for their expenditure on major maintenance items. However, if only one or a few owners undertake the investment, their property values alone might not increase sufficiently to compensate them if the area as a whole remains undesirable. Worse than this, if the area was already in a state of cumulative decline, house owners who invested might find they had done so in an asset that was actually declining in real value.[5] In this situation, nothing may persuade house owners to undertake major or even more minor repairs.

The problem, of course, is that while everyone may gain from joint action to improve an area, the benefits derived from housing renovation are substantially *non-excludable* in the sense that external benefits to other householders (who do nothing) occur in the form of an improved neighbourhood and, hence, higher property values. The 'residential environment' can be said, therefore, to have public good characteristics, and in consequence faces problems of suboptimal provision. Many households are likely to 'free-ride' and enjoy the benefits of an improved environment (and higher property values) without undertaking investment. Yet if everyone does the same, no renovation will occur, even though all may want it. This situation is referred to as the 'prisoner's dilemma'.[6]

One solution is for improvement grants to be concentrated on areas of greatest housing decay. This would provide confidence in an area and encourage owners to undertake improvements which they might not otherwise contemplate for the reasons just discussed. As long as the overall benefits to residents exceed costs to the state in subsidy and administration, plus the renovation costs paid by residents themselves, then the project will have produced a net improvement in social welfare.

Alternatively, or in addition, the state or local government could undertake selective compulsory purchase followed by renovation and eventual sale or letting on to the residential market. Lastly, with wider use of compulsory purchase powers, wholesale redevelopment of an area may be contemplated.

Whichever solution is chosen, some form of public intervention is required to ensure that existing residents do not lose out. They may suffer if, for example, excessive private redevelopment in more intensive uses (such as offices) occurs, or if over-extensive housing redevelopment causes large-scale residential displacement. If housing improvement programmes simply push existing residents into even more precarious housing conditions, then the change can hardly be described as a 'Pareto improvement'.

Public intervention in housing supply provides a further example. The case for public provision of subsidised housing has traditionally rested on three main arguments. First is the argument for redistribution in kind, which assumes that certain groups in society, for a variety of reasons, are likely to under-consume housing and remain ill-housed in spite of quite high levels of public spending on income support. Secondly, and linked to the first argument, is the view that society must ensure that a minimum standard of housing consumption is established and maintained. Although other reasons may exist (for example, to avoid overcrowding), the principle one may be that poor housing standards represent an environmental health risk. Public supply of low-cost housing may thus be

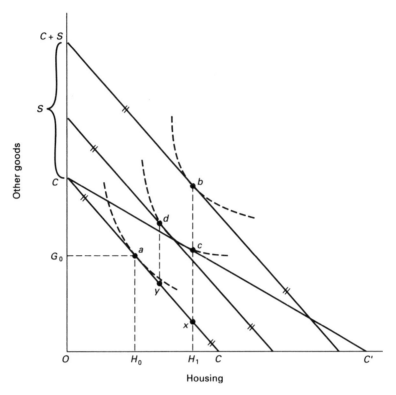

Figure 6.7   *Housing subsidies and the consumption of housing services*

seen partly as an alternative to controlling standards at the lower end of the private housing (and rented) sector. Thirdly, since a system of income subsidies alone may be unable to tackle regional and local shortages of adequate housing for low-income families, it may be thought necessary to intervene on the supply side to provide sufficient housing of suitable standard directly, at an affordable and controlled cost to residents.

The problem associated with a 'pure' income subsidy to tenants can be illustrated by comparing income transfers with price subsidies, such as low-cost housing provision. In figure 6.7, point a on the Budget line CC gives the initial position of the low-income household. At this point it is achieving its highest possible level of welfare, given its (non-subsidised) budget constraint. It is consuming H_0 housing and G_0 other goods at this point.

Assume that the government wishes to achieve a minimum standard of housing consumption equal to H_1. If it provides an income subsidy it will need to raise the household's income level to $C + S$ to achieve this ($C + S$ is parallel to CC but vertically above it by the level of subsidy). The household now maximises welfare at point b on the new budget line $C + S$. Note that if the pattern of household indifference curves had shown less preference for housing as income rose, then the degree of subsidy S required to achieve H_1 would have been much greater.

Alternatively, the government could lower the relative price of housing to CC' (say, via public provision) and could then enforce a minimum standard of housing H_1. Suppose this is what happens and compare this situation with the alternative of an income subsidy discussed earlier. By providing H_1 housing at a reduced cost to the household of CC', the total cost to the state is given by the vertical distance between CC and CC', that is, xc. The cost of the income subsidy which would be required to achieve the same objective is given by the vertical distance between C and $C + S$, and is equal to S or xb. It can be seen that xb clearly exceeds xc, illustrating the point that the least-cost method of achieving a target level of housing consumption is via direct provision/price subsidy.

In most European countries these aims have been achieved through the quasi-public sector – including co-operatives, housing associations and municipal housing corporations, which generally have received public subsidies in return for maintaining quality levels, a given proportion of low-income tenants and approved rents.

But what has happened to household welfare? It can be argued that since b lies on a higher indifference curve than c, the income subsidy has raised household welfare by a greater amount than the price subsidy. The point here, however, is whether society really wishes to achieve this degree of redistribution – if xb is judged to be excessive, then the price subsidy should be favoured instead. In practice, however, the state cannot even be sure that an income subsidy of xb will be sufficient to persuade all low-income households to consume a minimum of H_1 housing. Some may purchase considerably more and others less, yet it is impossible to vary the subsidy in line with individual preferences!

In conclusion, then, the view that income transfers are in some way optimal, in that they allow more individual choice than subsidies to housing provision, cannot be supported, assuming that the main reason for intervention is because of negative externalities (social costs) generated by low-standard housing. To make this point absolutely clear, a comparison can be made with an income support policy of the same budgetary cost as the price subsidy. This is shown by dy (equals cx) in figure 6.7. As shown, d corresponds to the same level of welfare as point c, but to a level of housing consumption well below the desired level of H_1. The situation could just as easily have involved both a lower level of welfare *and* lower housing consumption. A number of studies show that the income elasticity of demand for housing rarely exceeds unity, suggesting that rather large income transfers may be required to encourage housing consumption.[7]

In practice, local authority housing and housing association accommodation probably conform most to the idea of a 'pure' price subsidy (achieved through central government grant). Mortgage interest relief (MIR) probably conforms less; although MIR no longer has a 'perverse' income effect (lowering the relative price of housing *more* for *higher* income groups because of relief at higher marginal tax rates), it still does nothing to help those on low or variable incomes who could not in any case obtain (sufficient) mortgage finance.

COST-BENEFIT ANALYSIS

In the private sector, investment decisions are made with reference to the market mechanism on the basis of estimated monetary costs and benefits (see Chapter 5). Cost-benefit analysis (CBA) is basically an extension of these investment appraisal methods with modifications to make them suitable for project appraisal in the public sector. The main distinction is that public-sector CBA attempts to account for all the costs and benefits which affect the welfare of individuals, including those of a non-monetary nature. To facilitate comparison and assessment it is usual for such non-monetary costs or benefits to be translated in some way into monetary terms.

From the 1960s onwards, the CBA technique was extended to cover a wide range of applications, including water resource management, motorways, nationalised industries, airport locations, forestry, recreational facilities and a wide range of urban investment projects. While individual projects may pose specific problems, there are a number of considerations which are common to most.

(1) The first of these concerns the notion that projects in the public sector should be capable of achieving a potential Pareto improvement in social welfare. That is, expected social benefits should exceed expected social costs (all appropriately discounted to present values). Here social benefits involve any gain in welfare resulting from the project, including intangible – that is, non-market benefits (for example, investment in public transport may produce benefits in the form of lower congestion, accidents, noise and pollution). Furthermore, since many public facilities (such as parks) are provided free of charge to users, social benefit, determined by willingness to pay (WTP) criteria, may have to be estimated indirectly. Various methods exist and may involve one or more of the following:

(i) Consideration of demand for similar facilities elsewhere for which charges are made (such as historic monuments).
(ii) Extensive questionnaire analysis of potential users. Although the problem here is that in the case of public goods where 'free-riding' occurs, individuals may deliberately understate their preferences.
(iii) By implication from observed behaviour – for example, with recreational facilities (for example, in the Lake District) demand may be seen to fall with increasing distance from the facility. Willingness to pay can be imputed from the additional travel costs (in time and money) that users are known to incur as distance increases.

Social costs will include any intangible costs (such as environmental damage, noise, nuisance and congestion) as well as the construction and ongoing costs of the project – reflecting the production forgone (that is, opportunity cost) when resources are moved to the public sector. Concerning the latter, two problems may arise. First, if there is imperfect competition in the supply of goods (or factors) used in production or construction, then market price may exceed marginal cost – that is, the true cost of the good to society. Seen in another way, if the project's purchase of input X increases the output of a monopolist supplier, the relevant opportunity cost relates to the marginal cost of extra resources hired and not to the observed (and higher price) charged by the monopolist. Similarly, if workers being employed on a project would otherwise have remained unemployed, then hiring them at the going wage will not result in a reduction of output elsewhere in the economy – hence the marginal cost to society is, in fact, less than the wage rate paid to the labourer.[8] It can be noted that the net cost to the Exchequer will also be lower than the wage rate in this case, since the government benefits from lower unemployment and social security payments and receives higher direct and indirect taxes.

Secondly, market prices may require adjustment to take account of indirect taxes (subtracted) or subsidies (added), or because market prices may not reflect social costs adequately (for example, farmers may be unaware that their farming techniques are impoverishing the soil). However, while consideration should always be given to the need for adjusting market prices, in practice it may not always be feasible to do so; in many cases it may be too difficult or too costly to obtain the necessary information with a good degree of accuracy.

(2) The second set of considerations concerns the evaluation of non-market gains and losses. Here it is useful to distinguish two categories of intangibles. The first is where, although no direct market exists, there is nevertheless an indirect (or surrogate) market in other goods which is in some way influenced by the intangibles in question. The process of defining such alternative markets is known as shadow-pricing. For example, although there is no market for peace and quiet, if individuals buying and selling houses are observed to place higher or lower valuations on similar properties in quieter or noisier situations, then resulting differences in house values can be taken to represent the willingness to pay for peace and quiet. However, it is necessary to isolate all other factors influencing property prices; for example, although house prices may fall near motorways or airports, there may exist locational advantages which would tend to counteract the disadvantages. Hence, basing an analysis solely on observed price variations may tend to produce an underestimate of the willingness to pay for peace and quiet. Also, while individuals may be good judges of peace and quiet, they may be less likely to have full information about other environmental effects (such as lead pollution) – but even if they did, it is unlikely that the full effects would be reflected in the housing market, since many households may not have a real choice of relocating elsewhere. Overall, then, the presumption is that intangible costs of an environmental nature are likely to be partially, but not fully, reflected (or internalised) in the property market.

Another example is the valuation of travel time, widely applied in transport studies, where time savings may account for by far the largest category of benefit deriving from motorway or road schemes. A distinction is made between time savings in work-time and those in leisure-time. Concerning the former, hourly earnings (plus some savings on overheads) may be taken to represent production gained from the time saving of one hour (or *pro rata*), assuming that the wage rate is an adequate reflection of the workers' marginal product. One problem here is that, in practice, large rather than small time savings are more likely to result in productive work and, in reverse, longer travel times (for example, by train or aircraft) may not always result in lost production if, for example, businessmen are able to work while travelling. Time savings during leisure time could, theoretically, be valued at a similar rate, since if workers are able to choose their hours of work then, at the margin, they should be expected to value an hour's work at an equivalent rate to an hour's leisure. In practice such choice is rarely available, hence an alternative approach to the evaluation of leisure time must be sought. For example, if an individual is observed to choose a faster but more expensive means of travel in preference to a slower and cheaper alternative, then as long as no other factors (such as comfort) come into play, his/her willingness to pay for time saved on the faster route in terms of the cost difference can be measured. Using this method, various studies have suggested that leisure-time values are proportional to travellers' incomes, at around 25 per cent of the latter, although considerably higher or lower values cannot be ruled out.[9]

It is likely that, in practice, an individual's valuation of leisure time may vary from case to case and depend on many other factors, including frequency, length of trip and means of travel. Nevertheless, travel-time evaluation has played an important role in many studies, including the Roskill Commission Study on the third London airport, and the Victoria Line Study.[10] In the former, although the Foulness site produced the lowest estimates of noise-nuisance cost, the procedure adopted resulted in these benefits being vastly outweighed by its more distant location because of the high valuation placed on travel-time savings of relatively high-income air passengers. In the Victoria Line Study, the valuation of travel time proved less contentious. Since the new line would benefit passengers (over and above the revenue collected) it was reasonable to assume that users would have been willing to pay for the extra convenience (and time saving) of a direct line. Furthermore, since congestion would be reduced elsewhere in the transport system, some estimate of time savings here was essential.

A second category of intangibles involves those for which no efficient surrogate market exists. The Roskill Commission Study just mentioned, for example, placed no value on the loss of wildlife or preservation of countryside because of the difficulty of valuation. Yet even in these circumstances, a residual approach may be adopted. If a dam project, for example, is expected to produce an excess of measurable benefits over costs of £2 million, decision-makers can at least come to some conclusion as to whether they consider this figure to be sufficient to outweigh the loss of countryside and recreational amenities. The attractions of this approach may, however, be reduced if many intangibles exist.

(3) Distributional issues represent the third major consideration. Even if a project is expected to produce an excess of social benefit over social cost, there may still be some objection that the criterion of a potential Pareto improvement tells us nothing about *who* gains and *who* loses. In other words, as it stands, the criterion carries no distributional weight; it cannot, for example, help us to decide between, say, two projects where the first benefits everyone by £10 and the second benefits only the richest by £20 and all others suffer losses – since both could achieve a potential Pareto gain. It is worth stressing at this point that the distributional question does not arise when compensation is actually made, since the welfare of any losers is maintained and, overall, there is still a net improvement in social welfare (in theory by transfers from gainers who still remain better off). In contrast, when compensation is not made – which is, in fact, common because of the impracticality of lump-sum transfers – the distributional question becomes a key issue.

Clearly, individual monetary assessments of gains or losses (in terms of WTP) are likely to be strongly dependent on the level of personal income. It follows that project assessment will therefore tend to place relatively greater weight on the demands (or costs) of those on high incomes, and relatively less weight on the demands (or costs) of those on low incomes. For example, strict adherence to WTP criteria might suggest that road projects in urban areas should be located nearer to low-income housing than high-income housing, since the latter's WTP assessment of noise nuisance (reflected in house values) could generally be expected to exceed the former's.

If no adjustment of the WTP evaluation of gains or losses is made, then projects are being assessed implicitly on criteria that reflect the existing distribution of income. As Pearce has suggested, this is tantamount to saying that those who have been rewarded once (via higher earnings) should be rewarded once again in the choice of public projects. In contrast, in the above example one might wish to argue that a more widely acceptable assessment of noise nuisance would tend to put rather more weight on the number of individuals involved and the level of noise in alternative schemes than on the higher WTP of high-earning groups. A move in this direction could be achieved by weighting WTP assessments of intangible costs. Hence, values obtained for higher-income groups could be 'scaled down', while values for lower-income groups could be 'scaled up'.

The arguments in favour of adopting weighting procedures are undoubtedly strong since the main aim is to integrate considerations involving both efficiency and distribution. Failure to do so could result in glaring inconsistencies (for example, it might suggest that environmentally damaging projects should be located in 'poor' rather than in 'rich' localities). While it is possible that a weighting procedure would still sanction projects which made the rich richer and the poor poorer, weighting at least ensures that efficiency criteria will have been balanced against distributional considerations.

Although, as we have seen, distributional issues are less important when compensation occurs, even here many problems remain. In particular, compensation may often understate the nuisance caused – for example, houses will be valued at market prices which totally neglect any element of consumer surplus (that is, benefit exists in excess of the market price which an owner will derive from a particular dwelling or location).[11] Additionally, compensation is paid not by the beneficiaries themselves but out of general taxation. Although the cost to an individual taxpayer is minute, when multiplied over numerous projects distributional effects may be significant, especially if costs must be met by taxpayers, many of whom may be on low incomes themselves.

In conclusion, given the choice between two alternative projects producing the same net welfare gain to society, the appeal is clearly greater for the one where fewer people are to be made worse off. In practice, such handy alternatives are rare; in assessing public projects, planners should, at the very least point out the size and allocation of gains and losses together with recommendations concerning the feasibility of compensation.

(4) The fourth major consideration concerns the discount rate, the choice of which involves investment, savings and consumption decisions over time. All saving decisions involve the 'sacrifice' of lower consumption today in exchange for the promise of consumption at a higher level tomorrow. This is achieved by means of investment which places today's resources into production, which will yield results only at some date in the future. The decision of just how much saving and investment should be undertaken today by society can be illustrated, as in figure 6.8.

Consider the simplest case of a single individual in a 'Robinson Crusoe' world who is faced with fixed material resources.[12] His savings/investment decision over two time-periods (t_1 and t_2) concerns how much of his time and effort (in t_1) he should spend on projects (say, farming) which will yield a return in the next period (t_2). Spending his time in this way, however, involves Crusoe in a form of 'saving', since he will have less time to spend on activities (such as, say, collecting fruit) which yield an immediate benefit. This choice is illustrated by CC' which is Crusoe's *production frontier* (or production possibility curve). At the limit, he could consume nothing in t_2 but OC in t_1, or consume nothing in t_1 but (provided he did not starve), OC' in t_2. In general OC' can be expected to exceed OC because of technical advance and the use of capital-intensive production techniques; in Crusoe's case, by developing irrigation in t_1 he may ensure higher food output in t_2 than if he had attempted non-irrigated planting for consumption in t_1.

While Crusoe could achieve any combination of consumption levels given by CC', he will in practice choose that combination which gives him most benefit. This in turn will depend upon his relative preference for consumption in t_2 as against consumption in t_1. Crusoe's indifference curves, three of which are shown on figure 6.8, each tells us the combinations of consumption in t_1 and in t_2, which provide him with identical levels of satisfaction. As usual, higher indifference curves represent higher levels of welfare. In this case, Crusoe would reach his highest indifference curve by being at point s on CC'. This

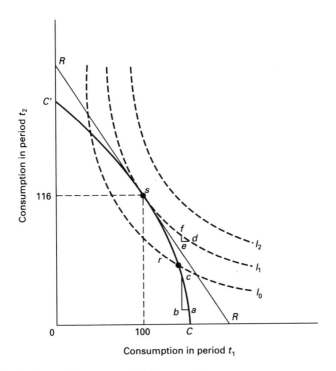

Figure 6.8   *Savings and investment decisions over time*

corresponds to consumption of 100 units in t_1 and 116 units in t_2. But in period t_1, if consumption accounts for only 100 units, this means that remaining resources ($C - 100$) must have been invested for future consumption. In other words, $C - 100$ represents both the level of saving and investment that occurs in t_1.

Point s is unique in that it equates the *time preference* of the individual with the marginal profitability or efficiency of available investment opportunities. These two rates are identical only at point s, and this is shown because the two curves (CC' and I_1) have the same slope (they are tangential) at this point. To show the importance of this, consider the two small triangles *abc* and *def*; *ab* and *de* represent one unit less of consumption in t_1. Considering I_1, it can be seen that (at the margin) Crusoe is indifferent between losing *de* in t_1 as long as he is rewarded by *ef* in t_2. But looking at the corresponding segment of the production frontier, it can be seen that the investment opportunities facing him are so good that he can achieve *cb* (which is greater than *fe*) by forgoing a unit of consumption in t_1. The reader should convince her/himself that the same conclusion applies to all units sacrificed in t_1 as Crusoe moves back from C to s. After this point the marginal efficiency of investment falls below Crusoe's rate of time preference. Only at s are these two rates identical and equal to RR. If RR represents points on the two axes of 200 units in t_1 and 220 units in t_2, then the rate of discount in the economy is such that 220 units in t_2 will have a present value (that is, in t_1) of 200. It can easily be seen that, in this case, the actual discount rate which will produce this result is 10 per cent. That is, given the discounting equation

$$PV = \frac{S}{(1 + r)^n}$$

where PV = present value of a sum S which accrues n periods hence, if r = discount rate (fractional) then

$$PV = \frac{220}{(1 + 0.1)^1} = 220$$

Projects which yield a higher rate of return than 10 per cent (those to the right of s along CC') will be accepted, and those with rates of return below 10 per cent (left of and above point s) will be rejected.

There are a number of features of the real world which very much complicate the above description of the Crusoe economy. In reality, there exist many individuals making separate investment and savings decisions, and these may not always coincide. There are numerous types of investment, long-term and shorter-term, high-risk and low-risk, and in consequence a variety of interest rates also, depending on the credit risks involved and the degree of liquidity.

In view of these considerations, it may be asked whether decisions on savings and investment made by individuals will necessarily prove optimal for society as a whole. For example, while individuals may 'know best' about their own welfare, can they realistically be expected to take a longer-term view involving future generations? If not, then society as a whole – which has such responsibilities – may need to adjust the 'market'-derived discount rate in making its own decisions about whether to invest, and how much.

In order to investigate these issues, figure 6.8 can easily be transformed so that CC' now represents the production frontier facing society and I_1 represents the *social* indifference curve (that is, the consumption patterns between which society is indifferent). Once again, at s the *social rate of time preference* (STP) given by the slope I_1 equals the *marginal efficiency of capital* given by the slope of CC'. The latter is often referred to as the *social opportunity cost* (SOC) of capital, meaning the amount of current resources which has to be given up (or is displaced) to produce a unit of consumption in the future. In practice, it is taken to be represented by the rate of return on marginal projects in the private sector.

Clearly, the only point on the diagram where these two rates, SOC and STP, are equal is at s. Any other point will correspond to a sub-optimal level of investment and savings. The question facing the public sector, then, is how to determine the appropriate discount rate to apply to its own decisions regarding public investment. The problem here is that while the marginal efficiency of capital (MEC) or SOC rate is, in principle, observable, the social time preference rate is not – at least, not directly. This would not matter too much if there were no dispute concerning the equivalence of the SOC and STP rates. The general presumption, however, is that the observable 'market' rate is likely to exceed the STP rate at *s*, so that the economy is in fact at a position such as *r* on the figure, corresponding to lower levels of investment, savings and welfare.

First, market interest rates reflect the *private* rate of return on investment rather than the *social* rate. The latter is likely to be higher than the former because of spill-over effects from one sector to another which raise the productivity of labour and other factors of production elsewhere. Yet only the private rate of return will enter into individual investment decisions. As a result, levels of investment and savings in the economy may be too low (that is, discount rate may be too high).[13]

By itself, company taxation would also cause the market rate to diverge from the STP rate at *s*, since for a firm to pay *RR* per cent to its creditors it must in fact earn a rate of return on its capital in excess of *RR* per cent.[14]

In addition, as Pigou[15] has argued, market rates reflect the fact that individuals are 'myopic' and have an irrational preference for present consumption. If this is indeed that case, then use of market rates reflecting 'myopia' will tend to penalise the assessment of benefits which accrue at some distant point, perhaps to future generations.

For public-sector projects of a long-term nature, the choice of a 'market'-derived test discount rate may, for these reasons, prove particularly objectionable. Pearce,[16] for example, illustrates this problem in the context of evaluating risks associated with the storage of nuclear waste. Say it is known for certain that an event causing £10 billion in damage at current prices will occur 500 years ahead (that is, in year 500). Discounting at 10 per cent using the above formula gives a present value of only 25 pence to the incident! More generally, the implications of this 'scaling-down' effect stretch far and wide to virtually all aspects of longer-term environmental importance.

Finally, the 'market rate reflects the inability of the private sector to "pool" risks across many projects (and taxpayers) in the way the public sector is able to do. As such market rates will reflect a positive "risk premium" which will be higher the greater the lack of risk-pooling by institutions in the private sector.'[17]

In practice, however, the opportunity cost approach – based on commercial rates of return – appears to have dominated thinking on public-sector discounting. In 1969 the Treasury test discount rate for public-sector investment was set at 10 per cent. This was subsequently reduced and most projects are now required to achieve an 8 per cent rate of return. It should be noted, however, that this represents a real rate of return with costs and benefits being expressed in real (that is, inflation-adjusted) values.

In defence of the SOC approach it is sometimes argued that setting a lower discount rate (reflecting STP) would redirect resources from the private to the public sector, since the latter would only need to secure a lower rate of return. Against this it can be argued that the cost of borrowing for the government (that is, the yield on long-term government securities) is in fact lower than for the private sector, reflecting the fact that lending to the government involves no element of risk (that is, it is 'gilt-edged'). While public-sector projects are not themselves without risk, a slightly lower rate than for the private sector would be justified since, as has been seen, a lower element of risk is inherent in public-sector investment as a whole.

Perhaps the strongest argument for adopting a SOC approach is in the case where private-sector output and investment compete directly, and could be displaced by public-sector investment (for example, in haulage). In this event one might wish to ensure that the public sector does at least as well as any private sector projects it displaces.

However, the assumption underlying the SOC approach – that because of increased competition for available savings, public-sector investment in some sense 'crowds-out' private-sector investment – is not entirely without criticism. First, since government revenue comes mainly from taxation (rather than from borrowing), it is not only savings but also consumption that is displaced. If individuals are not content with the rate of return on public investments financed in this way (perhaps reflecting STP), it is up to them to change it via the democratic process. Second, with growing capital mobility it is increasingly difficult to argue that domestic investment is restrained significantly by the level of domestic savings (the United Kingdom, for example, has traditionally been a net exporter of investment funds).

In contrast, the main argument in favour of the STP rate is that it more fully reflects the rate at which society as a whole is prepared to trade present for future consumption.

Thus there appears to be no clear-cut answer to the choice of discount rate and it has even suggested that a compromise approach would be to choose a rate that reflects both SOC and STP. In practice, a variety of rates is often used in sensitivity testing. This is certainly a useful addition to CBA methods, given not only that STP and SOC rates are perceived to differ, but also that estimates of either can vary over time. For example, in the late 1970s real interest rates were, in fact, negative. Equally, estimates of the STP rate are sensitive (and positively related) to future expected growth rates. In the final analysis, it is important to recognise that the outcome of using a higher SOC-derived rate will affect not only the level of public investment but also its direction – penalising public-sector projects where benefits are intrinsically long-term in nature.

Conclusion

While CBA raises many conceptual and operational problems – particularly regarding the valuation of benefits and costs and the choice of discount rate – it has nevertheless established itself as a useful technique. It may not be as exact a technique as might be wished but it does at least provide the decision-maker with a rational framework, and it allows systematic examination of all aspects of a scheme, including intangibles which would not be allowed for in any purely private appraisal. This is an essential part of public-sector investment; simply ignoring non-market effects does not make them go away, since even if CBA is not undertaken, any decision to go ahead or abandon a project carries an implicit statement about the present value of the social costs and benefits involved.

As Lichfield's planning balance sheet approach (PBS)[18] has shown, the technique can be an important aid in the planning process, making clear the types of cost and benefit involved and the groups who are affected. In this approach the community is divided into categories (for example, producers and consumers) and the costs and benefits are calculated for each sector. The totals for the various sectors are then added to establish whether the scheme as a whole produces a net benefit or cost. Many of the items in the planning balance sheet relate to non-monetary costs and benefits; these may often be measured in physical or time units or, where they cannot be quantified in any way, are listed as intangibles. The PBS approach has the advantage of making clear not only the net social benefit of alternative projects but it can also point to their distributional consequences.

For the urban planner, while CBA is potentially a useful aid to planning decisions it does not avoid the need to make value judgements in the comparison of intangibles arising from alternative projects and in the overall conclusions to be drawn from the assessment of costs and benefits. However, as long as such value judgements (for example, relating to distributional effects) are made clear, the analysis cannot be accused of 'subjectivity'.

CBA is least useful where the benefits of a project are intrinsically difficult to value. For example, if security considerations, or perhaps the long-term development of an area, are of overriding importance, then decision-making becomes a political issue. Similarly, where projects may have major irreversible consequences it can be argued that no decision should be made which limits severely the opportunities or options available to future generations. In contrast, CBA is perhaps most useful where a single project or only a few alternative projects are involved and where the range of intangibles is not too wide as to make comparison difficult. In practice, it is often the case that once decisions are made in principle (for example, the Roskill Commission on the Third London Airport), CBA is then brought in to facilitate the choice between alternative projects.

THE VALUATION OF ENVIRONMENTAL RESOURCES

Environmental resources such as clean air and water, peace and quiet, access to the countryside and recreational facilities are valued by the population at large. However, monetary evaluation of the benefits derived from such resources is often essential to support policies to control environmental pollution and the case for spending on projects which may secure environmental improvements.

In these cases, the general principle of valuation is that monetary estimates should reflect *either* what people are willing to pay to gain a benefit (for example, travel cost to recreational facility) *or* the compensation required to accept a cost (for example, increased noise).

A number of methods for deriving such values (for example, travel-cost and hedonic pricing techniques) have already been discussed in the context of CBA. Increasingly, however, environmental resources are being valued using contingent valuation methods (CVM) which involve asking people, under controlled conditions and often indirectly, what they would be prepared to pay to achieve an environmental gain (for example, improvement in air quality) or to preserve an environmental asset (for example a wildlife habitat).[19] Finally, actual markets for environmental resources should not be overlooked. For example, soil erosion or atmospheric pollution can be largely or partially valued by assessing their respective impacts on the value of crop production in farming.

In the case of conservation, it is important to recognise the concept of total economic value (TEV). The TEV of an environmental resource is comprised of two main components: total use value and total non-use value.[20] Total use value itself has two components:

(1) The value to individuals of uses made of the conserved area (for example, recreational visits) and any indirect benefits or functions that the area provides (for example, ecological functions such as drainage); and

(2) Option value, which refers to the value that individuals may place on retaining the facility for possible future use.

Non-use value comprises existence value which refers to the intrinsic value of the area or facility to individuals even though they do not intend to make use of it. Existence values are often associated with decisions to donate to causes involving, say, the protection of endangered species, rainforests, historic buildings and monuments and so on. Contingent valuation methods are particularly useful in encompassing both 'option' and 'existence' values, although one problem with using this method is that it is not generally possible to separate out the component parts of TEV.[21]

Lastly, concern for the future state of the environment underlies the recent philosophy of 'sustainable development', which suggests that current development should not take place at an unacceptable environmental cost to future generations. A 'constant natural assets' rule has also been advocated, which would seek to maintain the stock of environmental assets for future generations.[22] This is not generally taken to mean that no environmental damage should ever occur, but rather that whatever environmental damage is done by a development should be compensated for in similar terms, either through restoration or via alternative provision elsewhere. For example, woodland or wildlife habitats lost through a roadbuilding programme could, in theory, be recreated nearby. Problems arise, however, with unique environments if these are to a large extent irreplaceable.

Several authors have argued that environmental quality should be included

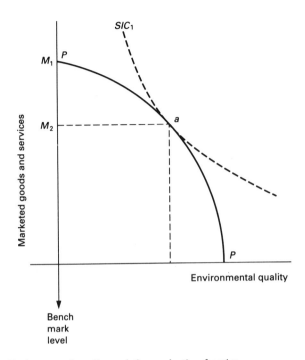

Figure 6.9   *Environmental quality and the production frontier*

in national measures of welfare. There are formidable problems in adopting such an approach, but the main aspects of this line of argument can be shown simply as in figure 6.9. Since the analysis is essentially the same as in the previous diagrams, it will be discussed only briefly. Assuming that an improvement in environmental quality will generally result in a lower level of material consumption (since resources may need to be diverted from the market sector) and vice versa, society's set of choices can be defined along the frontier *PP*. If environmental benefits are given no weight in this system, then it is likely that maximisation of production of marketed goods and services would lead to an extreme position such as M_1. However, if individuals place value on environmental quality (which it is assumed they cannot express via the market), the point which maximises society's welfare is in fact at *a* and SIC_1. At this point, however, measurable income has fallen to M_2!

In many cases, economic development proceeds at an unacceptable cost to the natural environment, to human health and ultimately, to the economy itself through environmental degradation of natural resources. Economies in this position may not even remain on the production frontier shown in figure 6.9. As such, improvements in both environmental quality *and* marketed goods may be possible. Estimates of both non-marketed pollution costs (for example, loss of recreational uses) and marketed pollution costs (for example, forestry and materials damage) in the former Federal Republic of Germany amounted to some

DM103 billion over the period 1983–5, equivalent to around 6 per cent of its gross national product (GNP).[23] The direct effects of environmental degradation on GNP (that is, marketed costs alone) may be around 5 per cent of GNP in developed industrialised nations, around 5–10 per cent in East European nations, and as much as 15 per cent in the developing world[24] – mainly through direct pollution damage, soil erosion, land degradation and deforestation. Improvements in environmental quality may thus lead to improvements in the economy as well as to environmental benefits. Although the solutions are not likely to be without cost, in many cases the costs of control may not involve major investments so much as simply changing the way things are done (see also figure 6.5 on p. 172). Where evidence exists concerning the costs and benefits of reducing pollution, it usually suggests that the benefits of control outweigh the costs. For example, the benefits of United States air pollution regulations have been estimated at over $37 billion in 1981 compared to the cost of regulations of between $13–14 billion in the same year.[25] In the United Kingdom, estimates of environmental expenditure came to £14 billion for 1990–1 (about 2.5 per cent of GNP). Over 60 per cent of this figure was on pollution abatement, the remainder being spent mainly on resource management, improvement of amenities, and conservation.[26]

POLLUTION AND PUBLIC POLICY

The problem of controlling externalities caused by pollution is, if anything, more important and also more complex than has been the case in the past. Central government control dates back as far as 1863, when public outcry against emissions of hydrochloric acid gas from the alkali industry led to the Alkali Act of that year. Subsequently, control of industrial processes not covered by this act was granted to local authorities under the Public Health Acts; however, the emphasis was clearly not on prevention, since action could only be taken if nuisance could be proved.

Following the great London smog of 1952, the Clean Air Act 1956 gave local authorities positive powers to control smoke, dust and grit emissions from combustion processes. These and subsequent acts have ensured improvements in urban air quality and substantial reductions in both smoke and sulphur dioxide emissions into the air.[27]

But while some of the old-fashioned environmental problems of smoke and dust appear now to be largely under control, scientific and public concern has shifted to the effects of toxic chemical pollutants, often at low levels of concentration. In particular, emissions of carbon monoxide and hydrocarbons have increased, while emissions of nitrogen oxides have not declined[28] (table 6.1). Other pollutants, especially photochemical oxidants such as ozone have only been monitored more recently and at relatively few sites, but there is growing evidence to suggest that at elevated levels the effects may be injurious to humans and plant life.

Table 6.1 *Emissions of selected gases and smoke, by emission source, 1990, United Kingdom* (percentages and million tonnes)

	Carbon monoxide (CO)	Sulphur dioxide (SO$_2$)	Black smoke	Nitrogen oxides (NOx)[1]	Carbon dioxide (CO$_2$)
Percentage from each emission source					
Domestic[2]	4	3	33	2	14
Commercial/public service[3]	–	2	1	2	5
Power stations	1	72	6	28	34
Refineries	–	3	–	1	3
Agriculture	–	–	–	–	–
Other industry	4	16	13	8	23
Railways	–	–	–	1	–
Road transport	90	2	46	51	19
Civil aircraft	–	–	–	1	–
Shipping	–	2	1	5	1
All emission sources (= 100%) (million tonnes)	6.66	3.77	0.45	2.73	159.55

Notes: 1. Expressed as nitrogen dioxide equivalent.
2. Includes sewage sludge disposal.
3. Includes miscellaneous emission sources.

Source: Warren Spring Laboratory; Department of Trade and Industry.

In the urban context, primary atmospheric pollutants can reach in the atmosphere to produce secondary pollutants such as photochemical smog – seriously
affecting major cities, particularly Los Angeles, São Paulo and Tokyo, and
many other cities under certain atmospheric conditions. The smog is formed by
the photochemical action of sunlight on pollutants, mainly nitrogen oxides,
aldehydes and certain hydrocarbons (from motor vehicles and industrial sources)
which react to produce elevated levels of photochemical oxidants and visibil-
ity-reducing haze. Chemical reactions of this type are very complex (ozone,
for example, may interact with other pollutants) and may occur over long periods
of time as air masses are transported over long distances. The effects of secondary pollution are not, therefore, restricted to urban or industrial areas but in
many cases take a wider geographical dimension.[29] A further problem generated by urban activities is that of acid deposition, which begins when sulphur
dioxide and nitrogen oxide emissions – largely from power stations, industry
and motor vehicles – are oxidised in the atmosphere to form sulphuric and
nitric acids. The resulting acidic deposits are often transported across national
frontiers, and are generally recognised as being a major cause of much of the
recent damage to forests, lakes and rivers in much of Europe, including the
United Kingdom. As many as one in five trees in the EU may have been
severely affected.

The complexity of problems brought out by urban pollution can be further
illustrated by reference to the findings of several surveys concerning spatial
differences in health. In a study in the United States, the concentration of three
measures of pollution (sulphur dioxide, nitrogen dioxide and suspended par-
ticles) was generally found to increase with city size. The study suggested that
major health benefits relating to respiratory diseases and cardiovascular diseases
(estimated at more than $1.5 billion annually in direct savings on earnings and
medical costs) could be achieved from a 50 per cent reduction in air pollution
in major urban areas.[30] While no such monetary estimates have been made for
the United Kingdom, the results of studies examining (standardised) mortality
rates from various diseases, particularly lung–bronchus cancer, show (for 1980–2)
that these have tended to be considerably higher in large urban areas when
compared to rural areas: large parts of the cities of West Central Scotland,
Tyne and Wear, Cleveland, Humberside, Merseyside, Greater Manchester, West
Midlands and Inner London appear to experience mortality rates more than 20
per cent above the United Kingdom average, rising in some cases to as much
as 80 per cent.[31] When compared with earlier studies (for example 1959–63)[32]
the overall geographical pattern seems largely unchanged, except that there
appears to have been a marked improvement in Greater London and the surrounding area, apart from Inner London.

Some types of pollution (such as mercury and cadmium) – when discharged
into rivers or estuaries – pose special problems in that they are bio-accumula-
tive and can become concentrated via the food chain, progressing, for example,
through various forms of aquatic life as far as birds (as well as humans) feed-
ing on poisoned fish. In such cases the effects of pollution are uncertain in

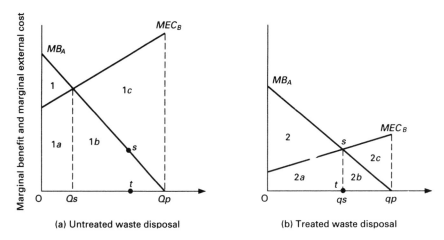

(a) Untreated waste disposal   (b) Treated waste disposal

Figure 6.10   *Private benefits and social costs in production: the optimum level of pollution control*

magnitude and liable to occur at a some distance or point in time from the initial emission. Moreover, since the effects are cumulative, reduction of emissions may not result swiftly in improved quality of the receiving environment. To achieve this, extensive clear-up of previous pollution may be needed. However, pollution problems do not always involve urban or industrial activities; for example, the over-use of nitrogen fertilisers by farmers in East Anglia and surrounding regions is blamed for the exceptionally high nitrate levels in drinking water that affect over a million people in that area.[33]

Finally, since some pollutants are considered to be very dangerous even in low concentrations, nothing short of a total ban on their import and use may be considered reasonable (for example, brown and blue asbestos, previously used in the building industry). For other types of pollutant where exposure costs could be high (such as radiation) the risk of exposure is fortunately minute if adequate precautions are taken. Nevertheless, the risk evaluation – derived from the probability of an incident occurring multiplied by the damage costs inflicted – may in fact be high if low risk is offset by high potential damage costs. Locating such activities away from densely populated areas would be sensible (that is, would lower the risk evaluation), but regular monitoring may nevertheless be required. Similarly, with the recently discovered problem of radioactive radon gas found in some homes, a reasonable suggested move would be to ensure that the problem is recognised when new housing is being sited and designed.

An example will illustrate the alternative policy approaches to pollution control.[34] Assume that *A* is a firm discharging its waste products into a river and that *B* is a town downstream of *A* through which the river passes. Figure 6.10a shows how *A*'s marginal benefit curve, *MB* (that is, marginal revenue – marginal cost) falls as output rises. If *A* were under no constraints it would maximise profits by operating at output *Qp*. The figure also shows *B*'s marginal external cost curve resulting from the effects of the river pollution. This is seen to rise from left to right since, with higher output and pollution, the town may experience higher water purification costs and may be unable to use the river for recreational purposes. If water quality deteriorates further, it may well become a nuisance for nearby residents. If *A* operates at output *Qp*, it can be seen that the total external cost inflicted upon *B* is given by the area under the *MEC* curve – that is, 1*a* + 1*b* + 1*c*. Similarly, the total benefit to *A* is given by area 1 + 1*a* + 1*b*.

Figure 6.10b illustrates the case where the firm has undertaken steps to treat or reduce its waste disposal into the river. This has the effect of reducing the firm's marginal benefit curve (since marginal costs are now higher), but since, for any level of output, pollution is now lower, there is a substantial reduction in the town's marginal external cost curve. Operating at its profit-maximising output (*qp*) *A*'s total benefit is now slightly lower at 2 + 2*a* + 2*b*, but *B*'s total external cost is greatly reduced at 2*a* + 2*b* + 2*c*.

However, from the point of view of society, the optimal solution is for production to take place up to the point where the marginal benefit to the firm of an extra unit produced is equal to the marginal external cost to the town. Beyond this point, marginal external cost to *A* exceeds the marginal benefit to *B*. In figures 6.10a and 6.10b, *MEC* equals *MB* at points *Qs* and *qs* respectively. However, point *qs* in figure 6.10b is clearly superior, since the net benefit to society is equal to area 2 (that is, 2 + 2*a* − 2*a*) while in figure 6.10a the net benefit at *Qs* is only area 1 (1 + 1*a* − 1*a*).

There are essentially three ways in which the level of output *qs* could be achieved: (1) taxation, (2) bargaining and (3) regulation.

(1) Taxation involves the 'polluter pays' principle. It was first suggested by Pigou, who showed how the optimal control of externalities could be achieved by charging the polluter a tax equal to the marginal external cost at the optimal level of production (*qs*). Since the tax would become part of the operating cost of the firm, the latter would need to take it into full account when determining the profit-maximising level of output. In the case of figure 6.10b, a Pigovian tax given by *st* (per unit of output) would have the effect of shifting *A*'s marginal benefit curve down, parallel to MB_A.

The problem with this approach is that where both the *nature* and *scale* of *A*'s activities vary, it will be necessary to adopt *two* controls rather than one. With reference to figure 6.10, it can be seen that *both* the level of output and the method of waste disposal (figure 6.10b) must be controlled to achieve *qs*. By itself, setting a tax equal to *st* will not achieve the desired result, since the firm would continue to produce (and discharge waste) as in figure 6.10a at a level of output slightly below *Qp*.

(2) If there is no impediment to negotiation between the parties involved, it can be shown that bargaining will always produce the optimal solution. In this case MB_A and MEC_B represent the bargaining curves of the two parties. If *A* is liable to pay compensation to *B* then the firm will choose to introduce waste treatment (figure 6.10b), will pay 2*a* in compensation to *B* and retain a net

gain of 2 (note: this is greater than 1 in figure 6.10a). Although the distributional consequences would differ, it might be possible for *B* to compensate *A* to achieve the same result; *B* would be willing to pay up to $1a + 1b + 1c - 2a$ to secure a level of *qs* output, as in figure 6.10b. Although this may seem unfair, there may nevertheless be circumstances under which it might appear reasonable – for example, *B* might represent a new housing development and the firm *A* may not see why it should incur additional costs if it had been operating for some time without causing externalities when there had previously been few residents in the area.

In practice, however, negotiation may be virtually impossible if there are many sufferers and polluters, or if the source of pollution is unclear.

(3) Regulation could operate if the firm were required first to undertake waste treatment (figure 6.10b), and secondly to reduce output (and corresponding pollution) to *qp*. As with the tax solution, this would require full knowledge of *A*'s marginal benefit and *B*'s marginal cost curve, with and without pollution control. The administrative costs of obtaining this information (as well as monitoring discharges) may themselves be quite high and could at worst outweigh any benefits from the scheme. Given the problems involved, a second-best solution may be appropriate; if only the total costs and benefits of production are known, then a total ban on waste disposal would be better than *Qp* output, in figure 6.10a (since total costs of $1a + 1b + 1c$ exceed total benefits of $1 + 1a + 1b$). If more is known about the alternatives, then a requirement that firms must undertake waste treatment (as in figure 6.10b) would be better still – giving a net gain of $2 - 2c$ at *qp*.

To sum up: first, if negotiation is possible, then a tax is unnecessary except where distributional considerations are involved; secondly, where alternative production methods exist then two controls rather than one may be required; and thirdly, if there are substantial costs in imposing a tax, some form of regulation may be preferable.

In many cases, however, the situation may call for discrete changes in practices or output, or the introduction of controls by firms rather than major changes in production processes. For example, in the previous example the firm or industry may be faced with a choice between different *levels* of waste treatment rather than a straight choice between untreated and treated waste disposal. In this case, it is generally more appropriate to view the cost to the firm in terms of the rising cost of abatement equipment rather than in terms of the value of lost output for a given technical process, (that is, *MB* of the firm).[35] This is shown in figure 6.11. The horizontal axis measures pollution, increasing from left to right. In the absence of controls, the firm(s) would be emitting *P* units of pollution. Assuming that pollution abatement controls are available and can be brought in gradually, the marginal control costs facing the firm are likely to rise along the *MCC* curve from right to left. This illustrates the point that, while the first few units of pollution may be relatively easy and inexpensive to eliminate, at greater levels of control, marginal control or abatement costs often rise sharply, as more elaborate and more expensive techniques are

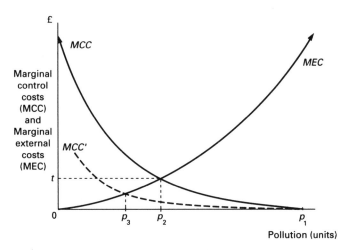

Figure 6.11 *Pollution control and abatement technology*

called for. As in previous diagrams, marginal external costs (*MEC*), sometimes also known as marginal damage costs, are shown as rising with greater levels of pollution emission. The optimum level of pollution can be seen to occur at point P_2 where *MCC*s just equal *MEC*s. The marginal cost of controlling further units of pollution after P_2 is clearly less than the external costs that these units would cause.

In order to achieve this outcome, the authorities could, for example, impose an emission standard equivalent to OP_2 units of pollution. Generally, this would need to be backed up by substantial fines for firms violating emission limits, otherwise there would be little incentive to comply. Alternatively, a tax of $0t$ per unit of pollution could be set. Firms would then cut pollution from P_1 to P_2, since (from P_1) up to P_2 units controlled, the (marginal) costs of control are less than the tax they would have to pay. However, up to P_2 units of pollution, firms would clearly prefer to pay the tax (since $0t$ is less than the *MCC*s). With improvements in control technology over time, the *MCC* curve would fall, for example to *MCC'* in figure 6.11. We can see that this would imply a change in public policy – either reducing the tax to the new point of intersection of *MCC* and *MEC*, or tightening up the emission standard to P_3.

Taxes and emission standards would both require the authorities to have detailed information on the MECs and MCCs, and they would both require precise knowledge regarding actual emission levels by firms. In the case of standards, legal sanctions would need to be applied in a consistent manner. Administrative costs and uncertainty could however be reduced by introducing emission standards in various stages. Further emission reductions might only be justified if the total control costs to firms were expected to be less than the reduction in external costs to society (that is, the benefits of pollution reduction). For example, in figure 6.12 a reduction in pollution from P_1 to P_2 would cost firms *ade* in control costs but would reduce external costs by *abcd*, and

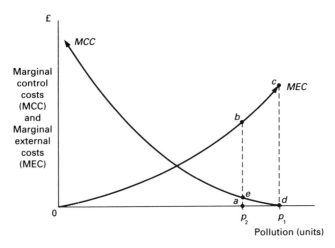

Figure 6.12 *Net benefits of pollution abatement*

would thus produce net benefits of *bcde*. While there are likely to be considerable problems in estimating *MCC* and *MEC* functions, the estimation of total control costs and benefits for smaller reductions may prove more straightforward. In the United States, the so-called 'net benefits' criteria has been applied since 1981 to assess regulatory action.[36]

Compared to taxes, emission standards are often criticised as doing little to encourage firms to consider further possible reductions in pollution. This occurs since standards effectively treat the environment as a 'free good' up to the permitted pollution levels. By contrast, since under the 'polluter pays' principle firms would pay tax on all units of pollution, they have a permanent incentive to seek cheaper ways of controlling emissions and thereby reducing their total tax bills. Furthermore, where firms face very different control costs (perhaps because some plants are much older and more difficult to adapt) a pollution tax is likely to be less costly overall than a policy of requiring each firm to undertake a given cut in pollution.[37] This occurs because, under a given tax, firms with relatively low control costs are likely to undertake proportionately more pollution reduction, whereas firms with high control costs would generally undertake less (and pay more tax instead).

It is sometimes argued that pollution taxes and emission standards do not always take account of the ability of the receiving environment to assimilate or disperse the pollution concerned. For example, smoke from domestic chimneys in rural areas may disperse easily and cause few, if any, problems, whereas in densely populated urban areas, this may not always be the case. One possible response to this problem – which is made more complex if many polluters and processes are involved – is to enforce environmental standards representing maximum allowable concentrations of the pollutant in air or water. Such standards are generally easier to administer since pollution is measured in air or water samples rather than at source where many polluters may be involved. However, by paying less attention to pollution at source, environmental standards can result in complex arguments about who or what is responsible (as with nitrate levels in drinking water) and it may be very unclear what the best method is to achieve compliance in cases where the standards are breached. Finally, as with emission standards, environmental standards also appear to provide a 'licence to pollute' up to the limits set.

Overall, the view of the Royal Commission on Environmental Pollution is that more traditional forms of regulation such as emission standards (sometimes known as consents) must remain in place. However, it also recognises that (water) pollution charging schemes – in addition to discharge consents – have been successful in reducing pollution in countries such as Germany and the Netherlands. The worry, as some studies have suggested, is that pollution taxes alone might not guarantee achievement of the necessary standards.[38] As mentioned above, some combination of taxes *and* standards, or even a system of tradable permits (which sets emission levels for certain pollutants and effectively auctions pollution rights up to these limits) may well be capable of producing a cost-effective and acceptable solution.

In practice, environmental control policies are generally developed around environmental or air quality standards (EQSs)/AQSs) or emission standards ESs. At present in the United Kingdom, EC directives set AQSs for lead, sulphur dioxide, smoke and nitrogen dioxide, while water quality standards exist for drinking water (nitrate levels) and bathing areas. Examples of ESs exist for classes of alkali and acid works and for cadmium and mercury discharges. To some extent, the advantages of EQSs and ESs can in practice be combined by introducing limit values (LVs) that require outer limits for both EQSs and ESs to be achieved. However, in setting standards, objectivity and scientific proof are not always easily achieved or obtained given the numerous issues and uncertainties involved; in the words of one specialist (on the problem of lead pollution) 'the things we would like to know may be unknowable, so there is some virtue in just getting rid of the problem'.[39]

Pollution Control in Practice

Traditionally, the United Kingdom has favoured a case-by-case approach, with emission limits being set at varying levels depending on local environmental conditions, financial implications and so on. However, most European countries and the European Commission favour uniform effluent emission limits based on the best available control technology. By 1987 it became clear that the United Kingdom would accept a new approach more consistent with EC thinking. Policy was streamlined in the late 1980s, and in 1987 a central body, Her Majesty's Inspectorate of Pollution (HMIP) was established.

The current system of pollution control stems from the Environmental Protection Act 1990 (EPA).[40] Industrial processes proscribed by regulations made under the Act may not be carried on without the prior grant of an authorisation by an 'enforcing authority'. In the case of more complex and potentially more damaging processes and substances, HMIP is the relevant authority. It operates within the framework of 'integrated pollution control' (IPC) exercisable in respect of any environmental medium. This enables a cross-media approach to be taken towards emissions into air, water and land. A greater number of less complex and less potentially polluting processes require authorisation from local authorities under the system of local authority air pollution control (LAAPC). IPC and LAAPC have common features regarding the regulatory framework, administrative provisions and standards and measures employed. In particular, one of the main statutory objectives to be achieved in every authorisation set out in Section 7(2) of the Act, involves ensuring that, in carrying out a prescribed process, the 'best available techniques not entailing excessive cost' (BATNEEC) will be used. In practice, this involves not only the provision of appropriate technology, but also its effective use, which may include the number, qualifications and training of persons employed in the process, and the design, construction, layout and maintenance of the building in which it is carried on (Section 7(10) of the Act).

In order to achieve consistency of authorisations, the Chief Inspector publishes guidance notes stating HMIP's views as to achievable standards and methods of achieving them. Applications that do not conform with the relevant guidance note will probably only gain authorisation if an applicant can establish that use of the best available techniques would entail excessive cost.

Overall, as technology evolves, it is generally anticipated that the application of the BATNEEC concept will mean that firms will be expected to meet higher control standards. Finally, the National Rivers Authority (NRA), established in 1989, provides consents for other non-prescribed discharges into watercourses, and is also responsible for monitoring water pollution. Further amalgamation of the NRA, HMIP and other regulatory bodies into a unified environmental protection agency seems likely to take place during the 1990s.

In the future, it is likely that economic incentives (taxes and subsidies) will increasingly become part of the European Union's (EU) environmental policy.[41] Indeed, the 'polluter pays' principle was confirmed in the Single European Act, Article 130R(2), and is forming the basis for the design of economic instruments.

Finally, environmental considerations and national planning and development control policies have been brought closer by the EU's Environmental Impact Assessment Directive[42] (1988), obliging member states to assess the environmental impact of major construction projects before they are implemented. Certain categories of project – crude oil refineries, thermal power stations, chemical installations, major roads and railways, large airports and trading ports – must be subjected to an impact assessment. Other categories of project may undergo an assessment at the discretion of the Member States. For example, other transport projects may require an assessment at the discretion of the competent authority (for example, highway or planning authority) if the project is likely to have significant environmental impact. Such projects could include other roads, harbours, other airfields, light rail, pipelines and marinas.[43] An environmental statement (ES) must accompany planning applications for projects which fall into the above categories. This must include a description and evaluation of the likely effects of the project on human beings, flora and fauna; soil, water, air, climate and landscape; the interaction of all these factors; and material assets and the cultural heritage. It should also suggest appropriate methods of mitigating such effects. Finally, the overall environmental assessment must take into account information and opinions received; and the public must be consulted and can propose alternatives.[44]

AIR POLLUTION – GLOBAL ISSUES

Global pollution arises because the effects of many types of pollutant can cross national boundaries, affecting those earth's resources that we all share such as the atmosphere and the world's oceans. Global warming, which we shall consider below, is one such problem, brought about by the recent and rapid increase in 'greenhouse gas' emissions.

Global Warming

Carbon dioxide is known to be the main contributor to the 'greenhouse effect'. This occurs as heat from the sun becomes trapped, reducing the rate of heat loss and raising the earth's temperature (figure 6.13). The burning of fossil fuels and deforestation have increased the concentration of carbon dioxide by a quarter over the past 200 years and on present trends, atmospheric CO_2 may double by the year 2030 (figure 6.14).[43] However, even with increased energy efficiency and conservation measures, and use of alternative fuels, carbon dioxide concentrations will probably continue to rise over the next fifty years as aggregate world energy demand increases. The possible effects are not known for certain, but it is expected that in the long term, global average temperatures could rise by between 1.5–4.5°C producing changes in sea levels, rainfall patterns and agricultural production. Given that around 3 billion people live in coastal regions, the effects of coastal erosion on infrastructure, housing and transport systems in these areas could be substantial. However, all countries would clearly be affected to some degree by changing climatic conditions.

It has been estimated that the capital cost for the United Kingdom of improving sea defences to cope with a sea level rise of up to 1.65m by the year 2050 would amount to at least £5 billion.[45] This figure begs the question of whether some areas might have to be left unprotected because the works involved would not be justified on cost-benefit grounds. Overall, Organisation for Economic Co-operation and Development (OECD) estimates put the cost of stabilising CO_2 emissions to 1990 levels by the year 2050 at between 1 per cent and 3 per cent of world GDP.

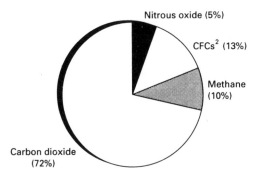

Notes: 1. Man-made emissions.
       2. Chlorofluorocarbons.
Source: Department of the Environment.

Figure 6.13 *Relative contribution to the greenhouse effect of various gases, 1990,[1] percentages*

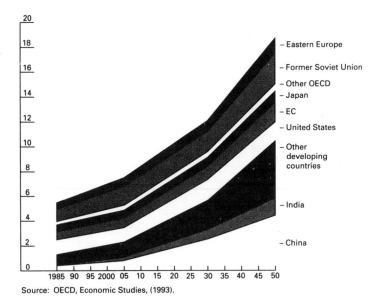

Source: OECD, Economic Studies, (1993).

Figure 6.14 *Projected carbon emissions (billion tonnes)*

In view of the potential seriousness of global warming, the EU has encouraged Member States to make commitments to stabilise emissions of CO_2 at their 1990 levels by the year 2000. However, this objective is likely to prove difficult to achieve. The government itself predicts that, given current trends, carbon emissions will rise from 160m tonnes to 170 tonnes over the 1990s – hence savings of around 10m tonnes need to be found.

In particular, the share of total United Kingdom energy demand accounted for by all transport activities – currently about 30 per cent of total energy

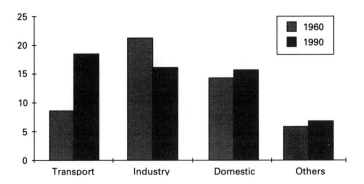

Source: *Digest of United Kingdom Energy Statistics* (HMSO, 1993). Crown copyright.

Figure 6.15 *Final users' energy consumption by sector, United Kingdom, 1960 and 1990 (billions of therms).*

demand by final users – has been rising steadily (although transport accounts for less than a quarter of United Kingdom CO_2 emissions). In 1988, transport exceeded the energy demand of both industrial and domestic sectors for the first time (figure 6.15).[46] Of the four main transport sub-sectors (road, rail, air and water), roads account for about 80 per cent (and car travel alone about 70 per cent) of energy used for transport. The Department of Transport's National Road Traffic forecasts suggest that road traffic volume may increase by around 125 per cent between 1988 and 2025. Without measures to moderate growth of car mileage or to improve fuel economy, CO_2 emissions from personal travel might increase by as much as a third as early as 2005.[47] However, particularly in built-up areas, congestion is already a problem and this will get worse as traffic increases, further reducing fuel efficiency and increasing urban pollution. At the European level transport accounts for 22 per cent of CO_2 emissions, with almost half of this due to urban traffic alone.[48] Improved public transport, light rail schemes and so on, combined with traffic restraint measures such as road pricing, would certainly help reduce congestion and improve the urban environment (see table 6.2). Schemes such as the Tyne and Wear Metro have undoubtedly been a success but in general (and outside London), bus patronage has been falling and in the late 1980s passenger kilometres declined steadily by 3–4 per cent a year.[49] Nevertheless, the EU is keen to encourage such schemes: for example, in 1993 the European Investment Bank provided a £98 million loan to enable the Jubilee Line extension in London to go ahead.

About 30 per cent of Britain's CO_2 emissions originate from heating and lighting and so on in domestic dwellings. While studies[50] suggest that considerable savings on space heating can be achieved without difficulty in 'new build', the rate of replacement of the existing stock is very slow. In existing dwellings, many of which are very old, the scope for cost-effective energy efficiency improvements (mainly through cavity fill and loft insulation, double glazing, improved boilers and controls, and improved lighting) is much more restricted. Domestic

Table 6.2 *Differential impact of transport modes on a number of environmental variables*

Environmental variable	Unit	Car	Car with 3-Way Cat	Rail	Bus
Land use	m²/person	120	120	7	12
Primary energy use	g coal equivalent units/pkm	90	90	31	27
Carbon dioxide emissions	g/pkm	200	200	60	59
Nitrogen dioxide emissions	g/pkm	2.2	0.34	0.08	0.02
Hydrocarbons	g/pkm	1	0.15	0.02	0.08
Carbon Monoxide emissions	g/pkm	8.7	1.3	0.05	0.15
Air pollution	polluted air m³/pkm	38 000	5 900	1 200	3 300
Accident risks	hours of life lost/1 000 pkm	11.5	11.5	0.4	1

Note: pkm = passenger kilometre. One passenger travelling one kilometre is 1 pkm; g = gramme.

Source: Based on D. Teutel, (1989) *Die Zukunft des Autoverkehrs*, Heidelberg, Report Nr 17 Umwelt- und Prognose Institut (UPI).

energy consumption may increase by as much as 20 per cent between 1985 and 2005. However, with increased application of energy efficiency measures, savings of around 5 million tonnes (as carbon) could be achieved representing around 11 per cent of 1985 CO_2 emissions from domestic sources.

One problem is that even if measures are cost effective, it is well known that individuals may fail to undertake the necessary investment. This might arise for a number of reasons: first, for major works, the required expenditure may be high in relation to earnings, and credit may be expensive; secondly, home owners who move frequently may feel that such investment is not fully reflected in capital values on sale; thirdly, consumers may lack the necessary technical information on which to base their decisions; and finally, many groups, particularly the poor and the elderly, may have high implicit discount rates (possibly as high as 80 per cent), meaning that they would only invest in more expensive energy-saving work or equipment if the long-run cost savings were very high indeed. Although grants exist for energy-saving investment in the home, other policy approaches could include requiring houses for sale to undergo an energy audit (as in Denmark, for example) which would help to raise the sale price of more efficient homes.

In terms of electricity generation, the government is working towards achieving 1500 megawatts (MW) of renewable energy (which, of course, produces no direct CO_2 emissions) by the year 2000. However, this will still only account for a very small proportion (3 per cent) of the United Kingdom's total energy requirements – the equivalent of only three modern 500 MW power stations. In 1991, the House of Commons Select Committee recommended a higher target of between two to three times this level.

In 1991 the European Commission (EC) announced its intention to introduce a carbon tax. This would have been placed on fossil fuels (coal, oil and gas) in proportion to their carbon content, thus taxing CO_2 emissions at source. Similar taxes exist in Sweden and have been considered in the United States. The proposed tax, planned to be phased in gradually, would have had many beneficial effects. First, it would have reduced energy demand through direct reductions in use. Secondly, it would have encouraged higher levels of investment in energy efficiency measures; and thirdly, it would have promoted a switch to less energy-intensive forms of transport. Finally, it would have encouraged a shift in energy generation towards less environmentally damaging fuels (for example, renewable energy sources such as wind and tidal power), and more efficient means of deriving energy from fossil fuel sources, for example, combined heat and power. Tax revenues – possibly as much as £17 billion – could have been used to reduce taxation elsewhere, to offset some of the effects on poorer households, and to subsidise energy-efficient public transport systems. However, some industries, particularly those using large quantities of electricity (for example, iron and steel, chemicals, cement, clay and glass), would be greatly affected by such a tax.[52] On the other hand, higher investment levels could result as firms would be likely to replace older, less efficient machinery and buildings at an earlier opportunity. The disadvantages lie pri-

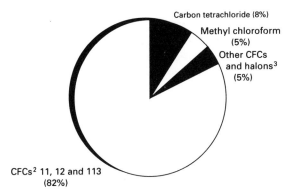

Notes: 1. Based on 1985 gas emissions.
         2. Chlorofluorocarbons.
         3. CFCs 114 and 115, halons 1301, 1211 and 2402
            and HCFC 22.
Source: UK Stratosphenc Ozone Review Group.

Figure 6.16   *Relative contribution of various gases to depletion of the ozone layer,[1] percentages*

marily in the undoubted regressive nature of the tax and its probable dampening effect on travel in rural areas. Also, trade distortions could arise if other countries did not introduce similar taxes, since domestic industries would be penalised. Furthermore, if world oil prices fell as a result of EU actions, energy consumption in non-taxing countries would probably rise, thus reducing net gains at a global level.

Other Global Problems

As with other aspects of global pollution, the reduction of greenhouse gas emissions presents certain *public good* characteristics and problems. Because it is shared by everyone, efforts to improve the global environment by one country will automatically be extended to others. There is thus an incentive not to implement costly environmental protection measures but to *free ride* on other countries' efforts to control emissions. Clearly, if everyone adopts this approach improvements will never occur, which is why binding international agreements are so essential.

Another of the major global environmental problems concerns damage to the ozone layer (see figure 6.16), caused largely by chlorofluorocarbons (CFCs), mainly of the type used in aerosols. Ozone depletion will increase the amount of ultraviolet radiation reaching the Earth, resulting in an increased incidence of skin cancer and serious effects on agricultural crops and marine life. In 1992, recorded concentrations of ozone in the atmosphere above Europe, Russia and Canada were at their lowest level in 35 years, and a 50 per cent destruction of the ozone layer above populated areas of southern Argentina and Chile was reported (World Meteorological Organisation). In 1987, the Montreal

Protocol, which was an attempt to reduce substances that deplete the ozone layer, was signed by all major CFC-producing countries. More recently, the EC has proposed to phase out CFCs by 1995.

On the international issue of acid rain referred to earlier, European agreement was reached leading to the Large Combustion Plant Directive in 1988. By 2003, emissions of sulphur dioxide will have been cut, in stages, by 60 per cent from their 1980 levels. Nitrogen oxides (NOx) are also to be reduced by 30 per cent, ending in 1998. Other northern industrial countries would have preferred larger cuts, but levels and progress will be reviewed again in 1995 and the United Kingdom could well be called upon to make greater reductions. However, since around 50 per cent of NOx emissions are due to road transport, the requirement to fit all new cars with catalytic converters from January 1993 should greatly reduce these emissions, as well improving the urban environment.

Finally, since some poorer European member states may find financial difficulty in adhering to EU environmental commitments, the Cohesion Fund proposed under the Maastricht Treaty will help to channel cash to environmental projects in Greece, Spain, Portugal and the Irish Republic.

REFERENCES

1. N. Kaldor, 'Welfare Propositions of Economics and Interpersonal Comparisons of Utility', *Economic Journal*, 49 (1939).
2. J. Hicks, 'The Valuation of Social Income', *Economica*, 7 (1940).
3. See R. Lipsey and R. Lancaster, 'The General Theory of the Second Best', *Review of Economic Studies*, 24 (1957); W. J. Baumol, 'On Taxation and Control of Externalities', *American Economic Review*, 62 (1972).
4. See D. W. Pearce, *Cost-Benefit Analysis*, 2nd edn (Macmillan, 1983).
5. W. J. Baumol, *Welfare Economics and the Theory of the State* (Bell & Sons, 1965).
6. O. A. Davis and A. B. Whinston, 'The Economics of Urban Renewal', *Journal of Law and Contemporary Problems*, 16 (1961).
7. J. Vipond and B. Walker, 'The Determinants of Housing Expenditure and Owner-Occupation', *Bulletin of the Oxford Institute of Economics and Statistics*, 34 (1972); M. Ball and R. Kirwan, 'Urban Housing Demand: Some Evidence from Cross-Sectional Data', *Applied Economics*, 9 (1977).
8. See C. M. Price, *Welfare Economics in Theory and Practice* (Macmillan, 1977).
9. D. W. Pearce, *Cost-Benefit Analysis*, 1st edn (Macmillan, 1971).
10. (Roskill) Commission on the Third London Airport, *Report* (HMSO, 1970, 1971); C. D. Foster and M. E. Beesley, 'Estimating the Social Benefit of Constructing an Underground Railway in London', *Journal of the Royal Statistical Society*, Series A, 126 (1963); R. Layard (ed.), *Cost-Benefit Analysis* (Penguin, 1972).
11. See D. W. Pearce, *Environmental Economics* (Macmillan, 1975).
12. R. Layard (ed.), *Cost-Benefit Analysis* (Penguin, 1972).
13. A. Sen, 'On Optimising the Rate of Saving', *Economic Journal*, 71 (1961); 'Isolation, Assurance and the Social Rate of Discount', *Quarterly Journal of Economics*, 81 (1967).
14. W. J. Baumol, 'On Taxation and Control of Externalities', *American Economic Review*, 62 (1972).

15. A. C. Pigou, *The Economics of Welfare* (Macmillan, 1920).
16. D. W. Pearce, *Cost-Benefit Analysis* (Macmillan, 1983).
17. R. Arrow and R. Lind, 'Uncertainty and the Evaluation of Public Investment Decisions', *American Economic Review*, 60 (1970).
18. N. Lichfield, 'Cost-Benefit Analysis in Town Planning: a Case Study, Swanley', *Urban Studies*, 3 (1966); N. Lichfield and H. Chapman, 'Cost-Benefit Analysis in Urban Expansion: a Case Study, Ipswich', *Urban Studies*, 7 (1970).
19. See *Journal of Environmental Planning & Management*, 36, 1 (1993).
20. D. W. Pearce 'Toward the Sustainable Economy', *Royal Bank of Scotland Review* (December 1991).
21. D. W. Pearce and J. P. Barde, *Valuing the Environment* (Earthscan, 1991).
22. D. W. Pearce 'Toward the Sustainable Economy', *Royal Bank of Scotland Review* (December 1991).
23. D. W. Pearce and R. Kerry Turner, *The Economics of Natural Resources and the Environment* (Harvester Wheatsheaf, 1990).
24. D. W. Pearce, 'Toward the Sustainable Economy', *Royal Bank of Scotland Review* (December 1991).
25. P. Portney 'Public Policies for Environmental Protection', *Resources for the Future* (Washington DC, 1990).
26. *Economic Trends*, No. 469, November (HMSO, 1992).
27. Royal Commission on Environmental Pollution, *10th Report* (HMSO, 1984).
28. Ibid.
29. Ibid.
30. I. Hoch, 'Urban Scale and Environmental Quality' in R. G. Ridker (ed.), *Pollution, Resources and the Environment* (US Commission on Population Growth and the Environment, Washington DC, USGPO, 1972).
31. G. M. Howe, 'Does it Matter Where I Live', *Transactions of British Geographers* (1985).
32. G. M. Howe, *National Atlas of Disease and Mortality in the UK* (Nelson, 1970).
33. *Guardian* (16 December 1986).
34. R. Turvey, 'On Divergencies between Social Cost and Private Cost', *Economica* (August 1963).
35. D. W. Pearce and R. Kerry Turner, *The Economics of Natural Resources and the Environment* (Harvester Wheatsheaf, 1990).
36. D. W. Pearce and J. P. Barde, *Valuing the Environment* (Earthscan, 1991).
37. D. W. Pearce, *Environmental Economics* (Macmillan, 1975).
38. A. Silberston, 'Economics and the Royal Commission on Environmental Pollution', *National Westiminster Bank Review* (February 1993).
39. Sir J. Gowans, quoted in Royal Commission on Environmental Pollution, *10th Report* (HMSO, 1984).
40. J. Pugh-Smith, 'The Loyal Authority as a Regulator of Pollution in the 1990s', *Journal of Planning & Environmental Law* (February 1992); Sir F. Layfield, 'The Environmental Protection Act 1990. The System of Integrated Pollution Control', *Journal of Planning and Environmental Law* (January 1992); 'Integrated Pollution Control in Practice', *Journal of Planning and Environmental Law* (July 1992); R. Harris, 'The Environmental Protection Act 1990 – Penalising the Polluter', *Journal of Planning and Environmental Law* (June 1992). S. Tromans and M. Clarkson, 'The Environmental Protection Act 1990: Its Relevance to Planning Controls', *Journal of Planning and Environmental Law* (June 1991).
41. J. Delbeke, 'The Prospects for the Use of Economic Instruments in EC Environment Policy', *Royal Bank of Scotland Review* (December 1991).
42. See Department of the Environment, Circular 15/88, *Environmental Assessment* (HMSO, 1988) and *Environmental Assessment – A Guide to the Procedure* (HMSO, 1989).

43. C. Ferrary, 'Environmental Assessment and Transport', *The Planner* (9 November 1990).
44. Commission of the European Communities, 'Environmental Policy in the European Community', *European Documentation*, 5 (1990).
45. L. Boorman, J. Goss-Custard, S. McGrorty, *Climatic Change Rising Sea Level and the British Coast*, Natural Environment Research Council, Inst of Terrestrial Ecology (HMSO, 1989).
46. Department of Energy, *An Evaluation of Energy Related Greenhouse Gas Emissions and Means to Ameliorate Them* (HMSO, 1989).
47. P. Hughes, 'Exhausting the Atmosphere', *Town & Country Planning* (October 1991).
48. Commissions of the European Communities, *Green Paper on the Urban Environment* (Brussels, 1990).
49. P. Hills, 'Private Transport – What Future for the Private Car in the City?' *The Planner* (13 December 1991).
50. Department of Energy, *An Evaluation of Energy Related Greenhouse Gas Emissions and Means to Ameliorate Them* (HMSO, 1989).
51. Ibid.
52. Commission of the European Communities, *European Economy*, No. 51 (May 1992).

7

Urban Congestion

There can be little doubt that population increase and urban decay rank among the world's biggest problems. The problems are severe in industrial countries with high population densities. In the United Kingdom, for example, the population increased from 27.4 million in 1870 to 57.2 million in 1991, and with an area of 22.7 million hectares the overall density of about 1 person per 0.4 ha is one of the highest in the world. For reasons of economic opportunity, over three-quarters of the rapidly growing population have left the countryside since the beginning of the Industrial Revolution to live in towns and cities – urban areas substantially increasing in size. An estimate by Best[1] in 1964, showed that in 1900 about 5 per cent of England and Wales was urban, by 1939 this figure was 8.6 per cent, and by 1950 it had reached 10 per cent. It was forecast that by 2000 it could conceivably reach 15–16 per cent.

But even if, as seems likely, population grows more slowly than in the recent past, or even falls, there would still be a tendency towards urbanisation. As accommodation standards improve high-density nineteenth-century housing is replaced by either lower-density overspill estates, or by relatively low-density development within the inner areas of towns. Best estimated that whereas in 1900 24.9 urban hectares were necessary to house 1000 people, in 1960 35.1 ha were required, and by 2000, 38.1 ha might be needed.

Urbanisation was both the result and the cause of an increase in GNP. Between 1870 and 1990 the GNP increased from £929 million to £517 824, million, or on a per capita basis, from £35 to £9053. But economic growth is not without its price – a figure largely omitted from GNP statistics. It has caused appalling traffic congestion in our towns and cities, it has brought about the decay of the inner urban areas since 'green field' locations have become more attractive for residential populations and more profitable for employers, and its effects have put increased pressure on local government finance.

ECONOMICS AND THE TRAFFIC CONGESTION PROBLEM

Transport plays an important role in determining the scale, nature and form of our urban areas. Although in Greater London the proportion of land occupied by roads is only 16 per cent, in other cities in Britain the proportions are often much higher, with the amount of land in central areas devoted to streets and parking rising towards the United States levels of 40 per cent in Cincinnati, 50

211

per cent in Detroit and 60 per cent in Los Angeles.[2] In addition, railway facilities, airports, docks and harbours make transportation land overall the major urban land use after housing. The efficiency of transport, and implicitly the efficiency of the use of land for transportation, contribute greatly to the level of productivity, growth and thus the standard of living. Ironically it is a higher standard of living, together with changing social habits and technical advance (permitting more convenient and personal travel over more extensive areas), which produce the problems of urban road transport.

ROAD USE AND DEVELOPMENT

In the years from 1910 to 1990 the number of road vehicles licensed in Great Britain increased very substantially from 144 000 to 22 million. It has been forecast by the Transport and Road Research Laboratory of the Department of the Environment that by 1995 the number of motor vehicles in Great Britain will reach 24 million, and by 2005 28 million (double the total of 1970). Over 80 per cent of these will be private motor cars.

Although there was an increase in total expenditure on highways from £312.2 million in 1963 to £5250 million in 1990, its share of gross domestic product (GDP) at factor cost decreased from 1.23 to 1.01 per cent – an appallingly low proportion of public expenditure despite the United Kingdom (by EC standards) having above-average traffic densities, with the degree of overcrowding substantially increasing (table 7.1).

Clearly, road-building and improvements have not kept pace with the growth of motor traffic. There is now less than 1 metre of trunk and principal road (including motorway) for each vehicle in Britain – largely the result of road expenditure being low by international comparisons and low in relation to road taxation (table 7.1). Even the £23 billion roads programme planned for the 1990s (of which £12 billion would be spent on motorways) is unlikely to provide Britain with similar main road and motorway provision to that found in other major west European countries. In densely populated areas, such as London, increased investment in roads and/or public transport seems to be necessary. Surveys have shown that these places are at crisis point as far as traffic is concerned and that urban renewal needs to take account of the desire for better mobility.

According to Roth,[3] however, there are four principal approaches to congestion and its effects:

(1) Doing nothing, and allowing congestion to be its own deterrent.

(2) Redeveloping cities to accommodate all the vehicles wishing to use them (assuming public funds are available).

(3) Restricting the use of motor vehicles in inner areas so as to reduce total traffic volumes to the capacity of existing streets.

(4) Imposing an economic solution by recognising that road space is scarce and rationing it by a direct form of pricing.

Table 7.1 *Some international comparisons of traffic density, taxation and expenditure*

| | Vehicles per kilometre | | | | Percentage of state revenue | | | | Road expenditure as a percentage of road tax | |
| | All roads | | Motorways and main roads | | Taxes incurred by motorists | | Road expenditure | | | |
	1985	1990	1985	1990	1985	1990	1985	1990	1985	1990
Great Britain	53	63	1 220	1 782	8.1	9.6	2.2	2.4	27.2	27.1
(The former) West Germany	55	65	679	1 034	3.7	3.8	2.4	1.9	64.9	53.4
France	30	35	697	993	13.8	17.1	5.1	n.a.	37.0	n.a.
Italy	75	91	438	614	22.9	16.7	13.4	5.2	58.5	31.6
European Community (average)*	40	61	611	1 434	10.0	10.9	4.6	2.9	46.0	33.0

Note: *The European Community averages relate to countries which were members in 1975.

Source: British Road Federation, *Basic Road Statistics*.

Following the publication of the Buchanan Report[4] in 1963 the second approach became widely considered, and influenced transport policies throughout the 1960s. The report proposed the provision of 'urban corridors' to take general traffic and particularly peak-hour (and through traffic), and a hierarchy of distributory roads filtering traffic of different sorts into 'urban rooms' or environmental areas. The aim was to ensure that in all places 'environmental capacity' would be realised – that is, the maximum level of permitted traffic would have to be compatible with the environment of the associated area.

Although new road patterns would best achieve these proposals, the existing road network could be modified temporarily by means of prevailing traffic management schemes and urban planning concepts. With limited financial resources, a choice would have to be made between accessibility and environmental requirements, but Buchanan believed that, with more financial availability, cities could accommodate the increased volumes of traffic forecast, provided the urban physical structure were redeveloped.

But the Buchanan thesis was subject to much criticism:

(1) It relied quite heavily on the depreciation and obsolescence of buildings and subsequent urban renewal brought about by massive investment. But given such opportunities for change, it would become possible to opt for a programme of decentralisation – the physical difficulties in accommodating the ultimate traffic level not then occurring.

(2) It may have over-forecast the number of vehicles in use in the future in Britain. As urban net residential densities rise there is usually a reduction in the proportion of residents owning cars, regardless of income groups. However, if substantial decentralisation were to take place, the proportion of car owners would increase, but the *raison d'être* for Buchanan's proposals would cease to exist.

(3) It was questionable whether financial resources would be available to implement the recommendations of the Report, except on a piecemeal basis.

Even so, the Buchanan Report highlighted the fact that transport planning is at the heart of the problems of urban planning. It recognised that transport can do great environmental damage through noise and air pollution, and visual intrusion and that developments in transport (in the form of increased car ownership and declining public transport services) may have contributed to social polarisation. There are two kinds of urban transport costs incurred by the community – direct costs and indirect costs.

Direct Costs

These comprise the initial costs of highway construction, ancillary capital costs of road servicing equipment, loan charges on capital, and ancillary costs on such things as lighting, signs, research, administration and policing – which totalled £5250 million in 1990/91. It can be argued that motorists should at least meet these costs, but although they contribute very large sums each year in fuel tax, value added tax (VAT) and vehicle excise tax, these payments (£19 200 million in 1990/91) are regarded as part of general taxation. The principle that motorists, by taxation, do not pay specifically or indirectly for the use of roads was established in 1935 with the abolition of the road fund tax.

Indirect Costs

Congestion costs

The most obvious indirect cost is that of traffic congestion. Congestion costs are imposed mainly by motorists upon other motorists and include the costs of time lost in delays and at lower speeds and the costs of higher fuel consumption – for example, when the average speed falls from 32 km/h (20 mph) to 16 km/h (10 mph), fuel consumption can rise by at least 50 per cent. The Road Pricing Panel of the Ministry of Transport estimated in the 1960s that total time-wasting costs per vehicle mile resulting from congestion were 2p at 32 km/h (20 mph) rising to 17.5p at 16 km/h (10 mph) and 30p at 13 km/h (8 mph). The costs of delay can be identified as those relating to the class of vehicle involved, to the driver's (and crew's) time, to the passenger's time, and to the police involved in traffic regulations.

The Road Research Laboratory calculated in 1959 that annual traffic congestion costs amounted to £250 million. In the same year, C. T. Bruner of Shell-Mex suggested that the probable cost was nearer £500 million. With inflation and the increase in the number of vehicles in the 1960s–1980s the cost now is considerably in excess of £1000 million per annum.

Congestion clearly adds to the cost of public road transport services; a 2 or 3 km/h increase in the average speed of urban buses could produce annual savings of millions of pounds.

In addition to delay, congestion and associated poor road surfaces result in motorists incurring a high rate of vehicle depreciation, notably because of tyre, brake and clutch wear.

Of course, motorists do pay these congestion costs but not equitably nor with any account being taken of the optimum use of road space or the individual's time. If motorists were forced to pay their full share of these costs, congestion might be greatly reduced.

But some congestion costs are clearly not borne in any form by motorists. This is when congestion reduces accessibility to such an extent that central-area land values diminish (as is the case in many United States cities). But up to now, non-economic factors such as prestige enable the central areas of British cities to retain their attraction as business centres, though the development of out-of-town shopping centres, geared to the motorist, may have an effect on central-area values in the future.

Environmental costs

Although the burden of congestion affects the community as a whole because of the resultant noise, fumes and visual affliction, the environmental spill over from motor traffic is not just confined to congested urban streets. Suburban and rural areas can be affected adversely even though roads may be used at well below their capacity.

Accident costs

Road accidents resulting from congestion or other causes are similarly difficult to value. The 'direct' cost of road accidents was estimated by the Royal Society for the Prevention of Accidents to be £136 million in 1950 and £200 million in 1960. By the 1990s the cost exceeded £1 billion. But these costs are partly based on outdated scales of charges laid down by insurance companies regarding ambulance services, treatment and limited hospitalisation.

Opportunity costs

Land and other resources for roads could be used for housing, hospitals, schools and open space. Roads, by having alternative use values, often impose high opportunity costs on urban communities.

Disequilibrium of Demand and Supply

The provision of road space, at a price to the motorist of substantially less than cost, results inevitably in excessive demand. Prior to an examination of possible solutions to the problems of excess use, the underlying features of demand and supply are considered.

Demand comprises journeys to work (the largest component of demand), travelling during work, and journeys for shopping or leisure purposes. More specifically there is peak demand – with longer-distance commuting becoming an increasingly important feature; revealed demand – the overall level of demand determined by population size and distribution, incomes and wealth, car-ownership preference and working hours; and suppressed demand – the traffic generated in response to the construction of new roads or the improvement of existing roads.

Supply consists of roads and railway track, and either private or public transport – private car, motorcycle, moped, bicycle or bus, train or underground railway. But although in mass-commuting the underground railway is four times more efficient than the bus, and the bus eight times more efficient than the car, the car is more flexible, convenient and comfortable and scores heavily over public transport over short journeys – all compensating the motorist's incurred cost of congestion.

Short-term solutions

Immediate reactions to the problem of disequilibrium have included the more intensive use of short-haul bus services, the adding of extra coaches to commuter rail services and the adoption of new traffic management schemes (such as one-way roads, linked signals and clearways), but the overall gain is usually minimal and at best stop-gap.

Long-term solutions

These have involved large-scale road development to allow for a freer traffic flow. This approach was used widely during the 1950s and 1960s, reinforced by the Buchanan proposals, and figured largely in the Greater London Development Plan 1969.

But new road development provides an unrealistic solution because:

(1) There would be an adverse environmental impact. The Crowther Steering Group to the Buchanan Report warned that United Kingdom cities could not accommodate United States-style road patterns.

(2) Despite higher speeds, real time-saving might not be reduced because greater distances would be involved. Suppressed demand would soon saturate capacity.

(3) Public transport would become uneconomic as diverted demand would reduce revenue, necessitating higher fares or reduced services.

(4) The cost of development would be enormous – over £19 million/km in inner areas, falling to £5 million in suburban areas in the 1960s. Investment in public transport would be much more cost effective – for example, the initial 18 km of the Victoria Line cost £60 million to develop in the 1960s and has a capacity of 40 000 passengers per hour; 18 km of an urban motorway would have cost £132 million and carried only 10 000 persons per hour (at an average of 1.4 persons per car). Yet public transport usually operates at a loss and will continue to do so until the motorist pays the full costs of his/her road usage.

In the very long term, excess demand could be eliminated by both strategic and detailed land-use planning. New linear settlements, out-of-town shopping and industrial and commercial relocation would extinguish inward and outward commuter traffic flows. The dilution of peak demand could also be brought about by a radical staggering of working, shopping and leisure hours.

Both in the short and long term, demand must be controlled so as to equate with the supply of transport facilities.

Road Pricing Theory

An economic system allocates factors of production and distributes goods and services so as to maximise social welfare. A traditional way of doing this is by means of the price mechanism, with competitive markets and prices determined competitively for each product, paid ultimately out of individual consumer incomes. With freedom to enter a market, suppliers produce on a maximum profit basis at a price equalling the cost of the last unit of output (marginal cost). Enough of each item is purchased by consumers to make the marginal benefits from spending an extra unit of income in all cases equal.

But in the case of roads, supply and demand considerations are entirely different. The motorist is influenced essentially by marginal private costs – those which s/he incurs directly and which expand as congestion increases. S/He will continue to use road space, however congested, as long as his/her marginal private costs are less than the marginal private benefits (monetary and non-monetary) which s/he enjoys through using his/her vehicle. It must be assumed that his/her marginal private benefits equal the price s/he is willing to pay and therefore are equivalent to demand. Marginal social costs equal marginal private costs plus the cost that the vehicle imposes on the rest of the traffic – that is, congestion costs.

The demand for road space is the relationship between the price of a vehicle-kilometre (determined largely by fuel and vehicle taxation) and the quantity of vehicle-kilometres required at that price. As the price of a vehicle-kilometre falls the quantity demanded expands, and as the price rises the quantity demanded contracts. For essential journeys, demand is relatively insensitive to price changes and is inelastic, but in the case of less essential journeys demand is fairly sensitive to price changes and is relatively elastic.

In figure 7.1, marginal private costs (MPC) equal demand D at t, the maximum traffic flow an individual motorist is willing to join. But at this level of flow, marginal social costs (MSC) are considerably higher – the individual motorist clearly not paying the extra cost of congestion that s/he is imposing on other road users. If the traffic flow was reduced to t_1, then marginal social costs would equal demand. The imposition of a road tax equal to an estimation of the difference between marginal social costs and marginal private costs at t_1 would lead to a contraction of demand from t to t_1 as the price the motorist would be obliged to pay would have risen from p to p_1.

Under such a direct road pricing system, the best use of existing roads would be realised, as each motorist would pay the marginal social cost resulting from his/her use. This would be equivalent to the optimum price and would be independent of the capital cost of the system. The major difficulty in applying this system is the determining the optimum level of traffic. Ideally, the price imposed should reduce the level of traffic to where the revenue collected equals the costs imposed by the vehicle upon the community in general and other vehicles in particular, but trial and error would be inevitable in pricing and establishing the optimum flow. Despite these difficulties, direct road pricing was recommended by the Smeed Report[5] in 1964. It suggested that variations from the optimum price might be made with little loss of benefit. If revenue exceeded total congestion costs, a self-financing road expansion or improvement programme would be feasible, but if revenue fell short of total conges-

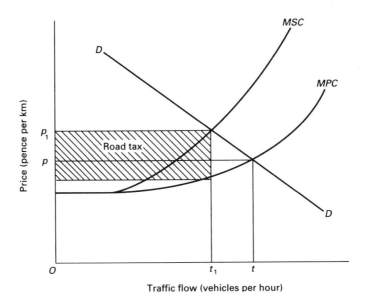

Figure 7.1 *Road tax and costs*

tion costs, road contraction might be necessary. Only in the long term should revenue equal total congestion costs.

A system of road pricing would thus involve road users paying more directly for the consumption of road space. Road space would be subject broadly to the economic principles on which we rely for the allocation of most of our goods and services. The advantages of this is that it would lead to the more efficient use of existing roads because users would be deterred by higher charges from using congested roads, and encouraged by low charges to use uncongested roads; and there would be a built-in criterion for investment, namely profitability. Currently, vehicle and fuel taxation assume as given the existing costs of the road system, and total costs are allocated among users and non-users without there being any reliable guidance as to which sections of the road network should be expanded and which contracted.

Methods of Road Pricing

The current method of taxing motorists (involving vehicle licences, VAT and petrol tax) fails to cope with current traffic problems in the following ways. It does not discriminate between locations where congestion costs are high or low; it fails to discriminate between times when congestion costs rise or fall; and although more petrol tax is paid on heavy-fuel-consuming vehicles than on low-fuel-consuming vehicles this is completely independent of location, time of day, or day of week and the degree of congestion. However slight the effect of petrol taxes in restraining congestion, it is probable that vehicle excise duties have even less effect. Taxes *in toto* incurred by the motorist unequivocally fail to control traffic flows in the right places at the right times.

Alternative indirect methods of charging motorists have been proposed in recent years. Outlined by Roth[6] these include:

(1) *Differential fuel taxes.* There would be different rates of taxation in different areas relating to the level of congestion.

(2) *Tyre taxes.* These could be seen as an alternative to petrol taxes.

(3) *Differential licences.* These could relate to zones of an urban area (for example, an expensive 'red' inner zone, and a less expensive 'blue' outer zone) and could be purchased for periods from a year to a day. Licence discs would need to be displayed on vehicles and there could be an exemption from licensing at night and at weekends. Because of its relative simplicity, differential licensing lends itself to experimentation, perhaps over a 5- to 8-year period. This system has been in use in Singapore for a number of years.

Whereas the above methods are indirect, relating to some product or requirement allied to road use, the optimal method may perhaps be a direct charge for road use. Direct charging could be by means of one or more of the following:

(1) *Toll gates.* Although these are the earliest and simplest method to have been used, in urban areas they can be costly and inefficient, can impede traffic flow and are impracticable where a large number of access points are required.

(2) *On-vehicle point pricing.* Meters attached to vehicles would pick up electrical impulses from cables laid across the road at selected pricing points. The meters would be read periodically by the pricing authority and accounts would be rendered.

(3) *On-vehicle continuous pricing.* Vehicles would be charged according to the time or distance travelled in a designated pricing zone. The meter would expire after a length of time or distance travelled in the pricing zone.

(4) *Electronic tolling. Either* a vehicle could be equipped with an identification tag which, on entering a pricing zone, could be registered by a roadside microwave beacon and the motorist's account debited, *or* vehicles could be equipped with meters which accepted rechargeable 'smart cards' (activated by roadside beacons) which displayed the remaining credit. Limited schemes are in use in Cambridge, Oslo and parts of some cities in the United States.

Both on-vehicle systems and electronic tolling could be based on a variable schedule – with maximum prices being charged during peak hours and in congested central areas. The point pricing system has advantages. It would not create the boundary problems inherent in the continuous pricing system; it could be employed for toll collection on bridges and in tunnels; and it would not encourage bad driving habits as motorists attempt to reduce payable time. The main advantages of the continuous pricing system are the ease of collecting payment (the main administrative difficulty of the point pricing system) and its relevance to motorists living and even driving entirely within one pricing zone – a situation which could not be controlled by the point pricing system. While not yet technically perfected, electronic tolling, on the other hand, offers most of the advantages of the on-vehicle point pricing system, while facilitating the easy collection of revenue. Both private and social costs could be reduced, however, if motorists installed computerised route guidance systems in their vehicles.

Some Economic Consequences of Direct Road Pricing

The disadvantages of direct road pricing are numerous:

(1) Many critics[7] predict that urban motoring would become the privilege of the wealthy.

(2) As a high proportion of low-income motorists travel exclusively in towns and largely at peak hours, a road tax would be clearly regressive.

(3) It was argued by Richardson,[8] however, that middle-income motorists would suffer the most. The low-income non-motorist might benefit from cheaper and more reliable public transport, the wealthy could afford the road tax without hardship, but the middle-income car owner might wish to continue using his/her car and thus incur the burden of the tax.

(4) If the road tax revenue was entirely invested into new and improved roads, congestion might ultimately reappear. Sharp[9] suggested that motorists would trade off the new tax initially against reduced travelling times.

(5) If a sufficient number of private motorists diverted their demand to public transport, overcrowded services and higher marginal costs of operation might result.

(6) Private traffic might be forced off congested routes by road pricing and begin to use less busy residential streets as 'short cuts' – thereby spreading environmental costs.

(7) Although it is technically possible to adopt a road pricing system by means of electronic devices, administrators and the police prefer a non-discriminatory system applicable to all sections of the community, and not one which is difficult to enforce or can be interpreted as being unfair.

(8) In the view of Munby,[10] continually changing conditions would make it necessary to adjust prices – the optimum price being difficult to estimate initially. It cannot be assumed that motorists (any more than non-motorists) always react rationally to changing economic circumstances. Road pricing would result inevitably in under-capacity or excess capacity of road space.

(9) A system of road pricing aimed at restricting the number of vehicles entering urban areas would necessitate the development of costly diversionary ring roads or bypasses for the use of through traffic. Often referred to as 'lorry routes', these roads might have no less of an impact on the environment than the existing full-capacity roads of the inner built-up area.

But the advantages of direct road pricing as seen by Hewitt, Lemon, Roth and Walters[11] are no less substantial:

(1) The resulting reduction in traffic in congested areas would produce a freer flow of traffic.

(2) The subsequent increase in average speeds would reduce the costs of delay.

(3) There would be a considerable saving in paid working time of people travelling during employment, and a saving in fuel – of great importance at a time of high energy costs.

(4) There would be greater productivity from buses and commercial vehicles. In the case of buses there could either be fewer crews and stocks required for the same level of service, or existing crews and stocks could produce a higher level of service. It is unlikely that road pricing would lead to an increase in fares.

(5) Road tax revenue would provide local and central government with funds for the improvement of road networks, the subsidisation of public transport, or for general purposes.

(6) Provided traffic did not become diffused over the road network and continued using (but at less volume) traditional routes, there could be a net reduction in environmental affliction.

In addition, direct road pricing – particularly if accompanied by improved public transport – could enhance property values. Better accessibility would increase both the efficiency of firms and the desirability of residential property. Depending upon the comparative costs and benefits of redevelopment and rehabilitation, *either* redevelopment would take place following an increase in the demand for sites and a consequential increase in site values, *or* rehabilitation would occur associated with the increase in the demand for buildings and their value. Figure 7.2a shows that with a rising site value, redevelopment would bring about the foreshortening of the economic life of the original building, while figure 7.2b indicates that rehabilitation would maintain the building's economic life following an increase in site value. In reality, the economic life of the building could be increased by more or fewer years than the number required to maintain the building's original economic life.

Road pricing has a number of general consequences. Motorists continuing to use road space would incur a higher cost, a cost previously passed on to other motorists. But they would probably attempt to minimise these costs whenever possible by travelling at cheaper times or by cheaper routes, by making fewer but longer shopping expeditions and by making greater use of vehicle passenger capacity. Road pricing might only be intended to reduce traffic flows by 10–12 per cent, and this reduction might only involve less-essential journeys, the 'second-car'-trip-makers and those middle-income commuters ready to transfer from the motor car to public transport as soon as the former becomes more expensive and/or the latter becomes more attractive.

Road pricing would probably not be difficult to enforce – certainly no more difficult than enforcing the 30 mph (48 km/h) speed limit, where it is estimated that only 10 per cent of offenders get caught. But rather than low fines

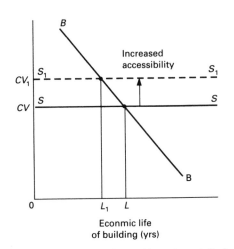

(a) Increase in the demand for a cleared site for the development of an alternative use.

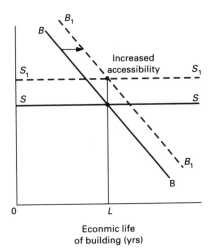

(b) Increase in the demand for a building (and site) in its existing use for the purpose of rehabilitation following an increase in the value of the cleared site.

Notes: BB = Capital value of building (and site) in existing use
SS = Capital value of cleared site in best alternative use
CV = Capital value of property

Figure 7.2 *The effects of increased accessibility upon the timing of redevelopment or rehabilitation*

and a low rate of enforcement, high fines could be imposed which would probably deter potential lawbreakers.

Investment

It is all too obvious that since urban roads are frequently congested, a solution to the problems of congestion would involve an increase in the supply of road space, at least on a selective basis, but sometimes extensively. In practice, investment techniques are not sophisticated enough to produce an optimum solution. Conventionally, the future unrestrained traffic flows over the urban road network are forecast, and there is then an attempt to allocate resources and provide facilities to meet this demand. Various *ad hoc* constraints may be proposed where flows would still be excessive.

Investment must take into account present costs and future needs. Although costs (at least direct costs) are predictable, benefits may not be. Information is required on how road development affects traffic speeds, delays, travelling costs, accidents, the environment, property values, commerce and industry – that is, how it affects vehicle operating costs and indirect costs. Road development is economically justifiable if total benefits exceed total costs.

The economist's role in road investment is to assess the relative costs and

benefits of the alternative proposals advanced by planners and highway engineers. An approach pursued increasingly is to undertake a cost-benefit analysis
(see Chapter 6). With regard to road investment, it was first used in Oregon in
the 1930s to help select a route between two points. Although the costs of
development were compared with the benefits of savings in fuel, time and tyre
wear, there was no consideration of the indirect effects on local economies.
Similarly, the London–Birmingham motorway was subject to a cost-benefit
analysis in the 1950s (after a decision had already been taken to build it). This
also ignored the more indirect benefits and costs.

But the main problem in undertaking a cost-benefit analysis, especially in
urban areas, is to quantify and value all the many intangibles obtaining to the
project. Since the pricing system is dominant, producers generally rely on the cost–
profit criterion as a means of assessing investment priorities, but in the case of
road development this simpler, less costly and possibly more effective approach
requires the establishment of an efficient road pricing system before it can be applied.

Road pricing would result in highway authorities adopting the attitude of a
competitive service industry, that is, expanding investment in the profitable
sections and reducing expenditure on the less profitable or loss-making sections. In the former, costs borne by the authorities would increase, but congestion costs would diminish. Lower congestion costs might then justify a reduction
in charges if the savings enjoyed were greater than the development, environmental and other costs. Although profits would be made on some roads and
losses on others (the flexibility of road pricing not being perfect) road pricing
would indicate the level of demand, identify the locations for development and
be very useful in investment decision-making.

To date, no effective solutions have been applied to the problem of urban
traffic congestion. Meanwhile, despite increasing energy prices, the shift from
public to private transport continues. It is over thirty years since the Buchanan
Report was published, but no technological answers have been introduced to
solve satisfactorily the problems imposed on people by cars and highways.
Architects, engineers and planners are unable to develop towns to accommodate traffic satisfactorily at present and future densities, even at unrealistically
high costs. Restricting traffic from entering large areas of towns and rerouteing
it away is not entirely feasible because of the numbers of vehicles involved
and the effect on populations elsewhere. Demand reverting to public transport
as it exists today is unlikely to take place (especially with rising fares), and
there are no technological developments anticipated which would eliminate the
attraction of the private car as a personal mode of transport.

Indirect methods of pricing currently ignore congestion as they do not relate
to the price users have to pay to the costs of road use. Although direct road
pricing systems seem complex, they would greatly simplify the overall problem of congestion by equating demand and supply. They would also assist in
ordering the priorities of use and increasing the efficiency of roads, ensuring a
more stable foundation for the operation of public transport services, improving the urban environment and providing a valid means by which public auth-

orities would be able to allocate resources for both road development and related public activities.

There is no reliable evidence to suggest that road pricing would reduce the attractiveness of town centres with regard to commerce or amenity. Road pricing would probably be less detrimental to the economic and social life of the town than current levels of congestion.

Yet road pricing has not been introduced. There have been political rasons for this; the motorists' lobby is very strong and in the public sector there are wide-ranging implications (not just confined to transport) in the concept that the consumer should pay the full marginal social cost for goods and services received. But central government may come around to accepting road pricing. In the 1970s, an official publication[12] suggested that the government was thinking along these lines. But even with political acceptability, it may take until the late 1990s before it is administratively feasible for an electronic tolling system to be applied.

It is probable that direct road pricing will be first applied to motorways, rather than to urban roads. In the 1993 Green Paper, *Paying for Motorways: Issues for Discussion*,[13] it was suggested that motorists will be charged 1.5p a mile for cars and 4.5p a mile for heavy goods vehicles on much of Britain's 2000-mile motorway network – generating about £700 million per annum.

Car Parking

At least since the Road Traffic Act 1956, which endeavoured to reduce congestion, local authorities have had powers to prohibit or restrict parking, and consequently (in theory) to restrict the total amount of traffic entering cities. The capacity of parking space (by time of day) is roughly related to the capacity of the road system. Parking restrictions and deterrents such as wheel-clamping are regarded as a first-stage traffic-management measure, something that can be applied before sophisticated methods of road pricing can be evolved.

But they do little to affect the volume of through traffic even during peak hours, they do not affect the total volume of peak-hour traffic, and they encourage motorists to take direct routes into central areas rather than circumferential ones. Motorists may cause congestion when looking for parking spaces; parking is often indiscriminate (it may or may not be close to the worst areas of congestion), much parking space is private and under the control of firms or individuals, and parking controls are difficult and costly to enforce.

Users of road space for parking should incur the full costs, both private and social, of doing so. If this is not done the parker is receiving a concealed subsidy at the expense of the community in general and other congested road users in particular.

The absence of an effective price mechanism for parking makes it difficult to assess demand. Roth[14] suggested that the need for parking space might be partly fulfilled by the following methods of allocation:

(1) *Queueing*. A specific amount of parking space is available on a 'first-come, first-served' basis. But it favours peak-hour car commuting; commuters may be the first to find a space and park all day.

(2) *Time limits*. These may be preferable to queueing as they eliminate all-day parkers, but may favour whimsical or frivolous users, and may add to congestion.

(3) *Equilibrium pricing*. Attempts to introduce equilibrium pricing have generally failed because charges have been too low to equate demand with supply. But if the motorist were charged an equilibrium price, congestion would be reduced and s/he would be meeting the full cost of parking. An equilibrium pricing system would ensure that parking space was filled most of the time, without there being unsatisfied demand at the price charged.

But since there is an absence of a pricing system reflecting the full cost of providing space, there is no economic yardstick to assist authorities in deciding whether parking space should be increased or decreased. 'Rule of thumb' decisions have resulted in unrealistically low parking charges, subsequent congestion and a demand (or 'need') for parking spaces in excess of supply.

PUBLIC TRANSPORT

Since the nineteenth century, public road transport has in many ways been regarded as an 'inferior good'. With the development of the motor car and rising real incomes, travellers have moved away from public to private transport. Congestion has largely been caused by the motor car. The London Transport Executive, referring to recent statistics, proclaimed that if 700 commuters travel to London they could fill 14 buses or 500 cars (that is, 1 bus for every 35 cars). One major effect of congestion has been that the efficiency and attractiveness of the bus has diminished.

There are no fundamental reasons why public transport should not be able to compete in speed, frequency or convenience with the private car if competition is on equal terms. Present conditions prevent this in the following ways:

(1) Private motorists are not being charged the full price (equal to their marginal social cost) for their use of roads.

(2) The increased congestion on roads and the subsequent rise in bus operating costs have necessitated ever-increasing fares.

(3) At off-peak hours and in outer suburban or rural areas, operators do not undertake marginal cost pricing as it is thought that fares would be intolerably high – cross-subsidisation of unremunerative services being necessary.

But the comprehensive subsidisation of public transport has its advantages:

(1) The present features of road transport tilt the balance in favour of the car and away from the bus. With road pricing applied to the private motorist the balance would be tilted the other way. Although the marginal costs of a car

journey may only be, say, 20 per cent of a bus journey per traveller, it is in fact considerably more; for example, 50 motorists would take up more space and impose higher congestion than 50 passengers on a bus. But the pricing of private motoring might not be itself attract back to public transport more than a marginal number of travellers. Bus services might have to operate at reduced fares, so that there is an absolute and not just a relative price advantage. This could be justified because whereas private motorists would be subject to a new road tax mainly on the basis of their marginal private costs being less than the marginal social costs they inflict on other motorists, buses incur higher marginal private costs (over long stretches of their cost curves) than the marginal social costs they impose on traffic in general. Therefore buses would be eligible for 'negative taxes' or subsidies.

(2) At a time of high oil prices, a rediversion of demand to public transport could have advantageous effects on the balance of payments.

(3) Subsidies would offset the regressive nature of road pricing by offering an alternative mode of transport.

(4) Generally, environmental costs are lower with public transport and a diversion to it would improve the situation.

(5) Reasonable mobility should be facilitated by local and central government for social reasons and the cost should be borne by the community as a whole.

(6) Highly subsidised or even free public transport would be warranted if the savings in travelling, congestion and administrative costs exceeded the extra rate poundage. By the early 1980s the Greater London Council (GLC) and most of the metropolitan counties were implementing cheap fare policies – for example, the GLC reduced London Transport fares by an average of 32 per cent in 1981. Even then only 46 per cent of the fare in London was subsidised, in contrast to 56, 61, 70, 71 and 72 per cent in Paris, Berlin, Brussels, Milan and New York respectively. Although in London, the cut in fares required a 6.1p in the pound increase to GLC ratepayers, the total increase would have been 11.9p in the pound because of a penalising decrease in the central government's block grant. Despite GLC policy reversing the trend of dwindling passengers for the first time in twenty years and cutting car commuting by 6 per cent, in December 1982 the House of Lords deemed cheap fares uneconomic and hence illegal under the Transport (London) Act 1969 – the Act not taking into account social cost-benefit considerations. Because of the reform of fare zones, London Transport was legally able to reduce fares in 1983 (by as much as 25 per cent), but at the cost of a 32 per cent increase in rates. Again, there was a marked increase in the proportion of commuters travelling by public transport and a decrease in commuting by car.

Under the Transport Act 1983, however, the Ministry of Transport could impose strict limits on the power of the (then) metropolitan counties to subsidise public transport (with inevitable increases in fares), and under the Transport Act of 1985, all bus routes outside London were opened up for competition from 1 October 1986. Unprofitable services were put out to tender by local authorities, with the probability that the bidder requiring the lowest subsidy would be offered the relevant routes. Underlying the 1985 Act was the government's desire to cut public spending by eliminating subsidy as far as possible, but also to extend untrammelled market forces by privatisation and deregulation. Within a year of the Act, 55–70 per cent of the formerly subsidised services were being run commercially, but with service cuts, lost routes, substantial fare increases, job losses and passenger confusion. Metropolitan areas were particularly badly hit. In London (after the abolition of the GLC and London Transport in 1986), the newly-established London Regional Transport Authority's initial subsidy of £190 million was reduced to £74 million in 1987–8 and to a targeted £59 million by 1988–9 – again with service cuts and lost jobs. Many of London's bus routes, moreover, were put out to tender and privatised, and it was planned to deregulate services in the capital by 1995. In the view of the all-party House of Commons Transport Committee, this plan would result in more congestion, unreliable services and a fall in the number of passengers.

The subsidisation of public road transport (except in the case of the abolition of fares) should not be seen as contradicting the principles of road pricing, but as part of the road pricing system where the basic parameters are marginal private costs and marginal social costs, and where the means of bridging the gap between these costs are taxes or subsidies. Since buses inflict very low congestion, environmental and accident costs on society, the marginal social costs of this mode of transport are often lower than its marginal private costs – and generally decrease with the volume of services (assuming a reciprocal reduction in the volume of motor car traffic). Figure 7.3 shows that if a subsidy were to fill the gap between these costs, bus operators could cut fares from f to f_1 but increase services from b to b_1.

Road pricing (involving both the taxing of private motorists and the subsidisation of public transport) would thus reduce congestion, improve accessibility and eliminate the need for commercial firms to relocate. In short, road pricing would improve the efficiency of the urban economy.

To date, no effective solutions have been applied to the problem of urban traffic congestion. Meanwhile, despite relatively high energy prices, the shift from public to private transport continues. A general trend in public policy initially towards zonal (differential) licensing and ultimately towards comprehensive road pricing and more heavily subsidised public transport may be seen as a solution to the problem of traffic and the environment. But in addition, the very special needs of the elderly and disadvantaged might require additional measures. Access credits have been recommended by a number of organisations[15] to enable the least mobile and less wealthy members of society to make use of the telephone or a home computer terminal to acquire information and to order goods for delivery, or to pay fares, road prices or hire taxis. Small, flexible-route, minibuses would also increase accessibility and provide an economic substitute for the private motor car or taxi.

It is perhaps reassuring that in the *Planning Policy Guidance Note 13* of

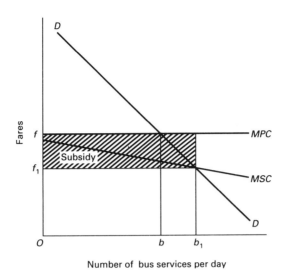

Figure 7.3 *Public transport demand, costs and subsidy*

1994, at last the Department of the Environment and Department of Transport recognised the need to plan for future employment, retailing and leisure facilities within the context of public transport networks, albeit a decreasingly subsidised network.

REFERENCES

1. R. Best, 'The Future Urban Acreage', *Town and Country Planning*, 32 (1964).
2. C. Doxiadix, *Urban America and the Role of Industry* (United States National Association of Manufacturers, 1971).
3. G. J. Roth, *Paying for Roads* (Penguin, 1967).
4. Ministry of Transport, *Traffic in Towns* (HMSO, 1963).
5. Ministry of Transport, *Road Pricing: The Economic and Technical Possibilities* (HMSO, 1964).
6. G. J. Roth, *Paying for Roads*.
7. M. E. Beesley, 'Technical Possibilities of Special Taxation in Relation to Congestion Caused by Private Users', *Second International Symposium on Theory and Practice in Transport Economics* (OECD European Conference of Ministers of Transport, 1968); L. K. Lemon, 'An Economic Examination of Traffic Congestion in Towns', *Administration* (1972); C. H. Sharp, *Transport Economics* (Macmillan, 1973).
8. H. W. Richardson, 'A Note on the Distributional Effects of Road Pricing', *Journal of Transport Economics and Policy* (1974).
9. C. Sharp, 'Congestion and Welfare: An Examination of the Case for a Congestion Tax', *Economic Journal* (1966).
10. D. L. Munby, 'Management: The Economist's Viewpoint', *Symposium on Traffic and Towns* (Annual Meeting of the British Association for the Advancement of Science, 1971).

11. J. Hewitt, 'The Calculation of Congestion Taxes on Roads', *Economica* (1964); L. K. Lemon, 'An Economic Examination of Traffic Congestion in Towns', *Administration* (1972); G. J. Roth, *Paying for Roads* (Penguin, 1967); A. A. Walters, 'Empirical Evidence on Optimal Motor Taxes for the United Kingdom', *Econometrica* (1961).

12. Department of the Environment, *Urban Transport Planning*, Cmnd 5336 (HMSO, 1973).

13. Department of Transport, *Paying for Motorways: Issues for Discussion*, Cm 2200 (HMSO, 1993).

14. G. J. Roth, *Paying for Parking*, Hobart Papers (Institute of Economic Affairs, 1965).

15. J. Ardill, 'Transport must face up to the future', *Guardian* (11 December 1986).

8

Urban Decline and Renewal

THE PROCESS OF URBAN CHANGE

Urban change has been characterized by declining populations, faster than average decline of manufacturing industry, lack of new 'hi-tech' industries and a growing predominance of the service sector. Poor housing conditions exist in many areas caused by on the one hand, a higher than average share of the older housing stock, and on the other, high concentrations of 1960s and early 1970s system-built high-rise dwellings – around three-quarters of which (nationally, one million dwellings) are situated in only six metropolitan centres.

The process of urban change has produced a complex set of social and economic difficulties for inner city areas. Although these problems were largely recognised as early as the 1960s and 1970s, by the 1980s it had become clear that inner-city problems involved not just isolated pockets of deprivation, but whole areas of the largest conurbations.

Population

Population movements have been at the forefront of urban change. Greater London, Birmingham, Sheffield and Bristol reached their peak populations in the census year 1951; Liverpool and Manchester even earlier, in 1931; and Leeds in 1961. While the conurbations (including the outer metropolitan areas of these cities) often continued to grow after the city's peak population has been reached – the West Midlands (Birmingham) and West Yorkshire (Leeds) conurbations declined only after 1971 – the general trend was downwards. Table 8.1 shows how this decline was part of a wider urban–rural shift in population which has gained pace over the post-war period.

Examining population change in the various area categories and over different time periods, we find that although population decline appears to be slowing in London and the principal cities, decline in other cities (for example, Bristol) is continuing at a similar, or even a higher rate than previously. Meanwhile, population growth in rural, mixed urban–rural, resort and seaside retirement areas and New Town districts has either continued at similar rates or has increased (figure 8.1).

More recently, in the case of Greater London, higher natural population growth (following, but above national trends) and a reduction in net (out) migration

Table 8.1 *Population change, intercensal periods* (percentages)

	1911		1931	1951	1961	1971	1981
Urban areas	13.5		10.6	4.3	3.5	−2.2	
Rural areas	1.2		5.3	9.6	14.8	10.3	

Notes: Population, urban areas 1981 = 37 324 (76%); rural areas 1981 = 11 687 (24%) (thousands).

Source: *Annual Abstract of Statistics 1993* (HMSO).

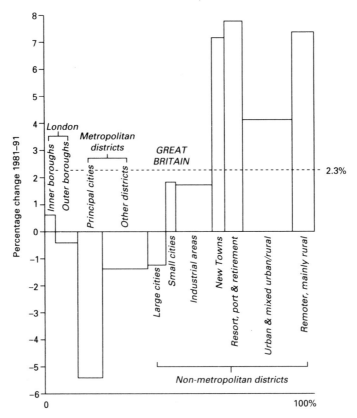

Source: *OPCS Monitor*, PP1 92/1 (HMSO, 1992).

Figure 8.1   *Population change, 1981–91, by type of district, Great Britain*

up until 1986/7 appear to explain the turnaround in decline in this area. While nationally, the natural change in population in the 1990s is expected to be roughly double that for the 1980s and will probably be at or above national rates in London, the metropolitan districts and other cities, net out-migration from the major cities and metropolitan districts is expected generally to increase. Nevertheless, as can be seen in table 8.2, higher net (out) migration will probably be more than offset by natural population change, so that apart from one case (Merseyside), population decline could be lower and some metropolitan districts may even achieve positive growth. If the predicted increase in out-migration from metropolitan districts over the 1990s materialises, this in turn will have profound implications for surrounding towns and rural areas in terms of service and new housing provision.

As for the conurbations themselves, the extent to which positive growth could be accommodated comfortably is also up for question. In the past, central-city population decline has generally occurred for three main reasons: first, slum clearance of the older stock of dwellings, often inhabited at high population densities; secondly, the conversion of residential inner-city areas for commercial uses; and thirdly, changes in average household size.[1]

While slum clearance in Britain's cities declined drastically from the mid-1970s to almost insignificant levels by the mid-1980s, some limited future increase cannot be ruled out, as the housing stock ages and as problems with 1960s high-rise flats become more intractable. Although new land has recently been released for housing in many inner-city areas (for example, the London Docklands) one view is that the most viable sites for new housebuilding may already have been exhausted.[2]

However, it is perhaps reductions in household size that have been one of the most universal causes of inner-city population decline. Not only has the average size of households declined nationally, but in urban areas average household size tends to be smaller and a higher proportion of households comprise single people (for example, the young and the elderly) or two-person, lone-parent households. Since the household forms the basic demand unit for independent dwellings, it is clear that this trend has the potential to cause significant mismatch between the total number of households and dwelling stock (units) over a period of time. Some indication of this problem is given in figure 8.2, which shows the relationship between population change and change in dwelling stock from 1981–9 in five major conurbations including the cities and outer metropolitan areas.[3] While the sample is not large enough to be significant in statistical terms, the trend relationship derived from this exercise does suggest that in order simply to maintain a given population, the urban housing stock would probably have to be increased by at least a half of one per cent each year. This figure, of course, represents a generalisation, and local circumstances may vary considerably, in particular with the possibility of converting larger houses into smaller units to more closely match household size. Excessive conversion might, however, have undesirable consequences if construction standards are poor (for example, sound-proofing), if parking space and so on is insufficient (especially in older housing areas that were not in any case designed to accommodate cars), or if as a result, floor space per inhabitant declines. It is also likely that nearer the city itself, expansion of the housing stock will prove more difficult, as initial population densities are usually much higher than in outer urban areas. Conversion levels here may already be high,

Table 8.2 Components of population change, 1981–9, 1989–2001 (thousands)

Region and metropolitan county (MC)	Population 1981	Component of change 1981–9				Component of change 1989–2001*				Population 2001
		Natural change	Migration	Total change	Percentage change	Natural change	Migration	Total change	Percentage change	
Greater London	6 805.6	175.4	−224.5	−49.1	−0.7	492.5	−415.3	77.2	1.1	6 833.6
Inner London	2 550.1	81.1	−127.6	−46.5	−1.8	226.0	−206.8	19.2	0.8	2 522.8
Outer London	4 255.4	94.3	−96.9	−2.6	−0.1	266.4	−208.5	58.0	1.4	4 310.8
West Midlands MC	2 673.1	65.4	−123.1	−57.7	−2.2	118.8	−169.1	−50.3	−1.9	2 565.2
Greater Manchester MC	2 619.1	35.1	−71.8	−36.7	−1.4	98.8	−113.9	−15.1	−0.6	2 567.3
Merseyside MC	1 522.2	13.2	−87.4	−74.2	−4.9	29.7	−123.9	−94.2	−6.5	1 353.8
Tyne and Wear MC	1 155.2	2.2	−29.3	−27.1	−2.3	16.8	−37.9	−21.1	−1.9	1 107.0
South Yorkshire MC	1 317.1	9.3	−31.3	−22.0	−1.7	27.5	−28.9	−1.4	−0.1	1 293.8
West Yorkshire MC	2 066.9	30.8	−31.1	−0.3	0.0	87.3	−56.7	30.6	1.5	2 097.2
England	46 820.8	621.4	247.2	868.6	1.9	1 646.8	−203.2	−1 849.9	3.9	49 539.3

Note: *Projections

Source: *Population Trends 66* (HMSO, 1991).

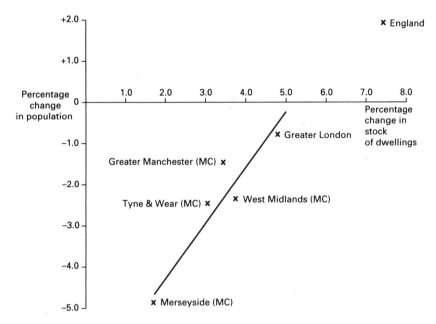

Source: *Housing and Construction Statistics* and *Population Trends*, (HMSO, various).

Figure 8.2 *Population change and change in stock of dwellings in five major conurbations, 1981–9*

while redevelopment would probably produce lower residential densities. As a further illustration, in the Dutch city of The Hague, an increase in housing stock of 3.2 per cent was achieved in 1975–9, but the population over the same period fell by 12.0 per cent.[4]

Employment

During the 1950s, employment in the conurbations grew more slowly than in the country as a whole, but during the 1960s and 1970s total employment there declined by 8.3 per cent and 11 per cent respectively. In particular, manufacturing employment in the conurbations declined substantially during these three decades. To a great extent this reflected national trends, with manufacturing employment peaking around the mid-1960s and falling thereafter. However, manufacturing decline in the conurbations continued at a faster rate than elsewhere because of the pronounced urban–rural shift in industrial location (see Chapter 2). Initially, this was felt most strongly in the central and inner areas of cities as firms moved to more spacious suburban locations, particularly during the early post-war period (over the 1950s manufacturing employment in the outer areas of the conurbations grew at the national rate). But by the 1970s, manufacturing decline in outer areas was not far short of the levels experienced

Table 8.3 *Employment change in the conurbations 1951–81*

	Great Britain (%)	Overall conurbations (%)	Central and inner areas	Outer areas
1951–61				
Manufacturing	5.0	−1.7	−8.0	5.0
services	10.6	7.7	6.7	9.3
Total	7.0	3.4	1.0	6.0
1961–71				
Manufacturing	−3.9	−17.2	−26.1	−10.3
services	8.6	−0.2	−8.5	13.6
Total	1.3	−8.3	−14.8	0.6
1971–81				
Manufacturing	−24.5	−34.5	−36.8	−32.6
services	11.1	1.8	−6.8	12.7
Total	−2.7	−11.0	−14.6	−7.1

Note: The conurbations are London, West Midlands, Greater Manchester, Merseyside, Tyneside and Clydeside.

Source: Derived from Begg *et al.* in V. Hausner, *Critical Issues in Urban Economic Development* (Clarendon Press, 1986).

in central and inner areas, which had itself increased (see table 8.3). The cause of such decline cannot generally be attributed to the past industrial structure of the conurbations – on the whole they do not appear to have had a higher than average share of declining manufacturing industries.[5]

Urban manufacturing decline would seem to be more easily explained by reference to locational factors rather than to structural factors. It is also worth noting that most employment decline has been associated with closures of complete firms or employment reduction by existing firms, rather than movement of firms away from the conurbations.[6] There is some evidence to suggest that multiplant firms may have been diverting jobs from plants in cities to existing branches elsewhere[7] and that post-merger rationalization may have played a role in some areas.[8] It is also likely that in response to the globalization of markets and production, the overseas workforce of multinational firms based in industrial heartlands, such as the West Midlands and North-West, has increased at the expense of plants in the UK.[9] Other locational factors have also been at work and one suggestion is that the profitability of plants located in the conurbations may be lower than elsewhere because of a range of urban problems. These include age and inconvenience of multistorey premises, higher rates and rents and higher labour costs. More recently, during the late 1980s, older industrial buildings were commonly converted to office uses, as demand for office space in many CBDs grew – a trend which was almost certainly helped by the introduction of class B1 (light industrial and offices) in the Use Classes order 1987.

Finally, the 'constrained location' problem (discussed in Chapter 2) is likely to be a major reason for manufacturing job loss in the conurbations. By itself, and assuming no growth in floorspace, the increasing capital intensity of manufacturing processes – necessitating higher average factory floorspace per worker – could alone have been responsible for a reduction in manufacturing employment by a third between 1964 and 1979.[10] Jobs would have been lost on cramped premises unable to expand floorspace, and new development would have been constrained by land availability, site constraints, and costs. Indeed, even if existing industrial sites were redeveloped, more modern buildings would achieve lower site coverage and would, of course, be single rather than multistorey. Nowadays, few firms are dependent on the skills traditionally found in the industrial cities and newer 'hi-tech' industries have locational preferences which can often be more easily met in areas outside the conurbations. These include good motorway and air links, proximity to research and development facilities, and access to low-density residential areas for management and research personnel.

The expansion of service sector employment has, until the early 1990s recession, been a more-or-less continuous feature of post-war growth. As table 8.3 shows, this increase has generally been slower in the conurbations than elsewhere, and (like industrial growth in the 1950s) has been limited almost exclusively to the outer metropolitan areas after the 1960s. Central and inner areas of the conurbations, taken as a whole, experienced a loss of 455 000 service sector jobs between 1961 and 1981 (the outer areas gaining 534 000).

Service sector employment grew by over 11.00 per cent nationally from 1985 to 1989. Because of the location of key financial and business activities in London, the city was able to reap the benefits of financial deregulation over the 1980s. Even so, service employment in London increased at a rate no higher than the national average over this period – accounting for an additional 307 000 employees. This growth in employment tended to mask the fact that manufacturing decline was continuing at or above past rates, and 97 000 manufacturing jobs were lost in London during 1985–9. We should set this figure in the context of a net loss of 125 000 manufacturing jobs in Great Britain over the same period.[11] These manufacturing losses in London are perhaps surprising, given that from 1987/9 nearly 8 per cent of all new industrial construction work took place in this area – a figure only slightly smaller than London's share of national manufacturing employment (8.9 per cent in 1989).[12] Employment changes were also accompanied by important gender differences; manufacturing decline tended to affect males relatively more, while service growth particularly increased opportunities for female employment. The net effect in London over the same period (1985–9), was an increase of 206 000 in female employment, whilst male employment remained static. One result was an increase in the proportion of households with two earners, and this fact, combined with an increase in part-time employment, may well have helped to reduce out migration from London (putting further pressure on the housing market) from the early to mid-1980s.

Table 8.4 *Percentage population and employment changes by type of local authority district*

District/Type	Population 1981–8	Employment 1981–7
London	−1.0	−1.5
Other principal cities	−4.5	−8.7
Industrial districts:		
Other metropolitan	−1.5	−4.6
Industrial areas	+0.1	−1.7
Remoter, mainly rural	+6.1	+5.0
Prosperous sub-regions	+3.2	+3.8
Great Britain	+1.3	−0.2

Source: Derived from A. G. Champion and A. R. Townsend, *Contemporary Britain*, table 7.8 (Edward Arnold, 1990).

Finally, table 8.4 illustrates the fact that up until the main employment gains of the late 1980s economic 'boom', the rate of employment decline was out-pacing population decline in the principal cities and industrial metropolitan districts.

COUNTERURBANISATION

One of the key questions posed by those studying recent population trends in Europe, the United States and Japan, is whether the share of national popula-tion in the largest urban areas of these countries has in fact peaked and whether further growth will in future be confined to smaller towns and rural areas. We have already seen evidence for the United Kingdom to suggest that the largest cities were not growing as fast as the country as a whole in the 1950s and that smaller settlements had already made some recovery by the 1960s. However, the more important consideration is clearly whether such changes form part of a more widespread process, affecting advanced industrialised countries in gen-eral. Whilst some studies have investigated overall population changes, others have placed more emphasis on migration patterns. Migration flows have often been more important than natural change in explaining spatial population changes and they more clearly reflect the place preferences of individuals. In all cases it is important to define settlements as being relatively self-contained units in terms of jobs and populations in order to exclude the effects of suburbanisation and local metropolitan decentralisation. This is desirable since these clearly represent extensions of existing urban settlements, rather than counterurbanisation as such.

In Britain urban population changes occurred only slowly at first, and although unexpected in terms of its eventual scope, some decentralisation was generally seen as being desirable to facilitate clearance of some of the worst slum areas (often in association with the New Towns programme). Elsewhere, however the decline of the largest metropolitan areas came as an even greater surprise. Indeed, in 1975, a report of the International Geographical Union went so far as to state that urbanisation had become a 'really worldwide phenomenon'.[13] In contrast, Berry in 1976[14] pointed out that since 1970, the United States metropolitan areas had grown more slowly than the nation as a whole and that this decline was mainly accounted for by the eight largest metropolitan areas, which had lost over a quarter of a million residents. Migration flows between these areas and the outlying non-metropolitan counties had also been reversed; while the largest metropolitan areas in the United States had gained (net) migrants over the 1960s they lost them over the 1970s. Although much of this growth took place in smaller metropolitan areas and in counties with substantial daily commuting to metropolitan areas, it also appeared that remoter rural areas had recorded a large upturn in population change. Taking a broader view of counterurbanisation (including all types of deconcentration) than might be used today, Berry attributed these changes to the residential preferences of individuals for low-density living. Housing and job markets would then adjust to these preferences to produce decentralisation of both population and employment. Economic, technological and transportation factors would play a role in influencing the speed at which counterurbanisation occurred. Berry clearly emphasises the role of 'values' in residential decision-making; this approach has, however, been given some support by later studies showing negative correlations between city size and respondents' assessment of their standard of living and neighbourhood ratings.[15] The drawbacks with this argument are, first, that not everyone has a true choice of residential location; and, secondly, that employment decentralisation is possibly at least as important in explaining population shifts as vice versa. For example in South-East England over the 1970s and 1980s counties with the highest levels of employment growth were largely dependent on in-migration of workers, so that employment growth and population relocation were interdependent. If residential location had occurred independently of employment relocation, in-migration of population would have been associated with increased out-commuting (to London), which was not generally the case.[16]

More recent statistics, shown in table 8.5, appear to show that counterurbanisation has gone into reverse in the United States, with metropolitan areas achieving higher population growth rates than non-metropolitan areas over the 1980s.

To what extent this is attributable to a fundamental reversal or merely a partial lapse in counterurbanisation is unclear. As in the United Kingdom, service sector growth and financial deregulation coupled with an urban property boom may have had some influence, particularly given their impact on the United States housing market.[17]

In Europe, in addition to Great Britain, the process of counterurbanisation – defined in terms of net migration patterns – appears to have generally held up

Table 8.5 *Population changes in the United States, 1960–90, by metropolitan type* (percentages)

Period	Large metropolitan area	Other metropolitan area	Non-metropolitan area
Ten-year change			
1960–70	18.5	14.6	2.2
1970–80	8.1	15.5	14.3
Five-year change			
1980–5	6.0	6.1	3.6
1985–90	5.8	4.4	0.3

Note: Metropolitan areas are defined according to constant boundaries as of 1990. Large metropolitan areas include 39 CMSAs and MSAs with 1990 populations of 1 million and over.

Source: Adapted from A. G. Champion, 'Urban and Regional Demographic Trends in the Developed World', *Urban Studies*, 29, 3/4 (1992).

in France, Belgium, Denmark and the Federal Republic of Germany (FRG) over the 1970s and 1980s (and Switzerland, based on population change). Sweden, however, appears to have experienced a shift back towards urbanisation over the 1980s, as has the Netherlands. In southern Europe, Portugal appears to exhibit an increasing tendency towards urbanisation, possibly due to declining agricultural employment in rural areas and growing industrialisation.[18]

Recent evidence suggests that counterurbanisation has now become a feature of Italian population change, with metropolitan areas of Turin, Milan and Genoa in decline over the period 1981–5. In the FRG functional urban regions with over one million population experienced absolute population decline for the first time during 1980–5.[19] With unification, however, it is possible, that these changes will be reversed because of in-migration. There are also signs of renewed acceleration in the United Kingdom and Denmark following a period of slower deconcentration in the 1980s.[20] For France, however, the 1990 census results suggest that the Paris conurbation in particular has recovered markedly from its losses during 1975–82, partly because of a strong natural rate of increase in the population and what appears to be a halt in the long-term decline of average household size (compare London on table 8.2). In Japan, rapid urbanisation took place in the 1950s and 1960s, with massive population movements into the metropolitan regions'. Urbanisation there appears to have reached a plateau after about 1975. While Tokyo continues to see net out-migration, its population is not in decline and overall a process of counterurbanisation cannot be clearly identified. In fact, a net migration outflow from non-metropolitan to metropolitan regions, although small, appears to have resumed since the early 1980s.[21]

Clearly, despite the general tendency for countries to have experienced population deconcentration at some point in the recent past, there are considerable differences between countries in terms of the timing and severity of this process. Some interesting generalisations can nevertheless be made, although many factors are obviously specific to certain countries or cities. One approach suggested by Frey[22] is to highlight two separate processes, the first being population deconcentration – a shift from heavily urbanised to less densely populated areas. The second being the 'regional restructuring process' – referring to the spatial effects of changes in the locational requirements of firms in the production and service sectors.

Population movements can in reality be considerably more complex than Berry's initial hypothesis envisaged. Movements away from large urban areas can be increased by improvements in transport infrastructure and the consequent expansion of commuting fields around large cities. In some countries this trend has been associated with a strong desire for different types of housing (especially houses rather than flats). In France, for example, as many as a third of new dwellings built after 1975 were for households setting up home in rural areas. To a large extent this may simply reflect a form of extended suburbanisation or peri-urban development with an associated increase in commuting.[23] Yet it also reflects the fact that relatively little new development of individual housing now occurs in many European cities.

Increasing international migration flows may be a factor tending to reinforce recent urban growth in the South and West regions of the United States, and may also have been important in London in the early 1980s. The increase in retirement migration towards areas such as the south coast and the South-West in Britain has had the opposite effect. Changes in the composition of households may also influence migration trends – one-parent families with limited means are likely to be less mobile and will try to minimise travel-to-work time/distance; similar considerations apply to part-time workers and two-income households where one job is part-time. On the other hand, households composed of divorced adults appear to be much more mobile over longer distance.[24] Particularly in the United Kingdom, the increase in part-time female work over the 1980s, and the subsequent increase in two-income households, together with the continuing rise in single-parent families is likely to have been important in reducing net out-migration from London during the early to mid-1980s. Finally, although cities such as London exhibit net migration outflows overall, in younger age groups (18–24) the net migration flows are often positive, thus an upturn in the proportion of the national population in younger age groups may help to reduce the migratory outflow.

It has been suggested by L. Bourne[25] that together, the effects of recession, reductions in employment in finance and related business services, a downturn in younger age groups and household formation, and an upturn in those of retirement age would combine to bring an end to the gentrification (residential upgrading) of many inner city areas over the 1990s. Others have argued that changes in the workforce and the composition of households, have widened permanently the social base for inner city resettlement. They point out that in some countries (for example, Australia) the gentrification process is already extensive and is therefore unlikely to be reversed.[26]

Turning to the employment effects of the 'regional restructuring process', we can contrast, on the one hand, the decentralising forces resulting from the urban–rural shift in manufacturing with, on the other the centralising forces brought about by the growth of financial and producer services over the 1980s. The processes involved have been examined in more depth by Fielding,[27] who describes how there has emerged a new spatial division of labour (NSDL), involving the increasing separation of command functions (for example, senior management, headquarters functions, and research and development) from production, and of white-collar employees from blue-collar. In large part this can be traced back to the growth of mass-market consumer industries from the 1960s; the rise of large industrial conglomerates and multinationals; and the boom in investment in branch plant operations – all from about the same time. More recently, corporate restructuring and the search for low-cost locations for routine production processes has contributed to the de-industrialisation of major cities. To a lesser degree, it has also influenced the dispersal of office workers to areas lying outside the main metropolitan centres.[28] One result is that relatively successful regions, seen as low-cost production locations with access to United Kingdom and EU markets, have been able to attract higher-than-average shares of inward foreign direct investment (for example, Wales, the West Midlands and the North).[29] On the other hand, the 'hi-tech' industries have tended to become polarised in the South and East of England (excluding London, however).[30]

The full implications of the NSDL are not yet clear. However, one result could be further concentration of service functions in a small number of major (especially capital) cities with prestige environments. Manufacturing losses in these areas would continue at much the same rate as in the past, with consequent upward effects on unemployment and social polarisation. Manufacturing employment growth would continue to gravitate towards the less urbanised areas; in the United Kingdom this would increasingly involve areas outside the South-East. Urban areas and regions will come to be characterised by the functions they perform, rather than the goods they produce or industries they host. Interindustry linkages in an area may thus decline in importance and growth centre strategies may consequently become less effective.[31]

Finally, comparative studies, such as those by Cheshire[32] have pointed to a growing polarisation between 'successful' and 'unsuccessful' cities. National or regional factors were shown to be important in explaining why cities performed better or worse than expected, as were the effects of local urban policies. For example, cities in south-western France, and south and south-eastern Germany (FRG) appear to have improved compared with their predicted performance. Also, European economic integration appears to be of greater benefit to cities in the more central (core) regions than to those more peripheral ones (including Southern Europe, the Republic of Ireland, Western Scotland and North-West England). In particular, there is some evidence to suggest that the problems of Southern European regions are becoming concentrated in urban as opposed to rural areas as low-skilled workers from the latter continue

Table 8.6 *Indicators of change in selected agglomerations in Germany* (FRG)

	(North) Ruhr-North	(South) Munchen
Percentage change in population 1970–85	−6.3	+10.1
Percentage change in dependent employment 1970–85	−20.1	+47.5
Percentage change in tax income per inhabitant 1979–85	+32.0	+46.4
Unemployment rate (1986)	13.7	5.4

Source: F. J. Bade Regionale Beschäftigungs entwicklung and Produktionsorientierte Dienst-leistungen, Deutsches Institut für Wirtschaftsforschung Sonderheft 143, Duncker & Humblot (1987).

to move to the cities in search of work (for example, in Naples and Andalucia). Other studies have identified stagnating cities linked to old industrial areas, ports or mining activities (respective examples being Birmingham/Turin, Genoa, and South Wales or the Ruhr), and dynamic towns or cities linked to tourist regions (for example, Spain) or dynamic rural areas with small/medium-sized towns (for example, north-east Italy).[33]

A recent study of urban development in Germany (FRG), showed clearly how the North–South divide in that country – because of the relative concentration of declining industries in the North and 'hi-tech' industries in the South – was especially evident in the performance of the agglomerations, influencing income and employment growth, unemployment and migratory balance (see table 8.6).

THE STAGES THEORY OF URBAN GROWTH

A more detailed picture of urban change can be obtained from various cross-national studies which have based their analyses on specially defined 'functional urban regions'. Such regions, based on recognised urban centres, also include their surrounding commuter belts. They generally cover a wider area than would national urban statistics, and this has the obvious advantage of encompassing more extended forms of suburban development. Indeed, these studies tend to place more emphasis on the relationship between population trends in inner (core) areas and those in outer (ring) areas, than on population change overall. The assumption is that urban areas undergo various stages of urban development, exhibiting particular characteristics at each stage. The stages model, initially suggested by Hall, was subsequently developed by Vanhove and Klassen, and Van den Berg *et al.*.[34]

Initially at least, the urbanisation process is invariably associated with growing industrialisation. As this process gathers pace urban areas move slowly from

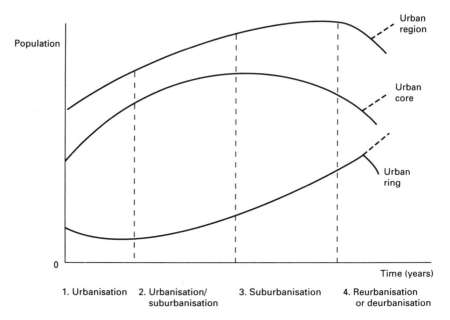

Figure 8.3 *Population size at stages of urban development*

one stage to the next (figure 8.3). In the first early stage of urbanisation agricultural labourers are drawn from the surrounding rural areas to the fast-grow-
ing industrial sectors located in the cities. Such changes began to occur more
than 100 years ago in Britain, but only towards the end of the nineteenth century or in the early twentieth century in most of Western Europe, and even
later in much of Eastern Europe. At this stage, population growth in the urban
'core' is fast, while population in the surrounding 'ring' may actually decline
as resources and population are drawn to towns and cities.

In the second stage, extensive transport facilities are created, as well as
public amenities and better housing. The role of services expands, and manufacturing industries are moved further away from the centre. With better public
transport, and especially growing car ownership, an increasing proportion of
households may take advantage of suburban residence to achieve lower-density
housing in a quieter environment while still maintaining reasonable access to
the city. Planning authorities rarely resist these tendencies and eventually population growth in the surrounding 'ring' comes to exceed that of the core area
itself.

By the third stage, the population continues to suburbanise but with falling
population at the core, since residential uses there are increasingly coming into
conflict with other uses, especially offices, which achieve higher land values.
Overall, however, the urban region continues to grow, albeit more slowly. It is
during this stage that the problems caused by excessive suburbanisation become acute; the existing road network in particular can no longer cope with

growing numbers of commuters and congestion reduces the accessibility of workplaces near the city centre.

During the final stage(s) these effects may also spread to the suburban areas, which then cease to expand. At this point, Van Den Berg *et al.* suggest that satellite towns 50–100 km from the 'core' city – themselves at an earlier stage in the urban life cycle – will benefit from decentralisation, thus encouraging job losses in the original urban system. As a means of reversing the decline of urban cores, these authors suggest measures to reduce congestion (in particular, by reducing traffic demand), to restrain suburbanisation and to support the residential function of central cities. Although the theory recognises the possibility of urban resurgence, this is not assumed to be a natural phenomenon but rather the result of concerted efforts on the part of central and local government to encourage urban renewal and introduce policies to deal more specifically with the problems mentioned above.

Studies which have examined the pattern of European urban development tend to support the validity of the stages theory. For example, the aforementioned study by Van den Berg *et al.* showed that only in Bulgaria, Hungary and Poland did the dominant stage of urban development (that is, urbanisation) fail to progress during the period 1950–75. All other countries moved up by one or two stages.

Countries such as Great Britain, Belgium and Switzerland were in the suburbanisation stage in the 1950s, so while metropolitan areas were still growing, they were decentralising people from 'cores' to 'rings'. By the early 1970s population decline in urban cores in these countries was not offset by growth in ring areas, and deurbanisation occurred. However, at the same time in countries such as France, Italy and Sweden, urban systems had moved only so far as the suburbanisation stage.

It would appear that countries which industrialised earliest, for example Great Britain and Belgium, generally found their urban system to be in more advanced stages in comparison with countries that were slower to industrialise. This may be due to the fact that in the former countries a larger proportion of cities date from the nineteenth or early twentieth centuries and cannot easily satisfy the requirements of today's modern industries. More recent studies by Cheshire and Hay[35] tend to confirm the trend towards decentralisation and also point to a tendency for northern European countries to lead and for southern countries to lag.

Finally, figure 8.4 illustrates how population change in London since the beginning of the twentieth century has followed the pattern predicted by the stages theory. In spite of the recent stabilisation of population it is too early to say whether de-urbanisation has turned to re-urbanisation. Moreover, unless economic development and employment can match any population upturn the term 're-urbanisation' itself is perhaps rather meaningless. Up to now, urban population decline has tended to be matched (or more than matched) by employment decline and decentralisation, so the prospect of a resumption of urban population growth in the absence of any accompanying improvement in

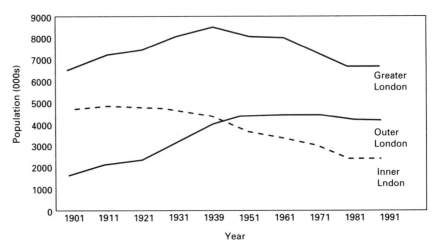

Figure 8.4 *London's population 1901–91*

urban employment opportunities must be one of particular concern to public policy-makers.

THE CHANGING INTERNAL STRUCTURE OF THE CITY

The process of urban renewal can be seen first as a reaction to changing requirements and demands being placed on the large conurbations, and secondly as part of the inevitable process of obsolescence and reconstruction. Redevelopment, rehabilitation and the relocation of activities are all part of the process of urban growth and renewal. As the economic life of buildings comes to an end, so the existing stock must eventually adjust to new demands.

Theories put forward to help explain changes in the internal structure of the city over time must therefore address themselves to these questions. As the city expands, however, and especially at later stages of urban growth, new development on the urban fringe may become an increasingly attractive alternative to redeveloping the existing central area. This outward movement of development and construction activity is invariably associated with the outward movement of population and population densities. Blumenfeld was the first to point out the wavelike characteristics of urban expansion.[36] By examining population change over fifty years in fifteen concentric zones extending outwards from Philadelphia, he found a similar undulatory pattern within each zone. Relative to the average density for a particular period and starting from the centre, each zone in succession reached a peak density, from which it gradually declined. However, as one moved outwards so this peak density itself became much lower and the variations in density over time became less pronounced. Boyce[37] noted that the fifty-year period required for an upward and downward

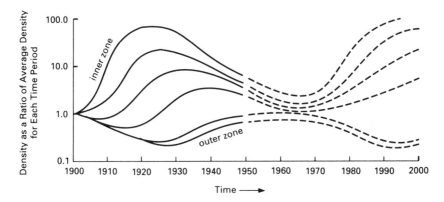

Source: Adapted from H. Blumenfeld (see note 36) and R. R. Boyce (see note 37).

Figure 8.5 *Schematic presentation of zonal density undulations over time in an expanding metropolitan area*

movement corresponded roughly to the economic life of buildings, and went on to suggest that the (then) current redevelopment of the central-city area could represent a new 'wave' and a repeat of the whole process (as illustrated by the dotted lines in figure 8.5).

According to Blumenfeld, at any point in time there is a particular zone of maximum growth. As illustrated by the already mentioned Philadelphia study, this zone would initially move outwards over time, representing a 'tidal wave of metropolitan expansion' at the rural–urban fringe of the metropolitan area. Boyce[38] argues that urban renewal and redevelopment is largely dependent on the ability to slow down or reverse the outward spread of this wave. In this sense, redevelopment at the centre can be seen as an alternative to further new development at the urban fringe.

Bourne[39] examines these processes in more detail, paying particular attention to the alternatives of development and redevelopment. Figure 8.6 illustrates a hypothetical view of development activity as we move outwards from the central business district (CBD). In the city centre, where accessibility is highest, the economic life of buildings may be relatively short, since new building generally requires redevelopment of the existing stock, and changes in demand affecting this stock are relatively frequent (for example, new shopping malls, 'hi-tech' offices and dealing rooms, and so on). Given that land values peak near the CBD, there is economic pressure to develop at high densities. Another peak in development activity may be expected near the suburban fringe, generally on green field sites, with lower costs permitting lower-density construction. Such development would tend to follow outward population movements, itself generating further demand. Accessibility may nevertheless be quite good in such locations, particularly given recent and prospective motorway programmes (such as the M25 orbital motorway which itself generated considerable development pressures outside the green belt fringe surrounding London). As a result,

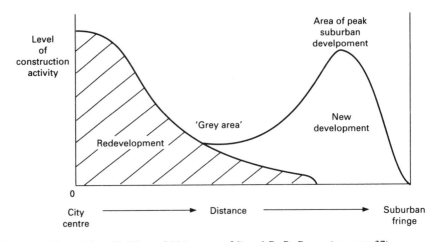

Source: Adapted from H. Blumenfeld (see note 36) and R. R. Boyce (see note 37).

Figure 8.6   *Cross-sectional view of urban development activity*

a wide range of development projects may be contemplated in such areas.

Over time, the central and suburban peaks of activity may gradually move outwards. However, physical expansion of the CBD will inevitably be much more restricted than that of the suburban fringe; indeed, in the case of London, many existing parts of the urban area were at some point in the nineteenth century villages at or beyond the rural–urban fringe. In between these two peaks available sites will already have been developed to varying degrees. Some redevelopment will occur in better locations, otherwise new development will generally consist of infilling. Available sites may be small, with mixed uses more common, and frequently, accessibility may be impeded by congestion and difficulty of improving the transport infrastructure.

Particularly around the transitional zone, these problems may be compounded by high demolition and site preparation costs (for example, old power stations or the effects of toxic land contamination on former industrial sites), making redevelopment more costly (see further Chapter 5). The overall atmosphere of decay in areas containing many redundant buildings and where improvement has failed to occur, may lead to even further decline; new investment may be considered to be too much of a risk, and owners of existing buildings may decide to neglect even essential repair and maintenance activity. This neglect may produce a short-term increase in returns but in the longer term buildings will tend to decay more quickly. Although it could be in the interest of all owners to invest in improvement works if capital values are sure to rise subsequently, such investment may nevertheless fail to occur. This is often due to the fact that, taken individually, any single investment would probably have little overall impact on property values in an area. As a result, it is likely that no owners will invest since they cannot be sure others will do the same (the so-called 'prisoner's dilemma' problem, mentioned earlier). Furthermore, the external costs and dereliction generated by such decisions may spill over, blighting surrounding areas where property values and the incentive for improvement may also become depressed.

In the case of housing, slum formation is the ultimate result.[40] Here, a 'filtering' process may occur, through which older dwellings vacated by higher-income households become available to (larger numbers) of lower-income households. This filtering may permit considerable change of use from single-family habitation to multiple tenancy before redevelopment or rehabilitation takes place. While this process, which increases the supply of low-cost housing, is generally regarded as being socially and economically useful, there may come a stage at which the pressure of demand from low-income groups in inner urban areas places considerable pressures on this stock. As a result, overcrowding becomes more common, rents soar, housing becomes increasingly adapted to temporary requirements and the pace of housing renewal grinds to a halt, since landlords find no shortage of tenants and owners have little incentive to undertake major improvements in a decaying environment.

Although development peaks, and even an outward wave motion, may be discerned, the pace of development activity from area to area may be very uneven. As we have seen, in residential areas the filtering process may delay the timing of redevelopment or improvement substantially. In other areas, urban decay may lead to a process of cumulative decline which eventually spills over into neighbouring areas. One further body of research suggests that since the intensity of site development at the suburban fringe is influenced by the stage of the development cycle in which it occurs, redevelopment in subsequent waves will tend to concentrate first of all on the less intensive land use.[41] For example, individual late Victorian villas (low-intensity, early-slump) are likely to be redeveloped sooner than early 1930s blocks of flats (high-intensity, early-boom) even where these happen to be in similar locations.

Finally, in addition to the influences discussed above, problems associated with the land market are also important. High land values will generally reflect high demand for a restricted number of sites, particularly within the CBD. However, especially in more outlying areas of the transitional zone, gross development values will often be depressed by uncertainty and locational constraints (for example, poor accessibility), and (re)development costs may be inflated by high site clearance and site preparation costs, and high reparcellation costs in trying to obtain sites of sufficient size for new uses. Consequently, the developer's (residual) valuation of available sites may often be below the values at which land owners may be willing to sell. Landowners must therefore be prepared to take a realistic view of urban site values if development is to proceed.

In conclusion, the above theories are all useful in helping us to understand the process of adaptation to change in urban areas. While the needs and requirements of various activities – retailing, industrial, offices and residential – may change at a fairly rapid pace with changes in technology and as fashions change, existing buildings are usually fairly fixed in terms of the services they offer. This problem of mismatch or 'functional obsolescence' can elicit a variety

of responses. In some cases existing buildings can be adapted, but more frequently there is a call for new buildings. In the latter case, the alternative to
redeveloping existing buildings within the urban area is often green field site
development at the rural–urban fringe. In this context it is sometimes suggested
that the existence of controls over the outward development of the city (such
as green belts) will help to turn back these waves of urban expansion – thus in
theory encouraging redevelopment rather than continuous urban sprawl. By raising
capital values for new uses in urban areas, redevelopment may well be encouraged, but other problems may be created. Rising land values would affect some
uses (for example, housing) more than others which could easily build at higher
densities (for example, offices), and the cost of providing some types of social
infrastructure (for example, roads) would also rise. Higher costs of living resulting from more expensive housing could well translate into higher wage
demands. Moreover, some activities could decide to leapfrog the barrier entirely rather than move back towards the city – possibly resulting in urban job
losses occurring at a faster rate than population decentralisation. On the other
hand, the unrestricted growth of urban areas would cause urban sprawl and
increased congestion, and thereby reduce the incentive for inner city renewal.

THE INNER URBAN AREAS

The interrelated processes of urban change examined above, and particularly
the causes of counterurbanisation and inner city decline, have been determined
substantially by market forces and have been broadly the same in most advanced capitalist countries. In Britain, however, and perhaps more than in most
other countries, planned overspill has compounded market forces. From the
Barlow Report of 1940 onwards, successive legislation (for example, the New
Towns Act 1946 and Town Development Act 1952) initiated programmes of
planned decentralisation. As a consequence, industrial development in the Midlands, London and the South-East was severely constrained by governments
unwilling to grant industrial development certificates (IDCs) in the period 1947–
82. For a combination of the above reasons, therefore, the decrease in population and employment in the major cities has been substantial – Greater London,
for example, losing 500 000 industrial jobs during 1965–80. In recent years,
the decrease in manufacturing employment in Greater London has been accelerating, in part because of the application of monetarist policy – different analysts
putting the manufacturing job loss at between 215 000 and 500 000 over the
period 1979–86.[42]

From the 1940s until the mid-1970s, urban and regional planners believed
that declining city populations would produce very real benefits. They argued
with conviction that smaller numbers would ease the housing shortage and improve
the residential environment; decentralisation would result in fewer commuting
problems; more urban open space would reduce crime rates and vandalism;
there would be less need for government subsidy; and less overcrowding and

more pleasant conditions would improve educational attainment. But none of these results has occurred – quite the contrary, in fact. In addition, rates of unemployment in the inner city are so high (over 15 per cent by the end of 1984 – with much higher levels among the unskilled and the young), that in the depressed regions it is this, rather than the decline of basic industries (coal, steel, textiles and shipbuilding), that is the principal cause of economic decline.[43]

These disturbing trends could be eliminated by massive investment in inner cities (by the public or private sector, or both), and other substantial benefits could accrue. First, there would result a superior pattern of resource allocation. There would be less wastage of land (in otherwise high-cost areas) since densities would be transformed towards an optimum level. Derelict areas would be developed for housing and employment, and overcrowded areas decongested. Some decayed residential areas would be converted into commercial and industrial uses and vice versa. There would also be less wastage of manpower. Reduced unemployment would raise income levels and, together with an inflow of middle- and higher-income households (with the development of owner-occupied housing and co-ownership) many inner urban areas would be 'transformed', both economically and socially. Property values would, on aggregate, rise and spill over into peripheral areas. Secondly, there would be considerable social benefits. An improved residential and work environment (and higher incomes) would result in less ill-health, fire damage and crime, reducing the cost of health and fire services and the police. A healthier, higher-paid labour force might increase the level of productivity and lower the rate of absenteeism, and less deprivation would reduce the cost of welfare services and payments. Finally, an improved environment and higher property values would widen the rate base and enable the local authority to provide better services where required. Ironically, areas with poor environments requiring the greatest amount of public expenditures are least able to raise revenue to facilitate it.

But to realise the above benefits, considerable costs would have to be incurred. These include research, survey and planning costs; administrative expenditure; the cost of acquiring decayed property; demolition costs; the cost of public and private developments; relocation costs (both economic and non-economic); and possibly the cost of land value write-down if sites are released for development at below their market value.

By identifying and quantifying the above advantages and costs of renewal investment carefully, cost-benefit analyses could be undertaken to a limited extent, and renewal projects ranked in order of greatest net benefit as a guide to decision-making (Chapter 6). Full account would have to be taken of the urban economic base and the effects of the multiplier (Chapter 2).

RENEWAL STRATEGIES

By the 1980s the inner cities of every region suffered a higher level of unemployment and poorer housing than that experienced in suburban areas or beyond, and the disparity was often greater than the imbalance between North and South. There was therefore a major shift of emphasis in government policy. Public expenditure on regional industrial assistance was replaced increasingly by government spending on inner-city renewal (table 8.7). Whereas the government spent £1325 million on regional assistance and £375 million on inner-city programmes in 1979/80, the respective sums were £220 million and £600 million in 1992/3 – increased expenditure on inner-city policy being more than offset by falling expenditure on regional policy. Since the Second World War, however, seven principle strategies have been employed in the United Kingdom – most of them pre-dating the shift of emphasis from regional to inner-city policy.

(1) *Filtration* This was based on the out-migration of households and employment followed by the clearance and redevelopment of vacated sites. It was potentially the most system-oriented of the approaches. Out-migration resulted from both planned decentralisation and market forces. Over the period 1946–66 under the New Towns Acts of 1946 and 1959, 21 Mark I and II new towns were designated in Britain. It was intended that, through the medium of development corporations, the new towns would provide overspill housing and employment for the major cities, and concentrate employment geographically to eliminate difficult journeys to work. More recently, between 1967 and 1970, seven Mark III new towns were designated, to act as 'countermagnets' of economic activity, to exploit the economies of scale in development and operation, and to meet social needs. From designation to 1985, the population of the new towns grew from 945 900 to 2 094 600, but probably only *one-third* of the increase was because of migration from Greater London and the major conurbations. Under the Town Development Act 1952, a total of seventy town expansion schemes had been initiated by 1980, when the government finally announced the winding-up of all expansion schemes still being undertaken. The expanded towns received even less overspill than the new towns. By comparison with planned decentralisation, the scale of 'voluntary' overspill – mainly in response to market forces (and environmental considerations – was enormous.

During the years of planned decentralisation, slum clearance schemes and massive public-sector housebuilding programmes were undertaken in the inner cities. In the period 1945–76, 1.24 million dwellings were demolished in England and Wales, but in the inner cities clearance was often followed by the development of high-rise housing at lower overall density. Clearance also had a severe effect on local employment – factories, workshops, retail premises and so on being sacrificed to facilitate housing redevelopment and infrastructure improvement.

(2) *Social planning* Except possibly for a few years in the late 1960s and early 1970s, governments have regarded this as being secondary to physical and economic planning. Social planning focuses on people rather than on urban space or property, and should first involve analyses of the basic causes of deprivation as a prelude to the application of needs-related policies.

Table 8.7 *Public expenditure on regional and inner city policies, 1979/80 to 1992/3,* in £m (at 1990–1 prices)

	Regional support*	Urban policy	Total
1979/80	1325	375	1700
1980/81	1120	360	1480
1981/82	1220	390	1610
1982/83	755	510	1265
1983/84	560	580	1140
1984/85	615	585	1200
1985/86	515	505	1020
1986/87	520	520	1040
1987/88	300	600	900
1988/89	460	720	1180
1989/90	390	800	1190
1990/91	340	860	1200
1991/92	250	750	1000
1992/93	220	600	820

Note: * Including general industrial support.
Source: Treasury, *Government Expenditure Plans, 1990–1991* (HMSO, 1990).

In the 1960s (and emanating from the United States) the social pathology view of urban deprivation emerged in Britain – the Urban Programme (UP) being introduced in 1968 in direct response to the growing concern about race relations, urban poverty and deprivation. Under the UP, the central government was empowered (by the Local Government Grant (Social Need) Act 1969) to award grants of 75 per cent towards the cost of 'approved' projects bid for by local authorities and voluntary agencies (in England and Wales) in areas of 'special social need' (there were separate arrangements for Scotland). In the early 1970s, moreover, the Home Office (considered than to be the appropriate government department to initiate inner-city policy), established twelve Community Development Projects (CDPs) – each with a team of local government officers and a team of independent researchers – to produce detailed analyses of inner-city problems in specific geographical areas and to identify solutions which would require implementation at a higher than local level. Prior to their demise in 1977, CDP teams were claiming that urban deprivation was not the result of social malaise, but the effect of unemployment, inadequate income maintenance, poor housing and a decayed environment. They called for more public ownership and control of industry, and substantial changes in income maintenance and public-sector finance.

In 1974, the Comprehensive Community Programme (CCP) was initiated to tackle urban deprivation by means of both a comprehensive Whitehall approach to urban problems and a new partnership between central and local government. However, since there was a conflict of interest between the Urban

Deprivation Unit of the Home Office on the one hand, and the various spending ministries and the Treasury on the other, the CCP 'experiment' achieved
very little. The Home Office was unable increasingly to exercise its responsibility for social policy in the inner city.

(3) *The boot-strap strategy* This involves rehabilitation (often with the aid of
grants) and is mainly confined to housing. It does not (or should not) involve
the displacement of occupants (Chapter 9), and it is often thought that in economic terms it is less costly than redevelopment, although evidence is conflicting.
Renewal theory evolved from the basic hypothesis of Needleman.[44] He suggested
that the comparative economics of redevelopment and rehabilitation depends
on (a) the rate of interest, (b) the future life of the rehabilitated property, and
(c) the difference between the running costs of the new and the rehabilitated
properties. Normally, rehabilitation would be worthwhile if the present cost of
clearance and rebuilding exceeds the sum of the cost of rehabilitation, the present
value of the cost of rebuilding, and the present value of the difference in annual running costs. In algebraic terms, rehabilitation would be more economic
than redevelopment if

$$b > m + b (1 + i)^{-\lambda} + \frac{r}{i} [1 - (1 + i)^{-\lambda}]$$

where b = cost of demolition and rebuilding
        m = cost of rehabilitation
        i = the rate of interest
        λ = useful life of the rehabilitated property in years
        r = difference in annual repair costs

Needleman extended his hypothesis by taking into account two additional variables – namely, the comparative quality and comparative density of new and
rehabilitated housing (normally, new housing would be of higher quality and
lower density than rehabilitated property). As Merrett[45] suggests, rehabilitation
would be worthwhile if

$$b > m + b (1 + i)^{-\lambda} + \frac{r + p + a}{i} [1 - (1 + i)^{-\lambda}]$$

where b = cost of demolition and rebuilding
        m = cost of rehabilitation
        i = the rate of interest
        λ = useful life of the rehabilitated property in years
        r = difference in annual repair costs
        p = excess of rent on (higher-quality) redeveloped property
        a = annual cost of 'decanting' surplus households from (low-density)
              redeveloped property.

Although Needleman's more comprehensive formula was incorporated in general terms in the Ministry of Housing and Local Government Circular 65/69,

Kirby[46] argued that planners may have found detailed formulae time-consuming and unwieldy in calculations. Lean,[47] possibly appreciating that less sophisticated methods were necessary to determine the most appropriate process of renewal, devised the capital value method to compare redevelopment and rehabilitation. This involves a comparison between the costs of redevelopment and the differences in capital values before and after redevelopment, and the costs of rehabilitation and the differences in capital values before and after rehabilitation. If, for example, £18 000 spent on redevelopment increased unit values by £21 000, and £6000 spent on rehabilitation raised values by £9000, then clearly £18 000 spent on rehabilitation would renew three times as many houses as the number supplied by redevelopment (and values would rise by £27 000 rather than £21 000).

In the 1970s, a limited amount of empirical evidence in the United States[48] and in Britain[49] seemed to suggest that rehabilitation was cheaper than redevelopment, although in Britain the evidence was by no means conclusive since it was difficult to compare the clearance and redevelopment of a whole area with the rehabilitation of a relatively small number of (often scattered) properties. Nevertheless, the government (particularly after the Housing Act 1969) made rehabilitation a major housing priority (Chapter 9).

The above considerations have ignored the question of timing – that is, when should redevelopment take place, or when should rehabilitation be undertaken? Even assuming that a site is redeveloped when the economic life of a building has expired (Chapter 2), the optimum economic life of a building is not fixed. The capital value of buildings and sites in existing use and the capital value of sites cleared for alternative use continually fluctuate and establish new optima.

The capital value of sites for alternative use will rise if the urban area experiences economic and population growth and benefits from an improved infrastructure. This will shorten the economic life of buildings and sites in existing use and encourage redevelopment. The value of cleared sites for alternative use will fall if reverse trends occur – a decaying infrastructure alone bringing down values and postponing redevelopment. In figure 8.7 the capital value of a site cleared for alternative use increases from SS to S_1S_1 and intersects the capital value of a building and site in its existing use at 80 years – reducing the economic life of the building from the original optimum of 100 years. Conversely, a decrease in the capital value of the cleared site could extend the economic life of the building.

The capital value of a building and site might, however, also change. It could be expected to rise as a result of rehabilitation and/or conversion from, for example, a single-family dwelling house into bedsitters, flats or bed-and-breakfast accommodation. Recently, deconversions of flats and bedsitters into single family freehold or leasehold properties have also increased the capital value of buildings and their sites. If rehabilitation and/or conversion (or deconversion) occurred when the age of the building was 80 years, the economic life of the building could be extended to 120 years, where values would again be in equilibrium. Conversely, if the capital value of the property is

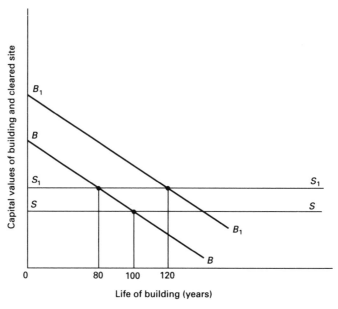

BB   = Initial capital value of building and site in existing use
SS   = Initial capital value of cleared site for its best alternative use
B_1B_1 = Increased capital value of building and site after rehabilitation etc.
S_1S_1 = Increased capital value of cleared site for its best alternative use

Figure 8.7 *Changes in the maximum economic life of a building (assuming general price stability)*

decreased (perhaps because of the building falling into serious disrepair), there would be a downward shift in the *BB* curve and the economic life of the building would be reduced.

The relationship of the capital value of the cleared site (for alternative use) to the capital value of the building and site (in existing use) is particularly relevant to the problems of the inner city. The inner city contains a high proportion of old dwellings – most of which have been modified over the years. Generally, the capital value of these buildings and their sites has increased to keep pace with the increase in the capital value of sites for alternative uses. Were it not for the conversion of houses into multi-occupied dwellings and other forms of accommodation, their demolition would have occurred many decades ago. The inner cities therefore often retain their nineteenth-century image which, except for a minority of buildings of architectural or historic interest, is one of gloom and decay. Yet it is not just the extended life of buildings (brought about by increases in their capital values) that is responsible for much of the inner city being a twilight area. In many cases, the capital value of sites cleared for alternative use is much greater than the current or potential capital values of the buildings, but the latter values have been kept artificially low by the effects of legislation. In 1915, 1939, 1965 and 1974,

Rent Acts subjected private landlords to rent control or regulation, while tenants were granted increasing protection (chapter 9). Although these measures should be viewed in the light of problems of housing need and affordability, the direct effect was that buildings which could neither be readily redeveloped nor maintained or repaired for want of an adequate return on investment were kept out of use. But after the Housing Act 1969, improvement grants became available increasingly for modernisation and these have raised the capital value of properties. Grants have thus had the effect of retaining in use the older housing stock of the inner city until such a time as redevelopment is feasible.

(4) *Replacement* Clearance is followed by sound redevelopment schemes. There are usually many social problems that need to be resolved, especially if redevelopment does not occur immediately after clearance, therefore it is essential that, not just for economic reasons, schemes are carefully selected, priorities determined and work programmed sensitively. Development is undertaken by either the public or the private sector, or by a partnership of both.

In the United States this strategy was introduced by the Kennedy and Johnson administrations as one of their 'Great Society' initiatives following ghetto riots in the 1960s. The federal governments set up a Department of Housing and Urban Development in 1965, which in turn introduced the 'model cities programme' in 1966. The programme aimed to concentrate and co-ordinate the provision of federal resources allocated to the urban areas and to involve local communities in improvement of their physical environment. Development programmes soon came to depend upon private-sector investment – for example, the successful Bedford–Stuyvesant scheme in Brooklyn which, while being managed by a community-based organisation, was partly funded by Wall Street institutions.

In the United Kingdom, replacement strategy emerged in response to the Inner Areas Studies (IASs) of Birmingham (Small Heath), Liverpool 8, and London (Lambeth) commissioned by the Department of the Environment in 1972. In contrast to 'blaming the victim' – the underlying rationale of the Home Office initiatives of the 1960s (see 'Social planning' above), the Department of the Environment acknowledged the conclusions of the IASs, which stressed that the economic causes of urban deprivation necessitated a new policy to channel additional resources to the inner cities.

Based on the White Paper, *Policy for the Inner Cities* (1977) the Inner Urban Areas Act 1978 brought about an increase in public expenditure on the Urban Programme (UP) from £30 million per year (in 1976–7) to £165 million per year (by 1979–80). In addition, the Budget of March 1977 set aside £100 million for a package of construction works in selected inner-city areas. Under the 1978 Act, a total of seven partnership, fifteen programme authorities and fourteen 'other' districts were designated in England (table 8.8), and each of the authorities had powers to make 90 per cent loans for the acquisition of land or site preparation, to make loans or grants towards the cost of setting up co-operatives or common-ownership enterprises, and to declare (industrial)

Table 8.8 *Urban areas designated under the Inner Urban Areas Act 1978*

Areas	Population 1981	Annual UP allocation
Partnership authorities		
Birmingham		
Liverpool		
Manchester–Salford		
Newcastle–Gateshead		
Lambeth	4 294 184	£66 m
Hackney and Islington		
London Docklands		
(Greenwhich; Lewisham;		
Newham; Southwark;		
Tower Hamlets)		
Programme authorities		
Bolton		
Bradford		
Hammersmith & Fulham		
Hull		
Leeds		
Leicester		
Middlesbrough		
North Tyneside	4 542 913	£25 m
Nottingham		
Oldham		
Sheffield		
South Tyneside		
Sunderland		
Wirral		
Wolverhampton		
*Other designated authorities**		
Barnsley		
Blackburn		
Brent		
Doncaster		
Haringey		
Hartlepool		
Rochdale	3 304 848	£ 6 m
Rotherham		
St Helens		
Sandwell		
Sefton		
Wandsworth		
Wigan		
Total	12 141 945	£97 m

Note: * In addition, there were 'other designated areas' in Wales: Blaenau Gwent, Cardiff, Newport, Rhondda and Swansea, which in total were allocated £4 million.

Sources: Derived from M. S. Gibson and M. J. Langstaff, *An Introduction to Urban Renewal* (Hutchinson, 1982); and *Town and Country Planning* (September 1981).

improvement areas (IAs). IAs were particularly important components of the 1978 Act. They were to be declared by local authorities to secure a stable level of employment in older industrial and commercial areas. Within them, grants and loans were available for the improvement of the environment, and grants could be obtained for the improvement or conversion of old industrial or commercial property. In 'special areas' within the partnerships, local authorities could make loans interest-free up to two years for site preparation, and award grants to assist with rents and to help firms that had incurred interest on loans for land acquisition and so on. Overall, assistance was co-ordinated by means of inner-city partnership programmes (ICPPs) or inner area programmes (IAPs) – the former being produced by teams of civil servants and local government officers in the partnership areas, and the latter emanating solely from programme and other designated authorities.

It was ironic that the 1978 legislation was introduced at a time of economic stringency – at a time when the Labour government declared in 1977 that 'it could not spend its way out of recession'. Although UP spending had increased in real terms up to 1980–1, however, macro-economic policies were being adopted simultaneously to curb the level of aggregate demand. The Conservative administration's 1980 White Paper, *The Government's Expenditure Plans, 1980–81 to 1983–84*, specified swingeing cuts in planned public expenditure, with the aim of cutting total public spending by 1984 to a level 4 per cent lower than in 1979–80 (at 1980 prices). Thus in 1981–2 and again in 1984–5 and the following two years, UP spending was cut in real terms. In addition to these reduced injections of resources into the inner city, rate support grants (RSGs) and housing subsidies were being cut in many cities, producing a net withdrawal of funds and a reverse multiplier effect on the local economy.

The provisions of the 1978 Act, however, did not apply to Scotland. Here the onus for urban regeneration fell on the local and regional authorities, and the Scottish Development Agency (SDA) set up in 1976. The SDA (now Scottish Enterprise) was given powers to reclaim derelict land and rehabilitate the environment, build and manage industrial estates, invest in industry, establish new companies and provide industry with finance and advice. Increasingly, the SDA entered into partnerships with both the private sector and local and regional government (for example, in the East End of Glasgow by the GEAR project) and has helped to change the image of Clydeside from a region of heavy smokestack industry to one of electronics, advanced engineering and energy-related technology.

The principal advantage of the replacement strategy, as applied in Britain, was that local and regional authorities were involved directly in the regeneration process (in partnership with central government in England and Wales, and with the Scottish Development Agency/Scottish Enterprise north of the border). Local or regional accountability was thus ensured, and job creation and other initiatives consequently benefited the local or regional economy (figure 8.8).

(5) *Guiding urban growth through investment* This method combines the

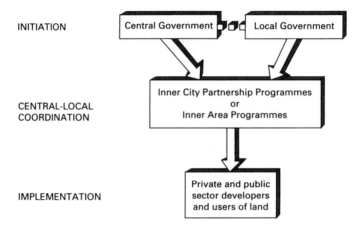

INITIATION

CENTRAL-LOCAL
COORDINATION

IMPLEMENTATION

Figure 8.8   *The funding of urban regeneration in England and Wales under the provision of the Inner Urban Areas Act 1978*

replacement strategy with market forces. Areas are ranked initially according to their renewal potential, related infrastructure may be improved, and private investment is attracted.

This form of strategy was introduced in the United States by the Nixon and Ford administrations in the period 1968–76. It involved direct co-operation between the federal government and private investors. Under a newly-introduced 'new towns intown' programme the federal government used its community development block grant to fund urban development in anticipation of complementary private investment, and the later Housing and Community Development Act 1977 (during the Carter administration) introduced urban development action grants (UDAGs) to 'lever' finance from the private sector for joint public/private schemes. Under the 1977 Act, city authorities could only obtain UDAGs (for joint schemes with the private sector) if their areas suffered from a high level of deprivation, but a fundamental characteristic of the UDAG was that it would have to enable private investors and developers to enjoy a level of return at least equivalent to that obtainable elsewhere. In addition to the above provisions, the federal government, under the Urban Growth and Community Development Act 1977, provides mortgage guarantees to encourage financial institutions to use mortgage-fund capital to finance urban development projects.

In the United Kingdom, with the return of a Conservative government, Urban Development Corporations (UDCs), appointed by the Secretary of State for the Environment (and answerable only to him) were designated in the London docklands and Merseyside in 1981 under the Local Government, Planning and Land Act 1980. Further UDCs were set up in Teesside, Tyneside, the Black Country, Trafford Park (Manchester) and Cardiff Bay in 1987; in Central Manchester, Leeds, Sheffield and Bristol in 1988; and in Birmingham in 1992. It was claimed that UDCs were intended to tackle the problems that local authorities could not or would not deal with alone, and where allegedly the private sector had been deterred from investing. Although UDCs became planning authorities and consequently gained compulsory purchase powers (usurping local authority responsibilities and lacking local accountability), they have been denied the powers once vested in the New Town Development Corporations (NTDCs) and are not permitted to acquire land except at market value (in contrast to the NTDCs, which could buy land at existing use value). Nevertheless, the UDCs have placed an emphasis on providing an adequate infrastructure including road development, reclaiming and servicing land, renovating old buildings and developing new factories – all in the hope of encouraging substantial development in the private sector. UDCs also provide practical assistance to potential developers and sometimes the offer of finance. The aim is to attract mainly private commercial and industrial development. The Conservatives believed that market forces would be the principal means by which the inner cities would be regenerated – provided the market was largely unfettered.

A great deal of leverage finance, however, has been supplied by government – over £500 million per annum by the early 1990s, while the largest UDC, the London Docklands Development Corporation (LDDC), absorbed £2.36 billion of public-sector funds between 1981 and 1992. It is probable that the government is nevertheless very satisfied with the return on this investment. Leverage ratios were often very high, for example nearly 5:1 in the London Docklands (where £10.6 billion of private-sector funds were attracted during the LDDC's first twelve years). Within the UDC areas, a total of 1679 hectares of land have been reclaimed, 75 miles of roads constructed, 35.4 million ft^2 (3.8 million m^2) of industrial and commercial property developed, 24 000 homes completed and over 93 600 jobs created, with nearly 26 000 of these in the London Docklands alone (table 8.9).

Despite their apparent success, it is probable that the UDCs and their activities are seriously flawed. It is rightly claimed that the UDCs lack accountability and are remote from the local community. It is also argued that there is an overemphasis on property-led development, which has meant that UDCs cannot provide the employment and low-cost housing that inner-city communities need. Clearly, stronger links between the UDCs and local government would be desirable, while at the same time UDCs would be more effective if they had (as with Scottish Enterprise) wider powers of intervention in the fields of industrial investment and housing. There is little evidence to suggest that the UDCs have helped to reduce unemployment in their areas (which remained at or above the national or regional average throughout the 1980s–early 1990s), nor has there been an emphasis on social housing development, in fact, quite the reverse. All too often, social housing has been squeezed-out despite lengthy waiting and transfer lists. But even market-led regeneration in the late 1980s–early 1990s was in jeopardy as many developers pulled out because of the downturn in the property market. Many had bought land at the peak of the market in the late 1980s, but by 1990–1 they faced a financial squeeze – the 14 million ft^2 (1.3 million m^2) Canary Wharf scheme in the

Table 8.9 *The development corporations: progress to 1992*

	Period of designation	Area (ha)	Population		Development since designation			
			At designation	1991	Industrial and commercial development (m^2)	Houses/ flats completed	Reclaimed Land (ha)	Miles of road built
London Docklands	1981–?	2 070	27 213	53 084	1 442 365	16 820	582	5.5
Merseyside	1981–1996/7	960	n.a.	34 000	n.a.	1 367	339	44.6
Black Country	1987–1997	2 345	70 500	73 100	484 376	1 248	60	3.1
Cardiff	1987–?	1 093	15 247	17 032	43 163	2 500	11	1.9
Teesside	1987–1996/7	4 565	15 000	21 618	193 750	n.a.	72	8.7
Trafford Park	1987–1996/7	1 267	24 950	33 181	362 000	315	38	4.9
Tyne and Wear	1987–1996/7	2 375	4 505	n.a.	519 061	70	87	0.8
Central Manchester	1988–1995 ?	187	n.a.	1 500	81 806	900	124	–
Leeds	1988–1995	540	31 971	37 733	301 390	180	37	2.7
Sheffield	1988–1995	900	n.a.	7 737	251 660	1 367	72	2.9
Bristol	1988–1995	360	14 000	18 000	710 418	1 400	12	0.6
Total		16 662	203 386	296 985	4 880 027	24 800	1 437	75.7

Source: Department of the Environment.

London Docklands being a well-known casualty of the property slump.

Although all the UDCs are expected to complete their work in the 1990s, the National Audit Office warned in 1993 that many would not meet their targets by the time they were wound up. It was thought in the case of the eight English UDCs set up in 1987 and 1988, and notwithstanding the effects of the recession, there was scope for improvement in planning, project control and departmental supervision.

In an attempt to stimulate market forces the government declared – under the Finance Act 1980 – a number of enterprise zones in which the following concessions were made: exemption from Development Land Tax; 100 per cent first-year depreciation allowance on capital expenditure on commercial and industrial buildings; simplification of planning procedures; abolition of Industrial Development Certificates; exemption from rates on all commercial and industrial property; handling of applications for warehousing free of custom duty, plus a relaxed regime for private warehousing; and a major reduction in government requests for statistical information. By 1981, thirteen enterprise zones had been declared – ranging in size from 57 to 364 ha. A further fourteen zones were created in 1984, but not all were in the inner cities (see table 8.10), and zones in Inverclyde, Sunderland and Lanarkshire were declared in 1989–92 – in the latter two cases in response to the cessation of shipbuilding and steel production respectively.

However, the enterprise zone concept has been subject to considerable criticism. It is thought that little new employment will be created if the zones attract superstore or warehouse development, and there will be few jobs for the local population if offices are developed. If manufacturing firms move in, employees will probably not receive training and remain unskilled and low-paid. In net terms, land values and economic activity will not increase but merely shift from adjacent areas, causing blighting and higher unemployment on the periphery. Only in the London Docklands and in Corby have industries been attracted from beyond the immediate vicinity. The Royal Institution of Chartered Surveyors (RICS) have claimed that landlords letting just outside a zone often receive up to £5000 less in rents on a standard 5000 ft^2 industrial unit than landlords receive inside a zone – higher zonal rents completely off-setting rate exemption. The RICS therefor suggested that the government should give more thought to the impact on surrounding areas if further zones were to be created.[50] It could be argued that land within the zones should be publicly owned (or that higher values should be taxed), otherwise benefits would accrue only to the developers rather than to the users of land. But many firms might have been deterred from locating in an enterprise zone since concessions were likely to be withdrawn at a later date ('rate holidays' were only granted for ten years initially).

From a monetarist point of view, the most damning indictment of the enterprise zone concept is the very high cost of job creation. Roger Tym and Partners have shown (in *Monitoring Enterprise Zones*) that in net terms only about 5375 jobs had been created by December 1983 at a total cost of £252.4 million

Table 8.10 *Enterprise zones: designations 1981–4*

Designations	Size (ha)	Date of designation
First round		
Team Valley	364	
Swansea	298	
Dudley	219	
Belfast	208	
Isle of Dogs (London Docklands)	195	
Clydebank	190	
Trafford Park	178	April–October 1981
Salford	174	
Speke	138	
Corby	114	
Hartlepool	109	
Newcastle	89	
Wakefield	57	
Second round		
Delwyn	1119	
Milford Haven	147	
North-west Kent	126	
North-west Lancashire	114	
Derry	109	
Scunthorpe	105	
Workington	87	July 1983–December 1984
Middlesbrough	77	
Invergordon	60	
Wellingbrough	55	
Glanford	50	
Tayside	3	
Telford	2	
Rotherham	1	

Source: Roger Tym and Partners, *Monitoring Enterprise Zones: Year Three Report* (Department of the Environment, 1984).

(equivalent to £46 958 per job).[51] The Association of Independent Businessmen also have severe reservations about enterprise zones – believing that the zones emphasise property development rather than the formation and growth of new enterprise, and that their artificial boundaries distort markets and create unfair competition; and the National Audit Office reported that enterprise zones cost the Exchequer £180 million (in 1984–5) and were of dubious benefit.[52] Although the Department of the Environment claimed that 20 000 jobs had been created and 2.9 million m² of floor space had been developed in the zones by 1986, the Secretary of State for the Environment conceded that enterprise zones had 'been rather expensive and have not given the best value for money'.[53]

By 1988–9, enterprise zones had cost the government a total of £856 million (mainly through compensating local authorities for rate revenue forgone). While 97 000 jobs had been created within the zones, it is probable that as much as half of these jobs resulted from short-distance moves in investment from surrounding areas. In recent years, enterprise zones have fallen out of favour, and most have reached the end of their ten-year life with a very mixed impact on the economy of the inner cities.

Although the equivalent of enterprise zones exist elsewhere in the EC, for example, in Copenhagen, Hamburg and Rotterdam, it must be borne in mind that in these cities public authorities first provided a modern infrastructure (particularly for transport) prior to releasing market forces. In the United Kingdom such infrastructure is generally absent in the inner city. It must also be borne in mind that free market forces prevail within the inner cities of the United States and have contributed greatly to their decline. It must also be remembered that in Britain many of the problems of the inner cities were themselves caused not by planning or by central government intervention, but by unbridled free enterprise.

Apart from setting-up UDCs and declaring enterprise zones, the government – in its attempt to unleash market forces – introduced a range of measures to benefit the private sector. The question of land was one of its first priorities. Although derelict land grants (DLGs) became available to local authorities under the Local Government Act 1972, the government extended eligibility to private developers by the Local Government, Planning and Land Act 1980. In the Assisted Areas and Derelict Land Clearance Areas, DLGs of 100 per cent were available to local authorities, and firms became eligible for 80 per cent grants. Elsewhere, both local authorities and firms received 50 per cent grants. Since 1981, the Department of the Environment has given preferential treatment to joint (public and private) schemes, particularly if high leverage ratios can be expected. In 1983–4, for example, DLGs of £32 million were allotted to forty-eight schemes in England, producing an anticipated £196 million of private-sector development. An allocation of £81 million of DLG in 1987–8 will thus be expected to attract private development for over £400 million *ceteris paribus*. Also under the 1980 Act, the Environment Secretary was given powers to direct local authorities to make an assessment of the amount of public land available for development, to register the information with the Department of the Environment, and to dispose of sites to private developers. By the end of 1983, local authorities had compiled 365 public land registers containing a total of 44 750 ha. But from this amount only 3951 ha had been sold and/or brought into use – most of the remainder having little or no development potential regardless of DLG pump-priming.

Urban development grants (UDGs) were probably the most important initiative to emerge from the Department of the Environment in the early 1980s. Like the UDAGs in the United States, their purpose was to promote the economic and physical regeneration of the inner cities by levering private-sector investment into such areas. UDGs were to be allocated to private firms via specified local authorities (that is, those designated under the 1978 Act and enterprise zone authorities). The Exchequer would meet 75 per cent of the grant and the local authority 25 per cent. The amount of the UDG was the minimum necessary to make a project commercially viable – any size or type of development being eligible. By 1986, grants totalling £120 million had levered £500 million of private investment, and created 24 000 jobs.

By 1985 it became clear to the government that the private sector might respond better to public-sector initiatives if there was a greater co-ordination in the provision of services. In 1985, therefore, five civil service City Action Teams (CATs) were set up in the partnership areas (Birmingham, Liverpool, Manchester, Newcastle and London) to bring together officials from the relevant civil service departments and managers seconded from private industry. (Further CATs were set up in 1988, in Leeds and Nottingham.) Their purpose was to eliminate blockages in the provision of services and to ensure a more efficient use of UP spending. Largely in response to civil disorders in Handsworth, Brixton and Toxteth in the summer of 1985, the government set up eight task forces by which ministers in a number of departments became responsible (under the Environment Secretary) for improving the provision of public services in the following areas: North Peckham and Notting Hill (London), Chapeltown (Leeds), North Central Middlesbrough, Highfields (Leicester), Moss Side (Manchester), St Pauls (Bristol) and Handsworth (Birmingham). In each location, civil servants were allotted £1 million to support existing agencies in providing help for training, regeneration and industrial development. However, although the task forces had started over 100 projects in their first year, only 600 jobs had been created, and at least three task forces managed to spend only one-tenth of their financial allocation – hardly the performance of dynamic management sought by the government. Nevertheless, in 1987 a further eight task forces were set up (in Coventry, Doncaster, Hartlepool, Nottingham, Rochdale, Preston, Wolverhampton and Tower Hamlets) at a cost to the Exchequer of £14 million.

The government's approach to urban problems has been subject to increasing criticism. The Archbishop of Canterbury's Commission on Urban Priority Areas,[54] for example, recommended a complete turnabout of policy, and proposed a large increase in the allocation of the rate support grant to the inner cities and an expansion of the UP; while the Town and Country Planning Association[55] proposed that local authorities should again have overall responsibility for the preparation and implementation of inner city renewal strategies. The government, however, continued with its strategy of stimulating private development. Under the Housing and Town Planning Act 1986, urban regeneration grants (URGs) were introduced and were to be paid directly to firms rather than indirectly through local authorities. URGs were intended either to bridge the gap between the cost of development and its value on completion, or to provide temporary finance before any income was received from the development. While URGs were only available for schemes which brought about substantial private investment, priority was given to areas which suffered from a severe loss of employment and where there were large amounts of derelict land or disused industrial and commercial property. Eligible sites had to be in excess of 5 ha, and eligible floorspace more than 23 000 m^2.

Following a Conservative win in the 1987 general election, the third Thatcher government attempted to reinforce urban policy by introducing city grants (which were to replace both UDGs and URGs and were to be paid directly to developers subject to a leverage ratio of 4:1), and giving the Department of Trade and Industry the task of spearheading the return of business enterprise to the inner cities. Measures needed to be taken to increase the cost-effectiveness of the UP and to reduce the extent of bureaucratic constraint. However, although the Department of Trade and Industry took over the running of the urban task forces, its inner city budget was minuscule compared with that of the Department of the Environment. In 1987–8, while the Department of Trade and Industry planned to spend £750 million on regional and industrial support, only about £100 million of this amount would be spent in the inner cities. In contrast, the Department of the Environment planned to spend £525 million specifically in the inner cities (including £230 million on the UP and £125 million on the UDCs) in addition to main departmental expenditure in these areas (on, for example, housing and rate support). The Department of Trade and Industry could, however, have played a major part in urban regeneration if it had employed English Estates as an agency to redevelop urban sites and provide small factories and offices. Although English Estates operated mainly in the Assisted Areas (and owned 5000 factories and 508 estates – in 1987), they could have become a bridge between the Department of Trade and Industry and the Department of the Environment.

There manifestly remained a mismatch between the characteristics of the inner city (large areas of derelict land with outmoded buildings, a high concentration of unskilled workers, an outworn physical infrastructure, fragmented property interests and an uncertain economic base) and the investment criteria of investors and occupiers. Investors in the commercial and industrial sectors require a stream of income, a rental which gives a hedge against inflation, a freehold or long leasehold interest, little onerous management involvement, and a large property in a satisfactory environment. Occupiers usually look for a conventional location, adequate physical access, security, a suitable labour force, and an acceptable working environment. These are generally not available in the inner city. Cadman[56] suggested in 1979 that solutions could be found to the problem of inadequate development if investors were very selective (focusing on the greatest opportunities – in contrast to public authorities which concentrate on the greatest problems); skilled labour and managerial and professional groups were attracted back into the inner cities; there was maximum consultation between the private and public sectors, and between private firms (possible

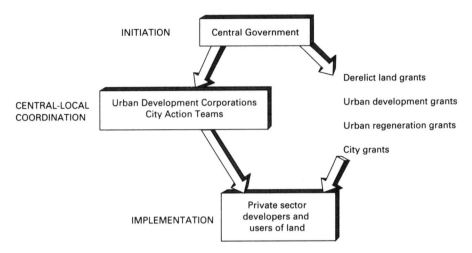

Figure 8.9   *The funding of urban regeneration in England and Wales in the 1980s*

through the medium of chambers of commerce and industry); new agencies were established to promote commercial and industrial development; local authorities and other public bodies released land for development; there was not too much emphasis on manufacturing since this would normally require large sites and these are not usually available; and there was only a little faith in the ability of small firms to regenerate the inner cities – the scale of the task of job creation is too great.

Cadman's proposals were reflected partially in government policy in the 1980s. Market forces were unleashed in areas of opportunity – Conservative philosophy seeing leveraged private investment as the only solution to the problems of the inner city. However, while UDCs and enterprise zones became the principal agencies of urban regeneration, ideologically their purpose was to shift the power balance from the local authorities to central government and to by-pass the normal planning processes and local accountability. Partnerships were established exclusively between central government and private-sector developers, largely ignoring the existence of local government (figure 8.9).

UDCs, enterprise zones, the extension of DLGs, the provision of UDGs, URGs and City Grants, and the setting up of CATs and task forces, all focused on private profitability; indeed, it is possible that the above grants were translated directly into the profits of recipient firms, thereby distorting the market. URGs and City Grants, in particular, were a cause for concern; since they were awarded directly by central government, neither the recipient firms nor their investment plans were subject to local scrutiny. Both public and private investment decisions, under the Conservative renewal strategy, thus not only failed to take into account the cost of job creation, but also ignored broad cost-benefit considerations.

(6) *A local government strategy*   By the early 1980s, a number of local auth-

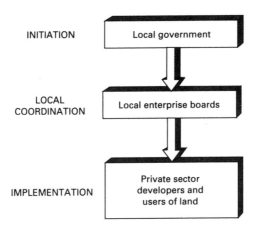

Figure 8.10 *The funding of urban regeneration through the medium of local enterprise boards*

orities began to see the irrelevance of Keynesian policy to the problems of the inner cities, were even more antagonistic to current monetarist policy, and were particularly alarmed at their loss of power. They saw the need increasingly for a 'bottom-up' (as opposed to a 'top-down') solution to the problems of the inner city. They may also have been aware of initiatives being taken in the United States. Urban authorities since the 1970s had been involved in joint private/public-sector development schemes. In Boston, Massachusetts for example, the Economic Development and Industrial Corporation not only helped the city retain and create industrial employment but also undertook joint enterprises with the Boston Redevelopment Authority – the city's planning, housing and commercial development agency.

In Britain, therefore, a number of Local Enterprise Boards (LEBs) were set up to provide equity and loan guarantees (to enable firms to borrow longer-term and for more risky ventures than would otherwise be possible), delayed-repayment loans, and 'seed money' for local ventures to attract consequential institutional investment (figure 8.10). For the most part, LEBs were funded from the product of a 2p rate levy under Section 137 of the Local Government Act 1972. The largest LEB, the Greater London Enterprise Board (GLEB), was set up in 1983 to help arrest industrial decline in the capital. Over the period 1983–5, it invested £60 million in London's economy – in total creating or saving 2500 jobs at a cost of about £4500 per job. This contrasts with the much higher cost of job creation in the assisted areas and enterprise zones – £35 000 and £47 000 per job respectively in the mid-1980s. LEBs included the West Midlands Enterprise Board, the West Yorkshire Enterprise Board and Lancashire Enterprises Ltd – each of which operated along broadly similar lines to GLEB. Apart from LEBs, many district authorities operate very strident employment and industrial development policies. Sheffield, for example, has used the product of a 2p rate to finance sixteen of the city's co-operatives, and has applied a policy of positive discrimination in favour of local firms in the placing of contracts to ensure that the local multiplier is not reduced by 'leakages' out of the area. Compared with the total amount of unemployment in the inner cities, local government initiatives have not created many jobs; for example, unemployment in Greater London, the West Midlands and Sheffield exceeded 725 000 in 1986 but only 9100 jobs had been created over the period 1982–5. However, with more funding and more co-ordination (perhaps within a regional framework), LEBs and the like might be capable of producing alternative urban strategies more effective than any of the strategies so far employed by central government.

(7) *A co-ordinated strategy*   In the late 1980s, the government recognised increasingly that not only were the many inner-city initiatives of the Department of the Environment uncoordinated but that several other departments were involved in inner city regeneration, operating within their own independent terms of reference. In March 1988, therefore, the government introduced *Action for Cities* in an attempt to co-ordinate its inner city policy and to hasten the pace of urban regeneration. Although the Department of the Environment had the greatest responsibility for inner city regeneration, spending £1312 million in 1988/9, the Department of Employment spent £1096 million (mainly on training), the Scottish and Welsh Offices spent £300 million, the Department of Trade and Industry £196 million, the Department of Transport £190 million, and the Home Office and Department of Education and Science spent £57 million and £14 million respectively – a total sum of £3165 million.

Apart from establishing a new UDC for Sheffield, doubling the size of the Merseyside Development Corporation, setting up new CATs for Leeds and Nottingham, and replacing the UDG and URG with the new City Grant, *Action for Cities* initiated an intensive drive to bring unused and under-used public-sector land on to the market, gave additional help to small businesses, and facilitated an additional supply of premises for new businesses in rundown inner city areas. Critics argued, however, that very little extra public expenditure was involved – resources were simply being spread more widely but more thinly. In total, moreover, cash allocations had to be contrasted with the £20 billion cut in rate support grant (1979–88).

Although Margaret Thatcher was replaced by John Major as prime minister in November 1990, elements of Thatcherism were far from dead. If local authorities were to have a role in inner city regeneration, they would now have to compete for it. In May 1991, therefore, a new initiative was introduced – *City Challenge*, an approach which, although it contained aspects of most of the strategies considered above, was fundamentally concerned with the diminution of the local state. If Urban Programme authorities required adequate funding, they were now obliged to bid for it – funds of up to £37.5 million per authority per annum (for five years) being available. At first, fifteen 'pacemaker' local authorities were invited to participate in the competition for funding, and eleven were successful. In 1992 the competition was broadened to all fifty-seven designated Urban Programme authorities, and the challenge produced twenty win-

Table 8.11 *City Challenge participants, 1992*

Urban programme authorities	Population	Area (ha)	Unemployment (%)
Pacemakers			
Bradford	42 997	1400	36.0
Dearne Valley	76 000	5750	16.0
Lewisham	28 000	494	20.8
Liverpool	4 000	138	27.0
Manchester	10 000	110	31.0
Middlesbrough	40 300	792	20.0
Newcastle	35 200	580	25.0
Nottingham	25 000	405	24.1
Tower Hamlets	13 500	145	21.8
Wirral	29 000	560	n/a
Round 2			
Barnsley	17 000	850	12.5
Birmingham	12 000	265	26.5
Blackburn	19 500	400	22.0
Bolton	19 500	506	17.0
Brent	20 000	320	30.0
Derby	26 000	240	25.0
Hackney	23 000	215	23.6
Hartlepool	11 200	280	22.7
Kensington	25 000	216	18.1
Kirklees	20 000	550	10.8
Lambeth	30 000	250	29.0
Leicester	13 600	370	13.6
Newham	17 000	518	20.8
North Tyneside	36 000	1128	15.4
Sandwell	27 000	606	16.0
Sefton	29 000	800	36.0
Stockton	23 600	695	22.8
Sunderland	37 000	2950	16.1
Walsall	15 000	470	17.2
Wigan	20 000	800	16.0
United Kingdom			10.1

Source: Department of the Environment.

ners (table 8.11). In making bids, authorities had to demonstrate that their programmes stressed four key points: (1) a comprehensive and ambitious vision
for the area selected; (2) full and effective partnerships with the private sector;
(3) participation and involvement of the local community; and (4) effective

Table 8.12 *Urban renewal expenditure, 1986/7 to 1992/3* (in £m cash)

	1986/7	1987/8	1988/9	1989/90	1990/1	1991/2	1992/3
Principal items							
Urban Programme	237	246	224	223	226	242	245
City Grants*	24	27	28	39	45	56	71
Derelict Land	78	77	68	54	62	76	95
Urban Development Corporations	89	134	234	436	554	502	332
City Action Teams	–	–	–	4	8	8	4
City Challenge	–	–	–	–	–	–	64
Total	442	490	563	763	892	884	813

Note: * Urban Development Grants and Urban Regeneration Grants until 1988.
Source: Department of the Environment.

arrangements for implementation and delivery – the most important criterion in at least the first round of bids.

In the forty-one unsuccessful Urban Programme areas it was unfortunate for the unemployed and those in housing need that the pace of urban renewal was held back, not necessarily because the problems of urban decay were not acknowledged, but because of the constraints imposed on the relevant authorities in presenting their bids.

In March 1993, inner city authorities suffered a further setback. It was announced that the Urban Programme as a whole would be phased out, from £245 million (1992/3), to £176 million (1993/4) and to £91 million (1994/5) with an inevitable adverse effect on urban regeneration. In Manchester, for example, 72 factories would not be built, 143 business not be started and 5680 new jobs not be created. Nationally, up to 34 000 jobs and 10 000 community projects were threatened by government cuts in the Urban Programme. The extent by which the Department of the Environment's urban renewal expenditure increased and decreased during the latter years of the Thatcher administration (1986–90) and the first period of the Major government (1991–3) is set out in table 8.12.

To a small extent, cutbacks in the Urban Programme were compensated by the introduction of a £22 million Urban Partnership Fund (UPF) in November 1992, administered by the Department of the Environment. In its first year (1993/4), the fund supported eighty-one projects in forty-six inner city areas, while the selected projects also received £33 million of local government receipts from the sale of council houses and other local authority assets under the provisions of the Autumn Statement of November 1992. While some of the fifty-seven Urban Programme local authorities undoubtedly raised large sums through the sale of assets, most of the worst-off councils raised very little and were forced to abandon many of their regeneration schemes.

Table 8.13 *The Single Regeneration Budget, 1994/5–1996/7*

Planned expenditure: (£m)	1994/5	1995/6	1996/7
UDCs	291	254	245
English Partnerships	181	211	221
Housing Action Trusts	88	90	90
Other programmes	887	777	768
Total budget	1447	1332	1324

Source: Department of the Environment, *Annual Report* (1994).

Further to cuts in Urban Programme expenditure the government established *English Partnerships* (EPs) – under the Leasehold Reform, Housing and Urban Development Act, 1993: (1) to take over policy decision-making from the relevant ministers or Secretaries of State in, for example, the Department of the Environment, Department of Employment and Department of Trade and Industry; (2) to complement the regional industrial policy of the Department of Trade and Industry and to take over the administration of the English Industrial Estates Corporation; (3) to buy and develop inner city sites, to assume the responsibility of much of the Department of the Environment's Urban Programme, to award City Grants and DLGs, and eventually to be responsibility for a large slice of the Department of the Environment's total budget; and (4) to administer City Challenge.

Even more co-ordination was planned with the creation of the Single Regeneration Budget in 1994. The Department of the Environment's City Challenge/Urban Programme, inner city task forces, CATs, English Partnerships, UDCs, Estate Action and Housing Action Trusts; the Department of Trade and Industry's regional enterprise grants; seven programmes of the Department of Employment, four programmes of the Home Office and one programme of the Department of Education were all brought together under a single budget. With administration devolved to ten new integrated regional offices, it was intended that public expenditure on urban renewal would be substantially rationalised and consequently reduced (table 8.13).

LOCAL AUTHORITY SOURCES OF FINANCE

In the early 1990s, local authorities undertook a large volume of capital expenditure, £31 billion (in England in 1991/2): approximately 22 per cent of housing and most of the community's expenditure on roads and schools. By 1990 total capital expenditure by local authorities was nearly half of the total outlay on capital projects in the public sector. Local authorities were responsible for about 25 per cent of total public expenditure and employed about 2 million people. The rate at which capital expenditure grew was substantially faster than the growth of the economy generally, as was the total of local authority debt, which exceeded £45 000 million by 1982.

Two aspects of this finance problem were of special significance: first, the interest charges on borrowing mounted as the outstanding total rose, a trend which in recent years was reinforced by high interest rates. Loan charges by the mid-1980s accounted for about 20 per cent of current expenditure and were virtually equal to net additional borrowing, exacerbating the problem of obtaining a surplus over current expenditure to help finance capital development. Secondly, local authority borrowing in the market competed with that of central government even if the latter lent to local authorities through the Public Works Loan Board (PWLB).

Local authorities depend on four sources for capital finance: government grants and subsidies, surpluses on current account (the margin of receipts over current outgoings), borrowings and the receipts from the sale of housing and land. In the short term, local authorities restrict their temporary debt to no more than 20 per cent of the total loan, and the amount repayable in three months or less to 15 per cent of the total debt. In the long term, the PWLB was established in 1875 to assist mainly the smaller local authorities who lacked the experience to raise funds in the money market. The Board is financed by the Exchequer, and the Treasury prescribes the interest rates to be charged. Up to 50 per cent of long-term capital requirements may be met by the Board, with three years as the minimum length of loan at current government borrowing rate plus a management charge. The PWLB is the main source of capital finance to local authorities.

There have been shifts in policy to the extent that local authorities may or may not borrow either from the Exchequer, or through the PWLB, or the market. Access has been encouraged by increasing flexibility and increasing substantially the amounts that may be borrowed. The central government wishes to reduce borrowing by local authorities from the banks and divert it to PWLB to facilitate its monetary targets.

Larger local authorities are able to raise funds by the issue of fixed interest securities which are quoted on the London Stock Exchange. Since 1933 local authorities have borrowed substantial sums by mortgages and bonds.

One other source of long-term finance used to a limited extent by larger authorities has been overseas borrowing. This is subject to Treasury approval and balance of payments constraints but is attractive at times of high home interest rates. The risk is that exchange rates may move against the borrower.

Governments in the United Kingdom have detailed and specific control of local authority capital expenditure and authorities cannot borrow money without the sanction of the appropriate government department. Since 1971 capital expenditure has been divided into 'key' and 'locally determined' services. The former includes services such as housing, principal roads and education, over which central control is exercised and for which local authorities may borrow only in respect of specific approvals. Locally determined sectors include services such as libraries, in respect of which a block loan sanction is allocated annually to each authority. The authority is then free to decide which projects to pursue and how much to borrow within the permitted figure. Since 1981 all capital expenditure has been subject to a national cash limit and this has had a marked effect on local authority activity; for example, the local authority sector accounted for only 2 per cent of the total starts in 1992.

The reasons for the control of borrowing have changed. Increasingly, there has been concern that local authority capital spending should conform with the government's overall economic strategy and with its patterns of priority. The regulation of local authority expenditure is seen as a useful tool of economic management. The heavy borrowing requirements of local authorities created problems for the Bank of England in seeking orderly financial markets. There have been shifts in policy to the extent that local authorities may or may not borrow, from the Exchequer, or through the PWLB or the market.

LOCAL AUTHORITY CURRENT FINANCING

Local government revenue expenditure increased in real terms throughout most of the 1970s. As a proportion of GNP between 1965 and 1975 it increased from 8 to 13 per cent, accounting for almost the whole of the rise in the proportion of total public sector to GNP. It was subsequently reduced by severe spending curbs, to 10 per cent in 1992. About 75 per cent of local authority current spending is on social services, principally education, and on environmental services; of the balance, over 20 per cent is on debt interest which increased to over £5000 million by the late 1980s.

There are three sources of income to meet this expenditure. First, income from rents, dividends and interest, and from charges for miscellaneous services provided. Secondly, there is grant aid from central government; thirdly, there are the proceeds of the general rate. In the 1980s the share of revenue raised through rates declined and government grants increased in importance. Whereas in 1960 rates accounted for 39 per cent of current revenue, by 1985 they accounted for only 22 per cent. Conversely, government grants, which in 1960 accounted for 40 per cent of revenue, had by 1975–6 reached over 66.5 per cent of relevant expenditure. (In the 1980s, rates rose within limits but grants slumped to about 40 per cent of expenditure by the end of the decade.)

In the 1980s, there was increasing concern that local authorities would be too much under the control of central government since they depended to an ever-increasing extent on central grants. A major reason for the increase in grant and the government intervention which accompanied it was the confinement of the local authority to a single form of local income – the rate – and the lack of buoyancy in this single source at a time of accelerating inflation and expenditure.

Rates and Rate Control

Rating had a long history as a means of providing revenue for local services. Rates were essentially a local tax paid by occupiers of land and buildings as a contribution towards local services. The rateable value of a hereditament was assessed by the Inland Revenue according to the rental value of a property and the rate poundage; the number of pence in the pound which the occupier consequently had to pay on his/her property was fixed by the local authority. It was calculated by dividing the total sum to be raised by the estimated yield of a 1p rate in the area. For example, with a rateable value of £5 million and £5 million required, the rates would be levied at 100p in the pound. By 1985 the annual yield from rates amounted to £13 796 million – about 10 per cent of the total fiscal revenue and a greater amount than the yield from Value Added Tax (VAT) and vehicle excise duties combined.

Despite the many acknowledged advantages of the rating system (including the fact that it was well understood, having been in use in some form since the seventeenth century), by the 1970s the disadvantages of rates were clearly apparent – not least their regressive impact on households. The appointment of the Layfield Committee[57] in 1974 led to a careful consideration of alternative forms of local taxation such as local income tax, local sales tax, employment and motor taxes, site value rating and service charges. By 1982, however, following the recommendation of the House of Commons Environment Committee, the government abandoned the idea of rate abolition – at least for the time being.

Instead, the government attempted to impose severe constraints on local authority spending as part of its policy of cutting back the money supply to Treasury targets. Central government grants to local authorities were reduced, and many large urban authorities were 'rate-capped'. The Greater London Council and the metropolitan counties were abolished in 1986 in a further attempt to reduced public expenditure. Cuts in local government expenditure not only had serious effects on the national economy, because the 'inverse multiplier' reduced demand and raised unemployment, but limitations on local spending also had harmful effects on the built environment and local services, consequently creating inefficiencies in the urban economy.

The reform of local government finance was eventually implemented under the Local Government and Housing Act 1989. Reform swept away the existing system of controls on local authority capital expenditure and replaced them with new 'credit approvals' – involving new restrictions on borrowing. Local authorities, in addition, were able to spend 25 per cent of their receipts from the sale of assets (with 75 per cent being used to repay debt). If they wished to spend more, they were empowered to increase the rate of poll tax (see below), although this would be electorally constrained and subject to capping in extreme cases. The rate support grant was retained under a new name – 'revenue support grant', and set at 47 per cent in England (and 70 per cent in Wales) in 1990/1.

THE REFORM OF LOCAL GOVERNMENT TAXATION

Based on the 1986 Green Paper, *Paying for Local Government*,[58] plans for the reform of local taxation in England and Wales were announced at the beginning of the third period of the Thatcher government in 1987. The new system, incorporated in the Local Government Finance Act 1988 and introduced in 1990–1, abolished rates and helped finance local authorities by means of the following four elements:

(1) A single uniform business rate (UBR) was fixed by central government in London (or Cardiff), and its proceeds were pooled and subsequently redistributed among local authorities on a pro rata basis related to the size of their adult population. UBR was to amount to an equivalent of about £240 per adult – equal to the average per capita proceeds from non-domestic rates in 1987–8.

(2) Each local authority received from the Exchequer a standard (top-up) grant of about £150 per adult.

(3) In addition, all local authorities (to be put on an equal footing) received a variable needs grant, averaging £140 per adult.

(4) The local authority fixed its own community charge, or 'poll tax', (intended to average £278 per adult in England, but averaging £357 per taxpayer when introduced). Poll tax was levied on every adult except the poor (who at the maximum received a rebate of 80 per cent), and those in prison, living in hospital, or under the age of 19 and still at school. Owners of second homes and dwellings empty for more than three months were taxed as if two adults occupied the property, and non-British residents were also eligible for the tax. A 'safety net' was introduced to ensure that the combined income received by each local authority by means of UBR and government grant was about the same as under the old system. The government's reasons for adopting this new form of local taxation was that it would ensure that, unlike domestic rates, (almost) every adult would pay the same for local services, it would (possibly) be a better reflection of the cost of these services than were the rates, and it would (supposedly) increase the degree of local accountability.

Overall, the new system was subject to considerable criticism. First, UBR has had a very uneven effect on businesses and on the local economy. With the revaluation of non-domestic properties in 1990 (which will continue at intervals of five years), southern and prime retail rateable values rose significantly more than northern and industrial values (notwithstanding a five-year phase-in). This affected businesses in very different ways, since some firms found that higher values were matched by lower rate poundages, or vice versa, and others were net gainers or net losers. As table 8.14 shows, 860 000 businesses were likely to lose, while only 560 000 firms would gain, both by as much as £1.8 billion.

A disproportionate number of winners would be located in the North, and most losers would be in the South. It is thus probable that commercial and industrial property values in the North will rise, while those in the South will

Table 8.14 *Predicted impact of the uniform business rate upon companies in England*

	Number of properties affected (000s)		Rate bill 1989/90 (£m)		Change	
					(£m)	(%)
Increases:						
5% to 50%	390		2260		+520		+23
50% to 100%	230	} 860	720	} 3420	+500	} 1790	+70
100% or more	240		440		+770		+175
Little or no change:	100		890		–		–
Decreases:						
5% to 50%	450	} 660	3650	} 4960	−1010	} 1800	−28
50% or more	110		1310		−790		−60

Source: Department of the Environment.

fall. Although criticised by the Confederation of British Industry, over the course of time UBR might become a means of reducing the North–South divide in terms of businesses expectations. It has been estimated that, of the anticipated annual £8.8 billion UBR yield, £1.8 billion will shift from the South to the North.[59]

Secondly, the poll tax was inevitably highly regressive. The 1986 Green Paper showed that individuals with gross weekly incomes in excess of £500 would gain from the new system to the extent of £5.84 per week, while those with weekly incomes of less than £100 would lose up to £29 per week. Generally, the gainers would be single-person households and/or those living in high-rated property, while the losers would be households with two or more adults and/or those living in low-rated property. It was estimated that, in total, as many as 75 per cent of adults paid more in poll tax than they would have paid in rates. Regionally, most of the affluent areas of the South and Midlands gained, but the North and London (and particularly the inner city areas) lost – as regional comparisons set out in table 8.15 broadly show.

In defending the poll tax, the government argued that a flat rate was not unfair, since nearly 50 per cent of local authority current expenditure is paid for by the Exchequer – in no small part from the proceeds of progressive taxation. Nevertheless, to limit the rate of increase in poll tax to £380 per head in 1991–2, the government capped increases in a number of local authorities, and provided a £3 billion package to cushion the impact of an escalation in local authority expenditure. In the Budget of 1991, moreover, the Chancellor gave the equivalent of a £140 per head rebate to every person eligible to poll tax, an obvious concession to mounting criticism.

Thirdly, poll tax was expensive to collect. The Chartered Institute of Public Finance and Accountancy and the Association of Metropolitan Authorities both

Table 8.15 *Local taxation in selected areas before and after the imposition of community charges*

District authority	Average rate bill per household 1987–8 (£)	Community charge per 2-person household (£)	Gain or loss (£)
Surrey Heath	519	280	+ 239
Woking	462	280	+ 182
Bromsgrove	433	270	+ 163
Slough	425	298	+ 127
Worcester	401	300	+ 101
Redditch	397	306	+ 91
Manchester	492	549	− 57
Liverpool	500	602	− 102
Newcastle upon Tyne	479	584	− 105
Hackney	765	1 382	− 614
Lewisham	684	1 354	− 670
Camden	843	1 564	− 721

Source: Department of the Environment.

estimated that the tax would cost up to two and a half times as much to collect as the cost of collecting rates – a major problem being to ensure that everybody liable to pay the tax was registered.

Fourthly, far from increasing the accountability of local authorities to their electorate, the new system reduced it. In the late 1980s, the rate support grant payable to local authorities in England and Wales was 45 and 65 per cent respectively, but when the revenue from UBR was distributed, English and Welsh local authorities had, respectively, a further 30 and 20 per cent of their spending met by the Exchequer. English and Welsh local authorities were consequently only 25 per cent and 15 per cent accountable (compared to 55 and 35 per cent before).

Finally, poll tax might have had a very substantial but not entirely beneficial effect on the residential property market. It was estimated that the tax might have resulted in 10 million households being better off by more than £1 billion per annum. Taking into account mortgage interest rates in the early 1990s, this sum could have been translated into an increase in property values of £12 billion (or, at least, when the housing market slumped in 1991–2, cushioned the fall in values by an equivalent amount) and represented, almost unnoticed, 'the greatest distribution of wealth unmatched since the great enclosure of common lands in the eighteenth century'.[60] Owners of small, low-priced and low-rated dwellings were, however, generally worse off, and the value of their properties fell – possibly more dramatically than the average fall in house prices during the slump.

Table 8.16 *Council tax bands, tax liability and comparisons with community charge, England, 1993/4*

| Band | Property value (£) | Tax imposed by a standard spending council on a 2 adult household (£) | Comparison with community charge 1992/3 (increased or decreased liability) | | |
			1-adult household	2-adult household	4-adult household
A	0–40 000	136	−11	−202	−766
B	40–52 000	420	+33	+143	−707
C	52–68 000	480	+78	−84	−647
D	68–88 000	539	+122	−25	−588
E	88–120 000	657	+211	+94	+470
F	120–160 000	776	+300	+212	−351
G	160–320 000	900	+393	+336	−227
H	Over 320 000	1 078	+526	+514	−49

Note: There are separate bands for Scotland and Wales, with maxima of £212 000 and £240 000 respectively.

Source: Chartered Institute of Public Finance and Accountancy.

Scotland's new system, specified in the Domestic Rates etc. (Scotland) Act 1987, took effect in 1989–90. Non-domestic rates were assessed and collected as before, although each year's rate poundages were indexed to the rate of inflation. A poll tax replaced domestic rates, and its effects were broadly similar to those in England and Wales – and became apparent sooner.

Because of considerable popular opposition and its many economic flaws, the poll tax was abolished at the end of the financial year 1992/93 and replaced by the council tax – as pledged by the Conservatives in their 1992 General Election Manifesto. Council tax is essentially a property tax (payable by all households), but people living on their own get a 25 per cent reduction and those on very low incomes or state benefits pay no council tax at all. Residential property values (based on 1 April 1991 valuations) are grouped into eight bands (A to H) and taxed to a limited extent proportionately (table 8.16).

There are undoubtedly disadvantages to the council tax; it can be inequitable. Compared to the poll tax, single people living in high-banded properties (and possibly on incomes just above the eligibility ceiling for state benefit) will lose, while large households living in low-banded housing (and possible with a high combined income) will benefit. There have also been a substantial number of appeals regarding valuation and banding. But compared to the poll tax, the council tax has a number of advantages. First, there is just one bill per household, which is easier to collect than one bill per adult (as was the case with the poll tax). Secondly, since the council tax is primarily a tax on property it is more difficult than poll tax to evade. Thirdly, the council tax is generally fairer to low-income families, the majority of whom live in low-banded property. Fourthly, government limits on current local authority spending are likely to keep the level of council tax down.

The effect on residential property values might be the opposite to that of the poll tax. There could be a downward pressure on house prices in the South-East and West Midlands (since households in these areas will generally be paying more than they paid in poll tax), while there could be an upward pressure on prices in the North and in parts of Inner London (where households will generally be paying less).

REFERENCES

1. P. White, *The West European City* (Longman, 1984).
2. A. G. Champion (ed.), *Counterurbanisation* (Edward Arnold, 1989).
3. Conurbations in Yorkshire are not included as their geographical area of definition is much wider than in the case of the examples given.
4. W. Van Vliet, *Housing Needs & Policy Approaches: Trends in 13 Countries* (Duke University Press, 1985).
5. *Cambridge Economic Policy Review*, vol. 8 (Gower, 1982).
6. P. Balchin and G. Bull, *Regional and Urban Economics* (Paul Chapman, 1987).
7. S. Fothergill and G. Gudgin, *Unequal Growth: Urban and Regional Employment Change in the UK* (Heinemann, 1982).
8. P. Gripaios, 'Industrial Decline in London', *Urban Studies*, 14 (1977).
9. F. Gaffikin and A. Nickson, *Jobs Crisis and the Multi-Nationals*, Birmingham Trade Union Group (Russell Press, 1984).
10. *Cambridge Economic Policy Review*, Vol. 8.
11. *Employment Gazette* (HMSO, August 1990 and November 1989).
12. *Housing and Construction Statistics* (HMSO, 1990).
13. See A. G. Champion, *Counterurbanisation*.
14. B. J. L. Berry (ed.), *Urbanisation and Counterurbanisation* (Sage, 1976).
15. See I. Hoch, 'City Size and US Urban Policy', *Urban Studies*, 24 (1987).
16. P. Congdon and P. Batey (eds), ch. 11 in *Advances in Regional Demography* (Belhaven, 1989).
17. K. E. Case, 'The Real Estate Cycle and the Economy', *Urban Studies*, 29 (1992).
18. S. Illeris, 'Urban and Regional Development in W. Europe in the 1990s', *Scandinavian Housing and Planning Research*, 9 (1992).
19. See A. G. Champion (ed.), *Counterurbanisation*.
20. A. G. Champion, 'Urban and Regional Demographic Trends in the Developed World', *Urban Studies* 29 (May 1992).
21. A. G. Champion (ed.), *Counterurbanisation*.
22. W. H. Frey, 'United States: Counterurbanisation and Metropolis Depopulation', in A. G. Champion (ed.), *Counterurbanisation*.
23. A. G. Champion (ed.), *Counterurbanisation*.
24. E. Moore and W. Clark, 'Housing and Households in American Cities: Structure and Change in Population Mobility', in D Myers (ed.), *Housing Demography* (University of Wisconsin Press, 1990).
25. L. S. Bourne, 'The Myth and Reality of Gentrification: A Commentary on Emerging Urban Forms', *Urban Studies*, 30 (1993).

26. B. Badcock, 'Notwithstanding the Exaggerated Claims, Residential Revitalisation Really is Changing the Form of Some Western Cities: A Response to Bourne,' *Urban Studies*, 30 (1993).
27. A. Fielding, 'Migration and Urbanisation in Western Europe since 1950', *The Geographical Journal*, 155 (1989).
28. See conclusion in A. G. Champion (ed.), *Counterurbanisation*.
29. S. Hill and M. Munday, 'The UK Regional Distribution of Foreign Direct Investment,' *Regional Studies*, 26, 6 (1992).
30. D. Massey, P. Quintas and D. Wield, *High-Tech Fantasies, Science Parks in Society, Science and Space*, (Routledge, 1991).
31. See J. Glasson, 'The Fall and Rise of Regional Planning in the Economically Advanced Nations', *Urban Studies*, 29 (1992).
32. P. Cheshire, 'Explaining the Recent Performance of the European Community's Major Urban Regions', *Urban Studies*, 27 (1990).
33. S. Illeris, 'Urban and Regional Development in Western Europe in the 1990's.
34. L. Van den Berg, R. Drewett, L. Klassen, A. Rossi and C. Vijverberg, *Urban Europe: A Study of Growth and Decline* (Pergamon, 1982); and N. Vanhove and L. Klassen, *Regional Policy: A European Approach* (Saxon House, 1980).
35. P. Cheshire and D. Hay, *Urban Problems in Europe* (Allen & Unwin, 1988).
36. H. Blumenfeld, 'The Tidal Wave of Metropolitan Expansion', *Journal of the American Institute of Planners* (Winter, 1954).
37. R. R. Boyce, 'The Edge of the Metropolis: The Wave Theory Analog Approach', *British Columbia Geographical Series*, 7 (1966).
38. Ibid.
39. L. S. Bourne, *Private Redevelopment of the Central City* (University of Chicago Press, 1967).
40. See B. Walker, *Welfare Economics and Urban Problems*, ch. 6 (Hutchinson, 1987).
41. J. W. R. Whitehand, *The Changing Face of Cities: A Study of Development Cycles and Urban Form*, (Blackwell, 1987).
42. Confederation of British Industry, *Economic Situation* (CBI, 1977); P. Townsend, P. Corrigan and U. Kowarzik, *Poverty and Labour in London* (Low Pay Unit, 1987).
43. S. Fothergill and G. Gudgin, *Unequal Growth*.
44. L. Needleman, *The Economics of Housing* (Staples Press, 1965).
45. S. Merrett, *State Housing in Britain* (Routledge & Kegan Paul, 1979).
46. D. A. Kirby, *Slum Housing and Residential Renewal. The Case in Urban Britain* (Longman, 1979).
47. W. Lean, 'Housing Rehabilitation or Redevelopment: The Economic Assessment', *Journal of the Town Planning Institute*, 57 (1971).
48. D. G. Bagby, *Housing Rehabilitation Costs* (Lexington Books, 1973); D. Listokin, *The Dynamics of Housing Rehabilitation. Macro and Micro Analysis* (Centre for Urban Policy Research, Rutgers University, 1973).
49. National Community Development Project, *The Poverty of the Improvement Programme* (CDP Information and Intelligence Unit, 1975).
50. A. Taylor, 'Property Market', *Financial Times* (19 June 1984).
51. Roger Tyn and Partners (1984), *Monitoring Enterprise Zones: Year Three Report* (Department of the Environment, 1984).
52. I. Wray, 'Enterprise Was Radical only in its Rhetoric', *Guardian* (30 July 1986).
53. N. Ridley, speaking on 'The London Programme', London Weekend Television (29 May 1987).
54. Archbishop of Canterbury's Commission on Urban Priority Areas, *Faith in the City* (Church House Publishing, 1985).
55. Town and Country Planning Association, Whose Responsibility?, *Reclaiming the Inner Cities* (TPCS, 1986).

56. D. Cadman, 'Private Capital and the Inner City', *Estates Gazette* (31 March 1979).
57. *Layfield Committee of Inquiry into Local Government Finance*, Cmnd 6453 (HMSO, 1976).
58. Department of the Environment, *Paying for Local Government*, Cmnd 9714 (HMSO, 1986).
59. A. Travers, 'New Year Rates Shock for Nearly a Million Businesses', *Guardian* (2 January 1990).
60. See *Land and Liberty*, 'How Thatcher Boosted Price of Houses', July–August 1987.

9

Housing

HOUSING MARKET

The housing market in the United Kingdom is composed of four distinct yet interrelated markets and tenures: private owner-occupied and private rented accommodation; the public sector, consisting of the local authority stock; and housing association accommodation, which provides social housing but is not in the public sector. These markets are related through a pattern of flows complicated by contractual obligations, ownership, property rights and government intervention: from privately rented either to owner-occupation or to the social sector; and from social housing to owner-occupation.

The housing market is dominated by the existing stock of buildings which represent a high proportion of the total supply of housing. Relative to the size of stock, the net annual addition is small. Supply is therefore relatively fixed even in the long term, and prices of the standing stock and its allocation among users are determined primarily by changes in demand conditions. The durability and immobility of housing imposes a brake on the pace of adjustment of supply to changes in demand. In layout and building pattern the market situation is fundamentally one of disequilibrium; since so much of aggregate stock is not of recent construction, its location pattern reflects past distribution of population and economic activity.

House purchase represents a very large capital outlay for the consumer which can rarely be financed out of income, thus borrowing is necessary and the availability of long-term credit is of critical importance in making demand for owner-occupation effective.

In the United Kingdom none of the housing sectors is left free to face market forces. Tax relief and exemption distort owner-occupation, and both private and local authority housing are subject to extensive intervention with marked effects upon supply and demand. Overall, the price system has not been allowed to carry out its function of allocating scarce housing resources between alternative users.

OWNER-OCCUPATION

The growth of owner-occupation began in the 1920s and 1930s, but the post-Second World War period saw its consolidation as the most important numeri-

Table 9.1 *Housing tenure, United Kingdom, 1981–91*

	Owner-occupied		Rented privately		Rented from local authorities		Rented from housing associations		Total stock
	(millions)	(% of total)	(millions)	(% of total)	(millions)	(% of total)	(millions)	(% of total)	(millions)
1981	12.2	57	2.3	11	6.6	31	0.5	2	21.6
1986	14.1	63	1.9	9	5.9	26	0.6	2	22.5
1991	16.0	68	1.7	7	5.2	22	0.7	3	23.6

Source: Department of the Environment, *Housing and Construction Statistics.*

cal, and therefore political, factor in the housing market. Favourable government policy, difficulties of finding alternative accommodation, the development of specialist financial intermediaries and an investment atmosphere favourable
for property caused the number of owner-occupied dwellings to increase from
3.4. million in 1974 to 16 million in 1991, or from 26 to 68 per cent of the
total stock of dwellings in the United Kingdom (table 9.1).

The growth in owner-occupation was mainly at the expense of the private
rented sector. Both the benefits of home ownership and the disincentives of
private landlordism (rent control, security of tenure and unfavourable tax treatment) resulted in an average annual loss of rented dwellings of approximately
125 000 in the 1970s. By 1991 only 7 per cent of the total housing stock was
privately rented: about 1.7 million dwellings. A decade earlier, 16 per cent had
been privately rented; in 1951, 41 per cent; while in 1914 it had been 90 per
cent. The proportion of new houses built for local authorities reached its peak
in 1951, with 87 per cent of houses erected. Because of economic and political
change, council-house building decreased rapidly after the mid-1970s and this,
together with council house sales, reduced the size of the council stock from
6.8 million to 5.2 million between 1979 and 1991 – its share of the total housing stock falling from 32 to 22 per cent.

The price of owner-occupied housing increased steadily up to 1989 (table
9.2). Until 1974 the rate of increase was greater than the rate of inflation, as
measured by the retail price index, and between 1971 and 1973 far exceeded
this. This apparently inexorable increase encouraged early entry into the housing market as the investment aspects of house purchase were emphasised. Between 1974 and 1982, however, there was a realisation that rising house prices
in real terms were not inevitable (in fact, between the First and Second World
Wars house prices had fallen), and in the early 1990s house prices fell in both
real and absolute terms.

Generally, the price of new houses will be determined by existing house
prices. Because of the durability of buildings, the supply of houses is dominated by the existing stock. The net average addition to stock by new building
is relatively insignificant; about 1.1 per cent per year between 1911 and 1991.
Thus the supply of houses is relatively inelastic even over a long period; price

Table 9.2 *Average house prices and retail prices, 1970–92*

	Average house prices		House price/ earnings ratio	Retail price index increase (%)	Real increase in house prices (%)
	(£)	(% increase)			
1970	5 190	7.0	3.25	6.4	0.6
1971	6 130	18.1	3.50	9.4	8.7
1972	8 420	37.4	4.29	7.1	30.3
1973	11 120	32.1	4.95	9.2	22.9
1974	11 300	1.6	4.25	16.1	−14.5
1975	12 119	7.2	3.65	24.2	−17.0
1976	12 999	7.3	3.40	16.5	−9.2
1977	13 922	7.1	3.34	15.8	−8.7
1978	16 297	17.1	3.43	8.2	8.9
1979	21 047	29.1	3.82	13.4	15.7
1980	24 307	15.5	3.61	18.0	−2.5
1981	24 810	0.8	3.30	11.9	−11.1
1982	25 553	3.0	3.13	8.6	−5.6
1983	28 593	11.9	3.23	4.6	7.3
1984	30 812	7.8	3.29	4.9	2.9
1985	31 188	7.7	3.30	6.1	1.6
1986	38 121	14.9	3.53	3.4	11.5
1987	44 220	16.0	3.80	4.1	11.9
1988	54 280	22.7	4.25	4.9	17.8
1989	62 135	14.5	4.43	7.8	6.7
1990	66 695	7.3	4.34	9.5	−2.2
1991	65 593	−1.7	3.90	5.9	−7.6
1992	63 425	−3.3	3.51	3.7	−7.0

Sources: Building Societies Association; Council of Mortgage Lenders; Department of the Environment.

changes are therefore normally caused by demand changes. Housebuilders will charge what the market will bear with reference to existing house prices but they can only pass on increases in costs to the consumer when the market is favourable. Consequently, there is a broad correlation between new and second-hand house prices (table 9.3) and between housing starts and prices of second-hand houses. Generally, when second-hand house prices increase at a faster rate (as, for example, in 1987 and 1988), there will be an incentive for developers to increase the supply of new houses, other things being equal. The trend will need to be well established before the level of new starts is noticeably affected. But when the rate of increase in the price of second-hand houses decelerates, or when the price falls, the supply of new houses will decrease – for example, between 1989 and 1992.

Table 9.3 *Indices of new and second-hand house prices (quarter ending 31 March 1983 = 100), housing starts and second-hand house prices, 1982–92*

	Second-hand properties		New properties	Housing starts private sector (000s)	Percentage change	Second-hand house prices (£)	Percentage change
	Modern	Older					
1982	90.4	91.4	94.8	140.8	19.9	25 167	3.3
1983	100.0	100.0	100.0	172.4	22.4	28 145	11.8
1984	112.7	113.7	112.5	158.3	−8.2	30 342	7.8
1985	125.5	127.8	125.0	165.7	4.7	32 673	7.7
1986	134.0	138.4	134.3	180.0	8.6	37 499	14.8
1987	153.7	160.9	150.3	196.8	9.3	43 427	15.8
1988	169.5	175.6	164.5	221.4	12.5	53 185	22.5
1989	225.8	233.7	211.1	170.1	−23.2	60 608	14.0
1990	224.2	239.7	205.1	135.2	−20.5	65 276	7.7
1991	212.7	217.9	190.1	134.9	−0.2	65 575	0.5
1992	204.6	209.4	187.0	121.0	−10.3	62 212	−5.1

Sources: Council of Mortgage Lenders, *Housing Finance*; Nationwide Building Society, *House Prices*.

There have been significant regional differences in price and site values; the highest have been in the South-East where site values reached over 35 per cent of price in 1972–3 and approached 50 per cent in the late 1980s. The premium established by this region reflected the higher incomes and relatively low levels of unemployment in the 1970s and 1980s. In the recession of the early 1990s, however, site values in the South-East slumped, both absolutely and as a proportion of house prices – narrowing regional differentials.

Population Trends

Population increase must result in increased demand for housing, and changes in the numbers of households are particularly significant. It is new households formed and existing households which move that generate the demand for new houses and put pressure on the stock of existing ones. Households which stay where they are have indirect effects. Those households which are most significant in considering housing demand include newly married people, elderly households dissolving, and the formation and dissolution of one-person households. The number of households formed is the result of a very complex pattern of relationships and flows including marriage, death, migration, divorce and elderly households going to live as part of another household.[1]

Between 1951 and 1991 total households increased by 28 per cent, with the most significant increase in the 26–30 age group, reflecting the sharp increase in the birth-rate after 1945. Single-person households increased from 11.9 to 29 per cent of total households between 1961 and 1991. The number of marriages increased substantially from the 1960s, reflecting the increase in the percentage of the population in the main marriageable age group, and easier divorce. Life expectancy increased, slowing down the recycling of houses as many more elderly households continued in existence. The impact of these factors was to greatly increase the demand for small dwelling units, not generally reflected in the types of housing developed. Between 1951 and 1991 the United Kingdom population increased from 50.2 to 57.2 million, while the total stock of dwellings increased from 13.8 to 23 million, outstripping the growth in household formation and producing a crude surplus of houses over households – illusory because it conceals serious discrepancies. It takes no regard of the geographical distribution of houses and people, the quality of the housing stock, the splitting of households, the increased demand for second homes, and the need to allow for a vacancy rate to promote mobility. This latter consideration is of increasing importance. In a modern economy, technological change leads to the existence of areas of decline and growth where new industries find favourable locations. There is therefore need for labour to move from areas of decline to areas of growth.

Finance for House Purchase

The effective demand for owner-occupier housing is critically dependent upon the availability of long-term finance, which in the United Kingdom is provided by a number of institutions including building societies, banks, insurance companies and local authorities. The market is dominated by the building societies, whose prime function is the provision of long-term finance for owner-occupation; this dominance is particularly clear in respect of finance for new dwellings. By 1992, building societies had over £211 000 million outstanding loans (62 per cent of all balances, compared with £121 000 million by banks, £4200 million by insurance companies and £1100 million by local authorities). In 1986, a peak year, building societies made 1 231 000 advances, 122 000 on new houses. Because of this dominance (table 9.4) the societies have had important effects on the nature of the housing stock – tending to favour traditionally built modern houses of two to four bedrooms. It may be difficult to obtain a mortgage on unconventional dwellings or conversions. Partly as a result of these restrictions there have been few changes in the type or method of construction of dwellings built for owner-occupation.

In deciding whether to grant a mortgage, the age, quality and type of house, and the likely length of the borrower's working life and his/her job security are important considerations. Generally, mortgages with low deposits and long repayment periods are more difficult to obtain for older properties. Older people usually have to accept shorter repayment periods or smaller loans and there-

Table 9.4 *Mortgages: main institutional sources, 1980–92, United Kingdom (£m)*

	Building societies	Banks and miscellaneous financial institutions	Insurance companies and pension funds	Local authorities	Other public sector	Total
1980	5 722	500	263	456	341	7 282
1981	6 331	2 265	88	271	353	9 308
1982	8 147	5 078	6	555	356	14 142
1983	10 928	3 531	126	−306	40	14 319
1984	14 572	2 523	250	−195	−42	17 108
1985	14 711	4 717	201	−502	60	19 184
1986	19 548	7 769	511	−506	54	27 372
1987	15 076	14 058	825	−433	49	29 573
1988	23 720	16 128	447	−329	144	40 111
1989	24 002	10 267	30	−230	134	34 203
1990	24 140	9 202	124	−322	−103	33 041
1991	20 927	6 795	−233	−370	−435	26 693
1992	13 767	4 536	−76	−342	−127	17 728
Advances outstanding at end of 1992	211 118	121 285	4 268	1 132	1 515	339 318

Sources: Council of Mortgage Lenders, *Housing Finance*.

fore need higher deposits or higher incomes to buy houses. Societies are vitally concerned with ensuring their reputation as safe investment media. In marginal cases, the non-manual applicant may be better favoured than the manual.[2]

The clearing banks have increased their involvement in mortgage lending beyond their traditional bridging finance. They began to offer a larger volume of loans for house purchase in the early 1980s, increasingly at the upper end of the market and in competition with the building societies. Loans increased from £40 million annually in 1970 to over £16 000 million in 1988. North American and Japanese banks and the Trustee Savings Bank also entered the market, the latter expanding its activity rapidly in 1979–80. Insurance companies have preferred to lend on commercial rather than residential property, thus housebuying loans are normally linked to an endowment policy – with higher repayments than with a conventional building society mortgage. Insurance companies have been significant in the higher mortgage range and on new houses, but their overall share of home loans has diminished since the 1960s.

Local authorities may grant mortgages under provisions of the Housing (Financial Provisions) Act 1958. They tend to limit their lending to borrowers unable to obtain a mortgage from a building society, either because of the financial status of the borrower or the age or construction of the property to be mortgaged; they also prefer to limit their lending to borrowers within their physical boundaries and also to a strict financial limit. They tend to act as lenders of last resort, mainly for older housing, and interest rates are normally fixed over the whole period of the loan. Public sector cutbacks meant that local authorities played a lesser role in the 1980s except in financing council house purchase, and recently loans have been less than mortgages.

Building Society Funds

Crucially, the ability of societies to lend depends upon the inflow of funds from savers, which in turn depends largely upon the rate of interest societies offer in comparison with other competing institutions within the money market. Thus the differential between building society rates and competing rates as indicated by the bank rate to October 1972, and minimum lending rate (MLR) and base rate since, is of significance in indicating the likely level of inflow funds. Typically, building societies borrow short and lend long but need to adjust their interest rates in relation to other short-term rates.

Although building society rate changes are slow over time, they follow other rates. For example, when the MLR is increased a new equilibrium occurs within the money market – building society rates appear to be relatively unattractive for the marginal investor. Thus funds flow out of societies, less money is available for advances, effective demand for housing falls and properties become more difficult to sell. This situation has occurred intermittently since the 1950s, usually at times of economic crisis associated with the balance of payments. The outflow continues until the societies are forced to increase their rates to lenders to restore the original equilibrium. Higher rates to depositors result in higher rates to mortgagors. Effectively, the higher the rate of interest the less capital can be raised by a borrower and the less the effective demand as maximum possible bid price is less. Therefore the overall impact of increases in the base rate is a slowing down in the rate of price increase in the private house market and eventually a slowing down in new developments as builders realise that anticipated prices will not be achieved and that they cannot sell completed developments. The reverse process occurs at times of falling interest rates. Thus there is a clear inverse relationship between interest changes and housing starts.

Incomes and Income Elasticity

For existing owner-occupiers, maximum demand, given financial constraints, consists of personal savings, the value of the existing dwelling and the maximum mortgage available. For households that are not already owner-occupiers, maximum effective demand is the maximum mortgage plus any personal savings. Mortgage potential is based on recipient's age, job security and earnings with a maximum mortgage normally set at between 2.5 and 3 times the head of households' gross annual earnings. With maximum mortgages linked critically to earnings, and mortgages being essential to house purchase, one would expect a fairly stable relationship between average earnings of fully employed men over 18 and house prices with a ratio of average price to income of approximately 3.5. This latter ratio held for most of the 1950s and 1960s, then between 1966 and 1970 it dropped to 3.4 before increasing steeply between 1970 and 1973 to 4.95 (rather higher for manual than non-manual workers).[3] Because of the significance of mortgages for house purchase there is clearly a limit to the increase in the price/earnings ratio before some slowing down in house prices occurs to restore equilibrium. This occurred in the housing market between 1974 and 1975. Similarly in 1989, the ratio reached 4.47 and was followed by a collapse in house prices between 1990 and 1993. Conversely, the relatively low ratio of 3.23 reached in the first quarter of 1985 indicated that house prices were due to rise at a faster rate, which duly occurred in 1986–7, and in 1993 the ratio fell to 3.2, which signalled an eventual increase in prices. The increase in the number of owner-occupiers means that the many transactions within the housing market are between existing owners rather than among households moving in from the rented sector. With a house to sell to partly finance the transaction through the resultant equity, the mortgage becomes marginally less significant and the ratio of price to income may tend to settle higher than hitherto.

The tendency to demand more and better-quality owner-occupier housing reflects the positive income elasticity of demand for housing. Income elasticity has been measured using either time-series analysis in which the available data on housing demand are analysed in relation to income changes over time, or cross-sectional analysis, in which housing demand is examined in relation to families within various income groups in a given period. The latter has advantages in that the time period is too short for other conditions to have changed substantially. In the United Kingdom, permanent income elasticity of demand based on cross-section analysis ranges from 0.6 to 1.0, largely depending on the considerations given to age of head of household and social class. Time-series analysis tends to show higher elasticities, probably because of the underlying conditions in the market for housing and in the population structure. Recent work carried out on price elasticity has found values ranging from 0.26 to 0.60 – that is, an inelastic demand.[4] The price elasticity of demand for a dwelling is, of course, less elastic than for housing as a whole.

There has been a consistent increase in the proportion of borrowers with wives working in paid employment whose incomes have been taken into account in the granting of a mortgage, although societies were reluctant to give a wife's earnings much weight since the continuity of that income was considered to be in doubt. However, by 1973 nearly 57 per cent of first-time buyers and 33 per cent of previous owner-occupiers had working wives.[5] Thus the average mortgage repayment as a percentage of average household income was lower than the price/income ratio suggests. The Nationwide Building Society suggested that repayments for normal mortgages represented 22.5 per cent of family income for first-time buyers, reducing to 10 per cent of income after 5.5 years (the average life of a mortgage). For all households, average expenditure on housing as a proportion of income increased from 9.5 per cent in 1966 to 14.9 per cent in 1976. By 1980, houses represented 20 per cent of personal sector net wealth. Generally, owner-occupiers tend to spend a higher proportion of their incomes on housing than tenants in either the public or private sector. First-time buyers under 25 required a deposit representing 66 per cent of income by 1978, compared with 50 per cent in 1966 (with the highest figures required in Greater London).[6]

There has, however, been an increased demand for owner-occupation from younger age groups. By 1992, approximately 16 per cent of all mortgages were granted to purchasers under 25 years of age and a further 42 per cent to the 25–34 age group. By the early 1990s, the proportion of owner-occupied dwellings in the United Kingdom (68 per cent) was in excess of most other West European countries, although in the United States some 66 per cent of dwellings were owner-occupied. It is of concern, however, that an increasing proportion of owner-occupiers (1.5 per cent) were affected by mortgage foreclosure in 1992 because of their inability to meet mortgage repayments.

Tax Concessions

A further incentive to owner-occupation has been tax relief at marginal rates on interest payments made on mortgages, although in 1974 this was limited to the first £25 000 borrowed (£30 000 in 1983). In the inflationary period of the 1970s and early 1980s, tax relief often meant that the owner-occupier paid a negative rate of interest. In addition, the steady increase in price emphasised the investment advantages of owner-occupation. If the increase in capital value is included, the effective rate of interest was further reduced. Tax relief on mortgages for owner-occupation was costing over £7000 million annually by 1990/1 compared with £75 million in 1962/3. It was clearly beneficial to be a borrower repaying in depreciated pounds in order to own an appreciating capital asset which was a fine hedge against inflation. The owner-occupier was also free of capital gains tax (on his/her main property) at an estimated cost of over £3 billion in 1988. Other tax changes favoured the owner-occupier. In 1963, Schedule A tax on the imputed rent income derived from a dwelling by its owner was abolished, at a cost to the Treasury of £48 million in a full year; the current cost of not having this tax could be more than £7000 million a year. In 1971, stamp duty on mortgages was abolished. In 1973, new housing was zero rated for VAT. In 1983 and 1993, thresholds for stamp duty rates on transactions were increased.

Mortgage interest relief, general exemption from capital gains tax and the abolition of Schedule A tax have been subject to widespread criticism. It is claimed by most economists that mortgage interest relief, in particular, is inflationary since it enables house buyers to bid-up the price of houses higher than would otherwise be the case. Conversely, house prices would be reduced if tax concessions were to be withdrawn or reduced.

Mortgage interest relief also provides inequitable assistance since it is regressively allocated, but while it increased from £1450 million in 1979/80 to £7700 million in 1990/1, it subsequently decreased to £5200 million in 1992/3 because of falling interest rates and house prices. Mortgage interest relief, however, is inefficient since the tax revenue forgone by the Exchequer could finance productive industry rather than lubricate the market largely for second-hand houses; it has adverse effects on taxation because the forgone revenue has to be made up by higher rates of taxation generally (including income tax); it adversely affects household mobility since during boom conditions it helps to widen North–South disparities (particularly boosting house prices in the South-East) and is a disincentive to trade-down; it distorts tenure preferences in favour of owner-occupation (to a greater extent than in many other advanced capitalist countries); it distorts rural values since commuters can easily outbid local labour for a fairly fixed stock of housing; and it fails to protect the poor because the system of relief pulls up house prices beyond their means. The reductions in mortgage interest relief in recent budgets (see later section), and likely reduction in the future, will undoubtedly decrease fiscal inefficiency and distortion, and give way to freer market conditions.

The House Price Cycle

The house price boom of the late 1980s

In the period 1985–9 average house prices in the United Kingdom increased dramatically, by 76 per cent in absolute terms, considerably ahead of increases in the retail price index and average earnings. The causes of the boom were numerous, but essentially derived from an increase in the overall level of demand for home ownership. First, there was a big rise in post-tax incomes, in part due to the reduction in the basic rate of tax from 30 to 25 per cent and the top rate from 60 to 40 per cent. Secondly, financial deregulation (for example, by means of the Building Societies Act 1986) made it easier for housebuyers to obtain larger mortgages.[8] The number of mortgages increased from 8.1 million to 9.4 million between 1985–6 and 1989–90, while net advances increased from £19.1 billion to £40.1 billion. Mortgage debt as a proportion of GDP therefore increased from 32 per cent to 58 per cent, compared to only 20 per cent in France, Germany and Japan, and the house price/earnings ratio soared to 4.43 in 1989. In the United Kingdom in the late 1980s, 100 per cent mortgages were common, whereas in France mortgages were no higher than 80 per cent and in Germany and Japan rarely exceeded 60 per cent. Since both realised and unrealised capital gains were greater than mortgage interest payments, the strong speculative motive in house purchase encouraged buyers to maximise their borrowing. With the end of multiple mortgage interest relief from 1 August 1988 (announced in the previous Spring Budget) there was a last minute surge in demand between March and the end of July which substantially accounted for the 22 per cent increase in average house prices in 1988. Demographic change (notably, high birth-rates in the 1960s) also stimulated demand; in the late 1980s there was a large increase in the number of young people wanting to buy.

The house price boom can also be attributed to a deficiency of supply. House building was increasing more slowly than were the number of new households – mainly because of planning constraints imposed by county councils (in attempts to protect green belts, other areas of high landscape value and the alleged interests of existing communities), and possibly due to private owners withholding land from the market for speculative reasons.

The effects of the boom

One major attribute of the boom was that it had a very variable spatial effect on house prices. There were very wide regional variations in the rate of increase in average house prices between 1985 and 1988, and in house price/earnings ratios (table 9.5). Whereas in East Anglia and the South-East (excluding Greater London) prices increased by 81 and 79 per cent respectively, in Northern Ireland and Scotland the rate of increase was as low as 30 and 17 per cent, and house price/earnings ratios ranged from 3.6 to 2.21 in 1988. Differential increases led to a divergence of average house prices in the late 1980s. By 1988, prices were as high as £77 700 and £73 000 in Greater London and the rest of the South-East respectively, but as low as £30 200 in the Northern region and £29 900 in Northern Ireland. Regional disparities clearly restricted household mobility. Households wishing to move from areas of high to low unemployment (for example, from the Northern region to the South-East) would not only have had to have paid substantially more for a house but also would have had to have secured more remunerative employment to have been able to afford to pay for their housing needs, as regional price and income statistics suggest (table 9.5). Conversely, few households would have been willing to move from high to low price regions (assuming jobs were available) since they would have had to forgo opportunities for substantial capital accumulation, and might also have feared that they would be priced out of the house market should they wish to return.

The effects on the macroeconomy in general were no less important. Since house prices were a major element in the cost of living of housebuyers, Muellbauer[9] argued that soaring house prices in 1984–6 put pressure on the labour market and added 4 per cent to the level of real wages (and predicted even larger increases in nominal wages in the late 1980s). Because wage agreements are often nationally based, house prices in the South-East thus influenced wage levels throughout Britain. The view that house prices during a house price boom, in effect, determine wage levels (rather than vice versa)

Table 9.5 *North–South disparities in house price change and incomes during the boom and slump, 1985–92*

Region	Average house prices £		percentage increase 1985–8	Average earnings of borrowers (£) 1988	House price/ earning ratio 1988	Average house prices (£) 1992	Percentage increase 1988–92	Average earnings of borrowers (£) 1992	House price/ earning ratio 1992
	1985	1988							
"SOUTH"									
East Anglia	31 661	57 295	81	15 936	3.60:1	64 610	−7	18 920	3.41:1
South-East (exc. Greater London)	40 487	72 561	79	20 180	3.60:1	75 189	−8	23 786	3.16:1
South-West	32 948	58 457	77	16 672	3.51:1	77 416	−4	19 950	3.88:1
Greater London	44 301	77 697	75	24 409	3.18:1	77 446	−6	26 597	2.91:1
West Midlands	25 855	41 700	61	15 130	2.76:1	58 405	17	19 601	2.98:1
East Midlands	25 539	40 521	59	14 533	2.79:1	56 527	14	19 818	2.98:1
"NORTH"									
Yorkshire & Humberside	23 338	32 685	40	13 387	2.44:1	54 699	31	18 213	3.00:1
Wales	25 005	34 244	37	12 886	2.66:1	49 502	15	17 797	2.79:1
North-West	25 126	34 074	36	12 257	2.57:1	58 169	38	19 172	3.03:1
Northern	22 786	30 193	33	12 693	2.38:1	48 624	30	17 672	2.75:1
Northern Ireland	23 012	29 875	30	13 490	2.21:1	39 240	30	18 009	2.18:1
Scotland	26 941	31 479	17	13 822	2.28:1	52 274	48	19 950	2.62:1
United Kingdom	31 103	49 355	59	16 040	3.08:1	62 265	14	20 819	2.99:1

Sources: Council of Mortgage Lenders, *Housing Finance*; Department of the Environment, *Housing and Construction Statistics*.

could be supported by the notion that people buy the most expensive house they can afford with the largest mortgage they can raise, but then need to earn more to maintain their customary level of consumption and savings.

Congdon and Warburton[10] have similarly argued that there is a link between rising house prices and retail price inflation. Although real house prices tended to rise on average by 2.63 per cent above the level of retail prices over the period 1957–86, occasionally they increased at a faster rate and pulled up retail prices. It is suggested that the mechanism by which this works is as follows:

(1) Housebuyers convert part of the increase in the value of their property into larger mortgages, or use part or all of the value of properties inherited to purchase consumer goods and thereby boost demand and raise retail prices. The Bank of England[11] estimated that equity withdrawal of this sort amounted to £7.2 billion in 1984, and by 1988 it had soared to £25 billion. The value of property inheritance alone had doubled over the previous ten years to £7 billion, helping to further fuel the consumer boom of the late 1980s.[12]

(2) The housebuilding industry responds to rising house prices by increasing output. Subsequent wage increases in the industry then inflate retail prices.

(3) House price inflation stimulates increased borrowing to invest in housing and this, it is suggested, increases the money supply and hence the rate of inflation.

The Muellbauer/Congdon-Warburton hypotheses have been subject to some criticism. Hamnett[13] has claimed that only a small proportion of equity withdrawal has been diverted into consumption and that most has been returned to the financial system to sustain mortgage lending; and there is little evidence that rising house prices stimulate output, or that earnings and wages generated in housebuilding are of sufficient significance to the rate of inflation. Yet there does appear to be a relationship between house prices and inflation. While the building societies argue that factors other than house prices are the main causes of inflation (for example, rising oil prices and increased VAT in the late 1970s–early 1980s), they claim that rising incomes cause rising house prices rather than the reverse. It is very likely, however, that there is an inflationary 'chicken and egg' relationship. An initial demand change might lead to a rapid rise in house prices (as workers find that their additional expenditure on housing only serves to raise the unit cost rather than the quantity consumed). This causes higher wage demands and, in turn, even higher house prices. If, as new evidence appears to show, widening differences in regional house price trends are producing substantial cost-of-living variations in different parts of the United Kingdom (with the highest prices in the South-East), then high money incomes in high-house-price regions might frustrate real wage demands in such areas – leading to spiralling money wage demands. If met, such demands could have a significant impact on the retail price index, particularly if they formed the bases of national wage settlements.

Clearly, the Treasury sees little connection between rising house prices and

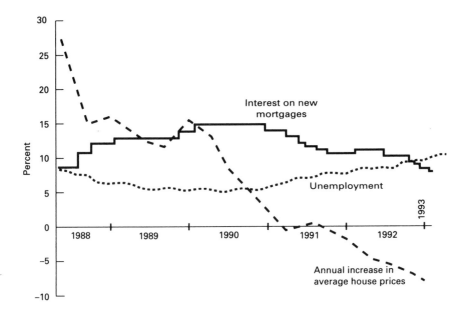

Figure 9.1 *Mortgage interest rate and unemployment constraints on housing demand*

inflation. While this situation persists, it is unlikely that there will be any radical reform to the current system of subsidising owner-occupation.

Critics argue that reform is long overdue. Although the government limited mortgage interest relief of 25 per cent (the basic rate of tax) in its Budget of March 1991, its Spring budget of 1993 announced that relief would be lowered to 20 per cent from April 1994, and its November 1993 Budget declared that it would be lowered further, to 15 per cent, from April 1995, there is a strong case for phasing it out altogether – a view shared by the National Federation of Housing Associations[14] and the Royal Institution of Chartered Surveyors.[15]

The House Price Slump

While average house prices in the United Kingdom increased by 10.9 per cent over the period 1989–92, the annual rate of increase decelerated from 11.1 per cent in 1989 to only 4.5 per cent in 1991, and in 1992 prices in fact fell by 2.6 per cent. The slump was particularly severe in East Anglia, the South-East, Greater London and the South-West, where house prices fell continuously from 1989.

A substantial decrease in demand was the principal cause of the slump. First, in response to an increase in bank base rate, interest rates on new mortgages rose from 9.5 per cent in April 1988 to 15.4 per cent in February 1990 and remained above 10 per cent until September 1992. Secondly, unemployment increased from 5.5. per cent in May 1990 to 10.9 per cent in January 1993, reducing the ability of many potential homeowners to buy, and lowering the purchasing confidence of others (figure 9.1).

Thirdly, other would-be buyers awaited further falls in prices and by remaining outside of the housing market helped to bring about the price reductions expected. Fourthly, in response to falling prices and decreased security, mortgage lenders were increasingly reluctant to provide 100 per cent mortgages, and advances fell from £40 billion to £27 billion between 1988–91. Fifthly, the ending of multiple mortgage interest relief in 1988 and the end of the 'stamp duty holiday' in August 1992 both decreased demand (from December 1991, stamp duty on transaction between £30 000 and £250 000 had been suspended, to encourage housebuying). Sixthly, the high level of demand in the late 1980s was very unstable and it was probable that house prices had risen to an unrealistically high level in relation to incomes during the previous boom and were destined to fall. The house price earnings ratio reached a peak of 4.43 in 1989 compared to an average of 3.7 throughout the 1980s and an average of only 3.3 throughout the period since the 1950s, but in the slump of the early 1990s the ratio plummetted to 2.99 in 1992, while demand decreased from 1.9 million to 1 million transactions during 1988–92.

The slump was aggravated by an excess of housing for sale. Many households afflicted with unemployment, failed businesses or bankruptcy were unable to sell their homes at an acceptable price (or at all) and were thus unable to repay their mortgage repayments. The number of properties repossessed (and often put on to the market at greatly reduced prices) increased from 19 300 in 1985 to 75 540 in 1991 (table 9.6). Although the number of repossessions fell slightly in 1992, there was a marked increase in the number of mortgages in arrears with the possibility of a resulting future increase in repossession and sale. There was also an increasing number of unsold newly-built houses on the market in the early 1990s which helped to depress prices.

The Effects of the Slump

The regional impact of the slump was the reverse of that resulting from the former boom. Instead of divergence, regional markets converged. Regional variations in the rate of change in average house prices narrowed and there was also a convergence in unemployment (figure 9.2). In the period 1989–92, whereas the South-East, East Anglia, Greater London and the South-West experienced a fall in prices and lower house price/earnings ratios, other regions (particularly Scotland and the North-West) appeared to be continuing to enjoy a boom. Despite convergence, however, house prices remained markedly higher in, for example, the South-East than in much of the rest of the country (and unemployment in this region was by then also high). Thus, convergence, as such, did little to encourage any notable increase in household mobility.

The effects of the slump in house prices on owner-occupiers and the macro-economy were, however, substantial. By 1993, over 1.5 million households (disproportionately in the South-East, East Anglia and Greater London) were

Table 9.6 *Properties taken into possession and mortgages in arrears, 1985–92*

	Properties taken into possession		Mortgages in arrears			
			6–12 months		More than 12 months	
	Number	Percentage	Number	Percentage	Number	Percentage
1985	19 300	0.25	57 110	0.74	13 120	0.17
1991	75 540	0.77	183 610	1.87	91 740	0.93
1992	68 540	0.69	205 010	2.07	147 040	1.48

Sources: Council of Mortgage Lenders, *Housing Finance*.

caught in the 'negative equity trap'. Since the value of their property was £3 billion below the mortgage debt, they were prevented from selling their properties and buying elsewhere – the market, to an extent, ceasing to work.

The increase in the number of repossessions (referred to above) was clearly not only a cause of the house price slump, but also an effect. Had house prices been buoyant, mortgagors facing repayment difficulty could have sold their properties and traded downwards. With the malfunctioning of the market, this was no longer possible and, at worst, dispossessed owner-occupiers found themselves homeless. To a significant extent, the substantial increase in homelessness and the increase in the number of homeless households in temporary accommodation (from 94 000 and 16 000 respectively in 1985 to 148 300 and 62 700 in 1992) was attributable to repossession.

With falling house prices and higher unemployment in the South-East, pressures on the labour market of the region eased in the early 1990s, with a stabilising effect on national wage settlements. The housebuilding industry, in particular, responded to falling house prices by decreasing output, reducing employment and lowering the rate of increase in wages in the industry, and thus helped to lower overall consumer demand. Falling house prices in the southern regions of Britain, moreover, deterred housebuyers from taking out second mortgages to purchase consumer goods and services, and equity withdrawal was further constrained nationally by the value of inherited properties rising less rapidly in the early 1990s than in the 1980s. Consumer demand was consequently reduced, with disinflationary effects on consumer prices.

If the government had failed to recognise the connection between rising house prices and inflation in the late 1980s, it was evident that, in the 1990s, it was beginning to acknowledge the link between the housing slump and the economic recession. This was apparent when the Conservative government (after its 1992 general election win) introduced a number of measures to increase the level of demand for home ownership as well as to decrease excessive supply.

First, building societies were allowed to raise the amount they could lend unsecured from £10 000 to £25 000 per person in an attempt to enable owner-

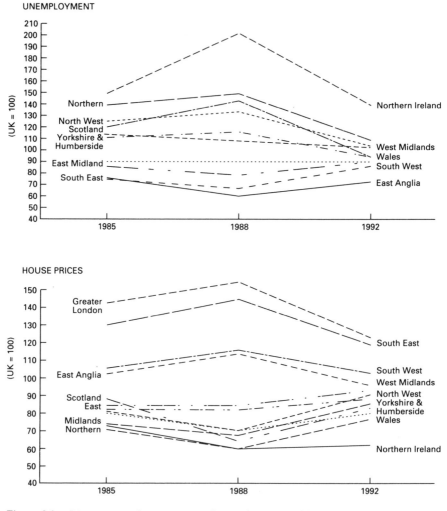

Figure 9.2   *Divergence and convergence of unemployment and house prices*

occupiers who had negative equity in their homes to sell and subsequently to buy elsewhere. Secondly, the Budget of March 1993 raised the transaction threshold from £30 000 to £60 000 on which stamp duty (at 1 per cent) would apply, and thirdly, the government, regarding low interest rates as being central to monetary policy, withdrew the United Kingdom from the Exchange Rate Mechanism (ERM) and brought down the base rate from 10 per cent in August 1993 to 6 per cent in January 1993. Consequently, interest rates on new mortgages fell from 10.75 per cent in September to 7.99 per cent by February 1993 – the lowest since the 1960s and, other things being equal, a stimulant to demand.

In an attempt to reduce excess supply, the government made £750 million available to the Housing Corporation (under the Autumn Statement of 1992) to allocate to housing associations to facilitate the purchase of unsold housing – mainly new stock and repossessions. By March 1993, over 21 000 empty houses were thereby removed from the market.

Prospects for Recovery

It might have seemed by 1993–4 that the stage was set for a recovery in the housing market. Owner-occupation had not been so affordable for generations. Apart from very low mortgage interest rates, the house price–earnings ratio had fallen to its lowest level since the 1950s – below 3.2. But a marked recovery did not occur. Unemployment in 1993 remained at a stubbornly high level (at over 10 per cent throughout the year), preventing many people from buying and dissuading those in work from risking house purchase. Unless there is a substantial decrease in unemployment, it is unlikely that house prices will rise markedly in the short term. The newly-introduced council tax, moreover, is likely to cost many households more than the community charge (poll tax) it replaced and will inevitably have a dampening effect on rising house prices in, for example, the South-East and possibly the West Midlands. A further adverse effect on prices was predicated as a result of the decrease in mortgage interest relief from 25 to 20 per cent in April 1994.

Possible Remedies

As with government policy, other possible ways of reviving the housing market focus either on increasing demand or decreasing supply. With regard to demand, at least two proposals have been voiced in recent years. First, mortgage interest relief, instead of being reduced, could be 'front-loaded.'[16] This could involve either an increase in the interest relief ceiling from £30 000 to, say, £40 000 (or higher) for first-time buyers, with the extra relief being phased out over several years, or interest relief could be raised from its present level to 50 per cent or more to first-time buyers, falling to nil after, say, 10 years. Second, cash grants of, say, £3000 could be made available to every household moving home – to increase demand for a specific period.[17] Although this proposal would almost certainly be unacceptable to a government aiming at decreasing its public-sector borrowing requirement, it would possibly be no more expensive than other methods of reviving the housing market.

With regard to supply, it has been suggested that a mortgage benefit scheme could be introduced to help low-income owner-occupiers (just as housing benefits are awarded to poorer tenants).[18] This would decrease the flow of repossessed properties coming on to the market and thus reduce the property glut, although the usefulness of a benefit scheme would have been greater when mortgage interest payments were high, as in the early 1990s, than when interest payments were low in 1993–4.

PRIVATE RENTED ACCOMMODATION

The decline of private landlordism has been due largely to the comparative advantage in selling vacant properties for owner-occupation, instead of letting, and the onerous task of managing rented housing compared with other forms of investment (many of which were not available in the nineteenth century when rented housing was the norm). The decline of the private rented stock (from 90 per cent of dwellings in 1914 to about 7 per cent in 1991) has also been attributable to several other factors: security of tenure, the tax positions of private landlords, the almost continuous intervention by successive governments in landlord–tenant relations, and rent control and regulation. From 1915 until 1974, rent legislation was intermittently introduced to control or regulate rents in the private sector, although in the inter-war period and again in 1957 decontrols were introduced – albeit for relatively short periods of time and specifically in relation to higher value properties (table 9.7).

A Labour government in 1964 brought an inevitable turn of policy. The Rent Act 1965, consolidated in 1968, brought within control all properties with a rateable value of less than £400 in London and £200 elsewhere (most of the houses which had been decontrolled under the 1957 Act). The Act followed upon the Milner Holland Report (1965)[19] and provided security of tenure for unfurnished tenants; tenants protected under the Act were 'regulated', while those protected by previous acts were still 'controlled'. New machinery was set up to fix and review rents for newly-protected tenants, while new safeguards were introduced to prevent harassment and eviction without a court order. Rent was to be assessed and registered by a Rent Officer after application by landlord, tenant or both. It was to be an objective and 'fair rent' although no fixed formula was given to officers in carrying out their assessment. Rent Officers were to have regard 'to all circumstances (other than personal circumstances) and in particular to the age, character and locality of the dwelling-house and to its state of repair'. Any improvement carried out by the tenant, or any damage caused by him/herself, should not be taken into account.

The most contentious aspect of the legislation was that Rent Officers were directed to assume that the supply and demand for accommodation in the locality was equal – this at a time of great housing shortage and where in most urban areas supply was far short of demand. The result of the disregard of the scarcity factor was that rents were fixed substantially below the market price, providing an additional deterrent to letting as landlords were unsure of obtaining a market return on their investment. On obtaining vacant possession, landlords often preferred not to re-let but to sell for owner-occupation, obtaining a greater price than if the property was sold as an investment. Once the 'fair rent' was registered it was fixed for a statutory two years. The 'fair rent' system placed enormous responsibility on the judgement of the Rent Officer, who often lacked suitable professional qualifications. There was a lack of consistency in rent assessments; appeal was possible to a Rent Assessment Committee which in the majority of cases increased the original fair rent, possibly

Table 9.7 *Legislation controlling rents, 1915–74*

Year of Rent Act	Main features		Rateable value (£)		
			London	Scotland	Elsewhere
1915	Rents controlled at 1914 levels	Not exceeding	35	30	26
1920	Rent controls continued	Not exceeding	105	90	78
1923	Decontrol by possession; letting freed from control when tenant left				
1933	(a) Decontrol of houses	Not below	45	45	45
	(b) Decontrol by possession	Not below	45	35	35
	(c) Decontrol on registration of possession	Not below	35	20	20
	(d) No decontrol by possession unless decontrolled 1923 to 1933 and registered	Not below	20	20	20
1938	(a) Decontrol of houses	Not below	35	20	20
	(b) No decontrol by possession of self-contained dwellings	Not exceeding	35	20	20
1939	Rents controlled	Not exceeding	100	90	75
1957	Rents decontrolled owner-occupied dwellings partly let and new unfurnished dwellings. Remaining tenancies had rents fixed at twice their 1939 rateable values	Not below	40	30	30
1965	Rent regulation	Not exceeding	400	200	200
	Rent controlled continued	Not exceeding	110	80	80
1969*	Controlled dwellings rehabilitated up to 12-point standard to be decontrolled and regulated	Not exceeding	400	200	

continued on page 304

Table 9.7 *continued*

Year of Rent Act	Main features	Rateable value (£)		
		London	Scotland	Elsewhere
1972**	Most controlled tenances to be decontrolled and regulated	Not exceeding	400	200
1973	Rent regulation extended to higher rateable value properties	Not exceeding	1 500	750
1974	Rent regulation extended to furnished tenancies	Not exceeding	1 500	750

Notes: * Housing Act 1969.

      ** Housing Finance Act 1972.

because landlords made more use of the appeal procedure and employed professional assistance. A further criticism of the system was that Rent Officers paid little regard to inflation in their original registration and the next after three years (up to 1980). The net effect of the 'fair rent' system was that unfurnished accommodation became almost extinct outside the controlled and luxury sectors of the market. In 1971 the Francis Committee[20] reported that, in general, the system of fair rents was working well, although it suggested a number of modifications. By 1975 the Department of the Environment (DOE) estimated that of all unfurnished tenancies with non-resident landlords, about half had fair rents registered compared with only 14 per cent five years earlier.

The supply of furnished accommodation was less adversely affected, as the 'fair rent' did not apply. Rent Tribunals assessed a reasonable rent as they were not specifically directed to disregard scarcity, thus the differential between rent assessed by the Tribunal and the market rent was not so great. 'Furnished' tenants did not have the security of tenure granted to the 'unfurnished' tenant; thus landlords had more incentive to let. However, there was a constant possibility of further legislation to give security of tenure to the furnished tenant. These considerations were justified with the Rent Act 1974, which included all properties with a rateable value of £1500 in London and £750 elsewhere. The furnished tenant of the non-resident landlord was given security of tenure and the right to apply for a 'fair rent'. The Rent Officer took over the Tribunal's functions. Compared with the previous 'reasonable' rents, the new 'fair rents' were often considerably lower – by a third to a half. Inevitably, there was a sharp decline in the supply of furnished accommodation and increased difficulty for the young and mobile in finding a home, as landlords preferred to keep their accommodation empty rather than to let and risk the reduction of income and loss of capital. The consequences were particularly serious in cities; about half of Britain's furnished tenancies were in London alone; approximately 10 per cent of London's households were furnished tenants.

An attempt to change housing policy radically was made in 1971, when the Conservative government published a White Paper, *Fair Deal for Housing*,[21] setting out a new system of housing finance for both private and public sectors. The Housing Finance Act 1972 implemented the major proposals. In the private rented sector all controlled tenancies, about 1.3 million, were to become regulated. As recommended by the Francis Committee in 1971, landlords and tenants were to agree a rent, and would be free to apply to the Rent Officer for a fair rent. Properties would need to be provided with standard amenities and be in good repair, and the increase would be phased over two years. The government hoped that the conversion to regulated rents would encourage more lettings and prevent deterioration of properties. It is unlikely that this incentive would have proved to be effective. In any event, the government's anti-inflation legislation of 1973 froze rent increases. On the return of the Labour government in 1974, the Housing Finance Act was repealed.

The major economic effects of government intervention in the rented sector are clear:

(1) The landlord's ability and incentive to maintain premises in good condition is impaired. Many landlords in receipt of controlled or 'fair rents' have found it impossible to meet maintenance charges. Much property degenerates into slums or is at best maintained at a level much below what is economically or socially desirable. Faced with the choice of running property at a loss or allowing it to decay, the landlord may sell. Tenants are also faced with a choice. They can either remain in unsatisfactory rented accommodation or become owner-occupiers – acquire an appreciating asset and benefit from tax privileges. An increasing number have chosen the latter option.

(2) Regardless of the condition of the accommodation, whenever a dwelling has fallen vacant, the landlord usually finds it pays to sell it for owner-occupation rather than to re-let. However, although it is often argued that rent control (or regulation) has resulted in the withdrawing from the letting market of most privately-owned houses suitable for owner-occupation or other uses, Harloe[22] has shown that in both Western Europe and the United States the private rented sector has been in decline whether or not it has been subject to control. In most advanced capitalist countries, owner-occupation is the most heavily 'subsidised' tenure and can outbid all other tenures for a relatively fixed supply of housing of land. The long-term effect of rent control/regulation is shown in figure 9.3. It is assumed that rents are fixed at r_1 (below their market level r), thereby creating an initial shortage of accommodation equivalent to $q_1 - q_2$. If landlords sell their properties for owner-occupation, the long-term supply of rented housing will decrease from SS to S_1S_1, but if, simultaneously, tenants become owner-occupiers, the demand for rented accommodation will similarly decrease (from DD to say D_1D_1), the eventual shortage becoming $q_3 - q_4$. However, if demand does not decrease (there might be a growing number of small households in search of housing) the shortage could be at least as great as $q_1 - q_4$.

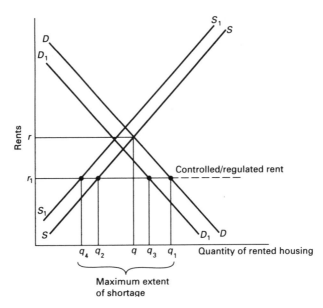

Figure 9.3   *Demand and supply in the controlled sector of the private rented housing market*

(3) The mobility of labour is impeded. Rent restriction involves what is in effect a tax on the landlord and a subsidy to the tenant, which the latter receives only so long as s/he stays in his existing house. The Rent Acts have reduced the supply of accommodation so that if a tenant wishes to move s/he may find her/himself unable to obtain alternative accommodation. The stock of rented property becomes 'fossilised', with a substantial proportion of old and poor-quality dwellings.

(4) Under-use of housing stock. Because tenants cling to their dwellings they prevent the adaptation of housing to changing requirements in size, amenities and standards.

(5) There is a distortion of consumer preference, land-use patterns and allocation of scarce resources.

(6) Landlords have been discriminated against by taxation authorities. A house is considered to last for ever and landlords cannot write down their investment. Even payments into a sinking fund to replace the dwelling cannot be treated as cost. This has led to further distortions within the housing market and further disincentives to letting.

Despite its often generally poor physical quality, largely explained by the succession of adverse legislation, the private rented sector is the only one with a large number of very small dwellings, such as bed-sitters and one- and two-roomed flats. This is very important since approximately 50 per cent of households in 1981 consisted of one or two people. Thus the sector is attractive for young households, particularly single people, students and couples without children. These groups – the young, the mobile, the newcomers to an area – benefit from the flexibility that is characteristic of the private rented sector. The very arbitrariness of allocation by private landlords may be an attraction to certain groups. Local authorities must observe equitable procedures in the allocation of their housing, which may be superficially fair but fail to provide for special needs or circumstances. The private landlord has a role to play which neither municipalisation nor housing associations can replace. Municipalisation, the process of local authorities buying sub-standard dwellings from the private landlord, often reproduces existing forms of council housing which do not benefit the marginal groups who benefit from private renting. In any event, municipalisation is expensive and local authorities outside a limited range of central London areas have shown a singular lack of interest in buying up tenanted property. The management problems involved in providing furnished bed-sit accommodation by local authorities have also not been solved. Similar considerations clearly apply to housing associations, who fail to cater for the marginal groups and 'floaters'. Fundamentally, private rented accommodation may be the only choice for many whose needs are greatest and whose resources are least, short of the availability of suitable public-sector housing.

It was largely for these reasons that the Conservative government, in its Housing Act 1980, introduced shorthold tenure. Shorthold was intended to reduce the landlord's uncertainty about letting, since the tenant's security of tenure was to be limited to the period of the shorthold agreement – a period of one to five years. However, the landlord's return on his/her investment was not improved. The shorthold tenancy in London was to be at a registered fair rent, set by the Rent Officer, which by definition could not take scarcity into account (outside the capital, market rents could be negotiated). A survey of attitudes to letting which the DOE carried out in 1976 showed that the one change which would be most helpful to landlords would be to allow more realistic rents. Shortholds might have some temporary effect: possibly to persuade landlords to let empty property while they are waiting to sell, but a change of government might make the 'shortholder' a lifetime tenant. The tenure is thus likely to have only a marginal effect on the supply of rented accommodation.

A novel proposal of the 1980 Act was that of 'assured' tenancy. Institutions such as building societies, insurance companies and pension funds wishing to build houses to rent could seek approval from the DOE to let property at freely negotiated market rents outside the provisions of the Rent Acts as long as building began after August 1980 and the property had not been occupied previously. This appeared to be merely a symbolic gesture given the political problems of the private rented sector, and it is unlikely that anything other than a very marginal contribution is likely to arise from this proposal since competitive returns may not be anticipated.

The House of Commons Environment Committee in 1982 examined critically the private rented sector.[23] It concluded that private rented housing compared unfavourably with other forms of investment in terms of risk, liquidity, expected returns on capital and management involvement. Landlords could not expect gross returns in excess of 2.75 per cent in London in the early 1980s, or net yields of more than 1 per cent (after taking into account management, maintenance and tax). To obtain a competitive yield of, say, 10 per cent, rents would need to rise considerably above fair rent levels, putting them beyond the means of most tenants. The tenure also fell short as far as tenants were concerned. It lacked the security of an owner-occupied property, while the average rent allowance was less than 10 per cent of the average relief on mortgage interest. The Committee recommended that the tenure could only be saved from further decline by subsidising both landlord and tenant via tax concessions and other means. However, the National Federation of Housing Associations' *Inquiry into British Housing* (1985) proposed that in order to retain and increase investment in private rented housing, rents should be linked to capital values.[24] Capital value rent would have three components: a basic element to provide a real return of around 4 per cent on capital value, an element for management and maintenance, and (if relevant) an element for service charges. As with the fair rent system, capital value rents would be set by rent officers.

In its third term in office, the Thatcher government attempted to build on to previous policy concerning shorthold and assured tenancies. It hoped that its new measures would bring back into use over 500 000 properties allegedly left vacant because of rent regulation. Based largely on the White Paper, *Housing: The Government's Proposals* (1987),[25] the Housing Act 1988 aimed to boost the private rented sector by reducing the minimum period of shorthold to only 6 months and to extend assured tenancies to the remainder of new lettings. Shorthold lettings would be at market rents that take account of the limited period of contractual security of the tenant. Assured tenants would have security of tenure but rents would be freely negotiated between landlord and tenant and would thus also be at market levels. Existing regulated tenants would (ostensibly) continue to be protected by the Rent Acts, and to deter landlords from forcibly securing vacant possession (to create shorthold or assured tenure, or to sell) the laws on harassment and illegal eviction were tightened and tenants forced out illegally could claim greater compensation than hitherto.

Critics of the 1988 Act argue that not only would rents rise dramatically, particularly in areas of housing shortages, but under shorthold arrangements tenants would have less protection than before, while assured tenants might have to pay exorbitant rents for dilapidated and unsafe housing. Even regulated tenancies would be under threat, since the right of succession at fair rent levels would be reduced, inflicting upon those 'inheriting' the tenure the option of market rents or eviction, and local authorities would lose their powers to apply for a fair rent to be registered. Many tenants would therefore find it more advantageous to buy rather than to continue renting, while others would be affected severely by housing benefits being paid only in relation to specific levels of rent assessed by rent officers on the basis of rules laid down by the Secretary of State for the Environment. Above these levels, landlords would be free to charge any rent the market will bear, with higher-income tenants inevitably squeezing out those in receipt of housing benefit. But even then, landlords might have found it more profitable to sell rather than rent.

The 1988 Act, claim its critics, thus gave the landlord a range of incentives and opportunities to secure vacant possession, with or without the use of illegal means. Therefore, far from bringing back into the market more than half a million properties, the Act could reduce supply still further until it reaches a core of about 5–6 per cent of the housing stock. If this proves to be correct, homelessness will increase among those sections of the population whose needs have been met traditionally by the private rented sector, and the mobility of labour will be decreased further rather than increased.

In a further attempt to revive the private rented sector, the Budget of 1988 extended the Business Expansion Scheme (BES) to individuals who invested up to £40 000 per annum in approved unquoted property companies supplying houses for rent under assured tenancy arrangements (eligible properties had to have a maximum value of £125 000 in London and £85 000 elsewhere. Individuals qualified for tax relief on their investment and companies were able to raise up to £5 million under the scheme. However, while the BES might increase the number of rented properties in the short term (benefiting investors and landlords more than tenants, since rents will need to be high to provide a competitive return), in the long term supply could diminish. Since tax relief was intended to cease in 1993, many individuals sought to withdraw their investments, while landlords become increasingly interested in realising capital gain – both situations resulting either in the selling-off of properties for owner-occupation or in leaving properties empty for longer-term speculative reasons.

By the end of 1992, only 16 000 additional rented homes were supplied under the BES scheme. Recipient landlords received two-thirds as much finance per dwelling as housing associations received, yet the scheme produced only relatively short-term accommodation with much higher rents.

Although the BES (withdrawn on 31 December 1993) cannot be claimed to have been a success, the government in the 1990s was intent on adopting other measures to assist the private rented sector – which was showing signs of recovery, albeit on a small scale. With the slump in house prices, many home owners, wishing to sell, instead let their properties on a shorthold basis to satisfy a demand among households unwilling to buy until house prices bottomed-out. There was also a long-term unsatisfied need among the many households who required the convenience, the lack of long-term responsibility and the ease of movement that renting offers, as well as a recent need among the growing number of homeless households – some of whom had suffered repossession during the house price slump of the early 1990s.

To respond to these needs, the following measures were introduced: first, selected housing associations were given the task of acting as intermediaries between private landlords and tenants in an attempt to bring back into use some 600 000 empty private houses. The associations were to act as management agents, choose the tenants, establish shorthold, collect the rents and improve the properties. Pilot schemes introduced in 1991 were extended subsequently, following the 1992 general election. Secondly, a 'rent-a-room' scheme was announced by the Treasury in 1992 whereby owner-occupiers would be permitted to let a room for up to £65 per week (or £3380 per annum) before being eligible for tax on the income received.

It was almost certain that if the government was serious about reversing the decline of the private rented sector then other measures were required. The sector had declined from 14 to 7 per cent of the housing stock between 1979 and 1981, despite a plethora of initiatives designed to revive private renting. In the 1980s, 800 000 private rented dwellings had been sold off for owner-occupation and almost as many private houses remained empty. The Joseph Rowntree Foundation[26] proposed that, in order to revive private renting, it was necessary both to unleash market forces and at the same time to extend measures to protect needy households. The sectors, according to the Foundation, should therefore be split into two parts: one, where the free market would prevail and where there would be no tax concessions, and the other where the sector would be regulated – with local authorities having the responsibility of approving landlords and housing conditions, and where rents would be limited to 4 per cent of capital values in return for capital tax allowances.

LOCAL AUTHORITY HOUSING

In the early 1990s, local authorities were the largest landlords in the country (owning 5 million dwellings or 22 per cent of the total housing stock) despite fluctuations in the economic and political philosophy of successive governments. Before 1914, local authorities had built a negligible proportion of houses. With a shortage of houses after the First World War of about 600 000 and a government pledged to build 'Homes for Heroes', the Housing and Town Planning Act 1919 required local authorities to provide working-class housing where the deficiency was not met from other sources. The Act also fixed minimum standards for new housing well above the conditions of previous working-class housing. A succession of Housing Acts related to the subsidy which should be paid to the local authorities for each unit built. Slum clearance received its first assistance under the 1923 Act, where the Exchequer bore half the losses local authorities incurred in slum clearance and rehousing. The Housing Act 1930 made local authorities directly responsible for slum clearance; it also made it possible to introduce differential rent or rebate schemes. A 1938 Housing Act made uniform the subsidies and rates contributions for both slum clearance and overcrowding, and by 1939 council housing had grown to about 1.3 million, or approximately 11 per cent of the total stock of dwellings. Between 1918 and 1939, local authorities built over a quarter of all permanent houses in Great Britain.

During the Second World War, over 200 000 houses were destroyed and another 500 000 were severely damaged. The result was a physical housing shortage in 1945 of at least 1 350 000, which took no account of obsolete houses that needed replacing. As after the First World War, the government's main weapons were rent controls and subsidised local authority housing on the basis of need rather than ability to pay. Between 1945 and 1951, of 1.01 million houses built in Great Britain, 89 per cent were for local authorities. The Housing Act 1946 made subsidies generally available to local authorities as the chosen instrument to relieve the housing shortage.

Between 1955 and 1961, subsidies to local authorities for new buildings were reduced to slow down the average annual rate of increase, and by 1960 only 35 per cent of new building was by local authorities. The subsidy an authority received depended on how many houses it had built and when it had built them. Authorities with a large amount of low-cost pre-war housing could, by averaging the lower annual loan-servicing charge of such houses with their more expensive post-war houses, ask a lower rent than others who had built most of their houses after the war. Rural authorities, most of whose houses were built post-war, had to charge higher rents than in urban areas even though incomes in rural areas were usually lower. New Town Corporations, whose houses had been built entirely since the war, were in a similar position. Thus local authority control of rents created a wide variety of rents for similar accommodation in different areas. The Housing Act 1961 was a step towards an approach to local authority subsidy based on need. Larger government subsidies went to the poorer authorities and encouragement was given to authorities to charge twice the 1956 rateable value as rent to cover their expenditure, including loan financing by introducing a two-level subsidy.

By 1964 there were about 4.2 million local authority houses let at rents lower than the economic level and which failed to cover costs of repairs, maintenance and administration, or loan-servicing charges, on an historic basis.

Between 1964 and 1970, with a Labour government, there was an increase in local authority building; during this period about half the total completions were by local authorities. The Housing Subsidies Act 1967 introduced a new basis for calculating the Exchequer subsidies to local authorities. This had always been a fixed sum payable for a certain number of years in respect of each house built. For approved new dwellings there was now to be an interest rate subsidy which meant that local authority housing was financed at 4 per cent (half the market rate). This measure attempted to deal with another weakness of the subsidy system, namely that no account was taken of the different rates of interest paid by local authorities on their total debt. The 1967 Act also provided for additional subsidies where blocks of flats of four or more storeys were built.

The change of government in 1970 was reflected in a slump in public housing, by 1973 only 34 per cent of total completions for Great Britain. By this time over 6 million dwellings, 30 per cent of the total housing stock, were owned by local authorities.

The Housing Finance Act 1972 attempted to rationalise local authority subsidies and rents. All existing housing subsidies to local authorities were to be phased out except for a slum-clearance subsidy which was to be provided automatically. A rising cost subsidy was to be payable, mainly in housing stress areas, when the costs of providing new housing rose faster than did rental income. Otherwise, except for a transitional subsidy, each local authority was to pay its own housing costs out of rental income. Thus, except in relation to new additions to stock in high-cost areas, local authorities needed to break even in housing for the first time since 1919. Local authorities were to lose their previously unchallenged freedom to set their own rent levels. Fair rents were to be charged for all public-authority dwellings, bringing them into line with the private sector. It was contended that 90 per cent of the 1970–1 £220 million subsidy had been used to reduce the level of council rents regardless of the needs of the tenants.[27] A system of rent rebates and rent allowances was to operate where there was inability to pay the new rent; subsidies would go to individuals in need. Opponents of this bitterly contested measure contended that the model provisions were insufficient and would result in mass means testing; yet it was estimated that the new legislation would save £200 million annually. The effort was abortive – an economic crisis, a rent freeze and finally the return of a Labour government ended in major changes: the repeal of the Housing Finance Act and the return to a subsidy system (Housing Rents and Subsidies Act 1975).

The amount of income the average tenant paid as a percentage of household income fell from 17.5 per cent in 1968 to 10.2 per cent in 1975.[28] Council tenants were paying less in real terms for their accommodation at a time when local authority finances were in a critical state. Rental income as a proportion of the Housing Revenue Account fell from 55.3 per cent in 1967–8 to 27 per cent in 1975–6. The share of the Exchequer subsidies increased from 27.8 to 54.0 per cent over the same period. It was clear that council rents would need to rise substantially as local authority improvement schemes were cut back drastically and the housing debt soared to over £16 000 million by 1975.

Recent Changes in Investment Policy

Until the late 1970s local housing authorities could borrow almost at will to invest in individual housebuilding and rehabilitation projects, subject to loan sanctions from central government. But in 1978 this practice was replaced by a process which required that each housing authority was to produce both a local housing strategy (setting out the needs of its area) and consequentially a housing investment programme (HIP) for the following year detailing what it planned to spend in order to implement its strategy. The DOE then considered both and allocated borrowing permission for the agreed total sum – instead of for separate items as before. The Local Government and Planning Act 1980 retained this procedure, but replaced block allocations of borrowing permission with block allocations of permitted capital expenditure. Expenditure could be supplemented by a proportion of the receipts from the sale of council houses (50 per cent of receipts in 1980, 40 per cent in 1984 and 20 per cent in 1985).

Under the Local Government and Housing Act 1989, however, there was a reversion to the control of borrowing. HIP allocations were to be controlled by means of a basic credit approval (BCA) for the following year – the Secretary of State taking into account usable capital receipts. In addition, supplementary credit approval (SCA) could be granted to permit borrowing for estate action (rehabilitation) schemes and initiatives to help the homeless. In addition to credit approvals, HIP allocations included capital grants for housing defects, renovation of private dwellings and area improvement and slum clearance.

Recent Changes in Rent and Subsidy Policy

Following the return of a Conservative government in 1979, a new and radical approach to local authority housing soon emerged. The Housing Act 1980 introduced a new rent subsidy consisting of a 'base amount' (equal to the total subsidy paid in the previous year) *plus* a 'housing cost differential' (representing the increase in the total reckonable housing costs over those for the previous year) *less* the 'local contribution differential' (the amount a government expects the local authority to pay towards housing via increased rents or rate fund contributions). In principle, the local contribution differential gave the local authority the choice between increasing rents or increasing the rate fund contribution, but since it was the government's intention to reduce Exchequer subsidies the DOE had powers to specify the target rate of annual rent increase. This resulted in rent increases considerably in excess of the amount that could be met fully from rate contributions. Over the period 1979/80–1984/5, therefore, Exchequer subsidies were reduced from £1258 million to £379 million (or from £255 to £84 per dwelling), while rents on average increased by 128 per cent (from £6.48 to £14.77 per week) compared with an increase in the retail price index of only 50 per cent.

It was argued, however, that rents were still below their economic level – put at about £28 per week by Nicholas Ridley, then Secretary of State for the Environment.[29] Ridley suggested that many people in local authority housing could afford economic rents (actual rents having risen from only 6.4 per cent of average earnings in 1979–80 to 8.3 per cent in 1985–6), and that low rents were a cause of the dereliction of much of the local authority stock. The National Federation of Housing Association's *Inquiry into British Housing* (1985)[30] had recommended that local authorities (as well as private landlords) should charge capital value rents, and that subsidies should be related to individual needs rather than to housing – a view shared by the Secretary of State. However, housing benefits in the mid-1980s were already being paid to two-thirds of the 6 million tenants of public-sector housing, therefore any substantial increase in rent would further escalate and extend welfare payments.

Housing subsidies to local authorities had, in cash terms, decreased from £1423 million to only £520 million between 1980–1 and 1988–9. By 1987, moreover, 80 per cent of local authorities did not receive any housing subsidy at all (although tenants continued to receive the rent rebates). Although rents had increased by only 39 per cent between 1982–3 and 1988–9, there was now a strong possibility that rents would rise by as much as 200 per cent in many areas. It was ironic that several local authorities in England and Wales (mainly in suburban and rural areas) were charging sufficiently high rents that they were able to transfer surpluses on their housing revenue account to their general rate fund – a sum amounting to £61 million in 1987–8.

Under the Local Government and Housing Act 1989, rent determination was reformed. The Department of the Environment would henceforth assess the total value of all the local authority housing stock in the country, with the value of each authority's stock expressed as a percentage of the total national value. The government would then decide what the total national increase in rents should be for the following year and would calculate how much each local authority's share should be. In effect, the government would use the capital value of each authority's stock, not to determine rents – as was proposed in the *Inquiry into British Housing* (1985), but to determine the amount of increase – regardless of current rent levels. Local authority rents consequently rose from an average of £20.70 in 1989–90 to £29.81 in 1992–3, a 50 per cent increase, greatly in excess of the rate of inflation. The system of subsidies also changed. A new housing revenue account (HRA) subsidy was introduced to replace the former housing subsidy and to include rent rebates (previously paid as a form of income support by the Department of Social Security). But although the increase in rents towards market levels brought about a reduction in the housing element of the HRA from £1356 million to £1027 million between 1990–1 and 1992–3, it led simultaneously to an increase in the rent rebate element housing subsidy from £2304 million to £2982 million over the same period.

Unlike the situation before the 1989 Act came into force, the housing revenue account is now 'ring-fenced'. No longer can rent surpluses be used to subsidise, in turn, rates, poll tax and the council tax (instead, surpluses help to finance the costs of housing benefit paid to two-thirds of all council tenants), and no longer can local tax revenue be used to subsidise rents.

Housing Management and Privatisation

Local authority tenants not only had to face soaring rents, but allegedly increasingly poor management. As Donnison pointed out, local government might be good at meeting needs but 'it is ... bad at meeting demands ... bad at listening to its customers ... bad at repairing and maintaining people's homes efficiently'.[31] He called for more housing to be handed over to housing trusts, co-operatives and associations, while management co-operatives should be set up to run the remaining stock of local authority housing. The Audit Commission in 1986 was equally critical. It claimed that 'standards of housing management give cause for concern ... where money is being spent on growing bureaucracy rather than on better services for tenants'.[32]

The Conservative government recognised that problems of housing management had long caused discontent among council tenants. It also recognised that public-sector tenants were aware of both the financial and non-financial advantages of owner-occupation. For electoral and ideological reasons, the government therefore embarked upon a policy of privatising local authority housing – almost without regard to the economic considerations. The Housing Act 1980 thus introduced right-to-buy (RTB) provisions giving tenants of three years' standing the right to buy their homes at a discount of 33 per cent – rising to 50 per cent for tenants of 20 years or more. The Housing and Building Control Act 1984 permitted tenants of only two years' standing to qualify for 32 per cent discounts – rising to 60 per cent for tenants of 30 years or more. In the case of flats, the Housing and Planning Act 1986 raised discounts to 42 per cent for tenants of only two years' standing rising and to 70 per cent for tenants of 15 years or more. Altogether, over the period 1979–93, over 1.5 million dwellings were sold-off in England and Wales under RTB legislation – nearly a third of 1979 total stock of 4.6 million.

Further measures were adopted to privatise the local authority stock.

(1) In 1983, as a means of supplementing HIP funds for housing rehabilitation, the government set up the Urban Housing Renewal Unit (renamed Estate Action in 1986) to attract private-sector capital for the purpose of rehabilitating council dwellings and estates in poor condition, prior to selling off a proportion of the dwellings as low-cost housing.

(2) The Housing Act 1985 granted local authorities powers to undertake large-scale voluntary transfers of complete estates (with their sitting tenants) to private developers or housing associations.

(3) The Housing and Planning Act 1986 Act gave local authorities wide-ranging powers to force recalcitrant tenants to move to alternative accommodation so that their estates could be sold off (with vacant possession) to private developers for conversion into owner-occupied housing.

(4) The Housing Act 1988 permitted tenants to form ownership and management co-operatives, authorised tenants to invite other institutions to acquire and manage their housing, and gave each local authority tenant individually the right to transfer the ownership of his/her dwelling to a housing association or any other approved landlord. In the case of very poor housing – for example, in parts of the inner cities – the Act empowered the government to set up Housing Action Trusts (unelected residential counterparts to Urban Development Corporations) to take over the local authority stock, rehabilitate it, and pass it on to housing associations or approved private landlords.

While the then Housing Minister, William Waldegrave, believed that these measures would 'wean people off the deadly drug of dependency'[33] on local and central government agencies, housing officials feared that, where rented housing transferred to new landlords, inevitably rents would rise since economies of scale would be lost if estates were fragmented; there could also be fewer rights for tenants and an increase in homelessness if private landlordism or owner-occupation replaced social ownership.

The Condition of Local Authority Housing

Regrettably, the condition of local authority housing has deteriorated in recent years. The *English House Condition Survey* (1991) using new fitness standards, reported that whereas in 1986 only 6.6 per cent of public housing was unfit in contrast to 9.4 per cent of the private housing stock, in 1991 the proportion of unfit public housing had risen to 7.6 per cent in contrast with the proportion of unfit private housing of 7.3 per cent.

Generally, however, council dwellings have been built to a good standard – major influences being the Tudor Walters Committee (1918), the Dudley Committee (1944) and the *Parker Morris Report* (1961). The latter was intended to apply to both public and private housing; its provisions were made mandatory in the public sector in 1967 for the new towns and in 1969 for local authorities as far as space and heating standards were concerned. It was not made mandatory in the private sector and thus many privately-built owner-occupied houses (particularly starter homes) did not conform to Parker Morris.[34] Thus in some respects some council housing is superior to that available in the private sector and certainly in the private rented sector. It was a pity, therefore, that Parker Morris standards were abandoned in 1979.

HOUSING ASSOCIATIONS

Complementary to local authorities in providing accommodation to rent are housing associations. Although with a long history in social housing, these became important under the Housing Act 1961 which set up a loan scheme to help associations both to build new dwellings and to buy up older property to rent without profit or subsidy. Some 7000 dwellings were built as a result, and in 1964 the scheme was expanded. A new government agency, the Housing Corporation, was established by the Housing Act 1964. It was to promote housing societies (a term which now took on a new meaning) which would provide 'cost-rent' accommodation or 'co-ownership' dwellings. The latter was a comparatively new concept for Britain in that all the society's accommodation was jointly owned by the members; cost-rent schemes have not been popular since their potential rent levels have been unattractive. Both kinds of society might borrow from the Housing Corporation and building societies.

The statutory definition of 'housing association' in the Housing Act 1957 is a broad one covering societies, bodies of trustees, or companies. Fundamentally, both associations and societies are organisations providing housing on a non-profit-making voluntary basis. They can be classified broadly into two categories although there is considerable overlap. Some look to the Housing Corporation to finance their development schemes, and from January 1973 the Corporation's lending powers were extended to housing associations building to let at fair rents and to those acquiring existing rented property for improvement and conversion. The other group are generally the longer-established associations, some of which began entirely from charitable sources and which obtained financial support increasingly from local authorities.

Housing associations traditionally have filled important gaps in the provision of housing for special groups such as the elderly or disabled; they also tend to operate in stress areas, providing housing for those in need but who are not eligible for council accommodation. They are often a greater force locally than the national average data suggest. By 1973, housing associations were producing about 15 000 new and improved dwellings per year and were providing approximately a quarter of a million dwellings – about 1.3 per cent of the total housing stock of Great Britain. Until the mid-1970s, new house building by associations, although growing in importance, was still small in relation to total output. The movement also had not yet grasped the opportunities offered for the improvement and conversion of existing properties under the Housing Act 1969. In 1973 they accounted for only 1 per cent of total improvements and conversions, a decline on a decade earlier.

The Housing Act 1974 was intended to encourage the expansion of the movement, largely under the auspices of the Housing Corporation whose powers of lending and control were greatly extended. Local authorities were to continue to provide support and financial assistance and to collaborate closely with housing associations, especially in stress areas. Under the Act, a new subsidy – the housing association grant (HAG) – was introduced. If housing associations needed to borrow from the Housing Corporation to acquire sites, meet development costs and pay contractors as the building work proceeded, virtually 100 per cent of the loan would be paid off by a HAG on completion and the grant would be repaid over 60 years. The same provisions applied to rehabilitation, although repayments in this case were over 30 years. Housing associations were also eligible for improvement grants. Unlike local authorities, however, housing associations have few, if any, old low-cost housing (producing profit rent) and cannot draw on rate fund contributions. There is thus the facility of a revenue deficit grant to cover rent shortfalls.

Although it is possible for non-registered housing associations to continue to operate with existing loan commitments honoured, clearly the majority of progressive housing associations will wish to register with the Housing Corporation. Records will be open for public scrutiny and there will be an opportunity to collect from a single source comprehensive and reliable information about the voluntary housing movement, its housing stock, current activities and its resources.

Housing associations had two major roles to perform. First, to expand their operations in inner urban areas, particularly by acquiring and improving unsatisfactory accommodation and to assist local authorities to deal with the problems caused by the declining rented sector. Under the Housing Finance Act and subsequent legislation, associations were brought within the fair rent and rent allowance scheme. Secondly, housing associations might become a significant force in the provision of new housing, but considerable difficulties remain. The substantial increases in costs during the 1970s adversely affected many schemes and there was also a decline in the number of grants approved for improvement and conversion. Many associations have to cope with decanting and rehousing in order to allow improvements and conversions to take place, and many experience problems caused by rapid growth and in the organisation of building work. The 1974 Act concerning registration, control, finance and subsidy provides conditions in which housing associations can expand and this expectation was justified by the 1974–5 results of the Housing Corporation. During this period it approved finance for 37 000 homes, over twice the number approved in 1973–4 and nearly 40 per cent of total approvals since the Corporation's foundation. Between 1975 and 1979, housing associations completed 95 500 dwellings, approximately 13.4 per cent of public-sector completions in the United Kingdom and 6.5 per cent of total dwellings completed. In 1976 alone there was a record 35 000 completions. Associations had over 70 000 improvement grant approvals over this period (13.1 per cent of total approvals).

In the 1980s, however, the housing association movement suffered reversals. Housing association tenants were, in general, offered the right to buy their homes under the same provisions available to local authority tenants. Also, the voluntary sector became adversely affected by cuts in public expenditure. Although the government wished to switch the emphasis in public-sector house-building and rehabilitation from the local authorities to housing associations, government funding on the Housing Corporation remained static and housing association completions plummetted to only 9700 in 1982–3. In consequence, by 1984, the Housing Corporation and some housing associations began to utilise private-sector finance (particularly from pension funds and building societies) to supplement (or replace) HAGs. The North Housing Association, for example (the largest in the United Kingdom with 20 000 dwellings), embarked in 1986 on a £112 million building programme using £100 million from the London capital market and the remainder from its own resources. In general, schemes were developed using assured tenancies (rather than fair rent tenancies) and private-sector finance was provided on an index-linked or low-start basis (with repayments rising in later years when rental income is increased in line with inflation). These innovations enabled housing associations to borrow more than would have been feasible previously and thus made it possible for the sector to develop viable schemes more effectively than hitherto.

Recent Changes in Investment Policy

Rather than complementing local authority housing, housing associations have become the principal providers of new social housing in Great Britain since the late 1980s, as prescribed by the White Paper, *Housing: The Government's Proposals* (1987).[35] Housing association net capital expenditure doubled from £1157 million to £2308 million between 1990/1 and 1992/3, while the number of housing starts in the sector increased from 12 905 in 1987 to 21 588 in 1991. Local authority starts, meanwhile, plummetted from 18 849 to only 3713 over the same period. Up to 50 per cent of housing association capital spending is now targeted at the homeless, with the development of new housing for the elderly (a traditional priority) dwindling to almost zero. Also, whereas much emphasis was placed on rehabilitation in the 1980, its share of capital investment within the housing association sector fell from just under 50 per cent in 1985 to about 14 per cent in 1993, since it was recognised increasingly that rehabilitation was becoming as expensive or more expensive than building, for example, high-density modern units on green field sites.

Over the three years 1992–4, the government aimed to spend over £1.5 to £2 billion per annum on housing association investment, and, planned, rather optimistically, to produce a total of 150 000 homes – each association setting out its investment plans in an approved development programme agreed annually by the Secretary of State. But with cuts in the size of the HAG for each completed dwelling, more had to be borrowed from the private sector. Although public funding continued (involving HAGs and loans from the Housing Corporation and local authorities), mixed funding schemes were undertaken increasingly – private finance enabling public funds to be stretched over a much greater volume of housing than hitherto.

In the November 1993 Budget, as part of a package of cuts aimed at reducing the size of the public sector borrowing requirement, the government announced a £300 million reduction in its funding of the Housing Corporation (for 1984–5), to be followed by a further cut almost as large in the following year – inevitably having an adverse effect on housing investment plans and clearly creating the conditions whereby the housing associations would have to rely more and more on private funding.

Recent Changes in Rent Policy

The cutback in the size of HAGs and increased reliance on private finance (which, by necessity, requires a competitive rate of return) has, however, not only had an unfavourable impact on housing standards but also an inflationary effect on rents. The consequences of mixed funding schemes could become even more marked if public funding is reduced to 50 per cent as was suggested in the 1987 White Paper.

Whereas existing lettings would be at fair rents as determined by rent officers, and be subject to rent increases every two years, under the Housing Act 1988 all new lettings would be at assured or shorthold tenure with housing associations setting their own 'affordable rents'. Although affordability is not defined by the DOE, it was interpreted by the National Federation of Housing Associations as a rent approximately equal to 20 per cent of the tenant's average net income. However, in order to ensure that private capital is attracted into housing investment in this sector, average rents for new housing rose to £48 per week in 1990/1 (notably in excess of average local authority rents), and by a further 21 per cent in 1991/2, compared with an increase of only 1.8 per cent in the retail price index and 5.8 per cent increase in the average income of new tenants. As a consequence, by 1991/2, rents consumed 29 per cent of the income of new tenants. Clearly, the underlying reason for these rises in rent was the government's intention to reduce its share of total investment in this sector. In 1994/5, it was reduced from 67 to 62 per cent, leaving the associations to fund the rest, primarily from private loans. Undoubtedly, rents will rise further, by 28 per cent in 1995/6 according to forecasts by the National Federation of Housing Associations.

But although low-income tenants might be able to afford higher rents (because of their eligibility for housing benefit, although the extent to which such benefit might increase in proportion to rents is uncertain), households with slightly higher incomes will be priced out, or face considerable hardship. With up to 50 per cent of households in new housing association dwellings previously being homeless, and with up to two-thirds of tenants being in receipt of housing benefit, housing association estates are far less likely to offer a broad social mix than hitherto.

Although several housing associations have been actively involved in acquiring local authority housing through large-scale voluntary transfers (and some housing associations have been set up by local authorities to facilitate transfer), many local authority tenants have been unwilling to opt for transfer because of the risk of higher rents. If, however, the associations acquire only 10 per cent of the local authority stock, they will not only double the supply of housing they owned in the late 1980s, but would possibly offer tenants a more sensitive and more efficient management service – albeit at a higher rent. Some associations, however (and particularly the smaller ones), might either be reluctant to expand their activities if this necessitates the adoption of commercial criteria in relation to investment and management, or to contemplate merger in order to respond effectively to their changing role.

SLUM CLEARANCE, REHABILITATION AND RENEWAL

Replacement demand is a function of slum clearance and other houses becoming out of date. With approximately 34 per cent of Britain's housing stock constructed before 1919, at a much higher density than in the inter-war period, any clearance scheme tends to worsen the situation. Density of development between 1881 and 1921 was at about 20 dwellings per acre (49 per hectare), between 1921 and 1941 it was at 13 per acre (31 per hectare) and prior to 1881 at 28 per acre (67 per hectare).[36] Inevitably, it is the older stock which will be replaced, thus creating more pressure for local authorities who, since the Housing Act 1930, have been obliged to see that people who have been displaced are properly rehoused. Demolition for slum clearance and for reasons such as road building can be as much as 0.5 per cent of the total housing stock per year. In the century from 1861 to 1961, approximately two million demolitions occurred, of which nearly one million took place prior to 1931.

Slum clearance is the main element in housing loss; it is an 'ongoing' process, as slums can never be eliminated. Clearance is the result of local government action taken with the help of central government subsidies. The real value of these subsidies varies considerably between authorities (depending mainly upon their past building behaviour) and over time. Local authorities have very different attitudes towards slum clearance, depending upon the general housing situation, the quality of local housing, and political philosophy. Consequently, the level of slum clearance varies greatly over the country, often being proportionately higher in Scotland than in England and Wales. The rate of slum clearance (table 9.8) has plummetted in recent years, reflecting economic recession as well as cuts in central government expenditure. The Housing Repairs and Rent Act 1954 laid down criteria to define whether a house was unfit for human habitation, including state of repair, freedom from damp, stability, lighting, ventilation, water supply and drainage. Because of the sub-standard nature of stock, demolitions are likely to continue, albeit at a reduced rate; designated slums must clearly be demolished and areas redeveloped even though since 1969 there has been a switch towards rehabilitation rather than clearance.

The number of properties demolished or closed will have effects upon demand for owner-occupier properties, particularly at the older, cheaper end, thereby forcing up prices. This may have a 'ripple' effect through the market as owners of cheap property find that values have increased and that they are able to move to a better class of property. Demand for this better property then increases, giving owners the opportunity to use their higher proceeds to push further up the ladder, assuming mortgage availability; thus all classes of residential property may be affected.

Rehabilitation

After 1945, because of the great housing shortage, there was a growing movement towards improving rather than clearing sub-standard dwellings. The 1949 Housing Act gave local authorities powers to pay half the cost of improvement of sub-standard housing in the private sector. In 1959 specific grants for the provision of standard amenities were introduced; these were available to owners of property, public or private, which did not have five basic amenities (bath, wash-hand basin, hot water supply, WC and a ventilated food store). Additional discretionary grants continued to be available but provided little inducement for landlords of tenanted property. To overcome this, the Housing Act 1964 gave local authorities power to establish improvement areas in neighbourhoods containing dwellings lacking one or more of the standard amenities. Provided it was possible to restore these dwellings to full standard, the local authority could carry out improvements and then charge the landlord. The Act also provided for subsidies towards improvement of dwellings let by local authorities or housing associations.

The Housing Act 1969 saw a major shift towards improvement and conversion.

Table 9.8 *Houses demolished or closed, Great Britain, 1975–91*

	1975–6	1984–5	1990–1
England and Wales			
Demolished:			
In clearance areas	41 772	6 472	1 954
Elsewhere	3 939	1 969	1 354
Closed	5 416	1 876	948
Total	51 127	10 317	4 256
Scotland			
Unfit	9 964	1 040	447*
Others	694	783	634*
Total	10 658	1 823	1 081*

Note: * 1989–90.

Source: Central Statistical Office, *Annual Abstract of Statistics.*

Grants covering half the cost of the installation of standard amenities were made widely available for both owner-occupier and tenanted properties; for the first time, funds were available for repair work. Improvement grants were discretionary and aimed at the provision of dwellings by conversion and for improvement other than standard amenities. These would cover half the costs up to a maximum of £1200 for dwellings provided by conversion of a building on three or more storeys, or £1000 for other dwellings. Special discretionary grants were also available for the provision of standard amenities in houses in multiple occupation. The Housing Act 1971 extended grants to private owners in development and intermediate areas to a maximum of 75 per cent of the cost of approved work, with a maximum of £1500 per dwelling. Under the 1969 Act and the Housing Finance Act 1972 landlords could convert tenancies from controlled to regulated as a result of improvements. The 1969 Act also made provision for grants for environmental improvement on the designation of general improvement areas (GIAs).

The 1969 Act took its cue from the national sample survey of housing conditions, carried out in 1967.[37] This showed that the dilapidation problem was much worse than had been imagined; at least 1.8 million houses in England and Wales were statutorily 'unfit' and more than 4.5 million lacked basic amenities or were in need of major repairs – about a quarter of the total stock. It also showed that the best conditions were in the South-East, and the worst in the North. Dilapidations and deficiencies were most extensive in the privately-rented sector, where 60 per cent of all unfit housing and 65 per cent of housing without baths were found, although this accounted for no more than 21 per cent of the total stock. The best conditions were found in local-authority housing, with owner-occupier housing in the middle position. A 1971 House Condition Survey showed the extent of improvement. The number of unfit dwellings had been reduced to 1.24 million, while 2.87 million still lacked basic amenities; the highest proportion of unfit houses, 51.8 per cent, were rented from private owners. By the end of 1973 less than 2.5 million dwellings lacked basic amenities.[38]

Thus the 1969 Act was a major factor in restoring many properties which otherwise would have remained derelict. There were also several side effects, for example, 'gentrification': the invasion of traditional working-class areas by higher-income households, often involving harassment and 'winkling' (persuading tenants to leave). Lower-priced houses were improved and converted, returning to the market at a very much higher price. In areas of acute housing need there was concern that grants were going to developers who were using them for profit. There was an added incentive for landlords to seek vacant possession to carry out improvements and subsequently charge a much higher rent. Thus the less wealthy local population was being driven from inner areas. The massive increase in house improvement work required much skilled labour, often drawn from new house-building. It was contended that only about a third of improvement grants benefited the lower-income groups; many went to owner-occupiers who obtained untaxed capital gains as a result of improvements. Until the Housing Act 1974 second-home owners were also eligible for grants. Grants have improved the standard of the housing stock and this must be balanced against the reduction of accommodation for lower-income groups (partly because of the operation of improvement grants), who cannot necessarily obtain council housing and are dependent upon the ever-diminishing supply of private rented accommodation.

The White Paper *Better Homes the Next Priority* (1973)[39] placed the emphasis on improvement of 'housing action areas' (HAAs). Measures were proposed to tackle, as a priority, the housing situation within the areas where conditions in human and physical terms were worst; new powers were to be made available to local authorities. A series of broad criteria were envisaged, justifying the declaration of a HAA, such as households living at high density per room, many furnished tenancies, and houses lacking basic amenities. Typically 400–500 dwellings would be covered, although local authorities with substantial resources might be able to tackle larger areas. Special powers included a discretion for local authorities to compel landlords and owner-occupiers to improve their properties to minimum standards, or themselves to act in default, and powers to acquire housing compulsorily. The proposals were largely incorporated in the Housing Act 1974.

Local authorities were to concentrate resources on the worst areas, that is, the HAAs, and were given wide powers to acquire property. The improvement grant system became more selective. Grants of up to 75–80 per cent of eligible expenses were available in the HAAs, 60 per cent in the GIAs and 50 per cent elsewhere (representing payments of £3750–£4500, £3000 and £2500 per unit by 1979). Larger eligible expenses were permitted for conversions. Financial help was also given for essential repairs, especially in HAAs. Anyone who obtained an improvement grant and then sold or left a house unoccupied within five years (seven years in a HAA) had to repay the grant at compound interest to the local authority.

But the 1974 Act largely failed to achieve its objective. There was a sharp decline in the number of improvement grants approved in the mid-1970s (table 9.9). Although the recession in the property market, high rates of interest, and the financial difficulties of building firms were all contributory, it is probable that the more stringent conditions of grant approval introduced by the 1974 Act had a major effect on applications. It was particularly regrettable that improvement in the HAAs progressed at a disturbingly low rate, and that although the number of HAAs and GIAs had increased from, respectively, 78 and 964 in 1975 to over 400 and 1200 by 1979, it was doubtful whether they had little more than a 'cosmetic' effect on housing within some of the inner urban areas. It was ironic that proportionately more money was spent on improvement in small provincial towns, where it was least necessary, than in the inner urban areas of greatest need. Housing improvement expenditure in real terms is seriously lagging behind the formation of new slums. Although there were less than a million unfit houses by the early 1980s, there were over 4 million sub-standard houses, consisting not only of those which were unfit or lacking basic amenities, but also those which required major repairs.

In an attempt to hasten the pace of rehabilitation, the Conservatives, in their Housing Act 1980, made the grant system more flexible, giving the Secretary of State powers to fix, for different cases, eligible expenses and grant limits; they abolished the five-year rule for owner-occupiers; and extended repair grants (the latter being particularly effective). These provisions were introduced at a time when public-sector housebuilding was at a (then) post-war low.

Thus government policy clearly moved away from demolition to renovation as the cheapest way of bringing the quality of housing to a minimum level with as little social upheaval as possible, particularly where many existing houses could be brought up to an acceptable standard as they stood. Certainly, the critical economic situation of the mid-1970s influenced policy. So too did the findings of the *English House Condition Survey* (1981)[40] (a survey of housing conditions in Wales produced similar results). Altogether, in England, the number of dwellings in serious disrepair amounted to 1178 million, a significant increase in the number recorded in 1976.

However, it has been contended that a commitment to a policy of rehabilitation 'is a vast exercise in putting off the evil day'. Failure to put a priority on new house building is creating enormous problems for future generations; the housing stock in Britain is the oldest in Europe. But worse still, in the private sector, even this commitment has not been sustained. Although government expenditure on home improvement grants increased from £159.2 million in 1980 to £1079 million in 1984, it was cut substantially to only £283.7 million in 1991. The number of renovations in this sector similarly increased from 95 000 in 1980 to 320 000 in 1984, falling to only 60 000 in 1991.

Of major significance was the Green Paper, *Housing Improvement – A New Approach* (1985)[41] which proposed means testing grant applications – which

Table 9.9 *Renovations with the aid of grant or subsidy, Great Britain, 1971–91*

	Dwellings (000s)			
	Grants paid to private owner and tenants	Housing association grant-aided	Local authorities	Total
1971	105	5	89	199
1972	153	4	137	294
1973	207	3	188	398
1974	242	4	121	367
1975	101	5	62	168
1976	83	14	75	172
1977	71	20	94	185
1978	72	15	106	193
1979	82	20	111	213
1980	95	18	100	213
1981	94	14	82	190
1982	139	22	109	270
1983	293	18	127	438
1984	320	21	123	464
1985	200	13	157	370
1986	163	15	208	388
1987	159	13	241	413
1988	157	15	250	422
1989	145	12	256	413
1990	138*	12	315	465
1991	60*	7	265	332

Note: * Excluding grants awarded under the Local Government and Housing Act 1989.

Sources: Department of the Environment, *Housing and Construction Statistics.*

by implication suggested either further cuts in public expenditure on improve-ment or more stringent conditions. The introduction of VAT in 1984 had al-ready reduced the rate of rehabilitation, and means testing would have a further adverse effect on the condition of the housing stock. By the late 1980s, there-fore, while rapidly-rising house prices and gentrification ensured a substantial amount of rehabilitation in London (both with and without grants), throughout much of Britain, particularly in the low-price regions of Yorkshire and Hum-berside and the North, valuation gaps (the excess of owner-incurred rehabilita-tion costs over resulting increases in value) deterred home improvement, except on a very minor scale.

The extent to which housing remained in a poor condition was indicated in the *English House Condition Survey* (1986)[42] (table 9.10). Although there had

Table 9.10 *The condition of housing in England, 1981–91*

| | Number of dwellings (000s) | | | |
| | 1981–6 fitness standard | | 1991 fitness standard | |
Condition	1981	1986	1986	1991
Dwellings lacking amenities	862	543	463	205
Unfit dwellings	1 116	1 053	1 660	1 500
Dwellings in serious disrepair	1 178	1 113	n.a.	1 420

Sources: Department of the Environment, *English House Condition Survey*, 1981, 1986 and 1991.

been a significant reduction in the number of dwellings lacking basic amenities since the survey of 1981, the number of unfit dwellings and those in serious disrepair remained much the same. The survey also showed that conditions were far worse within the private rented sector than in owner-occupation or social housing, and that low-income households and the elderly suffered the worst housing. Based on this and on the 1987 White Paper, *Housing Policy: The Government's Proposals*, the Local Government and Housing Act 1989 targeted grants towards the worst housing, and to households in greatest need.

The 1989 Act replaced the grant system of earlier legislation with a new and largely mandatory regime of grants, and reformed the system of area improvement. Renovation grants, housing in multiple occupation (HMO) grants, common parts grants, minor works grants, and disabled facilities grants were introduced and all were means tested. Owner-occupiers and tenants would be unlikely to qualify for grant assistance unless their incomes were at about the level which would render them eligible for income support or housing benefit; and landlords would not qualify unless (without a grant) their outlay on improvement and repairs exceeded their rental income (but that with a grant their return would be sufficient only to service a loan at 3 per cent over base rate for 10 years). With regard to area improvement, GIAs and HAAs were to be superseded by renewal areas (RAs). Each would have a ten-year life after declaration and contain between 300 and 3000 dwellings, of which 75 per cent would be privately owned and 75 per cent would be in poor condition, and over 30 per cent of households in each RA would need to be in receipt of housing benefit.

The impact of this Act on the volume of rehabilitation in the private sector is likely to be very mixed. While grants targeted at low-income households and the elderly (largely minor works grants) increased notably during the early 1990s, the remainder of owners (including landlords) were ineligible for grant assistance. The overall pace of grant-aided rehabilitation in the private sector remained depressed, although the extent to which means testing was largely contributory was uncertain.

The *English House Condition Survey* (1991)[43] had shown that, under new standards of fitness, the total number of unfit dwellings had decreased from 1660 million to 1500 million between 1986 and 1991 (table 9.10) and that this was largely attributable to the decline in the number of mainly pre-1919 unfit private dwellings as a proportion of the total stock, from 5.6 to only 4 per cent – a result mainly of non-grant-aided renovation during the house price boom of the late 1980s. If this degree of rehabilitation occurred when house prices were soaring, it is probable that a much lower level of rehabilitation took place when house prices became depressed in the early 1990s almost regardless of the type of grants available. Also, under new fitness standards, the number of dwellings lacking amenities decreased, but because of the lack of data it is unclear whether or not the number of dwellings in serious disrepair also decreased. It is possible that the number *increased*.

In the 1980s, it became recognised increasingly that the stock of public-sector housing was in an appallingly bad state of repair. The Association of Metropolitan Authorities (1983, 1984, 1985)[44] estimated that the repair costs to council houses built in the 1950s–60s using non-traditional techniques (such as steel frames and reinforced concrete) would amount to £5000 million, repair costs to council houses constructed in the 1960s–70s using systems-building techniques would cost a further £5000 million to put right, and the repair and renovation of council houses built in the 1920s–30s using traditional methods would cost £9000 million to rectify. In total, the £19 000 million needed to be spent on repairs can be contrasted with the government's capital expenditure plans for housing in 1985–6 – £3280 million. Nevertheless, the number of renovations undertaken by local authorities to their own stock increased from 157 000 to 315 000 between 1985 and 1990 (table 9.9), although it is little wonder that the government encouraged local authorities to sell off the worst of their estates to private developers.

THE SUPPLY OF NEW HOUSES

At any time the total stock of houses can be clearly defined and measured; however, only part of this stock will be available for sale. Households seeking to purchase will consider not only the present total available supply of housing but also how that supply is expected to alter in the near future. Households may postpone their demand for a short period if they feel that future trends are more likely to be favourable than the existing situation. Of particular interest is the anticipated net new supply of houses as a function of activity in the house-building sector. In fact, as we have discussed, the percentage annual addition to the existing stock is minute. However, generally the smaller the net new supply the faster the rate of second-hand price increases and consequently that of new houses, other things being equal. Increases in the value of established properties enable developers to ask higher prices for new.

The private housebuilding industry is essentially speculative in nature; houses are generally not custom-built but are constructed in the expectation of being

Table 9.11   *Houses started, Great Britain, 1950–92*

	Starts (000s)		
	Private sector	Social sector	Total
1950	19.8	184.4	204.6
1955	127.5	185.3	312.8
1960	182.8	126.3	309.1
1965	211.1	181.4	392.5
1970	165.1	154.1	319.2
1975	149.1	173.8	322.9
1980	98.9	56.4	155.2
1981	117.4	37.5	154.9
1982	140.8	53.2	194.0
1983	172.4	48.9	221.3
1984	158.3	40.1	198.4
1985	165.7	34.4	200.1
1986	180.0	33.4	213.4
1987	196.8	32.8	229.6
1988	221.4	30.7	252.1
1989	170.1	31.0	201.1
1990	135.2	27.2	162.4
1991	134.9	25.7	160.6
1992	119.9	35.8	155.8

Source: Ministry of Housing and Local Government; Scottish Development Department; Department of the Environment, *Housing and Construction Statistics*.

sold during or shortly after construction. Thus the industry is affected very directly by government economic policy. With the high risks of the industry, evidenced by bankruptcy figures, builders will generally charge the price that the market will bear. Thus, in 1971–2 prices originally agreed between the prospective purchaser and the developer were revised upwards by the latter during the construction period as demand pressures built up which could not be satisfied by supply. The prospective purchaser was left with the alternative of either agreeing to the new price or losing the house; 'gazumping' became commonplace. Confidence increased within the industry, contractors bought more land and started more houses. However, at other times, the developer was forced to accept a lower price than anticipated, confidence and expectations diminished, and the construction industry generally was depressed. Essentially, the developer has been a price taker and not a price maker (although this may be changing with the growth of giant firms). Thus in 1974 there were at least 30 000 new houses unsold on the market, reflecting a change in economic conditions including substantially higher rates of tax and interest. Developers' minimum selling prices were above the maximum bid prices of potential purchasers. Developers' potential profits turned into losses. Confidence declined as developers were unable to pass on sharply increased costs in the form of higher house prices as unemployment increased and disposable incomes fell. Potential purchasers became less willing to take on larger financial commitments. The best years for private housing starts were when mortgage and credit availability were easy and house prices appeared to be accelerating. The poorest years for housing starts were at periods of tight fiscal and monetary policy and rising unemployment. Thus much activity in the owner-occupier and housebuilding sectors is related to changes in economic policy.

The excessively cyclical nature of private-sector housebuilding and its relationship with the trade and building cycles has been evident over the past century and can be illustrated from the past three decades (table 9.11). The cycle of activity saw starts move from a peak of 247 000 in 1964, down to 165 100 in 1970, up to 227 400 in 1972, then rapid decline to 105 300 in 1974. Recovery to 1978 was then followed by savage decline to 1980, with the lowest level of starts since the early 1950s. These figures indicate a difference of some 147 000, or 60 per cent, between high and low.

The social sector declined sharply from 1955 to the mid-1960s, when a Labour government and New Town building led to a peak in 1967. The end of the 1960s saw a decline, with the low of 112 800 in 1973. A short recovery in 1975 was followed by a sharp decline through to the 1990s, with housing starts in 1991 being the lowest since 1919. It was notable, moreover, that by 1992 housing associations were building more houses than were local authorities: 33 400 starts compared to only 2400.

THE HOUSEBUILDING INDUSTRY IN GREAT BRITAIN

Whereas the Green Paper *Housing Policy: A Consultative Document* (1977)[45] estimated that it was necessary for a minimum of 300 000 houses to be built per year up to the year 2000 to satisfy national housing requirements, the average annual number of starts over the period 1985–9 was only 219 300 (compared with 281 000 per year, 1975–9, or 391 000 per year, 1965–9). It is remarkable that under capitalism, while more and better consumer goods are produced, often at lower and lower real prices for more and more people, in Britain there are fewer houses being built in the 1980s than in recent decades, they are inferior in size and quality to those built in the inter-war or post-war periods and are increasingly expensive. Between 1952 and 1980, whereas the Retail Price Index increased 6.5 times, the average price of houses increased elevenfold.

Over the past 25 years, the housebuilding industry has become dominated by a small number of giant firms – 'volume builders' (those constructing more than 500 houses per year) accounting for more than 50 per cent of the output of owner-occupied housing in the 1980s (compared with less than 15 per cent in the 1960s).[46] The top ten firms alone produced over 53 000 houses (or 28 per cent of the total completions) in 1986. Medium-sized firms have either been taken over by the volume builders (often to obtain their land banks) or have been rendered uncompetitive. Volume builders have been able to outbid all others in the acquisition of land, a process aided and abetted by the planning authorities who normally prefer to release blocks of land, rather than single plots, for development.[47]

Apart from public-sector contracting, the housebuilding process is largely speculative. As such, there is a high degree of risk and a very high bankruptcy rate. Timing is important at all stages from site purchase, through development, to sales. Most firms depend upon short-term bank credit during building (using the land and part-completed buildings as collateral). When interest rates increase it makes the situation extremely difficult – banks may cut finance to builders early in a squeeze. Private housebuilding thus tends to expand and contract cyclically in relation to the government's macro-economic policy.

To attempt to safeguard themselves against the vicissitudes of the economy, volume builders rely mainly on land development gains (often resulting from infrastructure improvement) and super-normal profits (reflecting their monopoly power) rather than on normal or 'building' profit (that is, the sale price of the dwelling in competitive conditions *less* the sum of wage, capital, material and land costs). There is thus little incentive to improve product quality, to increase productivity and to improve techniques of production.[48] Volume builders 'physically' construct few houses but concentrate instead on land banking (involving the purchase of land when prices slump to facilitate housing development when prices rise), and marketing. Housebuilding itself is undertaken by sub-contractors – the number of which increases when there is an upturn in the market and decreases when there is a downturn.

The construction process is thus largely in the hands of the small sub-contractor and the results economically are far from satisfactory. Volume builders tend to spread output over a very large number of sites to minimise risk – their sub-contractors constructing small batches of dissimilar houses normally with the use of hired plant and equipment, and employing almost entirely casual labour (individuals or gangs of self-employed operatives). Low productivity, retarded innovation, the lack of scale economies, minimal research and development, the absence of training in new techniques, and fragmented labour processes all militate against the lowering of unit costs of production.

Duncan contrasts the above characteristics of housebuilding in Britain with housebuilding in Sweden.[49] In Sweden in recent years there has been a high rate of housebuilding, standards have been improving and real costs have been falling. Since local authority land banks provide sites for housebuilding at low cost, and, in return for state housing loans to finance construction, builders have had to sell at prices set by the government, there are few opportunities for builders to realise land development gain and super-normal profit. Instead, they have had to rely on building profits via the construction process itself. There is therefore every incentive to increase productivity, improve the quality of the product, develop economies of scale, undertake research and development, ensure that there is proper training in the use of new techniques, and employ integrated labour processes.

House Prices and Land Costs

For the country as a whole there is a great deal of land; however, the supply available in urban areas is limited and is further reduced by planning delays, particularly in moving from outline to detailed planning permission. Thus it is not normally possible to substitute housing for other land uses and it may even be difficult to vary the intensity of use.

The quantity of land made available may be further reduced by landowners' own expectations. If they believe that in the future land prices are going to rise faster than other prices they will have an incentive to hold the land off the market and so shift the supply curve. This makes the builder's position difficult. If s/he holds a land bank s/he might do better to keep his/her land stock rather than to build because s/he expects the price to rise still further in the future. If s/he holds no land his/her profit from increased prices might disappear in higher land costs. In a competitive situation builders will bid against one another for the available land up to a level which leaves them a normal profit, and thus the whole price increase benefits the landowner. Thus builders' incentives to expand housing construction following house price increases may be reduced, if not completely removed, by the resulting increase in land prices.

Because land is heterogeneous there are enormous differences in individual plot prices. There is also the role of planning permission in determining prices. Official data show that from 1978 to 1980 prices per plot in England and Wales increased from £2367 to £4460, nearly doubling in these years (table 9.12). During the same period, average house prices rose from £16 792 to £26 131 – an increase of 56 per cent. From 1981 to 1983, however, average plot prices increased by only 28 per cent and average house prices by 15 per cent. In 1983, plot prices as a percentage of house prices ranged from 29 per cent in Greater London to as low as 10 per cent in Wales. By the late 1980s, however, both land and house prices were again increasing rapidly, and plot prices nationally were soaring as a proportion of house prices – exceeding 30 per cent by 1988 (and over 50 per cent in parts of the South-East).

But do house prices determine plot prices or do plot prices dictate house prices? While local planning authorities (and some economists) argue that the demand for land and thus its price is derived from the demand for housing, housebuilders (and other economists) believe that the supply of land and thus its cost is a determinant of house prices. As MacLennan suggests, attempts to disentangle the connection between land prices and house prices have been unconvincing and the relationship thus remains an important research issue.[50] In a report commissioned by the House Builders' Federation, Evans argued that a restricted supply of land resulted in both land prices and house prices being higher than they would otherwise be; that, by restricting the supply of

Table 9.12 *Private-sector housing land prices (at constant average density) and house prices, 1978–91*

	Weighted average price per plot (£)	Average price of houses (£)	Plot price as a percentage of house price
1978	2 367	16 792	14.1
1979	3 395	21 455	15.8
1980	4 460	26 131	17.1
1981	4 600	27 910	16.5
1982	5 200	27 914	18.6
1983	5 900	30 943	19.1
1984	6 600	33 416	19.8
1985	8 400	36 295	23.1
1986	10 700	42 319	25.3
1987	14 086	49 435	28.5
1988	19 254	61 551	31.3
1989	18 940	72 256	26.2
1990	17 321	75 403	23.0
1991	18 163	75 119	24.0

Source: Council of Mortgage Lenders, *Housing Finance*; Department of the Environment, *Housing and Construction Statistics*.

building land, planners were forcing up house prices and *either* squeezing-out first time buyers *or* adversely affecting the size of housing units; and that if agricultural land was converted into residential use it would significantly bring down the cost of new housing.[51] Ambrose, similarly, claimed that the planning system adds to Britain's housing problems by being excessively concerned with environmental protection and by 'not releasing the "correct" amount of land in the "correct" areas as assessed by the housebuilding industry'.[52]

In theoretical terms, it can be shown that there is clearly a relationship between the supply of land, land prices and the level of housebuilding. In figure 9.4 the supply of development land SL is completely elastic – possibly a result of government intervention (by, for example, public land banking). With an increase in the demand for housing (from DH to DH_1), more land is demanded for development (DL shifting to DL_1) but, since the supply of land (SL) is completely elastic, land is made available at a constant price – facilitating in turn an expansion in the supply of houses (SH) from q to q_1 without an increase in house prices. In figure 9.5, however, the supply of land is completely inelastic (for example, as a result of green-belt policy). With an increase in the demand for housing (from DH to DH_1), more land is demanded for development (DL shifting to DL_1) but, since the supply of land (SL) is completely inelastic, land supply is not increased and land prices rise sharply, preventing the level of housebuilding from increasing to satisfy the increase in demand. If

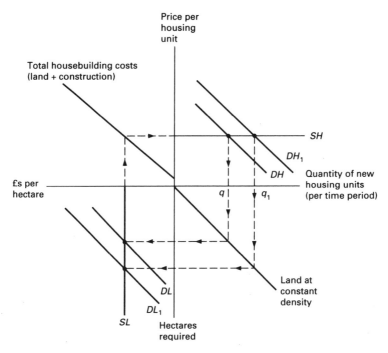

Figure 9.4 *The relationship between housebuilding and land costs under conditions of complete elasticity of supply*

the supply of development land were to be reduced from *SL* to *SL*₁ (by government policy or by landowners exercising monopoly power), then land prices would rise even more dramatically and the supply of new housing would be reduced from *SH* to *SH*₁. Clearly, the reverse could occur if the supply of land were to be increased.

It can, however, be argued that rapidly rising house prices (fuelled by an increase in mortgage credit and tax relief) have pushed up the cost of land since landowners have become aware of the prices builders can charge for new properties. Furthermore, rising house and land prices only serve to accentuate the problem of land supply since they encourage active land banking by major developers. It can be further suggested that in the South-East large wage increases (associated with the region's economic boom) have had an inflationary effect on house prices and hence land prices in recent years – land prices reaching £3 million per hectare in Greater London in 1989.

The House Builders' Federation are concerned specifically that there is much less inner city land suitable for private building than was generally believed, and that land shortages in inner cities will have an adverse affect on the provision of low-cost housing. This, if it is correct, could have serious consequences, since the supply of older private housing is being eroded through gentrification, and the public-sector stock is being decimated by 'right to buy' sales and major cutbacks in housebuilding.

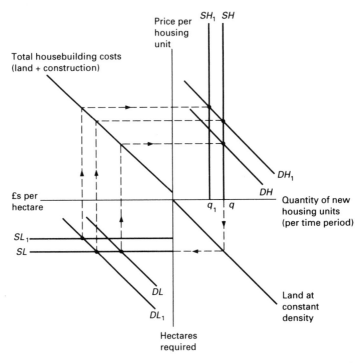

Figure 9.5   *The relationship between housebuilding and land costs under conditions of complete inelasticity of supply*

Overall, housebuilders lack information about the amount, availability and suitability of vacant land – both in the inner cities and the countryside. Builders claimed that they required nationally an extra 2000 ha per year in addition to the 6000 ha allocated by local planning authorities in the late 1980s. Only then, they estimated, could they build 250 000 houses per year – the number the government considered necessary. The extra land, however, according to the housebuilders, would need to have been made available in the green belt, but this would have been resisted strongly by the government on environmental grounds. It is within the South-East that the conflict between housebuilding and conservation is most apparent. Whereas housebuilders predicted that there was a need for an extra 880 000 dwellings in the region in the period 1981–91, the South Eastern Regional Planning Council (SERPLAN) allocated land for only 600 000 new homes. Similarly, Tyler and Rhodes forecast that an extra 770 000 new dwellings would be required during the years 1985–95, but SERPLAN predicted that only 550 000 extra homes would be needed.[53] By the end of the twentieth century, therefore, it is probable that local planning authorities will have allocated insufficient land to meet housing demand – ultimately with inflationary effects on both land prices and house prices in the region.

In addition to the inflationary effects of land shortages, the slowness of planning consents exacerbated the upward trend in house prices. In the 1970s, Pennance estimated a minimum of 6 months as the average time taken to secure planning permission, while about one in six applicants was refused.[54] The average time between appeal and decision was 36 weeks for those decided by the Inspectorate and 51 weeks for those decided ministerially. In 1975 the Dobry Report[55] recommended changes in procedure to hasten the process, but delays remain much in evidence (in part because of the time devoted to local enquiries) and indicate the extent to which the market is still hamstrung.

Material, Labour and Finance Costs

Since 1945 prices of housebuilding materials have risen steadily in comparison with prices of materials purchased by manufacturing industry generally. Between 1963 and 1973 prices of housebuilding materials doubled while those of manufacturing industry increased by approximately 60 per cent. Traditional housebuilding costs are affected more by internal inflation than by international factors; there are exceptions – for example, the price of timber imported from the USSR increased by 102 per cent in 1973 while devaluation in 1967 and the downward floating of sterling after 1971 adversely affected costs of building materials.

Accurate data on the labour content of costs are difficult to obtain; a particular problem has been the prevalence of labour-only sub-contracting among many highly skilled craftsmen (Chapter 10). Recorded labour costs in construction have not moved faster than industry in general; hours worked tend to be higher and are more variable to the level of economic activity. However, the relatively small changes in production methods in householding suggest that productivity increases may be less than in industry as a whole.

For most commodities, in the long term, it is reasonable to expect a stable relationship between the price of the product and its costs of production, with allowance for normal profit. If prices run ahead of costs then output will increase thereby bringing prices back into an equilibrium position with costs. Conversely, if costs run ahead of prices then output will fall, and reduced supply in relation to demand will lead to an increase in prices to reach an equilibrium.

However, there is no such relationship between house prices and housebuilding costs. Materials, land and labour costs are not major factors in the movement of house prices; with land, developers are unable to pass on increases in costs except at times of rising house prices. If costs rise, other things being equal, developers will either reduce the quantity of houses they build or cut the quality. The reasons are as follows.

(1) There is a long lag in the housebuilding process from site identification to completion. Economic factors may change or new legislation may be introduced which may affect tax relief on mortgage interest.

(2) The shortage of land for housebuilding may prevent an increase in house

Table 9.13 *Building society loans on new houses, starts and completions in the private sector, 1978–92*

	Building society loans on new houses (000s)	Number of new houses		Loans as percentage of completions
		Completions (000s)	Starts (000s)	
1978	134	149	157	90
1979	117	140	144	84
1980	94	128	99	73
1981	87	115	117	76
1982	94	125	141	75
1983	111	148	172	75
1984	130	159	158	82
1985	119	157	166	76
1986	122	170	180	72
1987	106	184	197	58
1988	118	199	221	59
1989	88	180	170	49
1990	78	156	135	50
1991	71	148	135	48
1992	63	138	121	46

Sources: The Building Societies Association, *BSA Bulletin*; Council of Mortgage Lenders, *Housing Finance*.

Table 9.14 *The number of dwellings and households, Great Britain, 1966–91 (millions)*

	1966	1971	1981	1991
Households	16.9	18.3	19.5	19.9
Dwellings	16.3	18.8	21.1	23.0
Crude balance	−0.6	10.5	+1.6	+3.1

Sources: Department of the Environment, *Housing and Construction Statistics*; Central Statistical Office, *Social Trends*.

prices from leading to an increase in the supply of housebuilding land – it may merely increase the price of building land.

(3) Building regulations and National House-Building Council (NHBC) requirements impose costs which might not be recoverable in the price that potential purchasers are willing to pay, because fundamentally the developer is a price taker.

Housebuilders have often had to contend with increasing interest rates. Most building firms have to borrow to cover construction costs as they do not have sufficient funds to tide them over until they have sold the houses. Increases in interest rates, usually coupled with credit restrictions, may have a deciding impact on marginal developments; increases are likely to increase builders' costs immediately and by larger-than-average amounts. Squeezes make building impossible because of builders' inability to raise funds. It is likely that the level of housing starts is determined almost entirely by the availability of funds and the level of sales (which free funds to start new dwellings), which in turn are determined by the availability of building society finance (table 9.13).

In general, the economics of housebuilding are predominantly demand-determined and fluctuations in demand merely serve to compound the inherent difficulties of developers. The operation of housebuilders is essentially determined by financial and structural characteristics quite outside the framework of land and other material supply and costs. In the South-East, however, land supply and land costs might be of at least equal importance in determining the level of housebuilding.

CONCLUSIONS

Since the 1970s, successive governments have appeared to believe that Britain's housing needs were broadly satisfied. A crude housing deficit had turned into a crude surplus, and in 1991 there were 3.1 million more dwellings than there were households – in contrast to a deficit of 600 000 in 1966 (table 9.14). However, the 1991 surplus did not indicate the true relationship between supply and need. Included among the 23 million dwellings were at least 200 000 second homes, while about 130 000 concealed households (such as couples living with their parents/in-laws) were omitted from the total number of households. Allowances must also be made for a vacancy reserve of about 800 000 dwellings to facilitate mobility. There were also great spatial variations in supply and demand, and an ageing population also produced a mismatch between housing occupied and housing required. There are also qualitative differences. In 1991, there were over 1.4 million unfit dwellings in England alone. Thus, far from there being a large surplus of housing, there is a very substantial deficit of at least 3.2 million dwellings according to the National Housing Forum,[56] a figure likely to be exceeded by the end of the twentieth century.

It could be argued that public expenditure on housing has increased from £7250 million in 1979/80 to £20 286 million in 1992/3 if housing benefit and mortgage interest relief are added to the housing expenditure of the DOE (table 9.15). But both housing benefit and mortgage interest relief are forms of income support and are not specifically housing subsidies. If deducted from aggregate public expenditure on housing, then the amount of public spending on housing increased in cash terms from £5600 million in 1979/80 to only £6200 million by 1992/3 – an increase of 11 per cent in cash terms, but a decrease of 55 per cent in real terms.

Table 9.15   *Public expenditure on housing and transfers, United Kingdom, 1979/80–1992/3*

	1979/80	1986/7	1992/3	Change 1979/80–1992/3
	(£m)	(£m)	(£m)	(%)
Department of the Environment (total housing expenditure)	5 600	4 100	6 200	+11
Housing Benefit*	200	5 050	8 886	+4343
Mortgage interest relief	1 450	4 670	5 200	+259
Total	7 250	9 150	20 286	+180

Notes: * Refers to rent allowances and rent rebates.

Source: Treasury, *The Government's Expenditure Plans, 1984–87*, Cmnd 9143, II; *The Government's Expenditure Plans, 1987–88 to 1989–90*, Cmnd 56, II; *Public Expenditure to 1995–96*, Cmnd 2219.

A major result of the net housing shortage and the real cut in public expenditure on housing is that the number of registered homeless households in England soared from 57 000 in 1979 to 148 250 in 1992. In 1992, 62 740 homeless households had to be housed in temporary accommodation since local authorities could not provide them with appropriate dwellings. Council waiting lists, moreover, had increased to 1.4 million by 1992. At the same time as homelessness and council waiting lists reached record levels, it was tragically ironic that there were well over 500 000 building workers unemployed (or 30 per cent of the construction industry's workforce). The principal reason for the plight of both the household in need and the unemployed building worker is the low level of housing starts in recent years, as indicated in table 9.11 on p. 328. Rather than demonstrating market failure, housing, possibly more than any other area of the economy, demonstrates that government intervention fails to satisfy needs for a large proportion of the population of Britain. Housing policy, in most of its manifestations, has been shown to be both inefficient and inequitable, and has failed to offer households a realistic choice between buying and renting.

It is thus a serious cause of concern that the White Paper, *Housing: The Government's Proposals* (1987)[31] – the basis of subsequent legislation – largely ignored housebuilding and failed to refer to homelessness. Clearly, the government assumed that supply and need were broadly in balance. While fiscal support for owner-occupation continues, the government evidently hopes that it will be able to attract sufficient private capital into the rented sectors to bring forward property lying empty, to rehabilitate social housing and (to a limited extent) to build anew. But private capital will only be forthcoming if rates of return are competitive with other forms of investment. This will either necessitate rent increases (with the poor paying an unacceptably high proportion of their disposable income) or housing benefit will rise dramatically and, in effect, subsidise private capital. As with tax relief to the owner-occupier, housing benefit will almost entirely increase the capital value of the property and have a negligible effect on supply. Not only are these policies inequitable but they are demonstrably inefficient. Because of this, current housing policy will do little to tackle the worsening housing crisis.

REFERENCES

1. A. E. Holmans, 'A Forecast of Effective Demand for Housing in Great Britain in the 1970s', *Social Trends*, No. 1 (Central Statistical Office, 1970).
2. G. A. Hughes, *Inflation and Housing* (Housing Research Foundation, 1974).
3. P. M. Hillebrandt, *Economic Theory and the Construction Industry* (Macmillan, 1974).
4. Ibid.
5. Nationwide Building Society, Occasional Bulletin 124, *Who Buys Houses?*
6. G. A. Hughes, *Inflation and Housing*.
7. Nationwide Building Society, *Who Buys Houses?*
8. Bank of England, *Quarterly Bulletin*, 1 (1991); Joseph Rowntree Trust, *Inquiry into British Housing*, 2nd Report (1991).
9. J. Muellbauer, 'How House Prices Fuel Wage Rises', *Financial Times* (23 October 1986).
10. P. Rodgers, 'Why Soaring House Prices Are a Pain in the Neck', *Guardian* (21 July 1987).
11. Bank of England, *Quarterly Bulletin*, 2 (1985).
12. M. Durham, 'Families Growing Rich in Inheritance Bonanza', *Sunday Times* (19 July 1970).
13. C. Hamnett, 'Making Money from Home Ownership', *New Society* (27 June 1986).
14. National Federation of Housing Associations, *Inquiry into British Housing* (1985).
15. Royal Institution of Chartered Surveyors, *Better Housing for Britain* (1985).
16. G. Marsh, in D. Bollver, 'Housing Demands 2 pc Interest Cut', *Guardian* (5 November 1992).
17. J. Wrigglesworth, in R. Kelly, 'Doomsday is Not Here Yet', *The Times* (14 October 1991).
18. R. Best, 'The Homeless Generation', Housing Report, *Observer* (5 July 1992).
19. *Report of the Committee on Housing in Greater London* (The Milner Holland Report) Cmnd 2605 (HMSO, 1965).
20. *Report of the Committee on the Rent Acts* (The Francis Report) Cmnd 4609 (HMSO, 1971).
21. *Fair Deal for Housing*, Cmnd 4728 (HMSO, 1971).
22. M. Harloe, *Private Rented Housing in the United States and Europe* (Croom Helm, 1985).
23. House of Commons, *The First Report of the Environment Committee*; Session 1981/2 (HMSO, 1982).
24. National Federation of Housing Associations, *Inquiry into British Housing*, Chaired by HRH The Duke of Edinburgh, *Report* (NFHA, 1985).
25. White Paper, *Housing: The Government's Proposals*, Cmnd 214 (HMSO, 1987).
26. Joseph Rowntree Trust, *Inquiry into British Housing*, 2nd Report (1991).
27. *Fair Deal for Housing*.
28. *Financial Times* (21 June 1975).
29. See D. Lipsey, 'Ridley's Home Base', *New Society* (7 November 1986).

30. National Federation of Housing Associations, *Inquiry into British Housing*.
31. D. Donnison, 'New Drama for a Crisis', *Guardian* (11 May 1987).
32. Audit Commission, *Managing the Crisis in Council Housing* (HMSO, 1986).
33. W. Waldegrave speaking at the Institute of Housing conference, Brighton, 19 June 1987.
34. *Homes for Today and Tomorrow* (Parker Morris Report) (HMSO, 1961).
35. Department of the Environment, White Paper, *Housing: The Government's Proposals*, Cmnd 214 (HMSO, 1988).
36. P. A. Stone, *Urban Development in Britain: Standards, Costs, Resources, 1964–2004, Vol. 1* (Cambridge University Press, 1970).
37. *National House Condition Survey*, 1967 (HMSO, 1967).
38. Ibid.
39. *Better Homes the Next Priority*, Cmnd 5339 (HMSO, 1973).
40. *English House Condition Survey, 1981* (HMSO, 1983).
41. Department of the Environment, Green Paper, *Housing Improvement – A New Approach*, Cmnd 9513 (HMSO, 1985).
42. *English House Condition Survey, 1986* (HMSO, 1988).
43. *English House Condition Survey, 1991* (HMSO, 1993).
44. Association of Metropolitan Authorities, *Defects in Housing, Part 1* (AMA, 1983); *Defects in Housing, Part 2* (AMA, 1984); *Defects in Housing, Part 3* (AMA, 1985).
45. Department of the Environment, *Housing Policy: A Consultative Document* (HMSO, 1977).
46. M. Ball, *Home Ownership: A Suitable Case for Reform* (Shelter, 1986).
47. Ibid.
48. Ibid.
49. S. S. Duncan, 'House Building, Profits and Social Efficiency in Sweden and Britain', *Housing Studies*, 1 (1986).
50. D. MacLennan, *Housing Economics* (Longman, 1982).
51. A. W. Evans, *House Prices and Land Prices in the South East – A Review* (The House Builders' Federation, 1987).
52. P. Ambrose, *Whatever Happened to Planning?* (Methuen, 1986).
53. P. Tyler and J. Rhodes, 'South-East Employment and Housing Study', *Discussion Paper No. 15* (Department of Land Economy, University of Cambridge, 1986).
54. F. Pennance, 'Planning, Land Supply and Demand', in A. A. Walters (ed.), *Government and the Land* (Institute of Economic Affairs, 1974).
55. *Review of the Development Control System* (Dobry Report) (HMSO, 1974).
56. National Housing Forum, *Housing Needs in the 1900s* (1989).

10

The Construction Industry in the United Kingdom

The construction industry covers a wide range of loosely integrated groups and sub-markets whose output varies, but which basically consists of the production, alteration or repair of durable buildings and capital goods involving the use of land combined with other scarce resources – a combination found in other industries, but construction has certain unique characteristics deriving largely from the physical nature of the construction product and its demand.

THE NATURE AND CHARACTERISTICS OF THE INDUSTRY

Much output is large, durable and expensive. Generally, value is high in relation to the income of the purchaser. A house can rarely be purchased out of income nor can a factory out of current profits; payment is either from accumulated reserves or from borrowings. Thus the prosperity of the industry is greatly affected by changes in the rate of interest and the availability of credit. Demand is geographically wide and much is unique to the requirement of the individual customer. Thus there are few opportunities for traditional building to develop mass production methods which would reduce unit costs. The industry's structure has changed little over the years, its methods of production are still mainly traditional and there are only small signs of technical change. A single contract may account for a large proportion of a contractor's output in any period; this may cause substantial diseconomies in the production process as well as increasing risks.

Repairs and Maintenance

The durability of buildings results in a high percentage of current output in repairs and maintenance – increasing from 27.5 in 1969 to 45 per cent in 1992 (Figure 10.1). Durability results in the existing stock of buildings being very large in relation to annual production; the total supply of buildings is very inelastic even in the long term. Therefore, small fluctuations in demand for the existing stock will have large effects on the price of new work.

Repair and maintenance is a sector in which productivity has risen more

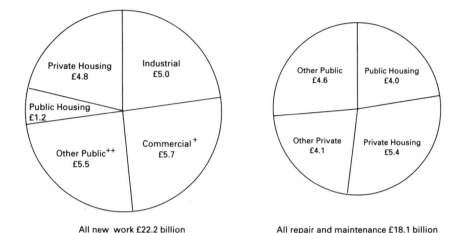

All new work £22.2 billion   All repair and maintenance £18.1 billion

Notes: [+] 42% of contractors output was in the office sector; 21% in shops; and 16% in the
         entertainment sector.
         [++] 26% of contractors' output in non-housing public-sector works involved education
         and health; 27% roads; 10% railways, air transport, harbours and waterways; and 5%
         sewage and water.
Source: *Housing and Construction Statistics*, (HMSO).

Figure 10.1   *Output of the construction industry by sector, 1992, at current prices (£billions)*

slowly than in new construction. Inevitably it is heavily labour-intensive and
techniques that have improved efficiency in new work are rarely applicable.
Capital expenditure per worker per year in construction is probably less than
half of the average for manufacturing industry, and in repair and maintenance
it is substantially less. Mechanisation is uneconomic for all except the largest
maintenance operations and returns to modern management techniques dwindle
as the scale of operations decreases. The smaller the scale of maintenance work
the more intractable are the problems of raising productivity. Small firms, of
25 employees or fewer, carry out over 60 per cent of repair and maintenance
in the industry; the smaller the firm the greater the percentage of repair and
maintenance work. In addition, the number of firms able to undertake this
work is swollen in periods of downturn in demand for new work, particularly
housing, and these have little incentive to improve capitalisation.

Site Work

Much construction activity is on site and thus vulnerable to climatic elements
against which it is often difficult to provide much protection, at least in the
early stages. The development of special plant and protective shelters has reduced these hazards but annual losses of building output are inevitable. Generally, United Kingdom winters are not severe enough for winter building techniques
to be economic. The problems of building in winter and the related economic

effects are international, and many countries, including Canada, Sweden and Austria, have found it necessary to provide economic incentives to avoid these effects.

Management problems on site may be great. Site labour accounts for about a third of the cost of construction. Much of this is casual, employed for one scheme only and often inefficiently employed.[1] Exposure to site conditions reduces the life of plant and in many large contracts it will be written off at the end of the contract. It is less efficiently used than under factory conditions – a factor in the growth of the specialist plant-hire company. Materials and components on site may account for as much as half the total cost of construction – and their assembly requires considerable managerial expertise, especially as a project may take five years or more to complete. In fact, management expertise is one of the scarcest resources of the construction industry in the United Kingdom, as in many other countries.

The Nature and Determination of Demand

The industry produces investment goods demanded not for their own sake but for their use in the production of less durable goods. This derived-demand for investment goods is unstable, and is difficult to forecast. There are three major categories of demand: commercial and industrial developments, whose construction will assist production; social types of development, such as schools; and housing, a unique investment good, which is also a consumer durable.

Tendering

In addition to the difficulty of estimating total work load for the industry, each construction firm is uncertain about future work loads. Because of the unique nature of so much of its output, the industry fixes its prices largely by competitive tender for individual contracts; tendering is either 'selected list' or 'open'.

Selected list

The selection of tenderers is made from a list or by an open invitation for firms to apply to tender. An objection to selective tendering is that lists may be too long and may not be an accurate reflection of the ability of firms. There is separation between design and construction, and the possibility of collusion between firms on the list. Since the Banwell Report (1964)[2] an increasing proportion of public-sector work is put out to selective tender, with generally up to eight firms invited to bid. The DOE uses selective tendering for almost all its work, whereas some local authorities, especially the smaller ones, have been slow to adopt the procedure, preferring the less economic yet superficially more competitive open tendering. Selective tendering is used extensively in civil engineering and almost exclusively in major road contracts.

Open tender

The project is openly advertised and any firm may bid. The major objections are the lack of control by the client over the competence of the builder being employed and the waste of resources when many firms tender for the same job because the prices for contracts obtained must include the costs of estimating on jobs not obtained. Tendering is an expensive and uncertain process, and while in theory open competition should result in the lowest cost for the client, in practice the lowest tender may not necessarily equal the best value. There is evidence that it is associated with less satisfactory performance.[3] Open-tendered projects are the least likely to maintain final costs close to contract sums, and average time overrun is greater than with projects let by other means. There may be grounds for 'spreading the net' in smaller projects but open competition tends to increase costs and uncertainties. There is also separation of design and construction.

It is not possible to anticipate very far in advance exactly what proportion of tenders will be successful. Research sponsored by the DOE indicated that the tendering success rate of firms is between 17 and 27 per cent by the number of bids.[4] There is therefore a tendency to bid for more contracts than are required, with the risk that at times the number of contracts and actual output will be far less than planned and at other times far more than can be handled efficiently. Thus contractors rarely know even within a relatively short time ahead upon which contracts they will be engaged. It is therefore difficult to plan future work loads so as to secure the most efficient use of resources, and wastage is inevitable. The contractor may therefore encounter rapidly increasing costs.

Negotiated Contracts

Most private work is negotiated with a contractor chosen by preliminary tendering or else brought in at the design stage of the project. The involvement of the contractors so early in the process can lead to improvements in efficiency and savings to the client. It overcomes the separation of design and construction, which is a major disadvantage of tendering systems. A negotiated contract is particularly likely if it involves a patented design system or the expertise of a particular contractor. Because public accountability normally requires acceptance of the lowest tender, negotiated contracts are less acceptable in the public sector as their price may be higher.

Serial contract or tender

This is a variation of the negotiated contract and is usually negotiated with a firm that has completed a similar contract successfully. Normally there is a legal understanding that there will be a series of similar contracts when the first is completed; this is advantageous to the contractor, who can plan a continuous programme of work. Lower costs to the contractor should result in the original price being keener than with normal contracts. Close collaboration is likely between design and construction, and both time and cost overrun is less than average.

'Fee construction' and management contracting

In the 1930s, Bovis pioneered the 'fee construction' system, a radical departure from competitive tendering in which the contractor and client agree on a fee to be charged for management services, while the client meets all construction expenses. Often, the management contractor does not undertake the construction work directly, but organises the site and manages the construction sub-contractors on behalf of the client. The contractor's risks are much lower but, in order to secure further business, s/he has every incentive to keep down the cost of construction. The system assures a close relationship between the client and contractor but is unacceptable to the public sector as the price for the project is not determined before work commences. In some cases the role of the management contractor may be expanded to include detailed design (design and management contract), although this will usually be provided through professional consultants.

Cost escalation on some recent major projects in London has, however, cast doubt on the management contractor's presumed incentive to keep costs down – especially when payment is on a percentage fee basis. Also, since the system does not provide privity of contract between client and sub-contractors, the client is unable to intervene should a dispute arise with the latter. This problem is largely avoided with construction management, which involves the contractor being engaged by the client on a management-only basis, yet retains privity of contract between client and sub-contractors.

Design and build

Instead of appointing an architect, the client may go to a company offering a complete service of design and construction. As well as achieving greater price certainty, design and build maximises the scope for overlapping the design and construction processes, and for adapting the design to achieve early completion. For these reasons it has been adopted widely by housing associations. On the other hand, problems of cost over-run may arise if variations are introduced at a later stage.

Once a tender has been accepted there is a variety of types of contract. Public-sector contracts are let on a firm price when their duration is less than one year. Even in the private sector, the majority of contracts are on a firm-price basis. Thus on most contracts, contractors are assessing their costs over the period of the contract and their price before it is executed. This is the complete reverse of the procedure followed in most of manufacturing industry, where the producer determines his/her price after the good has been produced and costs are known with reasonable certainty. In fact, with inflation in the 1970s, firm price contracts for local authority housing in England and Wales fell dramatically, from 88.9 per cent of all contracts in 1970 to 7.2 per cent by 1979. Contracts with fluctuation clauses rose from 11.1 per cent in 1970 to 82.7 per cent in 1979.

THE CONSTRUCTION INDUSTRY AND THE ECONOMY

The construction industry in the United Kingdom is of key economic importance because it is a major client of the government, and because of its size of output, numbers employed, and its contribution to the national stock of investment goods. It has been the subject of reports by numerous government bodies. The value of the construction industry's output in 1988 was approximately 6.5 per cent of GDP at factor cost. Employment (including self-employment) in construction accounted for nearly 7 per cent of the national workforce – hence output per worker is slightly below the average for the economy as a whole. In the same year fixed investment in dwellings and other new buildings and works accounted for just over half of total gross domestic fixed capital formation. Fixed investment by the construction industry itself in plant and machinery and new buildings and works amounted to £1.1 billion in 1988 – a figure representing less than 5 per cent of output of the industry. Construction is thus a relatively labour-intensive industry and in 1988 the capital stock represented a level equivalent to only three-quarters of annual output. By comparison, in manufacturing, the capital stock represented over three times the annual level of output. This low level of investment is almost certainly the principal factor influencing the productivity of construction workers relative to other sectors in the economy (see next section).

According to the United Nations, Great Britain, the Republic of Ireland and the United States were bottom of the international league table of spending on construction in 1991, with Britain spending only 9.1 per cent of its GDP on construction (compared to Switzerland's 17 per cent).

Some 30 per cent of new work and 48 per cent of repair and maintenance work in 1992 was for the public sector. Thus the government has a means of direct control over the output of the industry which is in consequence quickly and directly affected by any changes in economic policy. Thus its size – of critical importance as an investment goods industry – and its dependence upon the government as client, provide a key to understanding the interrelationship between the industry and the economy. Changes in the output of the industry are too significant to ignore as they affect the size of the national product and the level of employment both directly and indirectly through the multiplier effect.

Post-war economic management has aimed at balance of payments equilibrium, full employment, economic growth, and control of inflation. These ob-

Table 10.1 *Manpower in the construction industry, 1971–92*

Year	Contractors		Employees in employment (000s) Public authorities		All employees[+]	Self-employed	Total (000s)
	Operatives	APTC*	Operatives	APTC			
1971	826	219	252	110	1407	n/a	1606
1981	679	230	205	104	1218	385	1698
1991	516	251	120	63	950	657	1698
1992	437	221	112	56	825	597	1516

Notes: + All employees on register of DOE. Total figures include estimates of employees not on register.
* APTC: Administrative, professional, clerical and technical staff.
n.a. = not available

Source: Department of Employment, *Housing and Construction Statistics* (annual averages).

jectives have not always proved to be compatible and policy has varied. The easiest ways for the government to shift the economy in the direction required all affect construction either directly or indirectly. Interest rates may be increased and credit restricted, making it more difficult and more expensive to borrow; taxation may be increased; public expenditure may be reduced. Measures may affect construction directly; changes in government grants for house improvements, for example can cause fluctuations in construction work. One effect of raising home improvement grants in the early 1980s was a marked upswing in the repair and maintenance sector.

OUTPUT, BUILDING CYCLES AND PRODUCTIVITY IN THE CONSTRUCTION INDUSTRY

Construction activity in constant prices in 1990 was higher than in previous peaks in 1978/9 or even 1972/3, but *new* work was actually lower than in any year since 1973, a fact easily overlooked because of the expanded role of repair and maintenance in total work (figure 10.2). Even within the new work category, changes in the composition of output were significant. The late 1980s expansion was due largely to growth of demand in the private sector for commercial buildings, although all sectors of new work (apart from public-sector housing) showed some increase (figure 10.3).

Of long-term interest for the construction industry is the question of whether the level of new work will eventually rise beyond levels achieved during the 1990 peak. One would expect demand for new work (figure 10.4) to be linked to growth of production in general in the economy, yet it is only by including repair and maintenance activity that any real growth trend in total construction output can be observed over the post-war period since the 1960s (see figure 10.2). Analysis of growth in GDP and construction (gross) output (both in 1985 prices) in the post-war period as a whole (1950–89) suggests that while GDP would appear to double in value every 40 years, it would take over 55 years for construction output to do the same.

Up to 1968 (or possibly even 1973) post-war growth of construction activity was so significant that it tended to offset and smooth out much of the cyclical impact of macro-economic stop–go policies. The United Kingdom's *National Accounts* statistics show that between 1948 and 1968 new building and works increased its share of fixed investment in the economy – gross domestic fixed capital formation (GDFCF) – to well over half, at a time when fixed investment was itself rising as a share of GDP – from 12 to 19 per cent over this period. By the end of the 1980s, while fixed investment (GDFCF) had once again risen to around 19 per cent of GDP, the share of new building and works had declined.

For the past 25 years, therefore, the construction industry has had to cope with considerable fluctuations in demand for its product. A higher share (and more stable level) of fixed investment in the economy would clearly help the

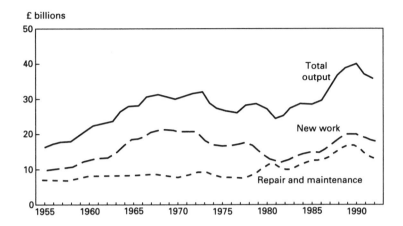

Source: *Housing and Construction Statistics*, (HMSO).

Figure 10.2 *New work, and repair and maintenance, 1955–92 (constant (1985) prices)*

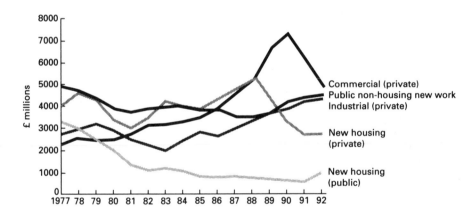

Source: *Housing and Construction Statistics*, (HMSO).

Figure 10.3 *Value of construction output (new work), Great Britain, 1977–92 (constant 1985 prices)*

construction industry. This would in turn require greater stability of public-sector capital spending on construction, as well as the long-term assurance of low and stable real interest rates. Instead, governments are often accused of treating the construction industry as a regulator of the economy,[5] either directly through cuts in capital spending programmes or indirectly through monetary policy and interest rates – influencing the cost of borrowing for both consumption and investment purposes.

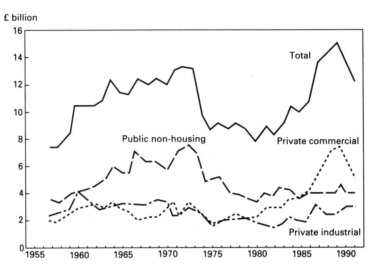

Source: *Housing and Construction Statistics*,   (HMSO).

Figure 10.4   *New non-housing orders, 1957–91 (constant (1985) prices)*

Building cycles

Building activity is typically subject to more pronounced cyclical fluctuations
than the national product as a whole. Rapid expansion of output frequently
results in over-supply and this is then followed by a phase of low development
activity. This problem is greatest in areas such as (major) office and retail
developments with long lead-in and construction times, since by the time they
are completed the underlying market conditions may well have changed. Output elsewhere, such as private-sector housebuilding, responds more quickly.
Nevertheless, even here, sudden fluctuations in demand, prompted, for example,
by changes in interest rates (as in 1989), can lead to a considerable backlog of
unsold properties in the housing market (see Chapter 9).

   Most buildings are not required for themselves but for the contribution they
can make to the production of distribution of goods and services. Thus construction demand is derived essentially from the needs of producers to increase
production of goods in factories, to improve or expand distribution networks,
to find extra capacity for retail sales or office staff, to expand public services
or to increase the production of raw materials (for examples, quarrying), utilities (for example, water), or energy. Although some proportion of the stock of
buildings will always be in the process of refurbishment or replacement, by
and large, new orders for industrial and commercial work are mainly required
in order to augment existing capacity. From 1985 to 1990, for example, manufacturing production rose by over 18.4 per cent, but new industrial construction work increased at more than twice this rate – by 40.9 per cent. Conversely,
in a downturn, relatively few new buildings may be required. This process, by

which a given percentage change (positive or negative) in demand may lead to a larger change in fixed investment, is known as the 'accelerator mechanism'. Macro-economic factors – such as changes in interest rates – will influence construction both directly and indirectly; by raising the cost of borrowing, development costs will increase, and demand will fall as a result of reduced investment and reduced consumer borrowing and spending.

Table 10.2 illustrates these points by examining downturns in the past two major building cycles. In both cases the fall-off in construction work was substantially greater than that of GDP as a whole. However, major compositional differences are revealed. The earlier recession affected most new industrial work and public-sector housing (because of cutbacks in government spending). The 1990s recession affected commercial work mainly, but also repair and maintenance activity (usually a fairly stable component of construction demand). In both cases downturns in private-sector housebuilding occurred earlier in the cycle and the effects were particularly severe.

It seems clear that although anything governments can do to reduce cycles in the economy in general is likely to reduce the severity of building cycles, on the whole, the accelerator mechanism will probably ensure that fluctuations in construction work continue to be more pronounced than in other sectors of the economy.

Nevertheless, the transition from new orders to output produces a considerable degree of 'smoothing' in output trends, especially in sectors with long lead-in and construction times. Hence orders received towards the top of a property 'boom' continue to provide work for some time after a downturn. This cannot hold up for ever, and clearly, any protracted slump in new orders will eventually filter through into similar reductions in building activity. Figure 10.5 illustrates this process well for the construction industry as a whole over the period 1988–93. Contractors' orders peaked in late 1988, 40 per cent above their average level in 1985. Output, however, increased over the much longer period up to early 1990, but achieved a lower peak level – just under 30 per cent of its average in 1985. During a lengthy downturn in new orders, output may continue to fall for some time, even when orders are picking up.

According to a study of post-war building cycles by Barras[6] the lags between new orders and output are shortest in the case of housing and longest for commercial development, with industrial property being in an intermediate position. For commercial new orders, major cycles have peaked in 1964, 1973 and 1989. The subsequent downturn in commercial construction output has tended to be less severe, as work received before or during the peak has carried over into subsequent months and even years. In fact, post-war commercial output does not appear to have suffered any significant periods of decline at all (in constant prices) until after the 1973 recession, and then again after output peaked in 1990. Recent evidence, however, suggests that the link between orders and output in this sector may be much closer than in the past, presumably because of faster completion times.

Fluctuations in industrial new orders are much more frequent and thus cycles

Table 10.2   *Major building cycles; construction output at constant (1985) prices**

	1979–81		1990–2	
Change in gross domestic product (GDP)	−4%			−3%
Change in all construction work	−14%			−14%
Change in new work	−21%			−11%
Sectors most affected:	(i) Private industrial	−22%	(i) Private commercial	−35%
	(ii) Public new housing	−47%	(ii) Repair and maintenance	−18%
	(iii) Other public new	−14%	(iii) Private new housing (1988–92)	−46%
	(iv) Private new housing (1978–81)	−34%		

Note: * percentage figures relate to annual averages. The full effects in some sectors may have continued beyond these dates.

Source: *Housing and Construction Statistics* and *Economic Trends* (HMSO).

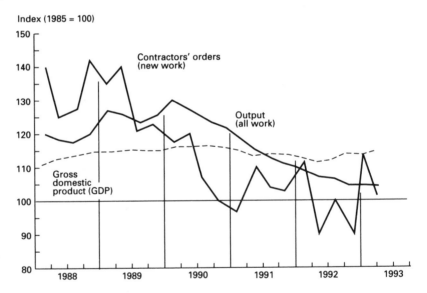

Source: *Economic Trends* (HMSO).

Figure 10.5   *Indices of construction output, contractors orders and gross domestic product (GDP) 1988–93 (1985 = 100)*

are of shorter duration. Peaks appear to occur on average every 4.5 years (1960, 1965, 1969, 1973, 1978/9, 1984, 1987); however, fluctuations in output are less marked, for reasons discussed above, and appear to be linked to a longer cycle of approximately 9 years (1961, 1969/70, 1979, 1992). In private-sector housebuilding, output closely follows new order cycles, both of which appear to be significant (recent peaks in new orders occurred in 1972, 1976, 1978, 1983 and 1988). Housebuilding (together with consumer expenditure) tends to be one of the first sectors to anticipate an upturn in the economy, and housebuilding cycles appear to precede the business cycle in the economy generally, by up to one year. Industrial and commercial new orders appear to be roughly coincident with the business cycle. Building cycles themselves are largely influenced by business cycles in the economy as a whole. The latter were first identified in the 1860s by an economist named Juglar (at the time they were called 'trade cycles'). Juglar claimed that it took eight to eleven years for a cycle to progress from peak to peak; other economists have claimed that the cycle takes only around half this time, and Kondratiev (a Russian economist) pointed to the presumed existence of long-wave cycles of approximately 50–60 years. Although there would appear to be a plethora of competing theories, they are not necessarily mutually exclusive, and they all follow the same pattern of expansion and recession around a long-run trend path of economic growth. However, some fundamental differences do exist concerning the economic influences at work. In particular, Kondratiev's long-wave theory (with later contributions from Schumpeter and, more recently, Van Duijn) stresses the role of new technologies in helping to develop new products and branches of industry. These in turn generate locational changes and infrastructure investment, and such long waves may be associated with several major building cycles. For example, the first phase of the Industrial Revolution, from 1780 to 1845, is generally associated with the first long wave or Kondratiev cycle – based, in particular, on the application of steam power to textiles and the growth of the Lancashire cotton industry. The second long wave (figure 10.6) was based on a wider range of industries such as coal, iron and steel, and heavy engineering; the development of the railways; and the increasing urbanisation of economic activity and population. The third cycle, from 1895 to 1945, involved the development of new industries based on the internal combustion engine, electric power, chemicals and the gradual development of consumer goods industries. The share of services in GDP overtook production industries after the turn of the century, reflecting the country's strong international commercial and financial interests. Two suburban building booms took place during this period, linked closely to developments in transportation (buses, trams and railways initially, later followed by the impact of the underground and the growth of car ownership), and the emergence of a stable white-collar workforce. In particular, the 1930s housebuilding boom was the first to be associated with speculative owner-occupied development in a significant way. This was further helped by a combination of low-interest rates, cheap land (the availability of which was undoubtedly increased by transport improvements), falling construction costs and the availability of government subsidies.

After the Second World War, massive expansion of the road network and the rapid growth of new consumer goods industries (particularly consumer durables) led increasingly to industrial and service expansion outside existing major urban settlements (see Chapter 8). Population growth now occurred mainly

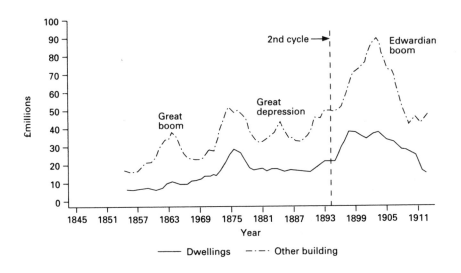

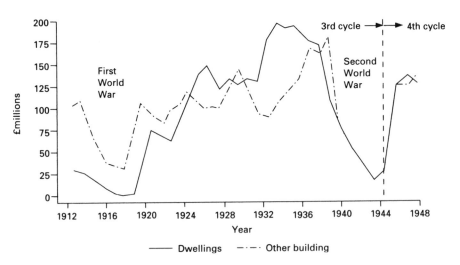

Source: Adapted from Feinstein (1972) and Barras and Ferguson (1985).

Figure 10.6 *Gross domestic fixed capital formation in building, at constant prices, 1856–1948*[7,8]

outside these areas as household mobility increased and new industries expanded. There have been clear implications not only for housebuilding and industrial development but also for associated services and the location of public infrastructure, schools, hospitals and so on.

The 1980s heralded the growth of new 'hi-tech' sectors associated with industries such as electronics, pharmaceuticals and biotechnology, as well as technologically advanced sectors of other industries and services. Arguably, many

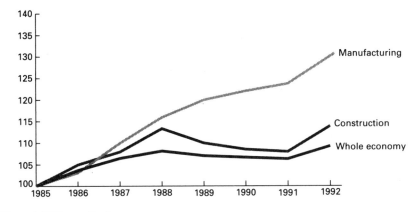

Note: * GDP contribution.

Source: *Employment Gazette* (HMSO, August 1993).

Figure 10.7 *Indices of productivity in the construction industry, manufacturing and the whole economy (output* per person employed, 1985 = 100)*

of the techniques upon which such industries are increasingly dependent – including micro-electronics and information technology, computer aided design and manufacture and so on – have yet to make their full impact. Such future developments could well represent the start of a new long wave of economic expansion but the full implications for construction – at this early stage – are unclear. Some insight may, however, be gained from trends already observable in the late 1980s and early 1990s: the clustering of new 'hi-tech' business parks in accessible locations such as the M4 corridor; the demands placed on new buildings (especially offices) by information technology; the increasing use of just-in-time delivery techniques in manufacturing and distribution; and development pressures for ever more out-of-town retailing.

Productivity and costs

Labour productivity over a given period is defined as output per worker, or output per hour. Given the difficulties of estimating accurately the total hours worked in construction (as a result, in particular of the large share of self-employment in the total workforce) the former definition is adopted. Other definitions of productivity are possible – such as capital productivity (that is, output per unit of capital employed) or total factor productivity. However, both of these are dependent upon achieving accurate estimates of the value of the existing stock of capital in construction (as in other industries) and this in itself is fraught with problems.[9] Estimates of output per worker are, however, readily available for a wide range of industries, and comparisons, as in figure 10.7, can be informative. It must always be borne in mind that (labour) productivity differences as between industries, as well as fluctuations over the business cycle, may be due to many different factors. Also, labour productivity is sometimes confused with 'efficiency', which can be misleading. While improvements in efficiency in construction may well improve productivity, workers might nevertheless remain less productive than in other industries if they have less capital in the form of plant and equipment to work with, and if their tools and equipment do not on the whole embody as much new technology as elsewhere. One long-term issue, to be discussed below, is the extent to which the stop–go nature of the industry discourages investment or the adoption of new techniques.

Productivity also tends to exhibit cyclical trends, rising fastest in the early stages of an upturn as a higher workload is spread over a largely unchanging capital stock and workforce. In a downturn, workloads often fall faster than capacity, and productivity declines. However, capacity constraints are often reached near the top of a major cycle, thus preventing further gains in productivity. Figure 10.7 shows that productivity in the construction industry fell by approximately 4 per cent between 1988 and 1990. Nevertheless, as Ball points out, significant productivity gains were achieved through reorganisation in the construction industry over the early to mid-1980s. Taking the period 1985 to 1992, although construction achieved faster growth of productivity than the economy as a whole, productivity in manufacturing (which accounts for nearly a quarter of GDP) rose more than twice as fast. Clearly, productivity growth in much of the rest of the economy, largely made up of services, is rather slow. Finally, the *overall level* of labour productivity in construction – as mentioned earlier – would still appear to be somewhat below the average for all sectors of the economy (although productivity appears to be above the construction industry average for medium- and large-sized firms).

Productivity can also have a significant impact on building costs in the long term. A recent study of the construction industry[10] suggested that over the twenty years from 1968 to 1988 construction output prices for new work rose nearly 25 per cent faster than prices in the economy as a whole (that is, the GDP price deflator). In the short term, construction prices tend to rise faster during an upturn than the output of other sectors, but in a recession the opposite occurs. Variations in tender prices may be even more marked (with firms taking higher profits in an upturn and reduced profits in a downturn). These trends are illustrated in figure 10.8 for the period 1985-1992. The strength of the recession facing the construction industry in the early 1990's is also evident from these figures.

Effects of Government Policy

An increase in interest rates raises the cost of projects and causes postponement or cancellation of marginal schemes not yet begun. Existing projects will probably proceed, but developers' profits are likely to be reduced (depending on the extent of borrowed funds). Future tenders will be increased. The effective demand for buildings will be reduced because, at higher rates of interest,

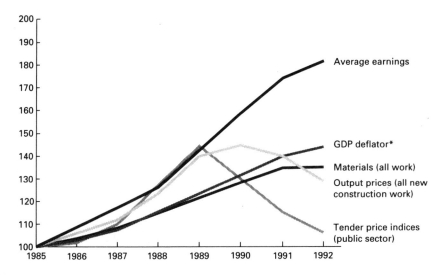

Note: * At market prices.
Source: *Housing and Construction Statistics* and *Economic Trends* (HMSO).

Figure 10.8   *Indices of construction costs and prices, 1985–92*

borrowers will not be able to raise such large sums. If interest rate increases are sharp or long-term, the speculative developer will be hardest hit, and overall there will be a downturn in construction activity. A credit squeeze will affect adversely many firms who depend on short-term bank finance during building: banks tend to reduce finance to builders early in a squeeze and not to start financing again until the squeeze is relaxed. Larger firms have a better credit rating and have access to alternative funds. The worst affected are likely to be medium-sized firms too big to exist on repair and maintenance work alone, yet too small to reap the benefits of a large contract which smooths the workload, and is probably heavily dependent on speculative new work. Prospective purchasers may not be able to raise funds and there will be a decline in the demand for new work. A reduction in credit availability and purchasing power in the economy will reduce demand for other goods and services. Plans for additional or replacement buildings are postponed; manufacturers postpone erection of new factories or offices. Thus there is a lower level of construction activity. Reductions in interest rates and easier credit have the reverse effect.

Cuts in government capital spending are likely to affect the construction industry in the longer or medium term rather than the short term as there will be existing work and contracts already signed. Although overall construction activity will be reduced, not all sectors will be affected similarly; this will depend on government priorities – for example, housing programmes may be cut back, whereas road building is maintained. Even within sectors the emphasis may change; for example, between 1985 and 1990 construction output for new public-sector housing fell by nearly 25 per cent in constant (1985) prices, but public-sector housing repair and maintenance activity rose by 10 per cent over the same period. Similarly, tax changes will have varying effects although any increase in taxation leads to lower real incomes and thus a decline in demand for construction output. Any specific taxes on property or gains from property will affect demand adversely. Conversely, tax concessions for owner-occupiers lead to an increase in demand for owner-occupied houses. The net effects of increased taxation on the industry depend on the way in which tax proceeds are spent. If some of the increased tax revenue is spent on public construction, then the decrease in demand for construction will be less than if none of the tax revenue is used to finance public construction projects.

Contractors have been affected substantially by the fluctuations in economic policy, which have in turn contributed to the increased importance of sub-contracting. As government action affects construction, so a change in construction output will affect employment, and hence incomes and ultimately output of other sectors of the economy. The decline in construction activity is, after a time lag, injected back into the system.

A major difficulty in economic management is the problem of timing measures so that the effects of the action occur at the optimum time to achieve the desired objective. The problems of using construction as a regulator are that lags (with the exception of housing investment) tend to be long and variable. If the government reduces its capital expenditure it will not normally cut projects where work has started, so the brunt of the impact must be borne by new orders. The build up of the workload on a contract is at first slow; it then increases rapidly, and towards the end of the project tails off. Thus if projects are cut, the reduction in the workload is not felt for perhaps a year or longer. This is a critical disadvantage as the major effect comes later and may co-incide with the desire to restimulate the economy.

Moreover, the longer-term consequences of such cuts can be serious: long-term programmes are completely disrupted; land already purchased for projects which are cut is held unproductively; design teams are dispersed and staff used less effectively. The repercussions tend to prove to be longer-lasting than the period of the cut itself since programmes lose impetus and cannot be fully reinstated for some time after the restrictions have been withdrawn, and the capacity of the industry to undertake the new work will have been damaged. There are also difficulties for the construction industry in switching resources between dissimilar sectors, such as civil engineering and housing. Between 1987 and 1992, for example, the proportion of new non-housing public-sector work on roads rose from 20 per cent to 27 per cent of the total.

Thus the manipulation of public capital expenditure for medium-term economic management has considerable drawbacks for construction, bringing with it unemployment; a net outflow of trained men (many of whom never return); reduced recruitment and training; excess material production capacity and stocks; non-utilisation of contractor's plant; and increasing bankruptcies. The effects of cutbacks under Thatcherism in the 1980s was therefore to disrupt and undermine confidence and damage the industry's overall efficiency. High interest rates and cuts in public spending between 1979 and 1984 produced a fall of 22 per cent in new private-sector industrial work and a 57 per cent reduction in new public-sector housing construction. Other new public-sector work fell by 7.5 per cent, and new construction work overall by 11 per cent between these dates. Although new private-sector work recovered subsequently, new public-sector work taken as a whole in 1992 was still 19 per cent below 1979 levels – a decline of 62 per cent in new public housing offsetting a small increase of 6.5 per cent in other public new work (all at constant 1985 prices) over this period.

THE STRUCTURE OF THE INDUSTRY AND ITS ECONOMIC ORGANISATION

The structure of the construction industry is largely determined by the nature of the production process – but this, according to Ball,[11] is fundamentally influenced by land rent. Land rent (syphoned-off from surplus value) alters the profitability and feasibility of production methods *either* by reducing the proportion of surplus value available for investment,[12] *or* by lowering the profitability of investment,[13] *or* by altering the conditions and terms under which investment is undertaken.[14] Ball suggests that while rent does not have a significant effect on the production process in modern contract building, since it is the client that bears the costs of land and not the contractor, land rent has a major impact upon speculative building. The speculative builder buys up land when the property market slumps to ensure an adequate supply of sites for development when the market picks up. But in recent years (and particularly in the South-East) the market power of the landowner has increased at the expense of the builder since restrictive planning and green-belt policy have produced an artificial shortage of development land. This, together with the volatility of the property market in the 1970s and 1980s, has forced developers to disperse construction over many sites and/or to concentrate on small standardised runs. Low rates of output and sharp variations in demand therefore have a marked effect on building techniques: casual labour becomes a necessity; and physically fragmented tasks are not amenable to effective management control. Land prices are therefore not just residual in the Ricardian sense but are often also synonymous with the concept of absolute rent. To compensate for being squeezed between high land costs and competitive product prices, builders are under pressure to maintain their profitability by adopting production methods which are neither conducive to sustained productivity nor to the permanency of a skilled workforce. The effect upon both construction costs and property prices has thus been inflationary in the long- term – to the detriment of both the quantity and quality of building work.

The construction industry in the United Kingdom, moreover, is typified by a large number of small firms with extremely low capitalisation and there are few signs of increasing firm size. The number of small firms rose dramatically over the 1980s, with an increase of 45 000 in the smallest firm size category alone between 1982 and 1990. Much work comprises small projects in repairs and improvements as well as in new housing. As there is little scope for technical or managerial economies of scale, this work is best undertaken by locally based firms. Efficiency will depend upon the skill of the operative rather than on the organisation and capital provided by the firm.

Number and Size of Firms

The fragmentation and numerical supremacy of the small firm is typical of the construction industry in most countries of Western Europe and the United States (table 10.3).

Little capital or qualification is required for entry into the industry, and trade credit is available from builders' merchants. When construction work is profitable and demand is increasing, workers may become 'self-employed' to benefit from the situation. Many small firms have little incentive to remain if work is short and, predictably, exit from the industry is high. In 1991 3812 receiving orders and similar were administered to self-employed individuals or partnerships in the construction industry and 3373 construction companies went into liquidation, a rise of nearly 40 per cent over the previous year.

Small Firms

Small firms employing twenty-five or fewer operatives account for 98 per cent of the total number of firms, but less than half of total employment by private contractors in the industry and only 36 per cent of construction work done. Generally, the smaller the firm the greater the significance of repair and maintenance. Small firms account for rather less than a quarter of new construction work but over 64 per cent of repair and maintenance activity (all figures for 1991). Small firms are to be found in all the main trades, such as general builders, building and civil engineering contractors (where over 90 per cent of firms are small), as well as in the more traditional craft-based or specialist trades.

Much of the output of the industry tends to be produced and assembled at the point of ultimate consumption, thus, except for large contracts, it is uneconomic for contractors to operate over long distances. Many small contractors regard their normal maximum radius as being 25 km; the small repair firm may restrict itself to a radius of only 8 km. There is a very imperfectly competitive market in which firms will compete mainly with similar firms in the same area. The small firm complements the larger because each is serving different markets. Much maintenance work must be handled quickly, and the larger firm may not have the flexibility to carry it out. The small firm will carry out new work which the large firm may not want. In new housing it will specialise where it has local knowledge and reputation – an important selling point.

Table 10.3 *Structure of the construction industry. Private contractors: number and size of firms, total employment and value of work*[+] *done 1982–91*

Firm size	1982			1991		
	Numbers[++]	Percentage of total employment	Percentage of work done	Numbers[++]	Percentage of total employment	Percentage of of work done
1 - 7	125 619	28.4	20.3	195 285	38.5	26.5
8 - 24	13 624	17.8	16.2	8 410	12.8	11.4
25 - 114	4 324	20.0	21.7	3 040	16.7	18.9
115 - 299	562	9.8	11.5	431	8.5	10.6
300 - 1199	228	12.7	15.9	195	11.9	17.8
1200+	38	11.3	14.4	39	11.6	14.8
All firms	144 395	100	100	207 400	100	100

Notes: + 3rd quarter 1982 and 1991.
++ October each year.

Source: *Housing and Construction Statistics* (HMSO).

Labour turnover is lower in small firms – many employees remain for long periods; less use if made of labour-only sub-contractors and demarcation is rarely a problem, partly because of low trade union membership (the national building strike of 1972 affected larger contracts and sites only). Output per worker is lower for small firms because of low capital input, largely a consequence of emphasis on repairs and maintenance, a difficult area in which to increase productivity.

Large Firms

While small firms prosper, it is the very large firms (employing over 1200 operatives) who are the most important employers and producers, and who have the highest output per employee. In 1991, this group accounted for only 0.02 per cent of all firms and 11.6 per cent of total employment, yet accounted for 14.8 per cent of work done (compared with 21.5 per cent in 1973). Substitution of new materials and processes for labour has improved productivity and benefited the large contractors, as they are most able to take advantage of these developments.

Large firms are better equipped, better financed and better organised but their number is limited by the nature of the construction process. Difficulties of centralised supervision and management are more acute in the construction industry than in manufacturing because firms may be engaged concurrently in work on widely scattered and constantly changing sites. The capacity of individuals to manage is limited, and organisations can outgrow the capacity of managements. The greater the size of the firm, the more complex the organisation and the more remote the control and level of incentive on site.

Size has advantages because finance may be obtained more easily and more cheaply; large buying orders may bring economies in price; there is more economic use of indivisible resources such as specialised skills; risks can be spread over a wide range of contracts; and selling organisations may secure control over markets. The very large contractors cover the whole range of building and civil engineering both nationally and overseas.

The size of the largest firms in the industry has tended to grow, often through amalgamations between contractors and property development companies. By the mid-1970s there were over 200 publicly quoted construction companies. In more recent years, however, the number of large take-overs or mergers has greatly declined. Diversification into other areas of construction is often seen as a means of spreading risk and workload, and for similar reasons, vertical integration into materials production and quarrying activities sometimes also occurs (for example, Tarmac). Some of the largest groups, such as Trafalgar House, may include non-construction firms within their organisation. Bouygues, for example, probably the largest European contractor, also owns a French television station. The larger size of firm reflects the industry's adaptation to changing demand conditions in which the big firm has an advantage; changing cost structures and labour shortages have encouraged mechanisation and system building. The increase in size and complexity of individual contracts, often beyond the resources of smaller firms, has increased the incentive to form consortia or to merge. Institutional involvement in property has brought links between property developers, institutions and major contractors. The latter, with proven ability to carry out large schemes, have benefited because of the availability of finance. This has ensured a continuity of work, allowing the very large contractor to survive variations in the construction cycle rather better than the small firm.

Although small contracts predominated numerically in 1990, contracts for commercial building of over £3 million in value accounted for £3.8 billion of work, or just under half of the value of orders for all commercial work. In public non-housing work, the other sector with very large contracts, 44 per cent of contracts were over £3 million in value.

Subcontracting

Increasingly, main contractors have become co-ordinators of labour, materials and sub-contract work. By 1975, about 40 per cent of gross output of civil engineers and builders was being sub-contracted. Fundamentally, this trend is caused by the increasing number and complexities of services demanded in modern buildings and the advantages of specialists in increasing productivity and speed of completion. In addition, the uncertainty of future work load emphasises the advantages of not maintaining specialists but of using them only when required. Only contractors with large financial resources and a steady workload can operate their own specialist departments; these tender for outside work if they are not required by the parent company, thus capital is not tied up and under-used. Similar considerations explain the growth of plant-hire firms. The continuing shortage of skilled labour and uncertainty of job continuity with general builders has induced many craftsmen to join specialist sub-contractors.

The organisation of sub-contractors demands managerial expertise and good communications between the specialist and the contractor. These qualities are often lacking on building sites, causing unnecessary delay, a high accident rate and lower productivity. Efficient organisation of sub-contractors requires the main contractor to draw up detailed construction programmes informing the sub-contractor well in advance when s/he will be required on site, or informing him/her of any modification in the programme, and to ensure that any necessary facilities are available. Sub-contractors may be unable to programme their work efficiently if the main contractor is deficient in this respect.

Where sub-contractors are nominated by the architect, because of expertise in specialised areas, they may adopt an independent attitude which may be resented by the main contractor, who is often chosen later. The latter prefer to have full control of sub-contractors; they may contend that the scale of appointment of nominated sub-contractors is so great that the organisation of the contract might be jeopardised since it is more difficult to co-ordinate nominated sub-contractors on the site. The practice may also reduce the competitive nature of contracting. There is a potential conflict of interest between architect and contractor; the former may carry the ultimate responsibility for poor-quality work as a result of the contractor striking a hard bargain with a sub-contractor. The main contractor must accept full responsibility for the organisation of the contract and the work of sub-contractors.

MATERIALS MANUFACTURERS

This sector reflects the industry as a whole, ranging widely in size, organisation and location. Generally, the extractive materials industries, such as sand and gravel quarrying, will be located at the source of the material, as will firms heavily dependent upon a key material such as Oxford clay for fletton bricks. Firms producing components are more likely to be located closer to their market. There is a clear trend towards rationalisation; the mass market for many building materials is dominated by a small number of producers, often only one. The development of capital-intensive plant has squeezed the small producer out, except where he can compete with the large manufacturer, either because the latter finds it uneconomic to deliver to some parts or because there are specialised products which can be made competitively by less automated methods.

The brick industry illustrates these features. By the early 1980s, the number of firms had fallen to about 200 compared with 900 in 1948. The fletton brick, which comprises about 45 per cent of the industry's output, is based on Oxford clay which requires no additives and is therefore cheaper to produce. London Brick produces about 95 per cent of fletton output from works concentrated in the Midlands. Its monopolist position has brought official enquiries into the supply and price position from the former Prices and Incomes Board and the Monopolies and Mergers Commission.

The non-fletton industry producing facing and specialised bricks is, in comparison, widely scattered and comprises some 200 firms, from public companies to family businesses. Whereas London Brick is heavily capitalised and automated, many of the smaller brick companies have low capitalisation and employ fewer than twenty-five workers. The small local producer has low transport costs, a big factor in the brick price, and this gives protection within the market. Specialised quality facing bricks, sometimes handmade, are in demand to give interest to buildings.

The fortunes of brick manufacturers are closely tied to housebuilding activity, as approximately 70 per cent of total brick output is used for new housebuilding. When housing activity booms, as in 1972/3, there is a great demand for bricks. This has led to bottlenecks and long waits in delivery – as the scope for importing is limited. At other periods, manufacturers have faced sharp declines in demand, mounting stocks of unsold bricks and underused capacity – as happened in 1980/1 and in the early 1990s, when brickworks were operating at only 50 per cent of capacity (figure 10.9). Such fluctuations in demand have adverse effects upon manufacturers' willingness to invest in additional capacity at a time of boom. Furthermore, in recessions, many smaller yet regionally important firms become bankrupt, brickworks become derelict and the industry is consequently less able to meet a recovery of demand.

The cement industry is dominated by a few large companies – Associated Portland being the largest producer of cement in the world. Small companies survive because transport costs are important in the price of cement. Cement manufacturers are affected by fluctuations in construction generally, but they are less dependent upon one sector than are brick manufacturers, and there is also a growing export trade. Sand and roadstone quarrying are dominated by small companies located at the source of material. The glass and plasterboard industries are monopolistic situations. Ceramic sanitary wares include companies which are among the largest manufacturers of ceramics in the world and about 30 per cent of output is exported. In 1980, the largest cement producer took over the largest ceramics manufacturer, after reference to the Monopolies and Mergers Commission. The timber trade has been rationalised considerably and great technological strides have been seen within the trade.

Government cutbacks in the economy will vary in effect. For example, a decline in house-building starts will affect brick manufacturers immediately, but plasterboard and flooring tile manufacturers rather later. Some materials are exclusively demanded by construction, whereas others – for example, glass, iron and steel – are widely used in other industries. The energy crisis in the 1970s and increasing oil costs affected materials manufacturers through changing demands. Building regulations' thermal insulation standards were improved to a point where they almost doubled the requirements for roof and wall insulation. Timber-framed housing, which could provide substantially greater lev-

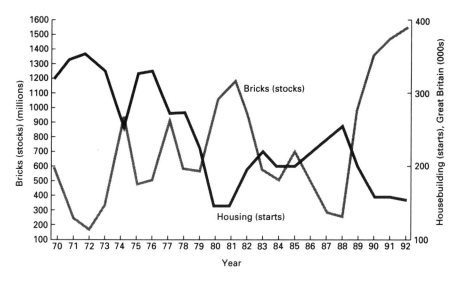

Source: *Housing and Construction Statistics* (HMSO).

Figure 10.9 *Brick stocks and housing starts*

els of wall insulation compared with traditional brick construction, became increasingly common as many of the larger builders switched to this form of construction. There was stimulus for the brick and block manufacturers to design materials with higher insulating qualities. The switch from metals to plastics continued, although higher costs meant that oil-based materials became less competitive. Although oil prices have since fallen (further encouraging the use of plastics), the continuing improvement of insulation standards has served to encourage energy efficiency in new buildings. As as result, housebuilders are showing a renewed interest in timber-frame methods.

Builders' Merchants

The great bulk of building materials, overall some £20 billion in 1991, is handled by builders' merchants. The merchants are widely located, and vary in size and capital resources. There has been a trend towards rationalisation and larger units, emphasising the economies of scale in material distribution. Many merchants specialise in 'heavy' materials and components such as bricks, cement and sanitary wares, or in 'light' materials, such as bathroom and kitchen fitments. The latter tend to be more profitable and with rising standards of living offer greater growth potential. The 'do-it-yourself' trade also offers higher margins. Self-selection centres have been developed which involve little bad-debt risk as goods are obtained on a cash basis.

The chief economic functions of merchants are to distribute efficiently materials and components and to collect and deliver where necessary to contractors.

Traditionally, merchants have acted as agents, passing on orders from contractors to manufacturers; most materials sold by merchants are delivered direct to the customer. Merchants maintain stocks, enabling contractors' demands to be met immediately; thus the latter do not need to rent storage space. Manufacturers are helped as merchants deal with the small, uneconomic order, breaking bulk and are thus able to give the purchaser a lower price than would otherwise have been possible. Stockholding also gives the manufacturer a more stable demand. Merchants give technical advice and advance the sale of new materials, especially when the manufacturers provide necessary technical literature. Traditionally merchants have granted trade credit to builders, although with higher rates of interest, credit control has improved significantly.

Generally, the sector is better able to withstand the cycle of construction demand than the materials manufacturers, although there is a strong dependence on the level of consumer spending and credit availability. Do-it-yourself and the emphasis on improvement after the Housing Act 1969 have provided a useful base, as demand from small builders engaged in renovation has cushioned merchants from the worst effects of any new housing downturn.

LABOUR

The construction industry is labour-intensive, much of it skilled, and there have been persistent shortages in the traditional building crafts since 1945. The industry was one of the first for which a training board was set up under the Industrial Training Act 1964. The prime objectives were to secure an adequate supply of properly trained workers; an improvement in the efficiency of training; and to share costs more evenly. The Construction Industry Training Board was set up to make levies on firms in the industry and to give grants for approved courses of training. The Act emphasised that demands upon the industry were likely to increase at a time when significant new techniques and methods were being introduced.

Labour turnover is about twice as high in construction as in industry generally. The greatest turnover is with large civil engineering firms where labour may be employed for one contract only and will not remain stable even for the duration of the contract. The percentage unemployed in construction at any time is often twice the national average and the gap widens in the winter period. The industry's vulnerability to the weather causes much casual unemployment. Winter unemployment in the United Kingdom is likely to be about 60 per cent higher than the summer total. Because of the imperfections of the market, high unemployment may exist alongside labour shortages.

About 80 per cent of operatives are employed by contractors, the balance by public authorities. Approximately half are craftsmen for whom apprenticeship or similar training is the usual method of entry. Apprenticeship was reduced from five years to four in 1963 to speed up the intake of skilled workers. However, the raising of the school-leaving age and a poor public image have adversely affected the flow of new recruits into construction. The fairly clear dividing line which once existed between the craft operatives and other labour has become blurred, especially in small firms, thus reflecting the diversity of building operations, and making it impossible to bring in different crafts every time a new material or method is introduced. In larger firms there has been the growth in new skills associated with new technological developments. Figures given by the Construction Industry Training Board show that between 1980 and 1989 the number of operative trainees in construction fell by a third to less than 50 000 in the latter year.

Labour-only Sub-contracting

Lack of personnel policy, poor site management and high labour turnover have all been factors in the growth of labour-only sub-contracting (LOS) in the United Kingdom. Under a labour-only contract, the main contractor provides the materials and most of the equipment required and pays the sub-contractor for his/her labour only. This differs from the predominant form of sub-contract in which materials and equipment are provided as well as the labour to perform the specified task. Generally, the labour-only sub-contractor provides only hand tools but s/he may be required to provide other equipment. The payment is usually a lump sum at the completion of the task – for example, so much per 1000 bricks laid. Over half of labour-only sub-contractors are self-employed, either as individuals or in gangs.

In the United Kingdom, LOS is most prevalent in the traditional crafts in private housebuilding, particularly in London and the South. The Phelps Brown Committee (1968)[15] indicated bricklaying, carpentry and plastering as the trades in which LOS predominated. It was less prevalent in the newer specialisms. Labour-only does not adapt itself easily to training. Operatives move from site to site carrying out a limited, fairly uniform range of operations; where there are new and unfamiliar techniques this is not possible.

Generally, payment to labour-only sub-contractors is on a 'piece work' basis, thus there is a clear relationship between effort and reward; they are able to achieve greater control over earnings than under a more complicated bonus scheme. Many employers see LOS as a way of raising productivity through simple forms of incentive. The 1968 Report indicated that 53 per cent of employers believed that LOS productivity was higher than direct labour employed. LOS also provided labour which could not be satisfied elsewhere – for instance, in remote areas where direct labour might not be willing or able to travel. LOS is useful for meeting peak demands for labour, providing an efficient, productive capacity which can be mobilised swiftly without the need to hire and then dismiss direct labour. A crucial incentive to LOS has been the increasing charges on employed labour. These have included the Construction Industry Training Levy, Selective Employment Tax (1966–73), redundancy fund contributions, employer National Insurance contributions, and holiday and sick pay. All these levies and their administration are avoided by the employer whose work is carried out by labour-only, self-employed operatives.

There are also difficulties largely reflecting poor site management. The quality of the work may be more variable although the 1968 Report commented that only 25 per cent of employers thought that quality was worse than that of direct labour. There were complaints of wastage of materials and unfinished work, and also a general impression of neglect of safety precautions, yet there is no evidence that accidents on site are more common among labour-only operatives compared with direct labour. There is a wide variety of labour-only sub-contractors ranging from the established craft operative maintaining very high productivity to the 'fly-by-night' operative with little pride in his/her work and no standards.

A major criticism of LOS is its effects upon training and apprenticeship. Clearly, workers whose aim is to complete a given task as quickly as possible do not want to include a learner in their team or to interrupt their own work to instruct him/her. There is great concern at the collapse of effective training in the basic craft skills in which LOS predominates.

There are administrative difficulties in dealing with LOS; in particular, there is the question of evasion of taxation and insurance. Various attempts have been made since 1968 to control the worst excesses of the 'lump', beginning with the recommendations of the 1968 committee, who suggested that all employers should be registered. In 1970, a Bill was introduced to set up a voluntary register for contractors. In 1971, employers were directed to deduct 30 per cent of payments to sub-contractors unable to produce certificates showing that they were known to the tax inspector. Registered companies were automatically exempted. In 1977, all building sub-contractors had to apply to the Inland Revenue for registration after meeting certain conditions. If accepted, they were issued with a tax certificate – the '714'. It was also suggested that the industry might be policed by an administrative board similar to those in France and Germany.

At best, LOS combines the continuous labour of the specialist sub-contractor, higher productivity and flexibility. At worst, it produces faulty work by irresponsible workers concerned only with the greatest possible gains in the short run. There is clearly a gap between the industry's collective approach which condemns the practice, and the individual companies who exploit it. This duality results in differentials in earnings on the same site and is a consequent source of disputes.

Trade union membership in the construction industry is currently running at around 20 per cent – although possibly as many as 40 per cent of hourly-paid employees of the larger private contractors belong to trade unions.[16] Yet the growth of LOS and the fragmentation of building work are not the only reasons why trade union influence is weak in the construction industry. From 1979, direct labour organisations (DLOs) were expected to show a return of 5 per cent on capital employed, while subsequently the Direct Labour Act 1981 compelled local authorities to put out for tender all but the smallest jobs. Yet

DLOs were required to adopt accountancy procedures which showed an antici-pated profit or loss on *each* of their activities. Under these conditions, DLOs found it difficult to secure work in the face of competition from the private sector not tied to the same constraint, or were wound up by the government for consistently not complying with official requirements. Since DLOs were highly unionised, a substantial reduction in their activity weakened trade union influence within the construction industry. DLO work fell from 12.5 per cent of construction output in 1981 to only 8.5 per cent in 1991.

A further reason for the weakness of trade unionism in the industry is the lack of unity. There are three main unions in the industry: the Union of Con-struction, Allied Trades and Technicians (UCATT), the Amalgamated Engineers and Electricians Union (AEEU) and the Transport and General Workers Union (TGWU). Other major unions maintain a significant presence in construction (for example, GMB) and there are also a number of smaller, often craft-based unions (for example FTAT, EPIU and MSF). There is, however, all too often an absence of cohesion in philosophy, policy and tactics – particularly with regard to the problem of LOS.

Although LOS has been an anathema to trade unions since it is associated with (in their view) the unacceptable exploitive nature of piecework, UCATT has recently showed signs of being willing to allow its members to work with bona fide sub-contractors – for example, UCATT (and the TGWU) signed an agreement in 1987 with the newly formed Federation of Brickwork Contrac-tors (a grouping of bricklaying sub-contractors operating in the South-East of England).[17]

TECHNICAL DEVELOPMENTS IN THE CONSTRUCTION INDUSTRY: SYSTEM BUILDING

As traditional building costs have spiralled, so increasing consideration has been given to switching from conventional methods to 'system' or industrial-ised building. This latter embraces many facets, combining aesthetic value and user satisfaction with economy of materials, factory production and quality control methods entailing the maximum use of off-site prefabrication. New materials and techniques will be used including the use of dry processes, increased mech-anisation of site processes, improved management techniques, the correlation of design and production, and better organisation and training of operatives on site, using new skills or fully rationalised traditional methods. Ultimately, more parts of a building will be in their final form when erected so that much site work becomes merely an assembly of factory-made components.

The advantages of industrialised over traditional building are economies in time and labour. The DOE has reported it possible to reduce the time required to build a house from over 2000 man-hours to 1300 when there was a series of large contracts each of about 500 houses.[18] Saving in construction time is effected by a division of labour between factory and site, using them as a single production line; by protecting labour from variable site conditions; by producing better quality and more complex components under controlled factory conditions free from factors which limit productivity on site; by reducing the number of operations and mechanising a high proportion of them; and by increasing the scope for modern management techniques, permitting complex operations to be organised smoothly. Quick completion brings an early return in rent, reduces site supervision, and enables capital to be released for further work.

Industrialised building (and to a lesser extent traditional building) will be more economic the larger and more repetitive the contract. The costs per unit of a manufactured product will fall as the production run is extended, although after a point the rate of reduction in costs falls off. In Finland the costs of doors fell by 14 per cent when the production run was increased from twenty to fifty, but by only 5 per cent when increased from 200 to 500.[19] The more times a system is used the more economic it is likely to be.

The manufacturer given a large order over an extended period can invest in new machinery, plan his/her production flow efficiently and thereby reduce waste. Fixed costs spread over a long run of production reduce unit costs. The contractor benefits, being able to programme more accurately, increasing efficiency and making continuous use of site labour. The designer benefits and techniques of briefing may be developed systematically and more thoroughly for the programme than would be possible for each individual building.

Although systems demand the development of new skills, notably in the site assembly of prefabricated components, the pressure upon the traditional crafts is reduced. However, the differential advantage in wage rates of skilled as against unskilled workers is smaller in the United Kingdom than in most other countries so there is less incentive to use techniques which replace skilled by unskilled workers. Also, labour costs of site labourers are generally less than those of factory workers. Thus there is less advantage in transferring work away from the site. However systems do reduce the amount of site labour and total worker-hours may be less than 50 per cent of the traditional figure. Seeley[20] estimates the labour requirements per dwelling using traditional building as about 1800 site worker-hours; in industrialised building, from 700 to 1300 per dwelling, depending on the buildings and systems. The difference between labour requirements for conventional and system building is likely to increase in tall buildings because these are better suited to industrial techniques.

Thus increased mechanisation can speed up production and may result in reduced costs of construction: for example, on small sites the use of power tools or larger cranes and fork lift trucks; on all sites the extensive use of prefabricated components which have eliminated many of the time-consuming 'wet' trades. In addition, the developments in organisation and materials in non-traditional building have stimulated the industry and represent an important gain.

Yet mechanisation of the industry has not proceeded as rapidly as might have been expected. Fundamentally, system building is only economic when high productive efficiency more than offsets additional factory overheads, and this will depend upon a high and stable demand to justify the high initial capital input. This stability has been absent in the United Kingdom; by 1977 the average size of scheme using industrialised methods had fallen to only 68 dwellings – hardly enough to achieve economies of scale.

In addition, the total costs of a building constructed by industrialised methods are not determined by factory costs alone. Problems may arise in fixing prefabricated parts on site because factory tolerances are much stricter than those on site. This has led to serious conflicts between the use of traditional methods and the installation of prefabricated components. Many of the potential advantages of prefabrication can be lost by poor design details, leaving awkward work to be carried out by traditional methods. Also, site handling costs for the largest prefabricated components are high. There is need for expensive capital equipment and highly qualified personnel, and materials costs will almost certainly be higher than with traditional brick and block construction.

Industrial building may have lowered the aesthetic quality of the built environment, and may have reduced the expected life of buildings and increased the maintenance liability of buildings erected. Economic use requires the minimum departure from standard design; thus the client has to accept a more restricted choice than with traditional building methods.

The difficulty in achieving economy by use of system building lies in the small proportion of the costs of the dwelling in which economies can be achieved in this way. Economies are limited largely to the structure itself and to services in walls and floors – probably no more than a quarter of the total costs. Moreover, to prefabricate and save on labour it is necessary to use precision materials and plant which are more expensive than traditional methods. Basically, in the United Kingdom the cost relationships are less favourable to systems than in many other countries. Traditional building is based on brick, which is very cheap compared with basic materials available in many countries.

Local Authority Housing and Industrial Building Costs

The amount of industrialised building (table 10.4) was relatively small in the early 1960s and costs, using more capital and less labour, were higher than dwellings built using traditional methods. However, between 1964 and 1967, as more resources were shifted to public housing, industrialised dwellings started increased from 28 000 to 66 000. By 1967, industrialised building was used in 42 per cent of public-sector starts, over half of this in high-rise flats. From 1968 to 1970, industrialised dwellings fell from 39 to 19 per cent of public sector approvals. Consequently, industrial building became less competitive with traditional, even for high-rise blocks of flats. Industrialised building faced a number of problems. In the first place there were too many competing systems (around 154) and the housing market was not in any case geared up to accommodate such techniques – between 1966 and 1977 the average size of industrialised schemes was only 120 dwellings.

Table 10.4 *Dwellings built by non-traditional methods: local authorities and new towns in England and Wales, 1965–79*

Year	Total	Percentage of all local authority dwellings
1965	25 527	14.4
1970	55 701	41.3
1971	38 314	32.7
1972	24 557	26.2
1973	17 660	22.3
1974	24 536	24.7
1975	25 792	21.0
1976	23 780	19.6
1977	19 697	16.2
1978	10 313	10.7
1979	4 566	6.3

Source: Department of the Environment, *Housing and Construction Statistics.*

Secondly, industrialised methods were really only able to gain significant cost advantage (of between 2 and 13 per cent) over traditional building for high-rise flats, but this type of dwelling was itself more expensive to produce than were houses or low-rise flats (by approximately 80 per cent and 35 per cent respectively).[21] Thus industrialised building failed to bring down the unit cost of high-rise dwellings to a level comparable with low-rise alternatives. The long-term future of high-rise was thus dependent on central and local government being willing to support higher unit costs. Subsidies were introduced in the late 1950s for high-rise flats on the basis that, first, economies in the use of high-value urban land would be achieved more easily by high-rise building.[22] The latter was felt to be important, especially where new local authority housing was meant to replace fairly high-density housing lost in inner-city clearance schemes over this period (although overall land use savings were later found to be much smaller than anticipated). By 1967 the worsening economic situation led to cost controls on new local authority house-building being introduced (which affected high-rise most). At about the same time, the special subsidy for high-rise public housing was removed for flats of over 6 storeys (but nevertheless retained until the mid-1970s for flats below this level).

High rise, in which industrialised systems have played such a dominant role, never recovered from the shock to public confidence caused by the Ronan Point disaster of May 1968. In addition there were growing doubts about the social and economic aspects of high-rise housing. In fact, by this date high-rise blocks were already in decline. There were three great weaknesses in the high-rise block, óne of which existed from the start while the others developed with the programme. The first was the inadequacy of the lift services. In council blocks, lifts were always on the extreme limit of allowable expenditure. They were neither fast nor large enough; provision was inadequate and they broke down often. The second fault was basic: as demand outstripped supply with the rapid post-war growth in population and new households, housing managers were forced to house families with small children in high-rise flats, for which the blocks were totally unsuitable. The third failure was in management and maintenance. The rapidly growing council housing stock was outstripping both. The fate of the notorious block of flats in Liverpool known as 'the pigeries' – rendered uninhabitable by vandalism and the collapsing social framework characteristic of the deprived urban area, and ultimately sold for a token sum to private enterprise – epitomised the failure of this attempt to cope with the problems of post-war housing. Large sums have been spent from the 1980s to the present on rectifying defects caused by poor design and inadequate erection procedures. In 1991 Newham Council was reputed to have spent over £3 million on demolishing each of the blocks built at the same time as Ronan Point, leaving one to be refurbished at a cost of £5 million.

The overall decline in public-sector housing from 146 000 approvals in 1965 to 55 435 in 1972 (in Great Britain) also affected system building adversely. Although the Labour government in 1974 indicated that more resources would be diverted to local authority housing, the economic recession of the early 1980s affected all public spending severely. With a new incoming government, housing expenditure as a percentage of total government expenditure declined from 10 per cent to less than 5 per cent by 1980. By 1979 only 4566 industrialised dwellings were completed for local authorities and most of these used timber systems as opposed to concrete. The biggest impact of systems outside local authority housing has been in schools, and by 1973 systems accounted for 44 per cent of all major projects started.

Any system depends upon the extent of its market to be profitable. Most of the early systems were 'closed' systems, whereby components were designed for use together in similar schemes, thus the market for a particular system was relatively restricted. Only a few of the many hundreds of systems evolved really succeeded. Open systems have evolved whereby components can be bought 'off the peg' and put together in any scheme and so provide the designer with a wider range of choices. The future of open systems depends upon the development of a mass market for prefabricated components. This has been limited by the non-standardised demand for construction output, lack of policies to rationalise demand, and long-term building programmes of public authorities. Fundamentally, production must be of a sufficient scale to allow the spreading of capital costs and sometimes expensive teething troubles. Costs may be higher initially than with traditional building but systems such as CLASP for schools have shown that industrial building can produce substantial economies over traditional methods provided there is sufficient size and continuity of contracts.

Perhaps the most radical prospect for the 1990s is a good factory-delivered house. If the costs are right, the potential benefits of quality, a more structured factory environment and avoidance of disruption by weather are obvious. Modern Danish systems for low-rise housing now use composite lightweight concrete panels which include facing materials and insulation. Internal fittings come in a modular form. While France and Germany also have small but significant levels of industrialised housebuilding, in Japan the factory production of low-rise housing units is said to have penetrated 15 per cent of the market.[23] As in France or Germany, one of the most significant impacts of industrialised housebuilding is the ability of prospective home owners to sidestep the speculative development process by designating the builder and style of their choice.[24]

CONSTRUCTION OVERSEAS

The European Union (EU) has yet to provide a substantial market for the United Kingdom construction industry. In-built restrictions in the various countries are very great and the Cecchini Report into the costs of a non-Europe estimated that the potential benefits of the Single European Market in building and civil engineering could amount to over 7 billion ECUs. In 1990, construction activity in the EU by British contractors amounted to less than 3 per cent of their total overseas construction activity.

Some steps have been taken towards harmonising conditions in each country within the basic principles of the EU that barriers, both fiscal and social, should in time be removed between the constituent states. Freedom of movement of labour and equal opportunities for employment imply that EU nationals have a right to employment in any member state. In the case of the quantity surveyor, there is no equivalent profession in Europe outside the United Kingdom, although some of the basic training is incorporated in other disciplines. This is an opportunity of which many United Kingdom consultant quantity surveyors are aware, and there has been some development towards the spread of this profession by firms opening up offices in centres such as Brussels and Paris. Elsewhere, professional education and practice differ considerably between countries. For example, in West Germany and the Netherlands, the education and qualifications of architects and engineers are closely related, while in France they are completely separate.

Since the formation of the European Economic Community (now the EU) there has been no significant increase in inter-community construction work brought about by its existence. There has been no great influx of work on a competitive basis. Clearly, the practical advantage lies with local companies for general construction work. The barriers against change are appreciable. Safety standards, technical differences and language difficulties all play their part, thus the relatively low significance for British contractors of the EU. Technical differences in material standards are, however, being harmonised through the European Commissions's Construction Products Directive, which came into force in December 1991. Products which satisfy the relevant requirements carry a special mark and may be sold anywhere in the EU without having to meet additional technical and procedural requirements.

EEC Directive 71/305 (1971) was the first practical step in the direction of giving contractors in each country similar opportunities of knowing what work was available for bidding. It is currently implemented in the United Kingdom by the Public Works Contracts Regulations 1991, and applies to public works contracts for construction and civil engineering work placed by central government, local authorities and their agencies where the contract value is over 5 million ECU (£3.5m). In general, public procurement by central and local government and its agencies is of considerable importance for the construction industry as it accounts for over 15 per cent of the national output of the EU. But by the late 1980s, less than 2 per cent of all public contracts went to non-national firms.[25]

There may be possibilities for increasing work not within the EU itself but with associated states eligible for financial aid through the European Development Fund; these include a number of Commonwealth territories in Africa and elsewhere. The more highly complex schemes may well depend upon international participation involving multinational consortia well suited to the expertise and financial resources of the largest United Kingdom contracting companies.

The value of overseas activity as a percentage of all work done by British contractors rose from 4.3 per cent in 1970/1 to 11 per cent in 1977/8. Overseas construction activity peaked again in the early 1980s only to decline sharply between 1984/5 and 1988, when it represented only 3.6 per cent of all work by British contractors. The contribution of consulting engineers to the United Kingdom balance of payments has also been significant. This grew sharply from the early 1970s to peak at over £500 million annually during 1982–6, but has not subsequently exceeded this figure.[26]

The dominant factor in the mid-1970s was the sharp fall in home construction demand coinciding with a great oil-financed demand overseas for construction on a massive scale. In the oil-producing countries there were national plans on a vast scale, of which construction projects constituted well over a half. For example, Saudi Arabia's second five-year plan called for spending of £63 billion over the period 1975–80, of which 60 per cent was to be on development. The Middle East was thus the major growth area. United Kingdom contractors with well-established reputations had much to offer in consultancy skills, manufacturing technology and project management.

By the mid-1980s, however, United Kingdom companies looking overseas for markets found that demand had slumped severely. Contracts won in 1985–6 were 37 per cent below their peak value of 1982–3 – largely as a result of falling oil revenues and the depressed Middle-East market. Although only a small number of United Kingdom companies undertake overseas contracts (ten firms handling as much as 90 per cent of the work), depressed demand overseas in the mid-1980s encouraged construction activity to shift back to the United Kingdom – increasing the degree of competition in the relatively comfortable home market.[27] By 1990, overseas construction activity by British companies had picked up slightly (in spite of a depressed Middle-East market) largely because of the effects of the property boom in North America. Nevertheless, at around £2 billion, overseas activity was still running at well below the levels achieved from 1982/83 to 1985/86 – even in cash terms.

Table 10.5 *Industrial and office building costs, 1989*

	Industrial building costs ($£/m^2$)	Office building costs ($£/m^2$)
France	284	714
West Germany	272	918
United Kingdom	366	1,410

Source: Hillier Parker, *International Property Bulletin* (Hillier Parker, May and Rowden, London, 1990).

Contracting activity overseas is dependent upon factors such as political stability, security of payment, local taxes and contract law, and the extent of competition. Tendering is expensive, complex and is likely to deter smaller companies. The United Kingdom Construction Exports Advisory Board has been formed to stimulate more effort by contractors in export markets. For large firms, overseas work is seen as a useful cushion against recession in the domestic market. It has also encouraged joint ventures and multinational consortia working.

Comparisons between construction projects in the United Kingdom, in Europe and in North America indicate the following features. The total time that elapses from the inception of a scheme to its completion is considerably longer in the United Kingdom than in other countries. The preliminary stages of design, pricing, application for and grant of planning permission in the United Kingdom are more complex and more time-consuming than elsewhere. Also, greater uncertainty exists for the applicant as to whether or not the requisite permission will be granted. Because of longer programme times, the final development costs of projects are greater in the United Kingdom. Some research has suggested that up to 45 per cent more worker hours are required to complete a project in Britain when compared with other northern European countries.[28] As Table 10.5 shows, these differences are clearly reflected in international variations in building costs.

Construction and the Macro Economy

The major problems facing construction are the continual pressure of land costs and the cyclical nature of demand for its output. The economic policy objectives of governments have conflicted frequently with stability in the industry; also, there are fluctuations in demand for construction output outside the control of government. Allowing that fluctuation inevitably will occur, the aim of the government and the industry must be to alleviate, as much as possible, the undesirable effects of these fluctuations. But both government and industry failed to do this. Under Thatcherism in the 1980s, the downturn in council-house building, public-sector contracts in general, and new industrial and commercial work, was particularly severe. There were fewer council houses built in 1986 than in any other peacetime year since 1923, and in 1986 public-sector housebuilding was accounting for under 10 per cent of the total new work of the construction industry by value compared with 20 per cent a few years earlier. There was a danger that there would be too few craftsmen available either to build new houses or to rehabilitate dwellings on the scale needed when economic recovery came. All sectors of the industry were affected – private firms, direct labour organisations, architects and planners. Even the normally resilient fields of repair, maintenance and improvement were not immune. Taking into account administrative and professional manpower, unemployment in the industry (broadly defined) reached 480 000 by 1982.

There was much concern within the Group of Eight (a pressure group representing management, the professions and unions within the industry) that since employers were becoming insolvent in increasing numbers, there would be very little left of the construction industry to respond to increased demand when the recession of the 1980s was over. Because of this scenario, both the Building and Civil Engineering Development committee and the Social and Economic Committee of the European Commission recommended that the government should introduce policies which would have a stabilising or expansionary impact on construction, so that the industry could plan ahead and increase its level of investment and training. However, the government failed to appreciate that the construction industry could help pull the rest of the economy out of the recession (believing instead that an eventual recovery in the economy would assist the construction industry).

Construction (especially housebuilding) is very labour-intensive, creating more jobs for any given volume of capital expenditure than most other activities. The industry also relies heavily on purchased materials. Any increase in investment, therefore – in, for example, housebuilding – has a multiplier effect on employment both 'down' and 'up the line'. The housing charity, Shelter, estimated that for every £100 million spent on constructing new dwellings, 5600 worker years would be created for on-site operatives and 3000 new homes would be built. An extra 1850 worker years' work would be created for architects, surveyors and clerical staff, and a further 7450 worker years for labour 'up the line' – for example, in building supply and transport.[29] The Trades Union Congress (TUC) calculated that there was an employment multiplier in the construction industry of two (that is, for every one extra person employed in construction, one extra job would be created elsewhere).[30] The creation of this amount of employment would save the Treasury up to £82 million (in terms of reduced unemployment pay and supplementary benefits, and a gain in tax revenue), therefore the net cost of building 3000 new homes would be only £20–£30 million extra on the borrowing requirement. On this basis, the gross cost of employing an additional 150 000 construction workers (on public-sector work) would be £2000 million, but the net cost could be as low as £400 million. Overall, increased public expenditure on housebuilding would not only increase or improve the supply of housing and safeguard the capacity of the construction industry, but would also reduce the level of unemployment substantially and reflate the economy as a whole.

Undoubtedly, the construction industry was showing distinct signs of recovery by the mid-1980s. But with a substantial decline in public-sector contracts and reduced opportunities overseas, the industry became increasingly dependent on an overheated private market at home, with the associated risk of eventually being squeezed by deflationary policies. The imbalance in construction activity was thus a major cause for concern, particularly in view of the depreciation of social capital.

The Charter for Jobs[31] estimated in 1987 that £93 billion needed to be spent on infrastructure investment – an injection into the economy which could produce 1 million jobs over six years. Of this sum, at least £30 billion was needed to remedy defects in the housing stock, £1.7 billion was required for hospital building, £500 million was needed for maintenance work on schools, and other large sums were required to repair water mains, sewers and roads. Britain was again bottom of the international league table of spending on construction and infrastructure in the 1990s, and its built environment was facing a renewal crisis of enormous proportions. The urban economy was yet again showing all the signs of private affluence and public squalor.

By 1992 construction output (in constant prices) had declined to its lowest level since 1986, and contractors' orders for new work were more than a third down on their peak of 1988. Unemployment in the construction industry was reputed to have reached 500 000 by 1993. Once again private-sector housebuilding was the first sector to suffer from the recession, and with the already low level of public-sector housebuilding, housing output (public/private) was lower in 1991 and 1992 than at any time over the 1980s. Although monetary policy had been eased and interest rates lowered after the United Kingdom's exit from the European ERM in late 1992, it seemed unlikely – by late 1993 – that without further public investment stimulus to construction, lower interest rates alone would provide a sufficient boost to demand in the short term for recovery to occur. As in earlier 'booms', it would take some time before demand in the economy increased the take-up of existing property enough to encourage new development. In the housing market, the number of people with negative equity peaked at 1.8 million in the first quarter of 1993, and this, together with the high but falling level of mortgage arrears and repossessions, seemed likely to depress the housing market for some time to come. Many of these effects (also paralleled in the United States and Japan) were the result of overlending to the property sector in general during the 1980s, a process which was in itself largely encouraged by financial deregulation and what now appears to be an over-relaxed monetary policy following the stock market crash in 1987. To this can also be added the impact of housing equity withdrawal as rising house prices, as we have seen, where in effect used to finance higher consumer spending. Undoubtedly, lessons have been learnt from this period and it can be expected that in the future more attention will be paid to the possible impact of monetary and fiscal policy on the property sector and to any feedback from this sector to the main macro-economic variables.

REFERENCES

Note: Unless otherwise indicated, statistical references are obtained from *Housing and Construction Statistics* (HMSO).

1. UK National Board for Prices and Incomes, *Pay and Conditions in the Building Industry*, Report No. 92, Cmnd 3837 (HMSO, 1968).
2. Ministry of Building and Public Works, *The Pacing and Management of Contracts for Building and Civil Engineering Work* (HMSO, 1964).
3. *The Public Client and the Construction Industries*, The Report of the Building and Civil Engineering Economic Development Committee (HMSO, 1975).
4. E. Lea, P. Harvey and P. Spencer, *Efficiency and Growth in the Building Industry* (sponsored by the Department of the Environment, 1972).
5. M. Ball, *Rebuilding Construction* (Routledge, 1988).
6. R. Barras, 'Technical Change and the Urban Development Cycle', *Urban Studies*, 24 (1987).
7. C. H. Feinstein, *Statistical Tables of National Income, Expenditure and Output of the UK, 1855–1965* (Cambridge University Press, 1972).
8. R. Barras and D. Ferguson, 'A Spectral Analysis of Building Cycles in Britain', *Environment and Planning A*, 17 (1985).
9. J. G. Lowe, 'The Fixed Capital Stock in Use by the UK Construction Industry', *Construction Management and Economics*, 8 (1990).
10. C. Daniels, *UK Construction* (The Economist Intelligence Unit, 1990).
11. M. Ball, 'Land Rent and the Construction Industry' in M. Ball *et al.*, *Land Rent, Housing and Urban Planning – A European Perspective* (Croom Helm, 1984).
12. D. Massey and A. Catalano, *Capital and Land: Landownership by Capital in Great Britain* Edward Arnold, 1978).
13. M. Ball, 'Differential Rent and the Role of Landed Property', *International Journal of Urban and Regional Research* 1 (1977); B. Fine, 'On Marx's Theory of Agricultural Rent', *Economy and Society*, 8 (1979).
14. B. Fine, 'Land, Capital and the British Coal Industry Prior to World War II' in M. Ball *et al.*, *Land Rent, Housing and Urban Planning – a European Perspective*.
15. *Committee of Inquiry under Professor E. H. Phelps Brown* (1968).
16. *Contract Journal* (9 September 1993).
17. I. McNeill, 'New Facade for Building's Bad Practices', *Morning Star* (11 March 1987).
18. I. H. Seeley, *Building Economics* (Macmillan, 1974).
19. P. A. Stone, *Building Economy: Design, Production and Organisation – a Synoptic View* (Pergamon Press, 1966).
20. I. H. Seeley, *Building Economics*.
21. R. McCutcheon, 'Industrialised Housebuilding in the UK – 1965–1977, *Habitat International*, 13, 1 (1989).
22. C. Couch, *Urban Renewal Theory and Practice* (Macmillan, 1990).
23. M. Ball, M. Harloe and M. Martens, *Housing and Social Change in Europe and the USA* (Routledge, 1988).
24. J. Barlow, 'Self-promoted Housing and Capitalist Suppliers', *Housing Studies*, 7 (1993).
25. A. Griffiths, *European Community Survey* (Longman,1992).
26. Central Statistical Office, *Annual Abstract of Statistics* (HMSO).
27. D. Turner, 'The Construction Industry in Britain', *Midland Bank Review* (Autumn 1987).
28. E. Koehn, 'International Labour Productivity Factors', *Journal of Construction Engineering and Management*, 112 (1986).
29. S. Hilditch, 'Build Houses, Build Hope', *Roof* (November/December 1981).
30. Trade Union Congress, *The Reconstruction of Britain* (TUC, 1981).
31. Charter for Jobs, reported in *Guardian* (8 June 1987).

Index